CONSTITUTIONALISM
IN AMERICA

VOLUME I

TO SECURE THE
BLESSINGS OF LIBERTY

First Principles
of the Constitution

EDITED BY
SARAH BAUMGARTNER THUROW
University of Dallas

UNIVERSITY
PRESS OF
AMERICA

Lanham • New York • London

D1153876

Copyright © **1988** by

University Press of America, ® **Inc.**

4720 Boston Way
Lanham, MD 20706

3 Henrietta Street
London WC2E 8LU England

Printed in the United States of America

British Cataloging in Publication Information Available

"Equality: The Framers' Views © 1988 by Mary K. Bonsteel Tachau

"Misapprehensions and the First Amendment" © 1988 by George Anastaplo

"Capitalism, Socialism, and Constitutionalism" © 1988
by John Adams Wettergreen

"To Secure These Rights": Patrick Henry, James Madison,
and the Revolutionary Legitimacy of the Constitution
© 1988 by Lance Banning

Library of Congress Cataloging-in-Publication Data

To secure the blessings of liberty

(Constitutionalism in America ; v. 1)
Includes bibliographical references.
1. United States—Constitutional history—Congresses. 2. Federalist—Congresses.
I. Thurow, Sarah Baumgartner, 1947– .
KF4541.A2C58   1988   vol. 1   342.73'029   87–31721 CIP
                                        347.30229
ISBN 0–8191–6776–2 (v. 1 : alk. paper)
ISBN 0–8191–6777–0 (pbk. : v. 1 : alk. paper)

All University Press of America books are produced on acid-free
paper which exceeds the minimum standards set by the National
Historical Publications and Records Commission.

Contents

iii

Preface

The essays in this volume were first presented as papers at a conference at the University of Dallas in Irving, Texas, on October 18 and 19, 1985. The concluding essays were written by the panel moderators and are meant in part to preserve the best of the conference comment and debate as well as to suggest how each essay relates to the overall concerns of the conference.

Both the conference and publication of this volume were supported by a grant from the Bicentennial Office of the National Endowment for the Humanities. The University of Dallas Bicentennial Project has been recognized by The Commission on the Bicentennial of the United States Constitution. The opinions in this volume are those of the contributors and do not in any way reflect official policy of the National Endowment, the Commission on the Bicentennial, or the University of Dallas.

I wish to thank my husband, Glen, for his constant support and encouragement of this project as well as his invaluable advice in formulating the issues and structure of the conferences. Both Glen Thurow and Thomas West deserve credit for selecting and inviting such a well-balanced program of conference participants. Finally, I wish to thank those without whose help publication of this volume would not have been possible: Kate Hohlt, who cheerfully mastered the word-processing machine; Calan Thurow, who invented ingenious means for electronic copy editing; and especially Nicholas Janszen, who labored long hours beyond the call of duty to assist me in compiling, editing, and typesetting the book.

Sarah Baumgartner Thurow
Irving, Texas
July 10, 1987

Introduction

I

There is no time more appropriate than the Bicentennial of the Constitution for citizens and scholars to lift their eyes from immediate concerns to reflect on the principles, institutions, and way of life that characterize the United States. Our 200-year-old Constitution forms the center of our public and common life. It is the fount of all our political authority and constitutes us as a particular people guided by certain fundamental laws, institutions, and principles. What shape does the Constitution give—or ought it to give—to the lives and character of Americans? How may its influence be deepened or improved? What are the obstacles which may threaten the continuation of constitutional government, or the possibilities which may allow for its perfection? The aim of this series is to encourage both scholarly and public reflection upon these and other issues of constitutionalism in America.

There are three habits or opinions which hinder reflection on the fundamental principles of constitutional government and which this project is meant to combat. Chief among these is the habit of taking constitutional government for granted because it has endured for so long. What was a difficult task of construction for our forefathers has become an easy inheritance for us. We need to be reminded that such a familiar phenomenon as the rule of law is an achievement attained with difficulty and with difficulty maintained. In the first *Federalist*, Hamilton conveys the conviction shared by many of the founders that constitutional government is a momentous and unprecedented undertaking. A wrong step would destroy the possibility of "establishing good government from reflection and choice," and would not only condemn future generations of Americans to governments founded on "accident and force," but be "the general misfortune of mankind." One aim of these volumes, then, is to recapture this sense of the importance and fragility of constitutional government. Our intention is to reawaken the knowledge that constitutional government must be constantly examined, constantly attended to, constantly cared for.

Connected with this danger of an easy complacency is the danger that constitutional government may be fundamentally altered without our being aware of the change or what it may signify. Not only may circumstances such as the growth of technology or industry bring about new conditions requiring new applications of old principles, but our principles themselves may change without our being aware of it. We may speak the language of the founding, the language of equality and liberty, but mean something very different from what our forefathers meant by the same words. We may then fail to understand both our present situation and the original constitution. To reflect upon our constitutional principles thus requires Americans to confront the different understandings of such concepts as liberty, equality, and political rights evident in the writings and deeds of the founders as well as in our contemporary debate. This is not to say that where there are differences the advantage is always with the founders, but reflection on these differences is always necessary to make certain we have not unconsciously declined, to understand where we have been and where we are going, and to provoke reflection about what we are by reference to what we ought to be.

Thirdly, Tocqueville long ago noted that the chief danger to democracy in America was that it would decline unawares into a soft despotism. Liberty, that rallying cry of the Revolution, would come to be understood as the easy life of private gratification. The life formed by such a conception would be that of "an innumerable multitude of men, alike and equal, constantly circling around in pursuit of the petty and banal pleasures with which they glut their souls." Such people are suited for tyranny, not for the arduous life of self-governing men and women. By liberty the founders seem to have understood, first and decisively, the activity of republican government, an activity characterized by public-mindedness, rigorous control of one's private desires for gratification or self-expression, and ceaseless devotion to the common good. The founders equated freedom with living under the law and contributing to the making of law. Perhaps the most essential activity for a free people, therefore, was the habit of continually reflecting upon the fundamental principles of government by constitution. Without such reflection public discourse was all too likely to become immired in partisan and legalistic concerns and to lose all sense of common purpose.

The three volume series, *Constitutionalism in America*, addresses the American experience of government by constitution, first, by examining the distinctive principles which went into the framing of our Constitution; second, by considering how those principles were incorporated into the structures, institutions, and practices of government; and third, by reexamining constitutionalism itself both as a theory of politics and as a mode of political order.

The chapters in each volume are composed of one essay examining the founders' understanding of the issue, one examining today's views, and a concluding essay intended to recreate a sense of lively controversy, both with respect to what exactly the founders meant to do—or did without meaning to do—and with respect to what we today ought to think and do.

II

Volume I of *Constitutionalism in America, "To Secure the Blessings of Liberty": First Principles of the Constitution*, addresses the founding principles of the American regime. In establishing constitutional government in the United States the founders made a series of choices which reflected their adherence to certain fundamental principles. These principles were known to political thought prior to the American founding, but were incorporated in the Constitution in a distinctive way. According to the 39th *Federalist*, the founders chose a democratic form of government as the only form compatible with the "genius of the people of America," with the "fundamental principles of the Revolution," and with "that honorable determination which animates every votary of freedom to rest all our political experiments on the capacity of mankind for self-government."

Aristotle states that the two great principles of democratic government are liberty and equality. In choosing to form a government which is, in the words of the *Federalist*, "wholly popular," the founders placed liberty at the heart of our regime. But how are we to understand the presence of slavery in a constitution dedicated to liberty, and how is liberty itself to be understood? Is there a conflict between liberty understood as individual freedom from public restraint and liberty understood as the activity of communal self-restraint? The meaning of the second great principle of democratic government, equality, is as controversial today as is the meaning of liberty. Is the meaning of equality to be restricted to the formal political rights to life, liberty, and property, or must the social and economic conditions which allow people to take advantage of their rights also be equalized?

Republican government also poses the problem of how to reconcile majority rule with minority rights—the topic of the third chapter—and how to transform the unalienable but insecure rights of human nature into the solidly buttressed rights of citizens—the topic of the fourth chapter. In creating a limited government based upon majority rule, the founders faced the problem of whether such a government was compatible with that freedom of conscience, thought, and speech which permits the highest human endeavors. In order to secure such freedom, does constitutional government require also the freedom to do what may be base or despicable? Furthermore, do non-citizens have civil rights? The Declaration of Independence states that the purpose of government is to secure men's unalienable rights. But these natural rights are transformed by the Constitution into civil rights—the rights of citizens. How is citizenship to be understood? What does our citizenship require of us that is not required of human beings generally? Do we have rights as citizens that we are not entitled to as human beings?

Perhaps the most important policy question facing the new regime was the problem of economic faction—the need to regulate the private pursuit of economic gain in a manner consistent with public rights and the common good. This is the theme of the fifth chapter. Does the form of government established by the Constitution rest upon particular economic requirements or a particular economic system? Was the Constitution intended to give political sanction to an existing economic order? As *Federalist* #10 makes clear, the founders thought that the character of economic life was important to the success of constitutional government; but as the quarrel between the Republicans and the Federalists makes clear, what that character should be was a matter of dispute. Can today's economic disputes be understood in terms of the debate over the larger principles of constitutional government?

The final chapter on the Declaration of Independence considers to what extent the political theory of our Revolution is embodied in the Constitution. The Declaration announced the principles justifying the American Revolution. Did these principles also provide the foundation of the American Constitution? Or did the Declaration set forth democratic principles which were abandoned by the Constitution in order to protect propertied interests? And how are we to understand the founders' treatment of slavery? These are some of the issues addressed in the essays contained in this volume.

The authors represent the disciplines of political science, history, law, economics, and literature, as well as the spectrum of partisan opinion. Some of the authors who have written on the founding are by no means partisans of the founders' beliefs, as the essays by Tachau and Nedelsky show. Tachau argues that the founders never meant to include women, Blacks, or Native Americans as equal members of their polity because at that time they were unable to conceive of these groups as political equals. Similarly, Nedelsky argues that it is doubtful whether we could ever institute a truly just economic order under a Constitution and a legal tradition so permeated by assumptions of inequality. Nor do the authors all agree on what it was that the founders intended: for example, Schaub believes that the founders intended the government to form the moral character of the people, while McWilliams believes that this is precisely what they neglected.

There is a similar range of positions with respect to what is wrong—or right—with America today and what to do about it. Barber calls for the establishment of a "strong democracy"—a species of participatory democracy based upon a classical understanding of citizenship modified by a modern understanding of rights. Anastaplo agrees that active, direct participation in politics is the foundation of good citizenship, but believes that the Constitution with the Bill of Rights—and especially the First Amendment—gives us all we need for such a regime; what is lacking is our willingness to use what we have. Both Arkes and Banning recover for us the arguments of the losing side in two crucial debates of the founding and demonstrate their relevance for policy deliberations today: Arkes does this for the Federalist argument against the Bill of Rights, Banning for the Anti-Federalists' arguments against the Constitution as a violation of the principles of the Revolution. Sandoz recreates the complex process of compromise involved in the founding and reminds us that it was as true then as it is today that politics is the art of the possible, and political decisions are an amalgam of principled aims and pragmatic calculations. Wettergreen shows how developments in political thought since the founding have led to a misplaced emphasis on the economic motives and principles of the founders, obscuring and diminishing the importance of their principle of individualism. Abraham critiques recent Supreme Court decisions to show the difficulty not only of agreeing on what equality means under the Constitution, but of discovering what it means in the abstract, in principle. And Thurow argues that the contemporary rejection of natural rights doctrine has led to the severing of freedom and constitutionalism—the principles of the Declaration and the Constitution—and a consequent loss of common purpose.

Taken altogether, these essays represent both the range of issues involved in the American experience of constitutional government and the range of partisan opinion about the Constitution itself, both at its framing and today. It is a truly *political* collection.

Chapter One

Popular Government: Liberty

Aristotle states that the two great principles of democratic government are liberty and equality. In choosing to form a government which is, in the words of the Federalist, "wholly popular," the founders placed liberty at the heart of our regime. But how are we to understand the presence of slavery in a constitution dedicated to liberty, and how is liberty itself to be understood? Is there a conflict between liberty understood as individual freedom from public restraint and liberty understood as the activity of communal self-restraint?

Justice and Honor, The Surest Foundation of Liberty: The Natural Law Doctrine in *The Federalist No. 10*

Sanderson Schaub

Natural Law

Our celebration is to take the form of a reflection on the American founding, in particular, on how the founders viewed the principle of liberty and the problem of popular government. Let our point of departure be a reflection made by Abraham Lincoln, in the light of Proverbs 25:11, on the blessings of liberty, as handed down from the founders to posterity:

> All this (said Lincoln) is not the result of accident. It has a philosophical cause. Without the *Constitution* and the *Union*, we could not have attained the result; but even these, are not the primary cause of our great prosperity. There is something back of these, entwining itself more closely about the human heart. That something, is the principle of "Liberty to all"—the principle that clears the *path* for all—gives hope to all—and, by consequence, *enterprise*, and industry to all.

> The expression of that principle, in our Declaration of Independence, was most happy, and fortunate . . . . [*W*]*ithout* it, we could not, I think, have secured our free government, and consequent prosperity. No oppressed people will *fight*, and endure, as our fathers did, without the promise of something better, than a mere change of masters.

> The assertion of that *principle*, at *that time*, was the word, "fitly spoken" which has proved an "apple of gold" to us. The *Union* and the *Constitution*, are the *picture* of *silver*, subsequently framed around it. The picture was made, not to *conceal*, or destroy the apple; but to *adorn*, and *preserve* it. The picture was made *for* the apple—*not* the apple for the picture.

Our Constitution, Lincoln is saying, is truly instrumental to securing the blessings of liberty; but it is so, insofar as it gives effect to the principle of our Declaration—"Liberty to all." That principle, as therein stated, is even more fundamental than the Constituion, for it is the very purpose of the Constitution. Now the Declaration's principle is expounded in terms of "the laws of nature and of nature's God." Natural law is understood by

Lincoln and by Thomas Jefferson, the author of the Declaration, to be a law higher than any law of mere human artifice, i.e., of the kind traditionally called postve law, such as the Constituion. Yet the Constituion, formed in accordance with and to give effect to this higher law, partakes in some degree of this higher law or is itself a kind of higher law; and must be viewed as the fundamental law of the land, being more permanent and stable than ordinary statute law. Just as the Constituion aims to accord with natural law, statute law must be made to accord with Constituional law, which cannot be created by ordinary majorities in our legislatures, but can only be formed by great acts of extraordinary majorities of the entire people, as at the founding epoch. If, then, the Constitution is the fundamental law of the land, the natural law, in this view of the matter, is its most fundamental part.

In this manner the principle of "Liberty to all" forms the guiding purpose of our nation, of the "*Union* and the *Constitution*." When, therefore, we look to the Declaration to comprehend the meaning of that principle—"that all men are created equal; that they are endowed by their Creator with certain unalienable rights; that among these are life, liberty, and the pursuit of happiness"—and its corollary principle—"that to secure these rights, governments are instituted among men, deriving their just powers from the consent of the governed"—we are celebrating, in a sense, the American Constitution as well.

Now in what respect are all men created equal? They are not created equally strong, nor equally good looking, nor equally smart, nor equally brave, nor equally skilled for a variety of pursuits. (Accordingly, while all have an equal right to liberty, they have no equal right to happiness *per se*, but only to its pursuit.) We must keep in mind that the Declaration is a political document. It means to say that all men are by nature equal, because they are equally possessed of political right. All men have naturally an equal political right to self-government. No man is naturally subject to the authority of another man, because no man has been granted a divine right to rule another man without the latter's consent. Considering man with a view to political authority, the Declaration contends that mature men are endowed by nature with enough reason to justify their equal right to consent to the authority of the government placed over them, while no man is sufficiently endowed with enough wisdom to justify the imposition of his authority upon mature human beings without their consent. Clearly, Jefferson meant to announce the principles of free, popular government and to renounce the divine right of kings.

As Alexander Hamilton (in *The Farmer Refuted*) had already pointed out in 1775, such a natural law doctrine does not correspond to the political thought of the monarchist Thomas Hobbes, according to whom man in a state of nature is "perfectly free from all restraint of law and government." For "good and wise men, in all ages," says Hamilton, "have embraced ... an eternal and immutable law, which is indispensably obligatory upon all mankind, prior to any human institution whatever." That is to say, from the perspective of the signers of the Declaration, just because men in their natural condition are free from the politicial authority of other men, this does not mean that as reasonable human beings, aware of their superiority to brute creation, they do not fall under an obligation to God and to themselves to act as men by fulfilling their moral duty to their fellow human beings and their political duty to their country. This understanding of natural law is implied by the whole Revolutionary and Founding effort. For when the signers of the Declaration and the people of the colonies dissolved their political ties and broke with their obligations to Great Britain, they did not (and could not) thereby renounce all obligations whatsoever, but rather did they take upon themselves a higher obligation. Such a conception of the bonds of duty which underlie the commitment to the principle of liberty for all, is shown most simply in the pledge of the signers that concludes the Declaration:

> And for the support of this declaration, with a firm reliance on the protection of divine providence, we mutually pledge to each other our lives, our fortunes, and our sacred honor.

The Problem of Popular Government
•

If the aim of just government is to secure liberty for all, its corollary principle is that just government must be based on the consent of the governed, or the opinion of society. Since unanimity is nearly always impossible, the closest approximation to it, the most consistent practical alternative to it, is the principle of majority rule. Free, popular government in practice means rule by majority decisions. Here a vast problem arises: there is no necessity that the opinion of society be fair enough to pursue liberty for those in the minority or even enlightened enough to pursue the political liberty of the society generally, including that of the majority itself. Man's very freedom, his power of reasoning and decision by which he is naturally separated from brute creation, precludes such a necessity. The principle of equal freedom, which puts ultimate authority in the opinion of society, means there can be no guarantee that popular opinion will prove just or enlightened. For if men are truly free to govern themselves, then they are free to act nobly or basely, sensibly or foolishly. "The noble things are difficult," said Aristotle. Surely it is not easy for popular government to prove just and enlightened. The Declaration opens a grand and imposing vista, the noble problem of political freedom. It was with a view to this fact that Lincoln at Gettysburg uttered the words: "We are engaged in a great civil war, testing whether that nation or any nation so conceived [in liberty] and so dedicated [to the proposition that all men are created equal], can long endure."

How, in practice, does one promote and sustain political liberty under a political system of majority rule? As this was the guiding question before the framers of the Constitution, so too did it form the central problem of *The Federalist*, the most celebrated defense of the Constitution. In a general way, in its attempt to solve the problem of popular government, James Madison's *Federalist* No. 10, the most famous number (perhaps along with No. 51), could be said to take its bearings from the Declaration. Yet the connection has been largely overlooked, perhaps for the following reason: in the 1790's Madison became Jefferson's ideological partner in founding the first Republican party; however, in order to do so, it has seemed to scholars that Madison was forced to break with his views concerning political parties as expressed in *Federalist* No. 10. It seems that its apparent differences with Jeffersonianism have tended to direct attention away from its link with Jefferson's Declaration. Now we do not wish to dispute the fact that Madison's views on broad vs. strict construction of the Constitution had shifted by 1798 in his Virginia Resolutions. Perhaps the case can be made, however, that in his view of political parties there is to be found a certain consistency between the earlier (*Federalist*) and later (Republican) Madison. It seems to me that it would be a fitting way to celebrate the bicentennial to show that Madison, at the time he fathered the Constitution, in his views on liberty and popular government, neither was inconsistent with the doctrine of the Declaration, nor with the later teaching of Abraham Lincoln, who used the Declaration's principle as his guidepost in all matters.

The Problem of Virtue

The appropriate starting point for comprehending Madison's teaching in *Federalist* No. 10, is to recognize the fact that Madison was as firm a defender of the equal natural rights of men as was Jefferson in the

Declaration. As Marvin Meyers has pointed out, "Madison and the founders ... had reached a state of conviction on the immutable laws of nature and of nature's God, prescribing the rights of man, [and] the ends of civil society."[1] *The Federalist* is everywhere filled with reference to rights: "private rights," "personal rights," "property rights," "the rights of individuals," "the rights of citizens," "civil rights," "religious rights," "the rights of states," "the rights of the people," "the rights of humanity," "natural rights," and "sacred rights." In 1785 Madison, in support of Jefferson's Bill for Religious Liberty in Virginia, had written a powerful and clear-cut defense of the right of conscience, "in its nature an unalienable right." But he did not separate right from duty: "what is here a right towards man, is a duty towards the Creator." He spoke of the natural rights teaching in the same manner as did John Jay at the very beginning of *Federalist* No. 2, which, if one discounts Hamilton's introductory remarks in No. 1, is actually the very beginning of the entire argument of *The Federalist*. The further fact that this is the only place in the entire work where the term "natural rights" is expressly mentioned, only serves to underline the primary and fundamental significance of the Declaration's teaching for *The Federalist* generally. "If 'all men are by nature equally free and independent,' " said Madison, referring to the Virginia Declaration of Rights, "all men are to be considered as entering into society on equal conditions; as relinquishing no more, and therefore retaining no less, one than another, of their natural rights." The equal right to the free exercise of religion, he also wrote, "is held by the same tenure with all our other rights. If we recur to its origins, it is equally the gift of nature." Consequently, the will of Virginia's government, or of its legislature, is not "the only meausre" of its "authority." The state is "bound to leave this particular right untouched and sacred."[2]

Madison himself alludes to this kind of higher law binding upon the state in *Federalist* No. 14. The argument in this number, it should be noted, is meant in defense of his call for an extended American republic in *Federalist* No. 10: "the mingled blood" of American citizens shed during the Revolution "in defense of their sacred rights, consecrate their Union." No. 10 describes a principle, newly discovered by political science, which is likely to help secure the rights of all citizens in a large republic and to appeal to the "friend of popular government." No. 14 indicates the reason

---

1. Marvin Meyers, ed., *The Mind of the Founder: Sources of the Political Thought of James Madison*, (Hanover: University Press of New England, 1981), p. xx.

2. *The Mind of the Founder*, pp. 7-13.

or cause for which Americans ought to be friends to popular government. Their blood was shed from obligation to a higher law, by which their natural rights are shown to be sacred for themselves and their kindred, so that their blood mingled with those rights—the blood *and* the rights— consecrates the Union. Ultimately, the unified republic and the attachment to popular government are justified only by those sacred rights. If all men are not created equal, attachment to popular government and concern for equal justice to all citizens, the core attachment and concern of No. 10, are of little moment.

In *Federalist* No. 43 Madison takes up two "very delicate" questions. On what principle can the Confederation legitimately be superseded, if ratification of the Constitution by nine states alone rather than by thirteen unanimously is enough to establish a new government? He appeals for justification to "the transcendent law of nature and of nature's God": the Confederation "*must* be sacrificed," and with sound reason, because it patently fails to secure the "safety and happiness of society." Political institutions which very poorly serve both the most urgent aim (safety) and the most complete—or perfect—aim of human society (happiness) cannot be permitted to deny the unalienable right to self-preservation of the vast majority acting sanely and prudently. Men are actually obligated not to proceed by means of imbecilic folly, continuing in a state of government so inadequate as to be virtually a state of anarchy, while meekly awaiting the stubborn blindness of an unreasonable minority. But what of the hypothetical relations between the new government and the four or fewer states still to ratify? These relations are not "political" but "moral"; the "claims of justice" and the "*rights of humanity* must in all cases be duly and mutually respected."[3] Plainly enough, I think, Madison refers in this instance, too, to the natural law. Yet in light of the sad experience of injustice under the Articles of Confederation, it is little wonder that Madison, aware of the dangerous passions of man, admonishes the ratifying states to forebear through moderation and the others to join quickly through prudence.

The state of near anarchy that existed under the Confederation leads us to an interesting point. As one scholar of the founding notes, "the view that a sense of common interest will lead states (as under the theory of the Articles of Confederation) to obey mere 'recommendations' is equivalent to the view that government is unnecessary."[4] Supposing that only man's

---

3. Here and hereafter the italics have been added, unless otherwise noted.
4. David F. Epstein, *The Political Theory of the Federalist* (Chicago: University of Chicago Press, 1984), p. 38.

reason were to rule him and his passions were powerless to control political affairs, anarchy, that is, the absence of governmental sanctions, might seem most appropriate to his condition. The crucial point is that during this period of the founding Americans lived, at the national level at any rate, in an unsatisfactory and utopian state of affairs, for the Articles did not represent a true "government" over individuals. This unsatisfactory condition brought about the Constitutional Convention in Philadelphia. Americans were living, so to speak, in a Garden of Eden from whence they had begun to fall and were falling further and faster. Reason and common sense independently of laws with teeth, that is, of the sanctions of government, were shown to be deficient. Thus they were called upon to impose a real government over themselves. Hence a kind of paradox might seem to arise: man's common sense must be persuaded to see that reason is too feeble without government to act reasonably. Accordingly, while still residing in a state without real government, he must be persuaded to act reasonably enough to set one up: this reasonable deed might seem to refute the premise of it. If self-government is possible on this point, why, after all, the need for government generally?

This inquiry brings us to the core of Madison's political thought, showing how he resolved the paradox. Man is a complex being, a mixture of reason and passion. He has a being in-between God and the brute creation. "But it is the reason alone of the public that ought to control and regulate government. The passions ought to be controlled and regulated by the government" (No. 49). Reason rules; passion serves. In this respect Madison was Aristotelian or classical in his thinking. He did not follow the modern, Hobbesian contention that the reason is only a scout and a spy serving the passions.

Defending the new Constitution before the Virginia ratifying convention, Madison argued against two contrasting positions, one expecting too little, the other expecting too much of the human character.

> I have observed that gentlemen suppose, that the general legislature will do every mischief they possibly can, and that they will omit to do every thing good which they are authorized to do. If this were a reasonable supposition their objection would be good. I consider it reasonable to conclude, that they will as readily do their duty, as deviate from it.

In *Federalist* No. 55 he had said, "Were the pictures ... drawn by the political jealousy of some among us faithful likenesses of the human character, the inference would be that there is not sufficient virtue among men for self-government." Madison entertained a different and more elevated view of human nature, for he was determined to "rest all our political experiments on the capacity of mankind for self-government" (No. 39).

But he recognized as well the power of the human passions: "nor do I go on the grounds mentioned by the gentlemen on the other side—that we are to place unlimited confidence in them, and expect nothing but the most exalted integrity and sublime virtue." In *Federalist* No. 51 he had said: "But what is government itself but the greatest of all reflections on human nature? If men were angels, no government would be necessary. If angels were to govern men, neither external nor internal controls on government would be necessary." Madison knew in advance how unlikely must be Lincoln's desperate plea and prediction in the face of impending civil disaster: "Though passion may have strained, it must not break, our bonds of affection. The mystic chords of memory . . . will yet swell the chorus of the Union when again touched, as surely they will be, by the better angels of our nature."

Yet Madison need not have been surprised by the presence of a Lincoln to lead the nation through the great time of crisis.

> But I go on this great republican principle, that the people will have virtue and intelligence to select men of virtue and wisdom. Is there no virtue among us? If there be not, we are in a wretched situation. No theoretical checks—no form of government can render us secure. To suppose that any form of government will secure liberty without any virtue in the people is a chimerical idea.

When Madison in *Federalist* No. 55 referred to those with a decidedly low view of the nature of men, he said that "nothing less than the chains of despotism can restrain them from destroying and devouring one another," if there "is not sufficient virtue among men for self-government." Using the same language in the Virginia convention, he continues: "if there be sufficient virtue and intelligence in the community, it will be exercised in the selection of these men [of virtue and wisdom]. So we do not depend on their virtue or put confidence in our rulers, but in the people who are to choose them." Madison expresses his commitment to republicanism in an almost formulaic fashion in No. 55: "As there is a degree of depravity in mankind which requires a certain degree of circumspection and distrust, so there are other qualities in human nature which justify a certain portion of esteem and confidence. Republican government presupposes the existence of these qualities in a higher degree than any other form." By now it should be plain that the presupposition of Madison's republicanism is the proposition that there is "sufficient virtue among men for self-government."

Indeed, this proposition forms one ground for Madison's adherence to the proposition "that all men are created equal," the other ground being that no man is wise enough to govern another man without his consent. For there can be no reason to guarantee liberty to men through free government, if they are not presumed at the same time to be morally free agents who may, as morally free, exercise virtue enough to govern themselves. Without this condition, that is, the possibility of self-restraint, "nothing less than the chains of despotism can restrain them." But in that case the enlightened and fastidious standard of wisdom which applies in the former instance—that no man can consistently know enough about the souls of other men to know how they would choose, nor is far-seeing enough to know the sure consequences of such a choice made on their behalf, nor, perhaps, can care enough to choose rightly without being answerable to them—must be lowered. In that case in other words, a standard of wisdom based on what Jefferson loved to call superstition— the right of divine inspiration, the divine right of kings, i.e., of one man, or of several men in the form of priests, to rule the rest without their consent or despotically—must take precedence over the higher standard. This application of the lower standard would follow with logical consistency. For the reason that no man can have that divine insight, that divine omniscience, that divine care of human beings, which we understand to be attributes of God, is that we recognize in men their free moral agency to decide the outcome of events for good or bad. The noble and free decision of Winston Churchill to stand and oppose Nazism at all costs had as its outcome that Adolf Hitler never would rule all Europe or the world. But there are very many, indeed, an infinite number of lesser decisions which also determine events, such as the decision of the German people to follow Hitler and the decision of the British people to elevate Churchill to the Prime Ministership. But mere men cannot have certain knowledge of, or predict in advance, what decisions, among so many, are being taken, or will be taken, or what their outcomes will prove to be. If, however, men were not understood to be in some sense free moral agents, free either to follow reason and virtue, or to succumb to passions opposed to them, then whoever recognized by some necessarily inexplicable divine insight his own fundamental madness, would at the same time, understand by this the madness and servitude to the passionate imagination of all others, that is, the necessary sameness of men among themselves and with the brutes, as opposed to the potential distinction among men and from brute creation by virtue of reasoned choice. Thus this madman could, with the aid of superstition and force, justly establish his own despotism in order to restrain men "from destroying and devouring one another." Yet even in this loathsome example is to be found a kernel of the truth of the enlightened conception of man, because this "divine" ruler would be acting in accordance with reason and some virtue by establishing a semblance of justice amidst the reigning chaos. He, at least, would be acting as a free moral agent.

Madison's view of human nature's capabilities for self-government suggests that there are several fundamental principles comprised within the proposition that "all men are created equal." One is merely a re-statement of the proposition itself: all mature men (excluding manifestly defective and therefore not fully human beings, such as those fit for insane asylums) are by nature free, moral agents. Yet we have seen two other principles folowing from this one.

The first is the principle of popular consent. Because of man's equality of moral freedom, no man is wise enough to govern another without his consent. All men possess certain natural rights, and it is republican government which, with the most just consistency, respects those rights by operating on the principle of the consent of all.

The second, equally necessary and fundamental, according to Madison, is the principle of virtue and equal justice to all, the presupposition of republican liberty. The precondition for establishing and preserving republican government (which is the embodiment of the principle of consent), is the existence of "sufficient virtue among men for self-government."

Yet it is clear that "this great, republican principle" is problematical for Madison. The American republic must be, and was by both Madison and Lincoln, understood to be a great test of "the capacity of mankind for self-government." For both of them this means that America is marked by the "honorable determination which animates every votary of freedom, to rest all our political experiments on the capacity of mankind" for justice and virtue. For that same human freedom which is recognized by the Declaration requires that the outcome in the struggle for justice cannot be predetermined. Fully consistent with this understanding, Madison states: "Justice is the end of government. It is the end of civil society. It ever has been and ever will be pursued until it be obtained or until liberty be lost in the pursuit" (No. 51). It is, therefore, in accordance with the teaching of the father of our Constitution, to say that Lincoln was right when he called the principle that "all men are created equal" "the father of all moral principle in us."

The Argument of Federalist No. 10

In the partisan battles that raged during the 1790's, Madison, who had supported Hamilton in the 1780's in his fight for a new federal Constitution, now sided with Jefferson and became an advocate for Republicanism against Hamilton's Federalism. He penned a series of articles which were published in Jefferson's party organ, the *National Gazette*. To "explain James Madison's articles for the Republican Party press," Harry Jaffa has said, is "a most painful and puzzling difficulty." "There is not yet a satisfactory, consistent account," says Jaffa, "of the anomalies presented by the words and deeds of James Madison."[5] While my discussion of *Federalist* No. 10, the theme of which is parties or factions, touches only briefly on the party press essays of Madison, my interpretation is intended to point in the direction of such a consistent account, insofar as one may at some time be found possible.

I doubt that Madison himself experienced any strong sense of inconsistency between No. 10 and his party press essays. The reason is that I believe the admittedly very rudimentary form of the Republican party lies beneath the structure of *The Federalist*. As Marvin Meyers has said of Madison: "Unlike the case of religion, the public right to frame a political creed raised no doubts for him." "It is certainly very material that the *true* doctrines of liberty," said Madison in a letter to Jefferson in 1825, "should be inculcated." In 1833 Madison, writing of John C. Calhoun's concurrent majority doctrine, called it a "new heresy."[6] Madison meant by this expression what Jefferson did when at the time Tom Paine's *The Rights of Man* appeared in America, he was quoted on the frontispiece of the book as saying that he was "extremely pleased to find it will be re-printed here, and that something is at length to be publicly said against the *political heresies* which have sprung up among us." But *Federalist* No. 1 already speaks of "heresies" in "politics," though it opposes "persecution" as the solution to them. More significantly, perhaps, No. 68 says of the book's authors: "we cannot acquiesce in the political heresy of the poet who says—*For forms of government let fools contest . . . .*" Wise men are enlightened partisans, *The Federalist* implies, of the republican form, which is worth contesting for. And as *The Federalist* speaks of policial heresy, so it speaks

---

5. Harry V. Jaffa, "The Madisonian Legacy: A Reconsideration of the Founders' Intent," in *American Conservatism and the American Founding* (Durham: Carolina Academic Press, 1984), pp. 205, 207.

6. *The Mind of the Founder*, pp. 348-49, 411.

of political truth: "No *political truth* is certainly of greater intrinsic value, or is stamped with the authority of more *enlightened patrons of liberty*" than that which "may justly be pronounced the very definition of tyranny" (No. 47). No. 9 speaks of "the friends and *partisans*" of "free government" and "the enlightened friends of liberty." And No. 10 speaks of the "friend of popular governments." Thus the friends, patrons, or partisans of free, popular government, insofar as they are enlightened, adhere to the political truth and oppose political heresy. The foundation was already laid in *The Federalist*, therefore, upon which Madison strove in his party press essays to build a national consensus of opinion and sentiment, an established Republican church, so to speak, for the nation.

Note: When Hamilton refers to the "friends and partisans" of "free government" in No. 9, he either uses "partisan" in a non-invidious, good sense, which the context implies, or else he demonstrates a certain neutrality between free and despotic forms of government which in No. 68 he says "we" call "political heresy." "We" could mean majestic we, or we authors as Publius, or we Americans, or all three. Hamilton either means to distinguish himself from Madison and the "genius of the American people" by using "we" ironically in No. 68 to exclude himself—and the context could suggest this, because he is worried about what he may "safely pronounce"—or he uses "partisan" non-invidiously in No. 9. Whatever his intent, I at least would not accept the facile explanation that he was merely confused on this central issue. I would add that if there is an implicit distinction between "friends" and "enlightened friends," this still does not mean that "friends" is used invidiously: such men still love justice even if they are not wise. The same would hold for partisans of free government, unless Hamilton were neutral to freedom and despotism— "*That which is best administered is best.*"[7] In my opinion, Hamilton was not neutral to despotism, but No. 9 does hint, perhaps, at a certain impartiality between monarchical or aristocratic liberty and republican liberty. Yet this means little because Madison's No. 10 also moves in its argument from liberty generally to republican liberty. It is just that the more guarded Madison does not praise the still free alternative to republican liberty as Hamilton does, and rather firmly at that.

Republican partisanship of the enlightened variety is clearly present in Madison's response to his query in No. 39, whether the Constitution is "strictly republican." "It is evident that no other form would be reconcilable ... with *the fundamental principles* of the Revolution; or with that

---

7. *Federalist* No. 68. Italics in the original.

honorable determination which animates every *votary* of freedom" (differently stated, that noble resolve which gives spirit to every religious partisan of liberty—such men as this will form the body of the church) "to rest all our political *experiments* on the capacity of mankind for self-government" (that is, to test republican virtue in mankind). Notice how Madison's rhetoric combines the language of ancient religion and the language of modern science to lend support to the principles of the Declaration—whose natural law doctrine points to classical political philosophy—while he forms the "strictly republican" political creed—whose republicanism points to ancient politics—for a broad, national consensus. Jefferson's rhetoric also comprehended these four tendencies. Religion was needed to give firm faith to the unenlightened. Science was needed in the technology of the free press to spread party doctrine. Classicism was needed to give the practical wisdom and moderation required in the long-range enterprise. Politics was needed to give the manly, fighting spirit which would bring victory to the lovers of republican liberty. This combination seems to be what Madison has in mind when in this same passage he mentions the "genius of the people of America." If present-day America is to win the many battles that lie ahead against Soviet tyranny, it must recover its genius; it is faltering in every category. This is not to say that such a combination is not a great task indeed for a contemporary political party to accomplish. But is it not the only way?

Harry Jaffa, in an unpublished article, has given an example of the kind of enlightened, or what might be called impartial partisanship which Madison seems to have had in mind even while writing *The Federalist*: "no less a *friend to popular government* than Thomas Jefferson, contemplating the invasions of the rule of law in his own Virginia during the Revolution, had written: "it was not an elective despotism we fought for . . . ." (Jefferson's remark is quoted in *Federalist* No. 48.) A passage in another of Jaffa's articles is also revealing: "Publius notes that it is *enemies of republican government* who say that 'there is not sufficient virtue among men for self-government.' "[8] Now Madison in *Federalist* No. 55 is discussing both the "sincere friends of liberty" and by implication the insincere. The latter, we learn in *Federalist* No. 57, are "the men who profess the most flaming zeal for republican government, yet boldly impeach *the fundamental principle* of it . . . ." Jaffa is correct to call them "enemies of republican government" because Madison demands a principled political partisanship. His

---

8. Harry V. Jaffa, "Phoenix from the Ashes," (unpublished) and Jaffa, "The Madisonian Legacy," p. 210.

position in 1787 is not, then, necessarily inconsistent with what he wrote on this point in 1792: "The republican party ... will naturally find their account in burying all antecedent questions, in banishing every other distinction than that between *enemies and friends to republican government*, and in promoting a general harmony among the latter, wherever residing or however employed."

Now the term "party" seems always to be used in *The Federalist* in its vicious or divisive sense except, perhaps, when Hamilton speaks of the "friends and partisans" of "free government." "Party" seems nearly always to mean "faction," which Madison defines in No. 10 as "a number of citizens ... who are united and actuated by some common impulse of passion or of interest, adverse to the rights of other citizens, or to the permanent and aggregate interests of the community." Yet frequently *The Federalist* uses the term "friends" (or "patrons") instead of "partisans." And it does so in order to suggest the elevated sense of an impartial partisanship, which meaning it clearly has in mind.[9] Madison wanted, insofar as possible, to form an enlightened republican consensus around the plan for Union. The enlightened friends to republican union were the natural leaders of this consensus or party. If the *word* "party" is nearly always applied in a pejorative sense, the *phenomenon* of a non-invidious partisan consensus is nonetheless present in *The Federalist's* approach, a consensus which is not factional or not adverse to the rights of citizens or to the public good.

The rhetoric of Nos. 9 and 10 proceeds along similar lines: We aim to be enlightened friends of liberty and popular government. But there is the problem of faction. We can solve it, however, in this way. Therefore we can be enlightened partisans—"friends"—to republican liberty, after all. Madison in No. 10 bottles up the reader's emotions longer than does Hamilton in No. 9, however, which has a heightened effect on both the restraint called for by Madison's argument and the passionate, partisan commitment invoked at its conclusion. He addresses the "friend of popular government," but tells him it would be "an unwarrantable partiality" to contend that the danger of faction has yet been overcome. Next, he appeals to "our most considerate and virtuous citizens," who are "friends of liberty," to attest to the danger. These men represent enlightened partisanship. Not until the entire argument has been completed and the

---

9. For an interesting discussion of nonpartisan politics partly in reference to *The Federalist*, see Harvey C. Mansfield, Jr., "Impartial Representation," in *Representation and Misrepresentation*, ed. Robert A. Goldwin (Chicago: Rand McNally, 1966), pp. 91-113.

reader enlightened does he let the emotion out of the bottle: "according to the pleasure and pride we feel in being republicans, ought to be our *zeal*" in pursuit of the proposed plan. Must we not conclude that it is a "warrantable and impartial partiality" to contend for the new republican union? Another question which may be asked is: how many references to republicanism in *The Federalist*—and there are many—refer implicitly to party in the elevated sense? We have already mentioned a few of the leading examples.

The great problem of republicanism lies in majority faction or what Tocqueville called tyranny of the majority. Madison argues that the extended union is preferable to the smaller areas of the states for the purpose of restraining majority factions. One cannot remove the causes of faction because the only practicable method would be to destroy liberty, which is folly because liberty is essential to political life. Madison seems to imply here that liberty is the condition for man to pursue the noble ends of justice, honor, and happiness as the aims of political life. At any rate, it becomes necessary, therefore, to control the effects of faction, which may be done through the principle of representation, tending to select out rulers of wisdom, patriotism, and justice; as well as by extending the sphere which will take in such a multiplicity and diversity of factions that they will act as restraints and mutual checks on one another. Thus, good rulers and counteracting factions will tend to create majority coalitions which are non-factional and formed on the principles of justice and the public good. This, in a nutshell, is the argument of *Federalist* No. 10.

John Zvesper, in a very informative study of party politics in the founding period, finds, as do others, a tension between Madison as Publius in the *Federalist* and Madison in his party press essay on "Parties." The Madison of 1792 consistently labels parties "unavoidable" and "evil" and suggests several ways to combat the vice:

> By establishing political equality among all . . . by the silent operation of laws, which, without violating the rights of property, reduce extreme wealth towards the state of mediocrity, and raise extreme indigence toward a state of comfort . . . . By making one party a check on the other, so far as the existence of parties cannot be prevented, nor their views accommodated.

> [Then he proceeds in mocking fashion:] Let us then increase these *natural distinctions* by favoring an inequality of property; and let us add to them artificial distinctions, by establishing *kings and nobles and plebeians*. We shall then have the more checks to oppose each other . . . .

[Finally he concludes:] From the expediency, in politics, of making natural parties, mutual checks on each other, to infer the propriety of creating artificial parties, in order to form them into mutual checks, is not less absurd than it would be in ethics to say, that new vices ought to be promoted, where they would counteract each other, because this use may be made of existing vices.

Now the reason that this essay is not used as a gloss on *Federalist* No. 10 appears to be that here Madison seems to be favoring a policy which fosters "an even distribution of wealth," whereas in No. 10 he had said that the "diversity in the faculties of men, from which the rights of property originate" is "an insuperable obstacle to a uniformity of interests." Moreover, the "protection of these faculties is the first object of government." Perhaps there is, in fact, some tension between Madison's two efforts. Yet Madison does repeat in 1792 that property rights must not be violated. Also, in another party press essay entitled, "Property," he subsumes all rights under property in the large sense—what is one's own including personal rights—in order, clearly, I think, to encourage and habituate men to give equal respect to the rights of property in the narrow sense. Then, too, by "faculties" he had meant natural faculties, and he explains here that this excludes wealth created by artificial or unfair advantages. It is not always easy to draw an exact line between "favoring" inequality and "favoring" equality of property. Is not Madison in favor of a moderate balance, recognizing natural differences and recognizing property rights, but leaning "towards" mediocrity and "towards" comfort? Were not the extremes to his mind the magnificent splendor of the French palace and the widespread poverty of the London city streets? Harry Jaffa has said that Aristotle's *Politics* "is addressed to precisely the same central problem which preoccupies Publius: how to moderate the conflict between the poor and the rich, so as to make possible a rule of law, a non-tyrannical way in which the citizens rule and are ruled in turn."[10] Is this not Madison's aim here, too? Did not Aristotle "favor" a broad middle class to give the tone to his polity? Perhaps Madison's essay is closer to the sobriety of Aristotelianism as opposed to the utopianism of Rousseau than might appear at first glance. However that may be, let us hear the contradiction detected by Zvesper: "Publius had sought to multiply rather than to prevent factions and had not been so concerned to correct directly the unequal distribution of property underlying them; Madison now

---

10. Jaffa, "The Madisonian Legacy," p. 211.

questioned the naturalness of parties produced by policies which favored 'an inequality of property'."[11] Now this, I fear, entails a real misunderstanding of the intent of *Federalist* No. 10.

Madison did *not* seek "to multiply rather than to prevent factions." Extending the sphere did not mean extending the influence of factions. It means delimiting or weakening their influence. Extension meant the inclusion of many factions, but it in no way multiplied their existence. By including the many, *pre*-existing factions within one government, the relative power of each would be weakened. It seems to me that Madison is showing us in 1792 how he expected his earlier argument to work. He begins *Federalist* No. 10 by calling the "violence of faction" a "dangerous vice." As he says in 1792, he does not wish to promote "new vices," but to use existing ones to weaken each other. Accordingly, if any multiplying is to be done, according to *Federalist* No. 10, new virtues are to be multiplied by habituating men to just principles of action. The obscurity seems to be in not making the following distinction: The natural faculties may be virtues while "the naturalness of parties" refers to the natural self-love which gives rise to vices. Madison's intent is to reduce the scope for extreme, violent, and unjust parties and to open the way for a broad consensus on just and patriotic principles. This means that if viciousness begins to spread by one small party growing larger, the majority can unite and justly oppose it. Some weak factions might be included in the majority, but if they begin to overstep their legal and constitutional bounds, it is to be hoped that the majority can unite with other factions previously in a minority, which have cause to oppose the new threat. The obvious problem is that by gradual steps the variety of vices, jockeying back and forth, soon grow out of hand, if a constant habituation and rededication to the principles of justice is not carried forward by political leadership. This kind of consensus, I think, Madison at least attempted to effect in the 1790's.

When Madison says that the aim should be to make "one party a check on the other, so far as the existence of parties cannot be prevented, nor their views accommodated," he is admitting that the larger the proportion of justice and virtue in society, of non-factionalism, the better the system works. To create virtue out of nothing but vice, would have seemed to Madison like trying to create reason out of nothing but passions.

Madison called for political equality in 1792 as he also called for a great

---

11. John Zvesper, *Political Philosophy and Rhetoric: A Study of the Origins of American Party Politics* (Cambridge: Cambridge University Press, 1977), p. 113.

harmony of sentiment within society, attached, of course, to just principles. But he had argued in No. 10 that "giving to every citizen the same opinions, the same passions, the same interest," could not be done, as "theoretic politicians" had "erroneously" supposed "by reducing mankind to a perfect equality in their political rights." It was "impracticable," that is, impossible. Was he himself now indulging in this error? The answer is that based on his contention in No. 10, he felt free to work for political equality. Because the theorists were in error, liberty and variety would still flourish. On the other hand, he had not said it was wrong to give men the same opinions, but that it was impossible. In addition, though he had said that "a *zeal* for different opinions, concerning religion, concerning government" divides mankind into parties, he did not say that all opinions were wrong. In 1792, he argued for a broad, harmonious consensus throughout America around the principles of justice. He could not possibly have expected the true opinion to be unanimously accepted. Nor did he advocate or favor persecuting false opinion out of existence. Rather he strove for the acceptance, within a broad majority—perhaps making some concessions here, but persuading elsewhere—of the true opinion about the just principles of government. This task is implied by his words at the end of No. 10: "according to the degree of pleasure and pride we feel in being republicans, ought to be our *zeal* in cherishing the spirit," of our republican constitutional union. Here was an enlightened and patriotic zeal, based on true opinion, which Madison expressly and quite obviously approved of already in 1787.

Addressing the issue of constitutionalism in America in 1792, he says of our "*great charters*": "How devoutly is it to be wished, then, that the public opinion of the United States should be enlightened . . . and that it should guarantee, with a holy zeal, these political scriptures from every attempt to add to or diminish from them." Madison wishes to add to the reasonableness of support for fundamental law, and not least for the new federal Constitution, a Biblical passion. He is aware of the significance of public opinion: "All power has been traced up to opinion. The stability of all governments and security of all rights may be traced to the same source." He clearly wishes to build on the already broad respect for the ancient religious scriptures and in some degree for the older state constitutions a like support for the new federal Constitution. His approach here corresponds to his earlier view as expressed in *Federalist* No. 49:

> In a nation of philosophers . . . reverence for the laws would be sufficiently inculcated by the voice of an enlightened reason. But a nation of philosophers is as little to be expected as the philosophical race of kings

wished for by Plato. And in every other nation, the most rational
government will not find it a superfluous advantage to have the prejudices of the community on its side.

Thus, Madison continues in 1792: "Liberty and order will never be *perfectly*
safe, until a trespass on the constitutional provisions for either shall be
met with the same keenness that resents an invasion of the dearest rights .
. . ." Public opinion knew its rights quite well; but it would have to learn its
duties and limits equally well. Madison seems to have been convinced that
attachment to the Constitution, respect for government and willingness to
grant power to that government would grow only from a leadership which
respected liberty. Of course, the problem was that countenancing local
liberty meant showing tolerance for slavery. But the compromises of the
Constitution required a provisional respect at any rate shown toward the
slave interest. Only gradually, it seemed, and after a time could it be extin-
guished. If the union and Constitution were to be secured, the compromise
with slavery would have to be made. Perhaps Madison felt that Hamilton's
political hands were too indelicate: that he would turn the people away from
respect for law, that he would force the issue of consolidation or anarchy,
and that consolidation of government would prove so popularly unacceptable that it could only be sustained by an anti-republican will outside society,
or else "schism" of the nation would result. Yet this is a wholly inadequate
account, since the case for Hamilton has been omitted and there are many
reasons on the other side to be weighed.

Let us return to *Federalist* No. 10. Is it not true that Madison thought the
entire society would be made up of vicious factions? His definition of
faction includes the phrase "a number of citizens." But he had just
mentioned the capability of "our most considerate and virtuous citizens"
who exemplify a non-factious number of citizens. He speaks of "enlightened statesmen" who exemplify the same thing, even if they will not
always be at the helm. Also, in touching on the principles of representation, he refers to "a chosen body of citizens whose wisdom may best
discern the true interest of their country, and whose patriotism and love
of justice will be least likely to sacrifice it to temporary or partial considerations." Here again is a non-partisan "number of citizens." Incidentally,
his remarks in No. 10 are perfectly consistent with his principle stated in
No. 57: "The aim of every political constitution is, or ought to be, first to
obtain for rulers men who possess most wisdom to discern, and most
virtue to pursue, the common good . . . ." Whatever auxiliary precautions
against vice he thought advisable, Madison clearly saw a realm for the free
exercise of virtue and statesmanship. Nor does *The Federalist* entertain a

low conception of the virtue demanded by the nation in her rulers. No. 71 states plainly that "the public happiness" requires men of "courage and magnanimity," the last being the classic virtue *par excellence*. Finally, Madison speaks of the "exemption" from "party animosities" that reigned at the convention and the member's "deep conviction of the necessity of sacrificing private opinions and partial interests to the public good." Noble statesmanship is certainly a distinct human possibility, according to Madison.

But is not the public good a common interest? Someone might cite *Federalist* No. 51: "If a majority be united by a common interest, the rights of the minority will be insecure." But Madison had just said that "different interests necessarily exist in different classes of citizens." He then means to say quite plainly that if a majority is united by a common ("different" or partial) interest, the rights of the minority will be insecure. Even though partial interests necessarily exist, the Convention had sacrificed "partial interests to the public good." Madison was surely no Leveller just because he called, in his party press essays in 1791, for an eradication of "local prejudices and mistaken rivalships," and for a "consolidation" of "the affairs of the states into one harmonious interest." He was merely following through on his intention in *Federalist* No. 10 of pursuing "great and national objects."

Why has Madison's intention in this number been misunderstood so often? "To secure the public good and private rights against the danger of [a majority] faction, and at the same time to preserve the spirit and the form of popular government, is then the great object to which our inquiries are directed." If Madison had only said so much, perhaps the argument of No. 10 would have been kept in proper perspective. After all, Madison mainly speaks only of probabilities. Furthermore, he takes as his point of comparison small republics or American states. He fails, it seems, to compare the extended republican sphere to monarchies or aristocracies and ask, in which is justice and security for liberty more probable? It is true that the most we can hope for in politics are good probabilities. It is true, too, that he thinks the probabilities are on the high side *in comparison to small republics* that majority faction will be prevented. But how much is this really saying? *The Federalist* admits that small republics and even the states were notorious for factionalism! Suppose a friend of monarchy or aristocracy were reading his account. Why would he be convinced? Why then does Madison introduce in the sequel an evidently grander claim for his discovery? "Let me add," he continues, "that it is the great desideratum by which this government can be rescued from the opprobrium under which it has so long laboured, and be recommended to the esteem and adoption of mankind." If his solution is merely a mechanical device and touches little or inadequately on the problem of virtue and self-restraint in government, could an enlightened aristocrat truly hold his planned solution in esteem?

It has not been sufficiently noticed, I believe, that although Madison's discussion of representation in *Federalist* No. 10 is no doubt very important, his whole argument leads up to really only one or two absolutely critical sentences in which he explains positively his core conception, beginning with the expression, "Extend the sphere . . . ."

> Extend the sphere and you take in a greater variety of parties and interests; you make it *less probable* that a majority of the whole will have a common motive to invade the rights of other citizens; or if such a common motive exists, it will be *more difficult* for all who feel it to discover their own strengths and to act in unison with each other.

Someone might ask: is that all there is to it? It is certainly to be hoped that the probability is high indeed that the variety of vices will be able to check each other or in the hands of good leadership be guided into noble and worthy channels, and that a common unjust motive may never exist. But what if a common motive should arise, as Madison admits it may? In an age of enlightenment, of improved technology for rapid communication, in a country which respects a free press and in which news travels fast by other means, such as through commerce, though such discovery will prove more difficult on the national than the state level, the difficulty may prove far from insuperable and, in fact, even rather insignificant. Yet there is a further reason which seems to persuade Madison or his readers to extend the sphere.

Given a common motive, however difficult or easy the discovery of it may prove, it will be more difficult for a national majority to act in unison with each other than for a state majority to do so. But is not even this a rather strange argument?

If one contends that it is harder *legally* to act in unison at the national level, its representatives gather together in one seat of government. Cannot the members of Congress, possessing a shared motive, and meeting in the capital, pass partisan legislation with as little trouble as do members of a state legislature under the like circumstances? Given the common seat of government and the recognition of the shared motive, the conditions for united action are met. If one wishes to count the greater likelihood of wisdom available at the national level, he could claim that united action is less likely there than at the state level. But the likelihood of good representation surely depended in Madison's mind on the people choosing it. Moreover, this is only a restatement of his earlier point, which is implausible for that reason, too. It would imply that his expressly stated "principal" point—extension for the sake of multiplicity of factions and difficulty in combination—in fact reduces to extension for the sake of better representation. This line of reasoning must be rejected.

Perhaps, then, we should recall that Madison has in mind the *violence* of faction. What of physical violence and illegal insurrection? This query, too, heads down an unlikely trail. The majority, unlike a minority, has little cause to resort to open violence since under the principle of majority rule, it can express its factional temperament quite peaceably through elections. Good representatives might indeed stand against a very temporary majority faction. But if such a faction has patience to wait two years for a largely new house, or four years for a new President and a new Senate up to two-thirds full of new Senators; or, if that is still not enough, though it is likely to be, six years for an altogether new Senate, then the principle of representation cannot stop it. Only, therefore, if the majority is exceedingly impatient can we imagine cause for openly violent measures on its part. Besides, these are clearly not the deepest dangers, and Madison knew it.

Previously, in discussing the violence of minority faction, Madison had said: "the republican principle ... enables the majority to defeat its sinister views by regular vote." But the sinister views of a majority cannot be so defeated. The monarchical or aristocratic principle might prove of service in such an instance, but Madison is opposed to setting up a will independent of society (as he tells us in No. 51). A minority faction "may clog the administration, it may convulse the society; but it will be unable to execute and mask its violence under the forms of the Constitution." Such masked violence is precisely what Madison fears from a will independent of society. Now, of course, an impatient tyrannical majority could bring the machine of government to a standstill or "convulse the society" in a bloody domestic war. But why engage in such activities when, with but a little patience, such a faction will be able, more easily, more subtly, and more quietly, "to execute and mask its violence under the forms of the Constitution."

Our inquiry to this point comes to this: in the question which is of far less moment, that of open violence, Madison is correct that united action is physically more difficult but by no means impossible, at the national level. Yet in the question which is of far greater moment, that of hidden violence by a majority faction, Madison is incorrect, if he means that united action is more difficult in Washington, D.C. than say in his own Richmond—except perhaps to the extent representatives of wisdom and virtue resist a temporarily inflamed majority passion, and tame, educate, and guide it out of its folly before it hurls them from office. National (and state) leaders must have fortitude, it is worth noting, to ride such a tiger. Yet to draw this conclusion can only mean that, once a common motive is formed, there remains neither a mechanical nor an institutional "solution" involved in extending the sphere, and that all depends on patriotism and good leadership.

Our findings have simply not proved satisfactory. Besides, Madison had promised that he would rely on "neither moral nor religious motives" as an "adequate control" against majority faction, and this is what his logic, as matters advance from bad to worse, seems to reduce to. Yet let us keep in mind that we have just now been examining only one critical sentence, though it forms the heart of his argument. Or does it? There is another sentence appended to it which is meant to cast light on the last part of the critical sentence, the very part we have found so problematical, the part that reads: "or if a common motive exists, it will be more difficult for all who feel it to discover their own strength, and to act in unison with each other." After all, by taking Madison's own words of explanation as our guide, we may be led to his true meaning.

Madison's only specific remark in his discussion of the advantage of an extended sphere supposing a common *unjust* motive to arise in a majority, actually does lead to an interesting consideration. "Besides other impediments," he says, "it may be remarked that where there is *a consciousness of unjust or dishonorable purposes*, communication is always checked by distrust in proportion to the number whose concurrence is necessary."

For years scholars have given too much attention to "other impediments" and neglected the one Madison singles out. Note that Madison is not relying on "moral or religious motives" as an "adequate" control, but on the motives of fear and "distrust." Yet he implies, first of all, that a teaching diffused throughout society about justice and honor is the first requirement to prevent the tyrannical action of a majority. Secondly, he means to say not so much that hypocrisy is the tribute that vice pays to virtue as that the fear and correspondent actual restraint in communication of evil designs which underlies hypocrisy is the real tribute that vice pays to the possibility of virtue in an extended republic.

Madison is not treating here in any explicit way the matter, to which we referred above, of wise and virtuous representation, which is necessarily one of the "other impediments" to united action for unjust purposes. In the repetition in the following paragraph, he speaks in a general way of the roadblocks to the "accomplishment of the secret wishes of an unjust and interested majority." Why do its wishes remain secret? What keeps the secret? What is the only roadblock he deigns to mention? Not conscience, not moral nor religious motivation, but fear and suspicion that others might prove just and honorable. Conspiracies, he means to suggest, are difficult in an extended republic, for accomplishing a tyrannical design is nothing less than conspiracy.

The longest chapter in either of Machiavelli's two great works is entitled "On Conspiracy." It is not clear whether Machiavelli wishes to teach how to succeed in a conspiracy or how to prevent one. Here then is another possibility which the name of Machiavelli might conjure up and which is perhaps equally implied in Madison: fear and suspicion that others will use the claims of justice or honor against those who betray their unjust and dishonorable designs, even if the former use these noble claims for less than noble purposes. Suppose, for example, that two unjust men share in their heart of hearts a common unjust policy motive. May not the less clever of the two, believing his views to belong only to a rather ineffectual minority, conceal his views from the other and actually join forces with the just against the unjust for selfishly ambitious motives? If the more clever reveals his true motives to the less clever man, may he not, through the ignorance of the latter, come to be exposed? Whether the bad man fears and suspects the other to be just and honorable truly or, alternatively, to be an incompetent crook and a foolish moralist might prove of little consequence. Could the unjust man not allow this distinction to enter very far into his calculations, and must he not ultimately show a certain restraint in his communications in either case? Perhaps Madison means to suggest such thoughts by what he says, but we do not wish to place undue weight on what is merely a subsidiary point.

The main point is that Madison certainly does mean that if there exists some genuine justice and honor diffused throughout society, republican government may still succeed in the face of a vicious majority, and conspiracy fail. In *Federalist* No. 1, Alexander Hamilton says in the name of Publius: "The consciousness of good intentions disdains ambiguity. I shall not, however, multiply professions on this head. My *motive* must remain the depository of my own heart. My arguments will be open to all and may be judged by all." The motives of men, as Madison as well as Hamilton realized, are very difficult to ascertain. If a bad man communicates his motives openly to one or several men who turn out not to be hypocrites after all, as he had mistakenly suspected, the conspiracy may be severely damaged. Madison enters into the plotting of the dangerous man far enough to reveal that in an extended republic, it is very difficult to distinguish the hypocrites from the just and honorable in order to form a working majority—when, at least, there exists "sufficient virtue" in the regime. In such a regime justice must give its tone to society.

It is critical to realize that the last determining factor in the argument of *Federalist* No. 10 is not quite what men for years have thought Madison to be driving at in that article. The final "obstacle," the last roadblock to tyranny, proves to be justice and honor after all, in the sense of fear of them. This is fully consistent with his honestly claiming that he does not rely on "moral nor religious motives" as an "adequate" control. They are necessary but not sufficient. For he does rely on fear of these motives as sufficient and, therefore, he relies on good motives as necessary. Nor, of course, does this mean that he does not rely on moral doctrines and principles as well as on the presence of *some* virtue. Evil men cannot always see very lucidly or know very certainly the real motivation behind this or that profession of goodness, nor behind the call to equal justice emanating from a society of allegedly good men. And since these evil men are conspiratorial and subject to all the dangers and pitfalls of conspiracy, Madison suggests they must either largely conform or at least pay lip service to the public teaching about justice or risk being put down by a majority formed on the "*principles*" of "justice and the general good."

James Madison and Thomas Jefferson knew what they were doing in the crucial respect. They were enlightened. And they were never more enlightened than when they announced the republican principles of justice and called for virtue in an extended sphere. Whatever one's final conclusion as to the precise truth and character of Madison's party press articles in the 1790's, it seems to me that he, at least, felt them to be wholly consistent with his object and with his implicit understanding in *The Federalist*. The Kentucky and Virginia Resolutions of 1798 and 1799 are another matter.

It seems obvious that, according to Madison, the teaching about justice must be the responsibility of the wise and virtuous representatives of the nation and not only of the families, churches, and schools. The responsibility of the nation's leadership is to promulgate the principles among the people. Of course, the people, or a large part of it, must have virtue in some degree and be able to select out leaders of wisdom, justice, and patriotism. But if the people should falter or if the leaders should falter, thought Madison, Jefferson, and certainly Lincoln, too, never should the principles come to be obscured and forgotten. For unjust, designing men would still find it difficult to unite an unjust and effectual majority until the principles had been overthrown, and by that time the nation may have recovered a sound leadership. Something like this seems to have occurred in the events leading up to Lincoln's Presidency. Jefferson certainly looked on the events leading up to his Presidency following these lines. Commenting on the value of an extended republic in 1801, he said: "While frenzy and delusion like an epidemic, gained certain parts, the residue remained sound and untouched, and held on till their brethren could recover from the temporary delusion."[12]

It is still more obvious and certain that Madison had a clear notion of what justice, honor, patriotism, and the public good were. I mean to say that to his mind these were real and intelligible qualities, that is, qualities of men and nations as displayed in their policies, utterances, and actions which were knowable as good and distinguishable from defective policies, words, and deeds. Men could and did differ in their opinions about them, but in principle they were qualities understood by Madison and the founders to be knowable to serious and enlightened thought.

The founders' views are not widely acceptable within the groves of academe today. Yet it follows from them that whoever would set himself up to oppose the promulgation of the principles of justice or deny the existence of such principles, is opening the way if not for his own unjust designs, for those of other men to win the day and to tear down the fabric of republican institutions—whether by loosing the tyranny of the majority to ride roughshod over the rights of other citizens or by so doing to create an anarchical state of affairs in which a select dictatorship over the people becomes necessary. This conclusion is implied in what Madison says about the prevention of the rule of faction, as it is by his teaching in *The Federalist* generally, and above all by the Declaration of Independence.

Someone is bound to ask, however: why did Madison not then develop more fully the theme of justice or virtue as a guard against faction in *Federalist* No. 10? The answer is, first, that under the circumstances, namely, the fight against small republicanism, there was no need. He knew that the attachment to republicanism in America was widespread. He could afford in this one essay (which, after all, is but one of a long series of papers) to take its principles and the general public's devotion to them for granted. Since his addressees were "jealous lovers of liberty," as one scholar has noted, Madison felt he would serve his cause better "by

---

12. Thomas Jefferson, Letter to Nathaniel Niles, 22 March 1801, *Writings*, ed. Lipscomb and Bergh, vol. 10, pp. 232-33.

arguments that acknowledge and promise a remedy for the known selfish ambitions of men than by unconvincing denials of the power of those ambitions."[13] To have talked at length about justice, virtue, and patriotism would have made it appear to the reader that he was contending (against the wisdom and experience of the ages) that republicanism requires (and can achieve, within the realm of sober possibility) an extended nation of good and just men in order to survive. He did not wish to appear to be advocating what he was not. Still more especially this appearance he had to avoid. Would it not have made him look visionary? Instead, Madison wanted clearly to bring out the fact that he was relying neither on "moral nor religious motives" as "adequate" or sufficient. But he was nonetheless relying on moral and political *principles*: the just principles of government announced in the Declaration and to which the vast bulk of the American people adhered, having displayed their respect for them in public utterances, such as the documents of their state governments, and in public deeds, above all in the revolutionary war of merely a few years past. His conclusion in *Federalist* No. 10 is perfectly consistent with this being his true outlook: "and according to the degree of pleasure and pride we feel in being republicans, ought to be our zeal in cherishing the spirit and supporting the character" of the union and the Constitution.

Perhaps the most important confirmation of our analysis of *Federalist* No. 10's argument comes from Madison himself when, in 1821, he restated his teaching on the protection of the rights of all citizens and in particular on "the security for the holders of property when the minority." The two final and surest props against majority tyranny that he mentions are: one, "The popular sense of justice enlightened and enlarged by a diffusive education" and two, "the difficulty of combining and effectuating *unjust purposes* throughout an extensive country."[14] These two points, precisely the ones we have stressed—extensiveness of the republic as a check against conspiracy, coupled with popular education in justice—were expressly conjoined in Madison's mind in 1821 just as they were implicitly conjoined in his teaching in *The Federalist*. It is noteworthy, too, that Madison, far from asserting that moral motives are unnecessary, maintains the reverse!

It was James Madison's view as well as Thomas Jefferson's that human slavery was wrong and contravened the principles of the Declaration. Both wished ultimately to have its existence expelled from the bosom of the

---

13. Epstein, p. 30.
14. Jaffa, "The Madisonian Legacy," p. 400.

country. Yet its gradual elimination seemed to both of them an extremely delicate practical problem. So it appeared to Lincoln, too, who at first aimed merely to set it "in course of ultimate extinction." But it should be emphasized that Madison and Jefferson adhered to the principles of equality and liberty as firmly as did Lincoln. They were the original American expounders of those principles which Lincoln adopted and took over from them. Neither Madison nor Jefferson ever adhered to the theory that slavery was a positive good, as opposed to a temporarily "necessary evil," and this was also Lincoln's position.

What has not been recognized, however, is that Lincoln, in opposing the theory that slavery is a positive good, when it reared its pernicious head among the apologists for the Southern slaveholders, was acting consistently with both the letter (although perhaps not wittingly) and the spirit, the Republican "zeal" and spirit, of *Federalist* No. 10 and its author, James Madison. (Let us also recall the charge of *conspiracy* made by Lincoln in his House Divided Speech.) If the principles of injustice were to become respectable in society, thought Lincoln, there were no limits to what tyranny bolstered by a confused, unenlightened, and vicious majority might perform in the name of democracy. However, even if the majority were not fully virtuous, even if large and significant elements of society were unjust in practice and even if many citizens were rather vicious in their heart of hearts, the public admission upon which policy must be based, that slavery is an evil (if a necessary evil under some unhappy circumstances) provided a firm foundation on which to construct a sound policy of extending the blessings of liberty. Indeed, in Lincoln's time, six of the original states had abolished slavery within their limits, although in Madison and Jefferson's time, it had been permitted in twelve of the thirteen states. In opposing the positive good school of slavery, Lincoln appealed to the only secure foundation of liberty, the conviction in the public mind that the principles of the Declaration of Independence are the true principles of natural and public right. In this appeal, Lincoln showed himself in the crucial respect to be a follower of Madison.

For Lincoln, who sometimes tolerated vice, even as he was willing to tolerate slavery, so long as it did not attempt to extend itself, refused to give countenance to the public enunciation of unjust and pernicious principles. "Public opinion is everything in a democracy," Lincoln said. James Madison had agreed in advance explicitly in his party press essays and implicitly in *The Federalist*.

What Madison saw was that in an exclusive government, whether of a king and his court, or of an hereditary aristocracy, or even in a small republic or democracy, it was far easier to penetrate a veneer of hypocrisy that might exist, to discern men's true motives, and, if they were vicious, to combine on this basis in pursuit of wicked and unjust designs. But he foresaw that in a large, extended republic, if the principles of justice and constitutionalism are widely respected by public opinion, it is much more difficult for dangerous men to separate the wheat from the chaff, to ferret out the true motives of the hypocrites, and to make conspiratorial connections with them before being denounced by the just. Madison was in favor of the teaching of public right and was convinced that it was necessary that its principles be accepted by the broad majority. His political efforts were aimed at holding public opinion together on this critical point. If political success were found to depend on the spirit of faction appealing to the principles of justice, to constitutionalism, and to the equal rights of all citizens; men would find themselves gently being forced to be free, and to act, broadly speaking, consonant with the principles of public and private liberty. The only sure foundation of this generous and liberty-loving policy is widespread public acceptance of the truth and justice of the Declaration's principles.

In Madison's time, such a commitment in the majority was manifest to him, although his party press essays aimed at bringing it out as the necessary foundation of republican government. In Lincoln's time, it could no longer be taken for granted. But Madison's task differed from Lincoln's insofar as his task was to secure the principles of the Constitution in a public mind already well-disposed toward those of the Declaration. Lincoln's task was to maintain that if you remove the principles of the Declaration the rock of republicanism, the Constitution, no longer having a firm foundation will eventually crumble away. We have argued that if you remove the Declaration, then Madison's *Federalist* No. 10, that defense of the Constitution which has been so celebrated for its political shrewdness, also has little to stand on. The surest foundation for the interplay of factions that liberty gives vent to is the public commitment to the "laws of nature and of nature's God," the commitment to that form of justice in whose support the signers of the Declaration pledged their "sacred honor." Justice and honor. That is what *Federalist* No. 10 comes down to in the end. It would seem that Jefferson, Madison, and Lincoln were right because the classic exponents of the natural law doctrine were right: natural law is the surest foundation of a free country.

The Discipline of Freedom

Wilson Carey McWilliams

I

"The world has never had a good definition of the word liberty,"
Abraham Lincoln told a Baltimore audience in 1864, "and the American
people, just now, are much in need of one."[1] Lincoln was speaking of the
struggle to end slavery and praising Maryland for repudiating the "wolf's
dictionary," with its idea of a freedom to hold others in bondage. Perhaps
he was speaking carelessly or for the moment, but taken at his word,
Lincoln was pointing to a problem more enduring and more fundamental. His assertion amounts to a criticism—startling, given Lincoln's reverence for the Declaration of Independence and the Constitution—of the
political theory of the American founding. Lincoln tells us that the
Framers, who "brought forth" a nation "conceived in liberty," did so
without a "good definition" of freedom, leaving a fault in the philosophic
cornerstone of the republic.[2]

---

1. Abraham Lincoln, "Address at Sanitary Fair" in *Collected Works of Abraham Lincoln,* ed. Roy
   P. Basler (New Brunswick: Rutgers University Press, 1953), vol. VII, p. 301.

2. That Lincoln refers to a "definition" of freedom indicates that he is concerned with the
   Framers' theory of liberty, their understanding of words and in speech, and not the
   practical decision to compromise with slavery. In his Address, Lincoln went on to
   describe two popular definitions of liberty, one allowing "each man to do as he pleases
   with himself, and the product of his labor," the second permitting "some to do as they
   please with other men, and the product of other men's labor" (*Collected Works,*vol. VII,
   pp. 301-302). While Lincoln's preference is obvious, both of these doctrines are familiar,
   and hence are included in Lincoln's criticism of previous definitions of freedom. The
   parties associated with the two views are only "called"; by the "names" of liberty and
   tyranny: the popular definitions, in other words, are conventional, limiting practice but
   falling short of the standard of theory, partisan rather than philosophic. As Lincoln's
   phrasing makes clear, both of the popular views rest on the principle that freedom is
   doing as one pleases. Moreover, he was too shrewd not to recognize that the first
   definition easily slides over into the second, since doing as I please with myself and my
   products can result in my establishing ascendancy over you. In addition, Baltimore's
   adherence to the party of liberty—was due to the success of Union arms (see the draft

He was right. The Framers' view of liberty is at best a partial truth, and Americans have reason to wonder whether that flawed foundation can bear the weight of the republic's contemporary problems. I will be arguing that American democracy needs to recall a teaching, more ancient than the Framers', which holds that liberty is found in and through political life, that civil manners are inseparable from civil liberty, and that liberty itself is no more than a means to higher ends, a great spirit but no god.[3]

The Framers taught us differently. They held that human beings are by nature free beings who are morally independent and primarily selfcentered. In this doctrine, nature is defined by origins, and hence by the body; the decisive evidence of human freedom is the fact that we come into the world in separate bodies, and so remain.[4] By nature, individuals

---

first paragraph, omitted from the final version of Lincoln's speech, vol. VII, p.303). The triumph of the party of liberty, in practice, depended on the Union's ability to do as it pleased with the rebel states and their sympathizers. In either of its popular forms, "doing as one pleases" fell short of Lincoln's standard for a "good definition of liberty." According to Harry Jaffa, Lincoln understood the "enjoyment of freedom" to be "conditional upon one's ordering of one's life and the life of one's community in accordance with the principle of the moral order." ("Is Political Freedom Grounded in Natural Law?," paper presented to the Claremont Institute Conference, "A New Order of the Ages," February 1984.)

3. Plato, *Symposium* 202B6-202E6.

4. Locke, for example, defined the identity of a man as "nothing but a participation of the same continued Life . . . like that of other Animals in one fitly organized Body . . . ." (*Essay on Human Understanding*, Bk. II, Ch. 27, Sec. 6). Similarly, the desire for self-preservation, part of the nature man shares with the "inferior animals," is "the first and strongest desire God planted in men," a "fundamental, sacred and unalterable law." It is prior to revelation, reason or any "verbal donation," and reason must assure man that by "pursuing the natural inclination to preserve his being, he followed the will of his Maker" (*Treatises of Government*, I. 86-87; II. 149). In other words, the body with its senses and inclinations has priority in the interpretation of revelation and the understanding of nature (*Essays on Human Understanding*, Bk. I, Ch. 3). Those among the American founders who spoke of natural obligation or sociability characteristically referred to a moral "sense" or "instinct," i.e., a part of bodily nature. As this suggests, even when they sought to uphold classical or religious ideas of virtue and morality, the Framers almost always cast their arguments in modern terms. In the debates of the late 18th century, for example, Locke is cited more than any other author (Donald Lutz, "The Relative Influence of European Writers on Late Eighteenth Century American Political Thought," *American Political Science Review*, vol. 78 (1984), p. 193; see also Gary Schmitt and Robert Webking, "Revolutionaries, Antifederalists and Federalists," *Political Science Reviewer*, vol. 9 (1979), pp. 195-229.) Whatever the Framers' intent, this modern way of speaking and teaching undermined traditional doctrine.

are unencumbered, without duties to others or claims on them. There is no natural restraint on our desires, and we seek to do as we like. Above all, we strive for self-preservation, "the first principle of our nature" and the hard core of human self-concern.[5]

---

5. Alexander Hamilton, "A Full Vindication" (1774), in *The Works of Alexander Hamilton*, ed. H.C. Lodge (New York: Putnam, 1903), vol. I, p. 12. In "The Farmer Refuted" (1775), Hamilton does call "absurd and impious" Hobbes' doctrine that there is no moral obligation in the state of nature (*The Works of Alexander Hamilton*, vol. I, pp. 61-62). But, in the first place, Hamilton is answering the Farmer's charge that Hamilton's principles, as enunciated in the "Full Vindication," are open to the imputation of Hobbesism, especially since Hamilton maintained that we are "bound by no laws to which we have not consented." (Samuel Seabury, *Letters of a Westchester Farmer* (White Plains: Westchester County Historical Society, 1930), pp. 109, 111). Second, Hamilton contends that Hobbes' error lies, not in a misreading of human nature in particular, but in Hobbes' lack of belief in an "intelligent, superintending principle who is the governor, and will be the final judge of the universe." Hamilton goes on:

> To grant that there is a Supreme Intelligence who rules the world, and has established laws to regulate the actions of his creatures, and still assert that man, in a state of nature, may be considered as perfectly free from all restraints of *law* and *government*, appears, to a common understanding, altogether irreconcilable (*Works of Alexander Hamilton*, vol. I, p. 62).

But this "common understanding" is only partially correct. God may have "established laws" for his creatures by giving them inward instincts, passions and motives, leaving them free from outward restraints. To obey such a law of nature, man must either (1) be free from the restraints of law and government, in the ordinary sense of those terms, or (2) be subject to laws and governments which are conformed to his inward nature. To obey the divinely-ordained law of nature, in this view, is to let human nature take its course. Hamilton subscribes to this view or something very like it. Repeatedly, he refers to the law of nature as the source of the *rights* of mankind; he makes only passing reference to natural duties:

> the Supreme Being gave existence to man, together with the means of preserving and beautifying that existence. He endowed him with rational facilities, by the help of which to discern and pursue such things as were consistent with his duty and interest; and invested him with an inviolable right to personal liberty and personal safety (*The Works of Alexander Hamilton* vol. I, p. 63).

In this light of natural endowments, duty, balanced by interest, yields priority to — and may even be derived from — the preservation and beautification of existence. Moreover, if our rights to liberty and safety are truly *inviolable*, they must, in case of conflict, be preferred to our duties.

Hamilton did consider blood kinship as a natural bond and source of authority. This is an important difference between Hamilton and Locke — see, for example, *Essay on Human Understanding*, Bk. I, Ch. 3, Sec. 12, or "The Reasonableness of Christianity," in *The Works of John Locke* (London: n.p., 1812), vol. VII, p. 143 — although Hamilton's principle attempts to derive obligation from the body. With this exception, Hamilton argues that since the law of nature gives "every man a right to his personal liberty," it "can...confer no obligation to obedience" in a state of nature, no man had any *moral* power to

This natural liberty, however, is insecure and obstructed in practice. Nature, indifferent or hostile, gives us little and in the end will deny our desire to survive. Our fellow humans, confronting the same fundamental scarcities, seek to despoil or dominate us: in the state of nature, Samuel Adams declared, "The weaker was *by force* made to bow down to the more powerful."[6] Yet even the powerful, as Hobbes had observed, could not rest easy, since "the weakest has the strength to kill the strongest, either by secret machination or by confederacy with others . . . ."[7] Hence, by the well-known logic of social contract theory, human beings eventually agree to give up some of their natural liberty in order to make what remains more secure and more effective.

Legitimate political society rests on consent of the governed, since morally free human beings cannot otherwise be bound. Consequently, it frees us from rule by the will of another, the "only distinction," Hamilton

---

deprive another of his life, limbs, property or liberty, nor the least authority to command or exact obedience from him, except that which arose from the ties of consanguinity (*Works of Alexander Hamilton*, vol. I, p. 63; compare Locke, *Treatises*, II. 54).

This negative doctrine — the absence of a right to harm or rule — does not entail any positive bond between human beings, not even a duty to respect the life, liberty and property of others. The absence of "any *moral* power...to command or exact obedience" excludes any right to make obligatory claims *on* others (and it is the weak, after all, who are likely to stand in need of "*moral* power"). To be sure, in the "Full Vindication," Hamilton declared that it is a "dictate of humanity to contribute to the support of our fellow creatures, and more especially those who are allied to us by ties of blood, interest and mutual protection." But this "dictate" is clearly *not* a duty. Quite the contrary — it is on this point that Hamilton insists that:

humanity does not require us to sacrifice our own security and welfare to the convenience of others. Self-preservation is the first principle of our nature. When our lives and properties are at stake, it would be foolish and unnatural to refrain from such measures as might preserve them because they would be detrimental to others (*Works of Alexander Hamilton*, vol. I, pp. 112, 15; compare Locke, *Treatises*, I. 6).

"The *supreme law* of every society," Hamilton wrote, is *"its own happiness"* (*Works of Alexander Hamilton*, vol. I, p. 66; the italics are his). Since civil society is created to secure natural right, this supreme self-interestedness must be a characteristic of individuals as well as polities. In the large analysis, for Hamilton as for Locke, "there is...an innate natural right, while there is no innate natural duty" (Leo Strauss, *Natural Right and History* (Chicago: University of Chicago Press, 1953), pp. 226-227.

6. Samuel Adams, *The Writings of Samuel Adams*, ed. H. Cushing (New York: Putnam, 1908), vol. II, p. 151; the italics are Adams'.
7. Thomas Hobbes, *Leviathan* Part I. xiii.

once remarked, "between freedom and slavery."[8] In an even more funda-mental sense, however, political society is created because we desire to be able, as far as possible, to *do* as we please. Civil society frees us—provides us with civil liberty—to the extent that it protects or adds to our power, especially when it enhances our mastery over nature.

In the Framers' teaching, civil society embodies the "two concepts of liberty" discerned by recent political philosophers.[9] We retain a consider-able sphere of "natural liberty" and moral independence, especially in our inward, theoretical freedom to want and choose what we please. In individual conscience and in private life, we enjoy "negative liberty," the absence of restraint. Civil liberty, on the other hand, offers us power, safety, and efficacy, the practical and positive freedom to act and achieve associated with participation in an ordered whole.[10] Government aims to afford the maximum power and safety consistent with the minimum limitation on natural liberty and individual rights, "the perfect balance of liberty and power."[11] However, since political society exists to serve the private purposes of free individuals, the balance must always tilt toward individual rights and liberties, the moral center of liberal civilization.

In our time, the balance at which the Framers aimed is threatened in two different ways. Most obviously, the institutions and organizations of civil society have come to constitute a power which overwhelms any practical notion of individual independence. Thinkers in the past—Jef-ferson and Rousseau come easily to mind—feared that this would be so; today, however, the power of civil society is not a fear but a fact, one close to the heart of modern political life and thought.[12] The power of govern-ment is unmistakable, armed as it is with weapons of destruction and technologies of surveillance, and capable as it is of great terrors and petty interferences. We need to emphasize, however, that the power of civil society is a *general* characteristic of our civilization, present in the private

---

8. *Works of Alexander Hamilton*, vol. I, pp. 5-6.

9. For example, Isaiah Berlin, *Four Essays on Liberty* (London: Oxford University Press, 1969).

10. Hence the appropriateness of Benjamin Hichborn's radically democratic and unusual definition of civil liberty as a "power in the people at large" rather than a matter of individual rights. "Oration Delivered at Boston, March 5, 1777," cited in Gerald Stourzh, *Alexander Hamilton and the Idea of Republican Government* (Stanford: Stanford University Press, 1970), p. 56.

11. Works of Alexander Hamilton, vol. II, p. 52.

12. Bertrand de Jouvenel, *On Power* (New York: Viking, 1949).

sector as well as in public life.[13] The vulnerability and dependence of individuals is ubiquitous, not only in economic and political practice, but also in the life of the soul. Modern civil society challenges the *moral*, as well as the practical, independence of the individual.

I will be developing this argument at some length in order to make clear that the protection of personal and civil liberties can no longer derive from the private resources of the individual. Contemporary freedom requires the support of political community. That argument, in turn, points to the more basic problem to which I have already alluded. The idea of an original, natural, individual liberty which we derive from the Framers threatens our most important civil liberty—our political freedom as citizens—and with it, our capacity to cope with the looming dangers around the republic.

II

We speak of the American economy as providing "freedom of choice," referring to the array of products, the range of services, and the diverse employments it offers us. For most of us, moreover, the economy provides freedom from want and affords us a chance, probably unequalled, to do what we do best.[14]

At the same time, our economy is a vast, complex, interwoven, increasingly international system of constraining interdependencies. It makes us free from particular persons and places, but only by involving us in a sphere in which individuals matter less and less. It protects the "diversity in the faculties of men," but it makes us more and more dependent on the economic whole, the great network of specializations of which our work is a part. The division of labor, after all, is a principle of dependence as well as individualism.[15]

---

13. "The autonomous forces of society," Hans Morgenthau wrote, have "engendered new accumulations of power as dangerous to the freedom of the individual as the power of government." (Hans Morgenthau, "The Dilemmas of Freedom," *American Political Science Review*, vol. 2 (1957), 721).

14. None of this denies, of course, that vast numbers of Americans live in virtually permanent privation, made more painful by its proximity to affluence.

15. The quotation is from Madison, *The Federalist* #10; see also Adam Smith, *Lectures on Jurisprudence* (Oxford: Oxford University Press 1979), A333; and John Dewey, *The Public and its Problems* (New York: Holt, 1927), pp. 96-99.

Of course, this is as the Framers intended. They preferred a large, commercial republic because such a regime could, at one and the same time, free individuals and promote national unity. They saw and valued the subtle ways in which commerce dovetails individuals and localities.[16] Yet it seems at least possible that the modern American economy has gone beyond even their Promethean vision.

Today, if our lives are to go on, millions of others must perform their specialized tasks. We "provide for" ourselves and our families by earning money, but very few of us can even come close to providing in the literal sense: we need public services to bring us water and rid us of garbage, and our homes and cities can scarcely survive without electricity. Even the freedom of choice we celebrate indicates the extent to which we are passive, dependent on alternatives created by others. Valuable though it is, the freedom of choice is a *civil* liberty which derives from the nature of the regime.

In fact, the civil discipline called planning has become incorporated into the definition of economic liberty. The interdependencies of modern life make it necessary for us to take thought about others who may be involved in what we do, and—if only as a form of traffic control—to give them notice of what we intend. If I want to fly to another city on a particular day, I will need to make reservations, but I do not experience this constraint as a violation of my liberty. I *do* feel interfered with, however, if the airline overbooks and decides to "bump" me.[17] Similarly, if I must spend time thinking about your business—wondering, for example, whether my bank is sound or whether the elevators I ride are safe—it impinges on my freedom to do *my* work. My freedom is bound up with the regularities of economic life; my self-determinations rely on people behaving in expected ways and making good on their implicit promises.

We are all exposed to economic and social forces, and to reasons and policies of state, on which our individual labor has little effect. American farmers have not been less productive or hard working in the last few years. They have suffered because the administration's economic policies, resulting in a strong dollar, have shut American products out of the

---

16. Ralph Lerner, "Commerce and Character: the Anglo-American as New Model Man" in *William and Mary Quarterly*, vol. 36, (1979), pp. 3-26.

17. My indignation decreases, of course, to the extent that I regard being bumped as a normal hazard of flying.

international market.[18] Especially because it is so often part of the problem, public authority has a duty to afford us, and our legitimate expectations, some insurance against our vulnerabilities.

At the same time, modern regimes are themselves noticeably fragile.
Disruption at any one of a number of strategic points can produce
disproportionate disorder. In fact, an individual's capacity to do harm to
society greatly outweighs the positive significance of his or her labor to the
economy as a whole. Outraged dignity is presented with a constant temptation to outrage.[19] Modern political life thus encourages a politics of
disruption, which in turn leads to demands for a government strong
enough to cope with the danger.

This is only a dramatic instance of a more general tendency toward an
expansion of the role of government.[20] Given the mutual dependence of
individuals in modern regimes, it is no longer enough for government to
protect my private resources, since those resources are not sufficient to
sustain me. I need a government which can guarantee that the economic
system as a whole will *provide* those things which are needful on terms
which are at least reasonably fair. As Michael Ignatieff observes, the
division of labor transforms needs into rights, claims on political society
mediated through public authority. The details are matters of political
controversy, but the principle is conceded: even the Reagan administration acknowledges a duty to maintain a "safety net." This public responsibility, Ignatieff writes, "gives us whatever fragile basis we have for saying
that we live in a moral community"; it is also a vital dimension of freedom.[21]

For most Americans, both political community and economic liberty

---

18. This explanation of the farm problem has been offered, among others, by Wayne
    Angell, one of President Reagan's appointees to the Federal Reserve Board (*Wall Street
    Journal*, 17 Oct. 1985, p. 62). The trade policies of other regimes also contribute. Given
    this, it is obtuse, and more than a little cruel, to claim that American farmers brought
    their fate on themselves by excessive borrowing.
19. Robert Coles, "The Politics of Ressentiment," *New Republic*, August 2, 1982, pp. 32-34.
20. Even Herbert Spencer, the great Social Darwinist, observed that increasing mass, com-
    plexity and range of activity in civil life necessarily entails and increased role for the
    "great nervous centers," despite the cost to individualism. (Herbert Spencer, *Principles of
    Biology* (New York: Appleton, 1874), vol. II, sect. 374.)
21. Michael Ignatieff, *The Needs of Strangers* (New York: Viking, 1985), p. 10.

are summed up by the phrase, "equality of opportunity."[22] Yet, in practice, equality of opportunity depends on civil discipline and public support. As a matter of theory, the idea of equal opportunity "assumes the possibility of a fresh start, regardless of past history."[23] In the contemporary United States, however, past history presses on us: property accumulates in some hands to the disadvantage of others; inequalities in early rearing give some a great advantage and others a fatal handicap; for a terrible fraction of our population—especially in families headed by women—economic inequality is radical and cumulative; and all of this says nothing of the ancient and durable barriers of race, gender and ethnicity.[24]

Soften the rebuke to the United States: the theory of equality of opportunity wars with the institutions of *any* complex civil society. Taken literally, it would require us to bring into civil society the conditions the Framers associated with the state of nature: a levelling of convention, reducing each of us to a "poor, bare, forked animal" without the burdens or the benefits of civil life and station.[25] Even memory, which brings past history into present life, limits equality of opportunity. In civil society, no start is ever truly fresh and equality of opportunity is never more than partial.

The promise of equal opportunity, however, encourages a "fatal passion for sudden riches," the dream of a miraculous moment that will put us on an equal footing with wealth. Traditionally, that yearning was held in check by the culture of work. Americans could argue with some plausibility that opportunities for instant wealth were phantoms. They told stories which emphasized the perils of speculation, and they left us with a great cautionary proverb, "Easy come, easy go." Earlier generations of Americans recognized that the *existence* of instant ways to wealth, even if rare and infrequent, threatens the discipline of work, and they outlawed

22. Jennifer Hochschild, *What's Fair: American Beliefs about Distributive Justice* (Cambridge: Harvard University Press, 1981); by reporting American devotion to the idea, I do not mean to endorse it. For one thing, the doctrine defines equality in terms of treatment (at a starting point) rather than seeing equality as a quality of spirit and a political goal. (See John H. Schaar, "Equality of Opportunity and Beyond," in *Equality*, ed. J. Roland Pennock and John Chapman (New York: Atherton, 1967), pp. 228-249.)

23. Harvey C. Mansfield, Jr., "The Forms and Formalities of Liberty," *Public Interest*, no. 70 (Winter 1983), p. 127.

24. John H. Schaar, "The Question of Justice," *Raritan Review*, vol. 3 (1983), p. 122; Michael Harrington, *The New American Poverty* (New York: Holt, Rinehart and Winston, 1984).

25. Ignatieff, pp. 27-53; the quotation is from *King Lear* III. iv.

gambling—an infringement of individual economic liberty—to encourage honest labor. The more positive basis of the culture of work was hope, the conviction that one's small gains might lead to a fuller measure of equal opportunity for one's children.[26]

In contemporary America, however, radical and unpredictable change threatens our sense of connection to future generations. Americans may have recovered their optimism, but they are borrowing against the future, not saving for it. Moreover, there are now a considerable number of nearly instantaneous routes to wealth. For the children of the disadvantaged, the lure of professional athletics, rock music, gambling or even less respectable ways of "striking it rich" helps to undermine work, especially given the attenuation of middle-income industrial employment, the traditional avenue for upward mobility.[27] In any number of ways, the demand for economic liberty to do as one pleases threatens to overwhelm the older bourgeois virtues.

The defense of *civil* opportunity is impossible without a government committed to encouraging a measure of social stability and protecting middle-income employment, the high wage labor we associated with manufacturing.[28] Employment is the heart of contemporary economic liberty, Most of us are wage-earners; we depend on jobs, and this makes us, to some extent, "unfree," even though we sell our labor voluntarily.[29] To the Framers, this was no small matter. "It is a general remark," Hamilton declared, "that he who pays is master" and Gouverneur Morris doubted that "mechanics and manufacturers" who "receive their bread from their employers" could ever be "secure and faithful guardians of liberty."[30] If such worries seem archaic to us, it is because we are less concerned with individual employers and more dependent on employment, and hence, on general economic conditions.

---

26. Hannah Arendt, "Revolution and the Public Happiness," *Commentary*, vol 30. (1960), pp. 413-427; on the culture of work at the time of the founding, see Edmund Morgan, "The Puritan Ethic and the American Revolution," *William and Mary Quarterly*, vol. 24 (1967), p. 7 and H. Trevor Colbourn, *The Lamp of Experience* (Chapel Hill: University of North Carolina Press, 1965), pp. 4, 76-77, 180.

27. The American dream, in its contemporary form, is probably exemplified by the twenty-one factory workers who shared New York's Lotto prize in August 1985 (*New York Times*, 23 Aug. 1985, Sec. ff, p. 1). On borrowing, see Richard L. Stern, "Tomorrow Will Take Care of Itself," *Forbes*, vol. 136, 16 Sept. 1985, pp. 38-40.

28. Robert Kuttner, "Jobs," *Dissent*, vol. 31 (Winter 1984), pp. 30-41.

29. Schaar, "The Question of Justice," p. l.

30. *The Federalist* #73; James Madison, *Notes of Debates in the Federal Convention of 1787*, ed. Adrienne Koch (Athens: Ohio University Press, 1966), p. 402; see also, *The Federalist* #79.

Nevertheless, the individual employee's need for work—a source of dignity as well as a way to provide—is virtually always far greater than an employer's need for his or her particular work. Employers are also freed from personal dependence by the market; they need labor the commodity, not laborers as individuals.[31] Consequently, as we have known for a long time, genuine freedom of contract for workers demands collective bargaining, recognized as a right and afforded governmental protection at least comparable to that given property.[32] Moreover, freedom for wage earners requires full employment at socially adequate wages. The vision of labor hired at ɔelow the minimum wage entrances some economists and employers; it does not promote economic freedom.[33]

I have been arguing that employment is comparable to property as an essential element of economic freedom. In fact, we are coming to view property in a rather new way. The Framers regarded property as a natural right, something very personal, closely tied to the self. They also thought of property as a "taste" which leads human beings into civil society; in that sense, property is the foundation of civil liberty, the bedrock of social stability. By contrast, corporate property is not possessed by individuals, and it is only by a fiction of law that corporations are defined as "persons" whose property is protected by the due process clauses.[34] The physical property of great corporations is not ordinarily connected in any integral way to the selves or the ways of life of its owners; the relation of stockholders to the corporation is largely instrumental. The owners and upper level managers of a large scale firm have no real stake in its operations; they are concerned with particular businesses only as investments. It is not enough, consequently, for a plant to show a profit; its rate of return must be competitive with other possible uses of its capital. These days, as the headlines tell us, capital is only too likely to move out of plants and between regions and countries. In fact, the corporation's physical assets and operations are much more likely to be bound up with the lives and liberties of its workers, its lower level managers, and the communities which depend on its taxes and payrolls. Property defined simply in terms of the rights of capital disregards and threatens the claims of social

---

31. Holden vs. Hardy, 169 U.S. 366 (1898); West Coast Hotel vs. Parrish, 300 U.S. 379 (1937).
32. Lincoln Federal Savings Union vs. Northwestern Iron and Metal Co., 355 U.S. 525 (1949).
33. "Labor at socially inadequate wages," after all, could stand as a definition of peonage.
34. Louisville, Cincinnati and Charleston Railroad vs. Letson, 2 Nov. 47 (1844); Santa Clara County vs. Southern Pacific Railroad, 118 U.S. 394 (1886); see also Justice John Campbell's dissent in Marshall vs. Baltimore and Ohio Railroad, 16 Nov. 314 (1853).

stability and civil freedom. That so many legislatures are now considering legislation regulating plant closings reflects an appropriate concern for those neglected aspects of the rights and obligations of property.

There is increasing support for defining property as right to participation in civil society. Citizens, Frank Michelman contends, have a right to "the maintenance of the conditions . . . of fair and effective participation in the constituted order," including the economic bases of citizenship. Michelman leaves room for considerable inequality and for loss. But his doctrine does introduce a public obligation to protect citizens against "sudden changes" in the "crucial determinants of one's established position in the world."[35] The Framers defined politics as existing to protect private rights, making civil freedom derive from natural liberty; contemporary theorizing is becoming more disposed to defend private rights because it conceives them to be necessary to political freedom.

This sort of thinking is not confined to theory. In recent years, the Supreme Court has acknowledged that expectations of benefit, encouraged by laws and policies, create a new kind of property right which cannot be abridged without due process of law. In 1970, the Court ruled that welfare benefits cannot be cut off without a hearing.[36] In 1976, it went much further, holding—against the historic practice of the republic—that non-civil service public employees cannot be discharged simply because of their political affiliations, a ruling it later extended to lower level policy makers.[37] In its most controversial decision, the Court found that the seniority rights of firefighters, established by collective bargaining, take precedence over programs for affirmative action unless there is evidence of discriminatory intent.[38] One need not agree with all decisions of this sort—to me, some of them seem plainly outrageous—in order to recognize that the Court is groping toward an understanding of economic freedom appropriate to our time. Individuals are not free if they are simply left alone; even private liberties have their roots in public freedom.[39]

---

35. Frank Michelman, "Property as a Constitutional Right," *Washington and Lee Law Review*, vol. 38 (1981), p. 1097; see also Bruce Ackerman, *Private Property and the Constitution* (New Haven: Yale University Press, 1977).

36. Goldberg vs. Kelly, 397 U.S. 254 (1970).

37. Elrod vs. Burns, 427 U.S. 347 (1976); Branti vs. Finkel, 445 U.S. 507 (1980).

38. Firefighters vs. Stotts, 104 S. Ct. 2576 (1984); see also California Brewers Assn. vs. Bryant, 444 U.S. 598 (1980) and American Tobacco Co. vs. Patterson, 456 U.S. 63 (1982).

39. Franz Neumann, "The Concept of Political Freedom," in *The Democratic and the Authoritarian State* (Glencoe: Free Press, 1957), pp. 160-200.

III

In politics and in the psyche, separate individuals also are more prone to frailty than to freedom. As Tocqueville observed, in a vast republic like the United States, democracy makes us depend on masses of unknown others. In a small group, a majority of 6-4 is no great matter; each member of the majority is perceived as a person with a face and with foibles, and I can turn the tables simply by persuading two people. In a national election, the same margin—Reagan's in 1984—is a landslide, a fact of nature. The majority is made up of many millions, far too many to be comprehended as individuals, and in order to reverse the verdict, I would need to change millions of minds, a task beyond my powers. Even powerful organizations and great leaders seek to read and adjust to the "mandate" of opinion. For an individual, isolation only accentuates weakness, pushing the soul toward the conviction that the only safety lies in conforming to the "tyranny of the majority."[40]

Up to a point, the Framers understood this. They knew and relied on the fact that individuals, set free and left alone among multitudes, would be "timid and cautious."[41] Part of their case for a large republic was this tendency to unite individual liberty with civil order. Yet while the Framers expected that individuals would be guarded, circumspect and even fearful in behavior, they believed that inwardly, the mind still would be free. They accepted and reasoned on the basis of Spinoza's proposition that the mind cannot be controlled as the tongue is controlled.[42] The fundamental condition of political liberty, in this view, is that the body be free from physical threats and restraints, leaving the soul to take care of itself.

Experience taught Tocqueville otherwise. The "civilization of our age has refined the arts of despotism" and no longer needs the "coarse instruments" of physical repression. The distinctly modern form of tyranny is:

---

40. Alexis de Tocqueville, *Democracy in America* (New York: Schocken, 1961), I:304-312; see also James Bryce, *The American Commonwealth* (New York: Commonwealth, 1908), II:358-368.
41. *The Federalist* #49.
42. *Tractatus Theologico-Politicus*, ch. XX; compare *The Federalist* #1: "In politics as in religion, it is equally absurd to attempt at making proselytes with fire and sword. Heresies in either can rarely be cured by persecution."

> ... as entirely an affair of the mind as that will which it is
> intended to coerce. ... Under the absolute sway of an individual
> despot, the body was attacked in order to subdue the soul, and
> the soul escaped the blows which were directed against it and
> rose superior to the attempt, but such is not the course adopted
> by tyranny in democratic republics; there the body is left free and
> the soul is enslaved.[43]

With hindsight, it seems clear that the Framers—and the liberal philosophic tradition of which they were a part—underrated the anxieties
which can imprison the human soul. The liberal tradition relied on the
lure and consolation of material well-being, but, Tocqueville noted, the
more devoted we are to material possessions, the more we will be haunted
by the certainty of their loss. The fundamental scarcity for human beings
is not lack of wealth, but lack of time.[44]

Enshrined in law and custom, individual liberty accentuates the desperate restlessness Tocqueville associated with the pursuit of worldly welfare.
The combination of individualism and change makes all social forms and
all relationships seem transient and insecure; home ranks high among the
things from which individual liberty sets us free. Having learned to expect
all bonds to be fragile, we fear to commit ourselves deeply to any relationship or community. To care about something or someone is to give part of
oneself as hostage, to make oneself liable to pain, desertion and loss. Love,
after all, scandalizes individual liberty: while it must be freely given, love
obliges. The logic of individualism, by contrast, makes "every man forget
his ancestors ... hides his descendants and separates his contemporaries
from him; it throws him back forever upon himself alone, and threatens in
the end to confine him entirely within the solitude of his own heart."[45]

Today, our rather frantic mobility and the juggernaut of change are
wearing away what remains of our communities of remembrance. Individualism continues to deny that we have any obligation to such communities, while change makes the past seem outdated and distant. Yet the
weakening of our bond with the past reminds us how swiftly our words
and days will be forgotten. In the Framers' teaching, human beings fear

---

43. *Democracy in America*, I:310-311.
44. *Democracy in America*, II:161-162; Ignatieff, pp. 83-103.
45. *Democracy in America*, II:120.

for their lives; contemporary Americans, as Tocqueville expected, are likely to fear for the self.[46]

It does not help that individual liberty tears down the social barriers to great achievement, encouraging each of us to aim high and to judge our worth by the standard of our dreams. Obviously, the more who compete for the highest prizes, the more who are certain to fail, and the more we feel at liberty to succeed, the more we will experience such failure as a personal defeat. A healthy realism, by limiting our aspirations, helps make us content with our achievements and ourselves. In our time, however, the dynamism of change undermines that discipline: "the impossible of yesterday becomes the possible of today, and the mind loses its sense of distinction between dream and risk."[47] An increasing number of Americans, drawing their aspiration from dreams, are destined to suffer shattering blows to self-esteem and to experience that "disgust of life" which Tocqueville already observed among the Americans of his time.[48]

In contemporary America, individuals are aware of their weakness and insignificance within the mass democratic public, and they are all too likely to be lonely and anxious. The mass media have an awesome power to shape our images of life and community by appealing to our desires for potency, for love without commitment and for heroic stature.[49] In fact, as Solomon Asch demonstrated years ago, isolated experimental subjects, confronted with an apparent consensus, came to have doubts about—and in a considerable number of cases, to deny—the contrary evidence of their senses.[50] The lesson is, by now, a familiar one: the more isolated we

---

46. The pace of change and the decline of community also encourage shamelessness, as Lewis Lapham observes: "The emotion of shame probably needs a small theater in which to make its effects. A man can feel shame before an audience of his peers, within the narrow precincts of a neighborhood, profession, army unit, social set, city room, congregation or football team. The scale and dynamism of American democracy grants the ceaselessly renewable option of moving one's conscience into a more congenial street." ("Notebook: Supply-Side Ethics," *Harper's*, May 1985, p. 11.)

47. Bertrand de Jouvenal, *Sovereignty* (Chicago: University of Chicago Press, 1957), p. 254.

48. *Democracy in America*, II:164-165.

49. Howard White, "Comment on Morgenthau's 'Dilemmas of Freedom," *American Political Science Review*, vol. LI (1957), pp. 731, 733; Todd Gitlin, *Inside Prime Time* (New York: Pantheon, 1983).

50. Solomon Asch, *Social Psychology* (Englewood Cliffs: Prentice Hall, 1952), ch. 16. "The reality of the world," Arendt wrote, "is guaranteed by the presence of others." (*The Human Condition* (Garden City: Doubleday, 1959), p. 178.)

are, the more likely we are to depend on opinion for our definition of reality.[51]

Alone, individuals are very likely to lack the psychological and social bases of freedom.[52] We need the support and counsel of friends to set us free from fears and, for that matter, to liberate us from lower motives allied with our fears. As the Supreme Court recognized in *Miranda vs. Arizona*, we have every reason to doubt the validity of consent offered by isolated individuals. A confession may be involuntary, the Court argued, even though no physical coercion is employed to obtain it. Consent, at least in the case of a confession, presumes an individual informed of his or her rights and provided with counsel.[53]

In fact, the quality of consent is a serious problem for our political institutions. The Framers taught us that "consent of the governed" is the sole basis for legitimate government, let alone political freedom.[54] Now, however, far too many of our citizens feel dependent, baffled and constrained in politics and, consequently, experience their consent as less than free.[55]

Even if we accept the narrow definition which equates citizenship with voting, it is clear that citizens are limited to alternatives defined largely by others. Primary elections were supposed to "open" the selection of candidates to ordinary citizens, but the mass electorates associated with pri-

---

51. David Riesman, Nathan Glazer and Reuel Denney, *The Lonely Crowd* (New Haven: Yale University Press, 1950); modern philosophers sometimes raise this to the level of principle. R. M. Hare writes that "if we can convince (someone) that everyone else can see a cat there, he will have to admit that there is a cat there or be accused of misusing the language." (*Freedom and Reason* (Oxford: Clarendon Press, 1963), pp. 1-2.) Hare attempts, without great success, to distinguish ethical arguments from this rule (p. 110); in practice, it is clear that no such exception applies.

52. For a similar view, see Larry Preston, "Individual and Political Freedom," *Polity*, vol. XV (1982), pp. 79-86.

53. Miranda vs. Arizona, 384 U.S. 436 (1966); Gideon vs. Wainwright, 372 U.S. 335 (1963).

54. In my own view, as will become clear, the "just powers" of government derive from the justice of the regime, a matter to which consent is no more than a relevant consideration, while the standard of political freedom is having a say—to that extent, sharing in rule—rather than giving consent.

55. Walter Dean Burnham, "The Changing Shape of the American Political Universe," *American Political Science Review*, vol. LIX, (1965), pp. 7-28.

maries are more apt to be swayed by the media, by money and by opinion polls. Primaries are probably less subject to influence by individual citizens than the convention system they succeeded.[56] Citizens chronically complain about the quality of their choice—with reason, in recent Presidential elections—and they know how little their individual votes matter. Consent given through voting—for those who go to the polls at all, and even for those on the winning side—is conditional and half-hearted, only marginally more voluntary than confessions made in ignorance of rights and without counsel.[57]

That citizens should be so constrained, and this constraint should weaken the quality of their consent, is in part as the Framers intended. Citizens who do not find their views and feelings perfectly mirrored in platforms and candidates will be restrained in their enthusiasm, resulting in a kind of political moderation.[58] Disenchantment constitutes a standing limitation on government.

Today, however, political disillusionment has taken on alarming proportions; the United States suffers from a chronic lack of legitimacy, a weakened sense of the obligation to respect and obey law.[59] Tocqueville trusted that in local community and in society, Americans would learn the "art of associating together," thereby discovering that affiliation and loyalty can give individuals a political freedom they could never know alone.[60] Now, local communities are attenuating and, in social life, organizations are yielding to purely private activities. Contemporary Americans are apt to see groups as a time-consuming and probably futile nuisance. For citizens who share this view, political life leads to frustration, not freedom. Whatever his other accomplishments, Ronald Reagan has not lessened our doubts about government and public life; many of Reagan's policies and more of his popularity are based on a radical distrust of government and politics. American democracy can no longer rely on the arts of association; it needs to promote them.

I suspect, moreover, that the Framers would be alarmed by the increas-

---

56. James Ceaser, *Reforming the Reforms* (Cambridge: Ballinger, 1982).
57. Benjamin Barber, *Strong Democracy* (Berkeley and Los Angeles: University of California Press, 1984); after all, despite Reagan's victory, most voters expressed disapproval of a number of his most important policies.
58. Of course, moderation in practice can conceal the most immoderate opinions, which are always liable to make themselves felt.
59. Seymour Martin Lipset and William Schneider, *The Confidence Gap* (New York: Free Press, 1983).
60. *Democracy in America*, II:128-133; I, 216-226.

ing role of organized power in our political life. Contemporary citizens confront a political world dominated by organizations so powerful that they amount to private governments. The media and the other great private associations have a considerable power to shape the market, to set terms for social life and to mold political opinion. Ordinary citizens, in practice, have little or no ability to create alternatives; these private governments can be controlled only by equally gigantic public bureaucracies.[61] But private governments are often so important that government, at least in the short term, cannot *allow* them to fail. This is not a matter of ideology: the Reagan administration rescued the Continental Illinois Bank just as the Carter administration delivered Chrysler. At a certain level and size, the great private governments virtually become institutions of the republic.

The relative invulnerability of private governments, however, emphasizes the distinction between such organizations and the small businesses and individuals who can be and are allowed to fail because they are not important to the republic as a whole. The lesson is not lost on citizens: for individuals, public life is a sphere of indignity as well as of weakness, a sphere of activity in which only a few are heard and still fewer matter.

Popular literature reveals our yearning for individuals who can outwit and undo bureaucracies. In crime fiction, our first heroes were private detectives, individuals who, though outside the system, were partisans of law. But the power of bureaucracy and large scale organization is making itself felt even in fiction: more and more, private detectives are yielding to the novel of police procedure in which the hero—his intuition and imagination intact—has moved *into* the bureaucracy.[62] There is, as we know, less and less room for the independent individual. Public careers require a strength of character that goes beyond individual freedom; Frank Furillo of "Hill Street Blues" chafes at bureaucratic politics, but he recognizes that the real enemy is "the despair that goes with the territory."

In one supremely dangerous way, after all, our politics does leave space for individual liberty. We can identify vicariously with the power of Presidents and leaders who we hope will prove able to master bureaucracy and political complexity, validating the voluntaristic ideal. Individu-

61. Clark Kerr, "Managing the Managers: the Distribution of Power in American Industrial Society," in *What America Stands For*, ed. J. L. Kertesz and M. A. Fitzsimmons (Notre Dame: Notre Dame University Press, 1959), pp. 89-98; Grant McConnell, *Private Power and American Democracy* (New York: Knopf, 1966).

62. John G. Cawelti, *Adventure, Mystery and Romance* (Chicago: University of Chicago Press, 1976).

alism has always taught us to suspect laws and forms, and millions of Americans—consciously or unconsciously—now see the law as their enemy. Ronald Reagan's favorite quotation from Tom Paine, "We have it in our power to begin the world over again," expresses the old faith in the possibility of mastering nature, and many Americans admire Reagan's assertion of the power of will and choice against those who speak of limits and necessities.[63] That our yearning for "strong leadership" has its dangerous side is obvious, and it is doubly perilous because, in practice, we cannot do without executive power.[64] Our fascination with leaders, like our adoration of celebrity, is strengthened by our passion for individual liberty, and we cannot be cured without a better sort of love.[65] We need a new appreciation of the liberative power of laws and civil forms, and a recognition that both love and freedom are founded on a common life.

IV

Despite all contrary evidence, however, the idea of individual liberty continues to dominate American thought and speech about freedom. Especially, Americans retain their belief in the moral autonomy of the individual, the heart of the Framers' teaching.

This persistence of thought is not surprising: political societies are even less willing than individuals to abandon habits of mind. It is more disturbing that, as Robert Bellah and his association found, contemporary Americans increasingly have no moral language *except* the idea of individual liberty. Our older traditions—Bellah and his associates identify them as civic republicanism and Biblical religion—are becoming inarticulate. Bellah's subjects justified themselves in the language of utilitarian or expressive individualism, calculated self-interest or spontaneous feeling, even

---

63. The startling impiety of this creed is clear from the context of Paine's remark (*The Complete Writings of Thomas Paine*, ed. Philip Foner (New York: Citadel, 1969), I:45).

64. Robert Eden, *Political Leadership and Nihilism* (Tampa: University of South Florida Press, 1983).

65. Loyalty to party, to take one humble example, makes us less dependent on leaders (George Reedy, "The Presidence in the Era of Mass Communications," in *Modern Presidents and the Presidency*, ed. Marc K. Landy (Lexington: Heath, 1985), p. 40), and more exalted illustrations come easily to mind (Psalms 146:3-4).

when their conduct seemed better explained in other terms (for example, by reference to a duty to one's community).[66]

It is a striking illustration that both sides of the abortion debate cast their arguments in terms of individual rights. Supporters of "choice" are willing to appeal to a woman's "right to property" in her body even if they scorn property rights in economic life. It seems even more dissonant that the religious opponents of abortion should speak of a "right to life" rather than a duty to nurture.

As a general rule, our growing recognition of the dependence of individuals in practice has only inspired a more determined defense of their freedom in theory, but without the philosophy of nature which gave the Framers' teaching its coherence and grandeur. The great philosophic dogma of the time, the separation between "facts" and "values" owes much of its intellectual popularity to the effort to protect individualistic values against the onslaught of disconfirming fact.

Total war and totalitarianism, for example, made political scientists and political philosophers zealous to guard individuals—so terribly vulnerable to repression and mass persuasion—against the moral claims of the state. In the years after World War II, political scientists became all but universally devoted to "debunking" claims to the public good, unmasking them as only this or that private interest.[67]

Relativism and positivistic scepticism were urged because, by denying the claims to superiority of any moral doctrine, they seemed to provide a kind of negative validation for liberal democracy.[68] The relativistic critique, however, also denies any superior claims to tolerance, to fairness or even to liberty itself.[69] Criticizing relativism for just these faults, Hans J. Morgenthau praised the liberal idea that "the individual is the ultimate point of reference for the political order and as such, owes nothing to any

---

66. Robert Bellah, Richard Madsen, William Sullivan, Ann Swidler and Stephen Tipton, *Habits of the Heart: Individualism and Commitment in American Life* (Berkeley and Los Angeles: University of California Press, 1985); David R. Carlin makes a similar point, while appreciating the virtues of the Framers' doctrine in his essay, "Negative Liberty," *Commonweal*, 6 Sept. 1985, p. 455.

67. For example, David Truman, *The Governmental Process* (New York: Knopf, 1951).

68. For a recent example of this sort of argument, see Bruce Ackerman, *Social Justice in the Liberal State* (New Haven: Yale University Press, 1980), pp. 368—369.

69. Liberal values, Michael Sandel writes, "can hardly be defended by the claim that no values can be defended." ("Morality and the Liberal Ideal," *New Republic*, 7 May 1984, p. 15.) See also Edward Prucell, *The Crisis of Democratic Theory* (Lexington: University of Kentucky Press, 1973).

secular order or institution" as an invaluable restraint on power.[70] But, as Howard White pointed out in response, Morgenthau was unwilling to maintain that this theory of natural rights is *true* as well as useful. Finding no basis for the teaching in political practice, Morgenthau also did not believe that nature grants, guarantees and limits our liberties. Without that grounding, however, natural rights are only one set of preferences, a doctrine which sets us free from decency as well as from nature.[71]

More recently, John Rawls and Robert Nozick have endeavored to find firmer footing for the doctrine of individual rights. Both Rawls' relatively egalitarian doctrine and Nozick's libertarianism begin with an idea of the individual as an "end in himself." In this view, human beings are separate persons and free moral agents, each able to establish his or her own idea of the good: "The self is prior to the ends which are affirmed by it." Since rights are prior to the good—and since nothing strictly can be said to be good by nature—any moral order must derive from and respect the moral autonomy which is our fundamental right. "Individuals have rights," Nozick writes, "and there are things no person or group may do to them."[72]

Beginning with these premises, Rawls follows Locke and the Framers, presuming that "free and rational persons concerned to further their own interests" will agree to limit their liberty in order to make their rights more effective, although individual liberty will always retain its "priority."[73]

Yet Rawls and Nozick do not speak of our rights as "natural." Both are unpersuaded that there is an order of nature; certainly, they doubt whether such an order can be demonstrated (and hence, Rawls' appeal to an abstract "first position" instead of a "state of nature"). Against teleolo-

---

70. Morgenthau, p. 720.
71. White, p. 730.
72. Robert Nozick, *Anarchy, State and Utopia* (New York: Basic Books, 1974), p. ix. Benjamin Barber calls this position "premoral without being nonmoral" (*Strong Democracy*, p. 31); see also Sandel, "Morality and the Liberal Ideal," p. 16.
73. John Rawls, *A Theory of Justice* (Cambridge: Harvard University Press, 1971), pp. 541-548; for a similar argument, see Ackerman, *Social Justice in the Liberal State*, pp. 54, 57, 373-374. According to Rawls, there is also an inherent limit to the size of legitimate government, which modern regimes may be approaching. Since our most pressing wants are satisfied first, Rawls argues, as civilization advances only less urgent wants remain. "Beyond a certain point, it becomes and remains irrational from the standpoint of the original position to acknowledge a lesser liberty for the sake of greater material amenities" (p. 542). The Framers, however, would have reminded Rawls that one unsatisfied desire— our desire to preserve ourselves—hardly ranks as an "amenity."

gical ideas of nature, Rawls argues that it is an advantage of contractarian theory that it needs "much weaker assumptions" about our natural attributes.[74] In any case, Rawls and Nozick must reject the idea of nature because any whole would limit the liberty of its parts, violating the claims of individuals to be ends in themselves.[75]

Rawls and Nozick, however, do rest their theories on an implicit idea of nature. The body and "the fact of our separate existences" is the foundation of our rights.[76] Our "natural talents and abilities," in Rawls' argument, are distinguished from "social circumstances" in the old distinction between nature and nurture, and—Rawls contends—we have a right to those natural abilities, provided the social process is "fair."[77]

Rawls recognizes the human need for social support; he knows that, to a considerable extent, the self is developed in and through politics and that civil society is needed to guide and nurture the individual. Nevertheless, Rawls seeks to retain moral autonomy for the self. As the fashionable idea of "realizing one's potentialities" implies, political society is limited to developing our "powers." The political order is only an instrument, restricted to the development of our individual means—our talents and our capacity to plan. Rawls confides that realizing our capacity as free moral agents will be associated with moral sentiments and psychology; these, in turn, prove to be a higher utilitarianism, similar to Tocqueville's "interest rightly understood."[78] Even if this is so, however, moral character is a by-product of politics, not its aim. Ends, even though they are developed in and through political society, are not a concern of political society. Despite the expanded role which Rawls allows to political society,

---

74. Rawls, *A Theory of Justice*, p. 509.
75. William Galston, "Defending Liberalism," *American Political Science Review*, vol. LXXVI (1982), pp. 521-629.
76. Nozick, p. 33.
77. John Rawls, "A Well Ordered Society," in *Philosophy, Politics and Society*, 5th ser., ed. Peter Laslett and James Fishkin (New Haven: Yale University Press, 1979), pp. 7, 15-16; Rawls, *A Theory of Justice*, pp. 72-74, 104.
78. Rawls, *A Theory of Justice*, p. 463ff, 515, 519.

he maintains in principle that political society exists only to enhance our capacity as moral agents to do as we will.[79]

The language of moral individualism, in fact, goes far beyond Rawls' utilitarian doctrine of rights. Inherently, it leads toward the nihilistic conclusion that any moral claim on the individual—even the existence of moral standards—restricts freedom. To be ruled or limited by a norm perceived as external to the self—the idea of an objective human nature, for example—is heteronomy, a surrender of liberty. Human freedom requires that all forms as well as goals be things of one's making, authentic expressions of the self. The Framers, in this doctrine, violated the principle of individual liberty because they believed in the existence of a self which needs to be "preserved." In reality, the argument goes on, "man makes his own essence": the self is produced (Marx) or created (Nietzsche) in an assertion of mastery.[80]

Most Americans, of course, do not yet carry the argument to so grand an extreme. Increasingly, however, they *do* reject almost all restraints on their private liberty to do as they please. The logic of individualism, as

---

79. William Galston, "Moral Personality and Liberty Theory," *Political Theory*, vol. 10 (1982), pp. 492-519. In a similar argument years earlier, John Dewey began an essay on "The Nature of Freedom" by defining freedom as a mind pursuing "purposes which are intrinsically worthwhile." Soon, however, Dewey defined this class of things good-in-themselves as ends, originating with "natural impulses and desires," which are deliberately chosen with knowledge of their consequences. Liberty is positive, a "freedom which is power," especially the power to "frame purposes" and to design means by which "chosen ends" may be pursued. (*Experience and Education* (New York and London: Collier, 1969), pp. 61-67.) Dewey's argument, in other words, emphasized farsighted and rational planning—a limitation in method—but his "intrinsically worthwhile" purposes prove, at bottom, to be *any* purposes, originating in genuine impulses and desires, which are freely and deliberately chosen.

80. Marvin Zetterbaum, "Self and Subjectivity in Political Theory," *Review of Politics*, vol. 44 (1982), pp. 59-82. For a defense of the modern view, see Marshall Berman, *The Politics of Authenticity* (New York: Atheneum, 1980). At this year's meetings of the American Psychological Association, Stanley Krippner of the Saybrook Institute told a panel on "The Concept of Human Potential in the United States and the U.S.S.R." that the Soviet concept of the "hidden reserves of personality" is similar to the American idea of "human potentials." He cited the work of a Russian scientist who allegedly improved the work of his students by telling them, under hypnosis, that they were historical figures— physics students, for example, were told that they were Einstein. (*Los Angeles Times*, 26 Aug. 1985, Sec. V, p. 8.) It does not seem to have mattered to Krippner that his Soviet colleague achieved these results by implanting in his students the idea that they were someone else. Krippner and his Soviet counterpart appear to share the conviction that identity, to a considerable extent, is an artifact, and that the most important "human potential" is that of creating or making the self.

Tocqueville foresaw, is being carried into private life. As the sphere of individual liberty shrinks, Americans are more likely to insist on being untrammeled in what remains.[81]

The signs are all around us: it is increasingly acceptable to be divorced, to remarry or to remain unmarried, and sexual conduct is regarded as a matter of personal taste, part of one's "life style" and hence an appropriate expression of freedom.[82] We are not accustomed to such arguments in secular society, but the same currents are visible in contemporary evangelism. The Christian life, in the new rhetoric, is portrayed as an "exciting, abundant adventure"; discipline and self-sacrifice are at least deemphasized, and Christianity is presented as version of expressive individualism in which "subjectivism has displaced . . . traditional asceticism."[83]

Yet this stress on liberties of private conduct and styles of life ignores the extent to which our lives and tastes are only too likely to be shaped by broad social currents, or by fashions and putative trends proclaimed by the media. "I could very easily imagine," Arnold Gehlen wrote, "a society of termites in which each one imagined itself free."[84]

V

That we so commonly speak of the "freedom of expression" is one indication of the privatization of liberty. Of course, the term also reflects a generous desire to broaden the definition of the First Amendment to include the arts and the symbolic acts which are so often necessary to capture public attention in this age of mass media and mass politics.[85] In that sense, we are compelled to refer to the "freedom of expression" by

---

81. *Democracy in America*, II:118, 257; Russell Jacoby, *Social Amnesia* (Boston: Beacon, 1975).

82. Joseph Veroff, Elizabeth Louvan and Richard Kulka, *The Inner American* (New York: Basic Books, 1981), pp. 147-151. In the l950s, Riesman described sex as a "last frontier" (*The Lonely Crowd*, pp. 145-148); today, Lewis Laphan writes, "Adultery . . . has become so minor an accomplishment as to be hardly worth mentioning in dispatches" ("Notebook: Supply-Side Ethics," p. 10).

83. James D. Hunter, *American Evangelicalism* (New Brunswick: Rutgers University Press, 1983), pp. 91-101.

84. "Je pourrais tres facilement imaginer une societe de termites dont chacun croirait libre." "L'Avenir de la Culture," *Bulletin SEDEIS*, no. 847, 10 Mar. 1963.

85. For example, see Larry Preston, "Freedom and Authority," *American Political Science Review*, vol. LXXVII (1983), p. 670.

the increasing ascendancy in our political life of what is visible over what is said.

Yet we can scarcely be deaf to the desperation in much symbolic expression. So often, it involves a kind of sacrificial witness in the face of forces one cannot hope to persuade. Thus, Camus, anguished by the Algerian war:

> If one dares to put his whole heart and all his suffering into such a cry, he will hear in reply nothing but laughter and a louder clash of arms. And yet we must cry it aloud . . . .[86]

The decision to "throw yourself into the machine," which Mario Savio urged in 1964, does not mean that one has freedom; it is more likely to signify that one has *lost* one's voice.[87]

In order to command attention—especially from the media—it is ordinarily necessary to reduce speech to slogans if not to violence, debasing the content of one's message to the point of inarticulateness. Justice Harlan's opinion in *Cohen vs. California* aside, a protester carrying a sign bearing a four-letter word is not writing lyric poetry. His evangel, if it is effective at all, is exhausted by the shock it is intended to produce.[88]

For citizens and for the republic, the freedom of expression is no substitute for the freedom of speech. Speech edifies in a way that mere expression does not. In dialogue with myself, "I" argues with "me" at the cost of my identity; passion is all too likely to gain the ascendancy and self-centeredness is the rule.[89] By contrast, if I desire to speak to an audience, my thoughts must be ordered in a way that makes them at least minimally intelligible. The silent, listening other gives reason a kind of ascendancy in speech which it is much less apt to have in private reflection.[90] Speech creates a whole which is ordinarily greater than the sum of its parts, a discourse more rational than would be possible for either party alone. Justice Brandeis was right: "It is the function of speech to free men from the bondage of irrational fears."[91]

---

86. Albert Camus, *Resistance, Rebellion and Death*, trans. Justin O'Brien (New York: Knopf), 1961, p. 128.

87. Robert Coles, "Civility and Psychology," *Daedalus*, vol. 109 (Summer 1980), p. 140.

88. In *Cohen vs. California*, Harlan argued that "one man's obscenity is another man's lyric" (403 U.S. 15, 1971).

89. Friedrich Nietzsche, *Thus Spake Zarathustra*, ch. 14.

90. Moreover, since one motive for speaking is the desire to be approved and admired, one's speech is apt to be as excellent as the audience it is intended to impress. In that respect, an excellent audience sets us free.

91. Dissenting in Whitney vs. California, 274 U.S. 376 (1927).

Free speech is more than a "right to utter." In the most fundamental sense, speech is a political act, a participation in deliberation.[92] Speech is not free without the opportunity to *be* heard by an audience which is *able* to hear: even if we gain the rostrum, we will be effectively silenced if the audience speaks a different language, unless it is willing and able to learn ours.[93]

The ability to hear implies an openness to deliberation, a willingness to receive evidence and to consider argument which has at least two vital aspects. First, it presumes confidence, a relatively low fear of being deceived, a conviction that one's critical skills will enable one to evaluate both the matter and manner of what is said. Second, an audience is able to hear only to the extent that it perceives listening as compatible with dignity. Listening is most dignified when one chooses to hear even though one might have spoken. Like other mass regimes, modern America denies that choice to all but a handful of citizens, depriving listening of its dignity. Moreover, dignity in listening varies with the matter being discussed. I am relatively willing to attend to a discussion of national politics even though I have no chance to speak myself, but I feel furious and ill-used when I must listen to a colleague ramble about trivia, even if I will have the chance to reply. In these terms, freedom of speech is enhanced by (1) civic education, including the study of rhetoric, and (2) access to forums in which we have the opportunity to speak, providing that these have at least some important powers and responsibilities.[94]

In our time, free government needs to foster, as well as protect, the conditions of free speech. Civic education is acknowledged already as a public responsibility, although that responsibility is discharged in an inadequate way. By contrast, public policy has ignored or undermined our local forums, which are now in urgent need of support. There are any number of ways of providing this assistance. We could mandate primaries by district caucus (as in Iowa) rather than by mass electorates; instead of requiring a certain number of signatures to qualify an initiative for the ballot, it would be possible to ask for the favorable vote of a number of district assemblies.

Perhaps most important, we could direct campaigning back to the local

---

92. Alexander Meiklejohn, *Political Freedom* (New York: Harper & Row, 1960).
93. Plato, *Apology* 17D-18A.
94. Barber, *Strong Democracy*, pp. 173-178; "The Greek *polis*," Hannah Arendt wrote, "was precisely that 'form of government' which provided men with a space of appearances where they could act, with a kind of theater where freedom could appear." ("What is Freedom?" in *Between Past and Future*, (Cleveland and New York: World, 1965), p. 154.)

level. Public funds, for example, could and should go to state and local parties as well as to candidates and national committees. Above all, it would strengthen the freedom of speech if we found ways to restrict the role of money in political campaigns. Of course, the Supreme Court has eviscerated the Campaign Reform Act by finding that monetary contributions are a form of expression protected by the First Amendment. In practice, this means that Congress may not limit the amount of money which an individual (or corporation) contributes to a political campaign, although it may require that the money be distributed through a number of nominally independent committees.[95] But money does *not* talk: we participate in politics by giving money, but most of us do so privately, without engaging in civic deliberation. The gift of money is an expression of sentiment which may or may not issue in speech.

Free expression in the form of money can, in fact, easily undermine free speech. In the first place, there are necessarily great inequalities in the extent to which citizens can participate by donating money, and the implicit indignity is likely to reduce the public's willingness to listen. Second, money tends to gravitate into the mass media, drawing campaigns with it. Even if we accept the Court's defense of unlimited contributions, we might choose to limit the amount of political advertising on television (on those networks and channels subject to regulation).[96] Such a regulation would rechannel money to the local organizations and forums in which broadly-based free speech is possible.

Finally, civil liberty implies the public protection of *civil* speech. When we argue about public questions, we have a right to attack the ideas and doctrines of our fellow citizens, but not their persons. The two things overlap, of course, but the principle is clear.[97] Moreover, the protection of the person includes more than the prohibition of assaults on the body. An attack on the identity or dignity of another citizen does violence no less than a physical blow.

The Supreme Court long ago noted that there are "fighting words" which public authority has a right and a duty to forbid in public speech,

---

95. Buckley vs. Valeo, 424 U.S. 1 (1976).
96. Other Western countries ban it altogether with no loss to democracy of freedom.
97. In the case of an overlap—when I am so identified with my philosophic position, for example, that I experience any argument against it as a personal affront—a free regime must ordinarily take the side of public argument against personal feelings. For us, given the First Amendment, this is especially true. For the general proposition, see Ronald Dworkin, *Taking Rights Seriously* (Cambridge: Harvard University Press, 1978), p. 272.

even though—to say the least—it has hesitated to apply that doctrine in recent years.[98] As Alexander Meiklejohn argued, rules of order and civil manners do not restrict content; such forms may challenge our creativity in speech and writing, but they do not make it impossible to say what we mean.[99]

For many years, we could take our civilities more or less for granted. Public debate was limited by a broad consensus on private morals—or at least, by the dominance of white, middle class, Protestant proprieties.[100] For many reasons, this is no longer the case: groups that were once excluded or invisible now demand consideration; things once unthinkable and unspeakable are now items on the public agenda; our militant insistence on individual freedom in private life has helped to shatter older ideas of respectability.[101] The social order, in other words, has only a diminished capacity to maintain civility. We are likely to need public authority to uphold the good manners appropriate to contemporary civil speech.

In a variety of ways, government already bars racist or sexist speech, and in forbidding sexual harassment, governments look behind words to determine their intent.[102] This is as it should be. Our persons are not defined simply in terms of our separate bodies, but by the groups with which we identify. A slur on a gender or on a racial or ethnic group involves an offense to its members, and is intended to do so. This is especially true in mass society, since where individuals are dwarfed, the group takes on added significance as a source of strength, dignity and

---

98. Chaplinsky vs. New Hampshire, 315 U.S. 568 (1942); the Court's recent reticence is indicated in Gooding vs. Wilson, 405 U.S. 518 (1972).

99. Alexander Meiklejohn, *Free Speech and Its Relation to Self-Government* (New York: Harper, 1948); Leo Strauss, *Persecution and the Art of Writing* (Glencoe: Free Press, 1952), indicates the possibilities in far more confining situations.

100. *Democracy in America*, I:33-34.

101. Even in 1956, Harold Nicolson observed that American manners were "nervously" changing (*Good Behaviour* (Garden City: Doubleday, 1956), p. 15).

102. To argue that a "classification" using race is "suspect"—or that one involving sex is "semi-suspect"—involves the assertion that such language may not be used, without exceptional justification, by public institutions or in the law. Through civil rights statutes, this affects a variety of private institutions as well. (For example, see Craig vs. Boren, 429 U.S. 190, 1976; Runyon vs. McCrary 427 U.S. 160, 1976; see also Morroe Berger, *Equality by Statute* (Garden City: Doubleday, 1968), pp. 116-117 and Catherine MacKinnon, *The Sexual Harassment of Working Women* (New Haven: Yale University Press), 1979.

personal freedom.[103] Given the unsettled state of civil manners, there is a good case for entitling the victims of such group libels to some sort of civil damages.[104]

All of this presumes, however, that civil freedom ranks higher among the liberties than the right of individuals to do as they please. As a matter of theory, however, that is a proposition which the Framers' teaching denies.

VI

This brings me back to the fundamental point: part of the contemporary problem of freedom derives from the inadequacy of the Framers' view. Of course, the Framers were wiser than today's fashions in political thought and opinion, especially in the value they set on government and civil restraint. Nevertheless, the Framers' doctrine inherently involves a threat to the order of civil life since it makes private, pre-political rights the end of human society, superior in principle to all the forms (i.e., contracts and laws) created to "secure" these rights.[105] The Framers hoped that the principle of natural liberty could be contained within scientifically designed forms, and Madison disagreed with Jefferson, his mentor in so many things, by seeking to make any "recourse to first principles" rare and extraordinary.[106] Even so, the Framers' theory gives the rights of morally free individuals a priority in defining the terms and setting the direction of political life.[107]

---

103. Hadley Arkes, *The Philosopher and the City* (Princeton: Princeton University Press, 1981), pp. 23-91; Harry Kalven, *The Negro and the First Amendment* (Chicago: University of Chicago Press, 1965); Donald Downs, *Nazis in Skokie: Freedom, Community and the First Amendment* (South Bend: University of Notre Dame Press, 1985). Joel Grossman would limit public intervention to cases in which the threatened group faces a "likelihood of actual harm." By any reasonable definition, however, "actual harm" includes more than damage to one's body or property, to say nothing of the injury done to public speech and public life (Grossman, "The First Amendment and the New Anti-Pornography Statutes," *News for Teachers of Political Science*, no. 45 (Spring 1985), p. 20.)

104. Beauharnais vs. Illinois, 343 U.S. 250 (1952); in an important sense, this is part of the intent of programs for Affirmative Action.

105. Mansfield, pp. 129-130; Schaar, "The Question of Justice," pp. 127-128.

106. *The Federalist* #49; as Stourzh indicates, this helps account for the reliance, in *The Federalist*, on theorists the Framers associated with the study of the *forms* of government (i.e., Montesquieu) as opposed to thinkers who were concerned with *principles* (i.e., Locke) (Stourzh, p. 6).

107. Rawls' defense of the "priority" of liberty essentially follows the Framers' argument (*Theory of Justice*, pp. 243-251).

By contrast, Aristotle held that human beings develop in and through political society. The ends of political regime are not established in some pre-political state; they are characteristic of the political society as a whole. In this view, the forms and ends of a regime are closely related, defining a "way of life" which constitutes the political society.[108] In Aristotle's terms, the end of a democracy is political freedom, embodied in the form of equal citizenship, ruling and being ruled in a shared responsibility for the common good. The danger to democracy, Aristotle argued, lies precisely in that idea of liberty which the Framers made their first principle—that individuals are most free when they can do as they please.[109]

As Aristotle's argument suggests, there is something base about the Framers' idea of liberty. Freedom is a relationship with three parts. I am free, in ordinary speech, when I am not kept from doing what I choose, a notion which involves (1) subjects, (2) the goals they pursue, and (3) the restrictions which are absent or the means which are available in the attainment of these goals.[110] If this is so, then unfreedom in *any* of these parts will limit liberty. Modern political doctrine, however, focuses entirely on the question of my power to do as I will.[111] Doctrines of negative liberty contend that I have the power I need, provided that you do not restrain me; ideas of positive liberty insist that I lack the power unless you help me, and hence, that I am restrained by your indifference.[112] For both, power virtually subsumes freedom.

At least implicitly, these modern ideas of liberty identify freedom with domination, the struggle to master nature which cannot be separated from the ability to master other human beings.[113] To that extent, as

---

108. Aristotle, *Politics* 1276b10-12.

109. Aristotle, *Politics* 1310128-38, 1317a40-b17.

110. Gerald MacCallum, "Negative and Positive Freedom," *Philosophic Review*, vol. 76 (1967), p. 314; Rawls, *Theory of Justice*, p. 202.

111. Stanley Benn and W. L. Weinstein, "Being Free to Act and Being a Free Man," *Mind*, vol. 80 (1971), p. 197; De Jouvenel, *Sovereignty*, p. 249ff; Charles Taylor, "What's Wrong with Negative Freedom," in *The Idea of Freedom* ed. Alan Ryan (Oxford: Oxford University Press, 1979), pp. 175-193, especially p. 183. It ought to be clear that, given the diversity of subjects, any notion of liberty must also involve an element of inequality or, to put it more precisely, of difference between us.

112. C. B. Macpherson, for example, defines freedom as the "absence of humanly imposed impediments" including those institutions which deny us equal access to "the means of life and the means of labor" (*Democratic Theory* (London: Oxford University Press, 1973), p. 96).

113. The desire for power, De Jouvenel writes, "is not the story of liberty but of human imperialism" (*Sovereignty*, p. 259). See also Helmuth Plessner, "The Emancipation of Power," *Social Research*, vol. 31 (1974), pp. 155-174.

Lincoln appears to have understood, one cannot reject the "wolf's diction-ary" without rejecting the Framers' teaching as well. When freedom is separated from ends and defined in terms of an independent self, Schell-ing recognized, any "objective power" is a limitation on liberty. Even in the sphere of ideas, any "system of theoretically universal applicability" threatens my subjective freedom, since it denies my uniqueness and limits my creativity. It follows that I am free only to the extent that I can overcome nature in *theory* as well as in practice.[114] In other words, the idea of natural rights—which makes my independence derive from nature—has a tendency to destroy itself.

The ancient teachings which the Framers rejected spoke of freedom in a more comprehensive way. In the first place, they regarded liberty as a quality of soul, an attribute of a particular *kind* of subject—one who is "free in spirit"—rather than a characteristic of subjectivity as such. Sec-ond, the older doctrines denied that freedom can be separated from worthy and appropriate ends. Whatever the means at our command, and whatever the opportunities open to us, we are not free if we slavishly pursue a goal which enslaves us.[115]

Freedom is more than a matter of outward form. The fact that my body is physically separate does *not* endow me with moral autonomy. Quite the contrary, as Aristotle reasoned, the body is essentially slavish. On its own terms, the body, devoted to "mere life," pursues pleasure and self-preser-vation. It can, consequently, be controlled by pain or by threats to life. The processes of the body offer automatism, not liberation; we must look elsewhere to find freedom.[116]

In his essay, "The Turning Point of My Life," Mark Twain begins with hyperbolic determinism, deriving the events of his life from Caesar's crossing of the Rubicon (and explaining that only limitations of space kept him from going back to Adam and Eve). Later in the story, however, Twain makes clear that the real turning point of his life came during his early adolescence. The town was visited by an epidemic, and Twain's

---

114. P.W.J. Schelling, *Sammtliche Werke*, ed. K.F.A. Schelling (Augsburg: Cottaa, 1860), I:179, 304, 336; VII: 351. For Schelling, this implied that we must see nature as something which is "becoming"—that the "essence of nature" is, in fact, only being approached *through* freedom (VII:348, 362). See also Geoffrey Clive, *The Romantic Enlightenment* (New York: Meridian, 1960).

115. The Framers recognized this, whatever the other shortcomings of their argument, when they referred to rights as "inalienable." In these terms, a phrase like "the freedom to establish National Socialism" reflects, at best, a truncated idea of liberty.

116. Arendt, "What is Freedom?", p. 168.

mother, following the practice of the day, kept him isolated in a darkened room. Twain decided, he tells us, that "life on these miserable terms was not worth living." He escaped from his room and visited the sickbed of a friend, succeeding in his attempt to catch the disease rather than live in fear. It was this particular act of defiance which led Twain's mother to apprentice him: it was, in other words, a transition from the estate of a child to that of a man.[117]

This decisive "turning point," Twain is telling us, is premised on a liberation from the body and its fears. We are emancipated by the sort of courage which, acknowledging that death is fearful, recognizes that there are things still more dreadful. The free spirit will, like Twain, prefer to share death with a friend rather than live alone. To that extent, the need for friendship and conversation—the heart of politics—works to set us free.[118]

Similarly, an ageless wisdom instructs us that a free person is able to do without many things. In this understanding, the modern notion—that we are unfree unless we have what we want—bespeaks enslavement to desire.[119] Instead, one becomes free by distinguishing what is humanly needed from what is needless, trivial or merely pleasant. Freedom is not so much an ability to *do* what we want as it is the capacity to *be* what we are.

In this sense, freedom expresses itself through a desire to know and be what one truly is, to be oneself fully. Yet this nobler self-seeking implicitly includes a need to know the whole of which we are parts, and hence, to see ourselves in our partiality. Freedom, in this elevated sense, strives to become unfree, and the higher dependence sets us free from lesser things.

---

117. *The Favorite Works of Mark Twain* (Garden City: Garden City Publishing, 1939), pp. 1129-1135.

118. This is no esoteric teaching. In this year's Disney movie, *The Black Cauldron*, the half-human Gurgi, who ordinarily flies from trouble or danger, emerges as the hero because, in the end he is willing to sacrifice his life to save his friend. Gurgi has no warrior's honor; he is moved by humbler motives, but he is still free. This freedom, however, stops short of full self-rule: Gurgi chooses to be ruled, like a body disciplined to accept its limitations.

119. Epictetus, *Discourses* IV, 75, 81, 83, 89; the extreme versions of this doctrine hold that any desire or affection restricts our liberty, but radical asceticism sets a standard which, because it is fundamentally inhuman, also leads toward the effort to master human nature, aiming at a kind of tyranny in the soul. Orwell recognized this imperious element in Gandhi's teaching (*The Complete Essays, Journalism and Letters of George Orwell*, ed. Sonia Orwell and Ian Angus (New York: Harcourt Brace and World, 1968), IV: 463-470).

Any such exalted idea of freedom, however, presumes that we have learned in humbler ways that attachments—the bonds of love and friendship—can make us free. An education in human freedom needs the kind of civil society which leads us, without indignity, out of the isolation of the body.[120] In that fundamental sense, the discipline of civility is the school of freedom.

---

120. Michael Platt, "Leo Strauss: Three Quarrels, Three Questions," *Newsletter*, Dept. of Political Science, University of Dallas, vol. II, no. 2 (Winter 1978) pp. 5-6.

Constituting Liberty

Jeffrey K. Tulis

Many Americans have died in wars fought to secure the blessings of liberty. One might therefore think that establishing liberty as a political *purpose* was easy and painless, especially compared to the practical political tasks of securing it. This would be so if the meaning of liberty were simple to grasp. We sometimes forget that our founding and subsequent political life not only constituted institutions and arrangements to make liberty safe and secure—but also constituted liberty itself, that is, certain peculiarly American meanings. Moreover, attempts to recover or analyze the constitution of American liberty inevitably reconstitute it, altering its meaning for us by privileging some of its expressions and concealing others.

The discussion of liberty at this conference revolved around the locus of responsibility for the political vices that attend an overly individualistic understanding of liberty. All panelists (with the possible exception of Marvin Meyers) began from the premise that excessive freedom for autonomous individuals, a concomitant privatized society, decline of public spirit, and contempt for honor and social responsibility are characteristic of American life today. Sanderson Schaub adopted an avowedly "moral majoritarean" standpoint; Wilson Carey McWilliams appealed to a forgotten Aristotelian world (while acknowledging his Presbyterian slant on that perspective) and Michael Sandel articulated a classical republican, communitarean perspective. No one spoke in behalf of the bourgeois virtues, of acquisitiveness as a value, or of the relativity of all values, as for example, a libertarian might. No one expressed a Marxist longing for utopian freedom, for freedom from nature. Nor did anyone (with the slight exception of Meyers) contest the shared perception that our political condition is troubled and our current conception of the meaning and demands of liberty insecure. Despite a sizable contingent of supporters for Ronald Reagan at the conference, the President's optimism regarding our moral condition did not display itself at this session.

Sanderson Schaub attempts to correct alleged misreadings of *The Federalist*. His discussion traverses considerable portions of *The Federalist* in an effort to show, following Harry Jaffa, how that text can best be interpreted as a modern expression of Aristotelian natural law. Liberty itself is not discussed much, but rather justice, honor and virtue. Sometimes Schaub

64

suggests these political qualities to be necessary means to secure liberty, but in other places he suggests the reverse.

His most sustained argument is a reinterpretation of *Federalist* 10. This essay is commonly thought to be an especially cogent argument for a polity that does not *substantially* rely upon virtue, moral instruction, or religious sentiment to secure liberty and individual rights, but instead rests upon the depoliticization, if not destruction, of religious and ideological factions, the proliferation of other factions, a commercial political economy, a vast territory, a representative government, and a *modicum* of virtue.

By contract, virtue, justice, honor, and zeal assume central places in Schaub's interpretation. According to him, Madison attempted to prevent majority tyranny by establishing a new majority around new political principles. This virtuous majority, rather than some political equivalent of the invisible hand, would protect liberty and individual rights. "For the surest foundation for the interplay of factions that liberty gives vent to is the public commitment to the 'laws of nature and of nature's God,' the commitment to that form of justice whose support the signers of the Declaration pledged their 'sacred honor.' Justice and honor. That is what *Federalist* No. 10 comes down to in the end."[1]

An adequate review of the argument that leads to this conclusion requires more space than I am permitted. But readers may wish to consider three issues as they read the essay and *The Federalist* for themselves. First, one must surmount the difficulty of distinguishing rhetorical from theoretic expression. Mr. Schaub treats all references as part of a philosophic argument. Imagine yourself a founder who wished to transform a religious community into a secular one. How would you address your audience? You might refer to God, Providence, or to the sacred while at the same time altering their status in the political construction you bring into being. "Nature's God" is no longer the God of Abraham.

Second, you might wish to ponder the place of zeal and zealotry in Mr. Schaub's position. Schaub notes Madison's attempt to quiet religious fanaticism, but he suggests that the Father wishes to redirect zealotry to a defense of moderate republican principles. ("Extremism in defense of liberty is no vice . . . !") This intention presumes that the most offensive aspect of religious fanaticism is religious opinion rather than the temperament and passion that attend such opinions. Could it be that the problem of religious or ideological fanaticism is the *form* of opinion more than

---

1. Schaub, p. 30.

opinion, per se, and that redirected obnoxiousness will still be obnoxious? Moreover, can a redirected zealotry successfully abandon its affinity for religious opinion—can there be a Madisonian "moral majority" that does not inevitably degenerate into something like the familiar Jerry Falwell version?

Finally, readers might want to bear in mind the distinction between political explanation and political aspiration. *The Federalist* has long been heralded as providing the most profound account of the political logic animating American politics as well as, and connected to, the ideals to which the nation should aspire. The familiar *Federalist* provides useful explanations of the *conduct* of political life today. If we accept Mr. Schaub's new *Federalist*, we are left wondering why American politics is not actuated by and devoted to justice and honor. Just what makes America tick?

Wilson Carey McWilliams provides an exceptionally thoughtful answer to the last question. He tries to identify and understand salient characteristics of American politics today in light of the political logic of the founding principles.

Conceding that several "voices" contended at the founding, indeed sometimes *within* the thought of individual founders, McWilliams suggests that one philosophic voice dominated all others and continues to animate and structure our politics and psychic economy. The founders may have spoken about the common good, about public spiritness and honor, and they certainly exemplify political virtue in their public conduct. But their Constitution and its defense rested upon a Hobbesean atomistic materialism and *that* commitment governs all others. The founders "held that human beings are by nature free beings who are morally independent and primarily self-centered. In this doctrine, nature is defined by origins, and hence by the body; the decisive evidence of human freedom is the fact that we come into the world in separate bodies, and so remain. By nature, individuals are unencumbered, without duties to others or chains on them."[2]

The movement from man's natural condition to an artificial civil one requires consent: consent to give up enough natural freedom to secure peace. Because institutions necessary for this purpose require civic-mindedness to function, the founders view of civil society embraces both the "negative" freedom of precivil life and the "positive" freedom to participate in an ordered whole. But "the balance [between these two sorts of free-

---

2. McWilliams, p. 32-33.

dom] must always tilt toward 'negative' individual rights and liberties, the moral center of liberal civilization."[3]

McWilliams invites us to consider the *context* and *logic* of appeals to virtue, justice, and honor in American political discourse. Examined closely, he argues, they all reflect a Hobbesean core: they are almost always deployed in the service of individual liberty. McWilliams' keenest insights concern the paradoxical result of these "first principles" for American political development.

As Americans have become physically more secure—safer, healthier, materially better off, in short *independent*—they have become psychologically insecure, vulnerable, fearful, and more and more *dependent*. What's more, they have become dependent on strangers. For example, the complex American economy increases "freedom of choice" and provides material conditions for the exercise of diverse talents but it also establishes a vast network of impersonal interdependencies.

Michael Sandel summarized well McWilliams' paradoxical insight: as rights and entitlements expand, individuals become less and less in control of the forces of their own lives. The most arresting sections of McWilliams' paper illustrate this paradox in detail.

McWilliams urges a return to pre-liberal thought, because for individuals to overcome their predicament, even in the service of autarkic individualism, they would need resources unavailable to them in our political tradition. Friendship and other virtues that might combat the anomie McWilliams describes cannot be grasped in thought or successfully defended without appeal to a tradition other than one that derives all from the body and its self-preservation. McWilliams urges return to an earlier conspectus of opinion in which the notion of a *free people* as distinct from *free individuals* was a guiding idea around which other political norms radiated. Such a notion in turn would rest upon a metaphysical alternative to the corporeal concern that McWilliams locates beneath the surface of all contemporary American thought.

It seems as if McWilliams intends to leave the amelioration of our grave condition to college professors. He does not discuss the political institutions that would embody his republican soulcraft or the political difficulties that would accompany those institutions. Acutely aware of the practical problems of establishing liberty, the founders did not simply prefer their large modern construction but argued its superiority over previous polities in contending with many perennial political problems. Professor

---

3. McWilliams, p. 35.

McWilliams reminds us of antiquity's Aristotle, but Alexander Hamilton was concerned too with that "fierce rapacity" that characterized so many actual ancient regimes.

Reflections like these prompted Marvin Meyers to charge that McWilliams offered only utopianism (perhaps the first time an Aristotelian has been burdened with an epithet usually reserved for Platonists). Yet because Meyers also argued (in agreement with Schaub) that the founders' thought is not as individualistic as McWilliams supposed, containing within it some of the pre-liberal elements McWilliams seeks, why not consider the founders to be utopians too?

Professor Meyers concluded his remarks by noting that McWilliams' paper "shows so little respect for what we have here" since it neglects to note how well our "flawed" success compares to other regimes. Just as McWilliams' paper seems to echo Solzhenitsyn's critique of American politics, Meyers calls to mind the irate journalists who couldn't fathom how the great Russian could be so critical of *both* the U.S. and the U.S.S.R. (If Professor McWilliams doesn't like it here he should go back to—New Jersey?)

The last commentator, Michael Sandel, agreed with McWilliams' diagnosis of American ills, but argued that now neglected American political traditions contain resources sufficient to ameliorate our condition. If liberty is thought today to be in opposition to democracy and if rights are depicted as "trumps" to be used against the majority, there was an earlier American tradition, a democratic-republican tradition, in which liberty was thought an attribute of republican institutions, not of individuals. Government attempted to secure *civil liberty* not civil liberties. He pointed to the long line of 19th century Supreme Court cases which did not depend upon arguments for individual rights, but instead focussed upon the appropriateness of exercises of institutional power. And he suggested that political thought beginning with the Anti-federalists and extending through Jefferson and his intellectual heirs provides an alternative to the rights-based liberalism that has become so pervasive today.

How fundamental are the differences between our democratic-republican and individual rights traditions? The Anti-federalists did not articulate a classical case for virtue as its own reward, but rather wished to inculcate virtue for the protection of individual rights. And it was the Anti-federalists who led the cause for adding a Bill of Rights to the Constitution. Have there been coherent American political doctrines that did not rest, in the end, as McWilliams would argue, on Hobbesean premises? Whatever the answer to this question, Sandel's thoughtful remarks force us to wonder whether the most vulgar expression of found-ing ideas must inevitably carry the day. If they must, does self-government have a future?

Chapter Two

Popular Government: Equality

The meaning of the second great principle of democratic government, equality, is as controversial today as is the meaning of liberty. Is the meaning of equality to be restricted to the formal political rights to life, liberty, and property, or ust the social and economic conditions which allow people to take advantage of their rights also be equalized?

Equality: The Framers' View

Mary K. Bonsteel Tachau

Going back to the 18th century to reconstruct the views of the Framers is an exercise in imagination as much as it is an act of scholarship. It is somewhat like immersing oneself in an aquarium or going scuba diving. We see those things that we have read about, but the light in which we view them is refracted differently, and the details are unexpectedly complicated. There is beauty and harmony, but great dark depths of ignorance are always along the periphery. Everything is in motion; nothing living is still. Most of all, we see what we are looking for. It is impossible to comprehend the entire watery universe, and our perceptions and 20th century postures distort reality just as do the filtered sunshine and the shadows. Despite all the things we share with our forebears, theirs was a world almost as different from ours as water is different from earth and air and fire.

For example: we live in a crowded, urban, post-industrial society made up of many people with different ethnic and racial characteristics. We can travel the Atlantic in two hours, telephone China in a minute, and our missiles go almost as fast. Every day we eat food that has come to us fresh, frozen, freeze-dried, or canned from all over the world. We can choose clothing, household appliances, furnishings, and automobiles that have similarly exotic points of origin. Our children think that money comes from automatic tellers, water from faucets, electricity from switches, and milk from paper cartons. We air condition our homes with fuels and machines that were unimaginable two hundred years ago. Our technology is the wonder—and the fear—of the entire universe. We are so powerful that it is a mark of distinction in some international groups for angry people to storm our embassies, bomb our military installations, or commandeer our aircraft and make hostages out of vacationing Americans.

The Framers' world was very different. For one thing, they all spoke the same language; they all shared the same culture. They all read and discussed the same books, although some read more widely and reflected more deeply than others. One might have had a French grandmother and another a German grandfather, but most of them were British, and they looked more or less alike: white and Anglo-Saxon. Their faces were marked by an earlier bout with smallpox; many had survived malaria, typhoid, and yellow fever. When their children got what until recently were considered normal childhood diseases, they feared for their lives: half of all children even in their society died before the age of six. They did not expect themselves or their wives to live much beyond the mid-forties, although some did. They generally anticipated a life after death, for all were reared as Christians, as were almost all of the people they knew. They wore homespun most of the time because machine-made fabric was expensive and rare. Their comfort in summer depended upon the thickness of the walls of the buildings they worked and lived in, the shade of trees, or the prominence of hills almost as much as upon latitude. In winter, it depended upon their personal proximity to a fireplace. Some lived in farmhouses, others in townhouses, a few in mansions, but none of them ever had to climb more than three stories (although sometimes their servants did). All were sufficiently prosperous—at least at the time of the Convention—that they could take months and even years away from their livelihoods, which usually involved lawyering. All of them knew about farming because many were farmers, as were ninety-seven per cent of their compatriots. They shared landladies, butchers, bankers, candlestick makers, and information on where to stay when traveling. They all rode horses and knew how to take care of them. None of them ever tasted hot dogs or saw a baseball game; none of them had any toothpaste or Right Guard.

They shared so much that it was not necessary for them to explain or define many of the words they commonly used among themselves: words like liberty and republicanism. But equality was not such a word; it was not commonly used. Instead, they discussed, disagreed, agreed, or argued about how much democracy could or even should be attempted in a republic founded upon a common goal of liberty. They doubted that the nation would be secure if there was too much equality or democracy in it; for them, the words were synonymous. Everything they knew about democracy came from their reading about the Greek city-states, which were much smaller in area and in population than the United States. The republic with which they were most familiar was the Roman republic, and it had fallen victim to demagoguery and tyranny. The Framers were determined to learn from the lessons of history and avoid the failures of the past. They knew that they were engaged in a momentous experiment, that America would be (as John Winthrop had said of the Massachusetts Bay Colony), "as a Citty upon a Hill, the eies of all people are uppon us." Meanwhile, the United States was an embarrassingly poor and unimportant cousin in the western family of nations, often bullied both by France, its former friend, and Great Britain, its former enemy.

The Founders were men of extraordinary political experience. They had risked revolution because they did not fear that anarchy would accompany their Declaration of Independence. The American colonies had been largely self-governing for seven generations. Every one of the Framers had seen his own colony's charter transformed into a state constitution; many had assisted in that process. They had survived a war against the most powerful country in the world, and had conducted that war through an ad hoc legislative body and thirteen loosely allied states. By 1787, they had lived through one experiment in national government. Even though it appeared to have failed, they were eager to try again to devise a more perfect union. They knew that there were many models for government: some as ancient and distant as classical Greece and Rome, others as recent and as nearby as the constitutions of the thirteen states. Thus, although they lived in what was in many ways a technologically primitive society, the Framers' political sophistication was of a quality matched in that era by Mozart, by the great Georgian architects, by Arkwright and Watt, and by all those farmer-experimenters (including some of the Framers themselves) who brought about the third important agricultural revolution in human history.

The greatest problem in describing accurately the Framers' beliefs about equality lies in the fact that they wrote and spoke surprisingly little about it. Charles Pinckney made a long speech in the Convention on June 25 giving an optimistic but rather general definition of what it meant. But there was no response, no debate following, and therefore no evidence about whether he spoke only for himself or whether his ideas were typical. Things might have been different if Thomas Jefferson had been present because he had such uncommon faith in common people, but he was in France doing the nation's business. For those in Philadelphia, equality was simply not a major item on the agenda. What the Framers were concerned about were concepts like liberty and republicanism; how to devise techniques that would check and balance political power, divide authority between the national government and the states, limit the central authority while still giving it enough power to sustain itself; and how to protect the states and their citizens from encroachment by what they called "a general and consolidated government." Therefore, if we are to discover what the Founders meant by "equality," we must judge by their deeds, not their words, and see how much equality they provided for—or made possible—in the Constitution.

This kind of investigation is familiar to me because it is similar to my research field. I study court records in a systematic way in order to discover how the Constitution and constitutional principles were actually carried out in federal and state judiciaries. I recreate the court records and carry the cases through to disposition to find out how the Constitution and the laws actually functioned. In the course of my work, I have often found that what we have believed to be true is not borne out by the evidence. The frequency of this phenomenon suggests that people tend to impute to the past what they know of the present. It is a human tendency, but it is not rigorous scholarship.

Although inquiring about the Founders' views of equality is essentially an exercise in presentism, it is an important exercise. There is no question that achieving equality for all Americans is the major challenge of the late twentieth century. To borrow a phrase from Franklin Delano Roosevelt, that issue marks our generations's rendezvous with destiny. Still the kinds and degrees of equality with which thoughtful people must be concerned today are issues of 1987, not 1787.

Paradoxically, it is the very fact that equality is so important an issue today that prompts us to go back two hundred years to the world of the Framers to see what they may have meant by that word. After all, *they* were part of a generation that had proclaimed the revolutionary idea that "all men are created equal." No one had ever made that assertion before in order to establish a government, much less to justify a rebellion. No other people have ever tried harder since then to realize that principle, to convert an inspiring abstraction into reality. All of us know how far we have yet to go to achieve a just society characterized by many kinds of equality. Our inquiry into the past may bring some perspective to that goal.

It would be an exaggeration to say that fifty-five men had fifty-five different ideas about equality because, as in any group, there were clusters of consensus. It would be boring to quote some aphorism characteristic of each of those clusters. Similarly, it would be futile to try to line up all the Framers at one point or another on a scale that measured their ideas about equality; such an exercise would be as inaccurate as it would be arbitrary. For one thing, they sometimes shifted their positions according to the issues before them. For example, some who believed in legal equality did not believe in political equality. Some believed in political equality when it meant choosing representatives for one house of the legislative branch but not the other, others believed in it for both houses, or for neither. Some may have honestly changed their minds, others may have made arguments that went beyond their convictions in order to achieve political victories. As in the simile about the underwater world, nothing living is still, and we are talking about living and mortal men.

The one thing that we do know about the Founders is that they did not want their intentions and their definitions to control the future. For that reason, their proceedings were held in secret and they did not publish whatever notes that had taken until many years after the Convention. Much of what we have learned was written in private letters, which they certainly did not expect to reach publication. Occasionally their intentions are clear, as when they consciously departed from English precedents. One example of this is in their narrow definition of treason. Other examples reflecting their commitment to open and accountable government are seen in the requirements for recording votes, publishing the journals of Congress, and having the executive deliver what has become the State of the Union address. Such evidence is clear but anonymous. It reflects consensus but not the opinion of any individual. For that we rely upon another source.

One member of the Convention provided posterity a remarkable body of data from which we can discern the views of many of the Founders. That person, of course, is James Madison. Madison has a well-earned reputation as the Father of the Constitution. He knew where other people stood on the issues, and he used that knowledge effectively, although he was not a consensus-builder and was more nationalist-minded than many of the other members. He was both a theoretician and a realist. His own opinions were generally more enlightened than those of his contemporaries (except for Thomas Jefferson's and in the Convention, James Wilson's), but they were not so unusual as to have been atypical. More important for this inquiry is the fact that he was internally consistent. Happily for us, he not only took careful notes every evening about what had gone on in the Convention; he also carried on an extensive correspondence at the same time. He made it possible for us to know a great deal about what happened, what he thought, and by extension, what many of the others probably believed, also.

One way to approach the subject of equality is by identifying those whom Madison and the other Founders assumed to be unequal. The first to be considered are the first Americans. The Founders' ideas about Indians were complicated and ambiguous. The prevailing sentiment was a Rousseauesque admiration for the children of the forest, coupled with condescension for these strange people who thought that the land was theirs to use and who stubbornly resisted European civilization. This frame of reference was tempered by genuine fear of the native Americans' prowess in war and by a general acknowledgment of their status as members of independent nations, at least temporarily. Such opinions often coalesced in a patronizing attitude not unlike the worst B movies of the 1930's. Jefferson's rather respectful anthropological interest in native Americans does not seem to have affected Madison, who—at least publicly—thought of himself as the great white father who knew what was best for his children. In any event, there was so little discussion about Indians in the Convention that it is clear that whatever the Framers meant by the word "equality," it did not extend to Native Americans.

It also did not extend to that half of the population who were female. The Framers were reared in the English legal system, where coverture prevailed. Married women were "hidden from the law" and had no legal rights. They could not manage the property they inherited or the money they earned; they could not be the legal guardians or custodians of their children. In theory, there were no grounds upon which they could divorce their husbands (who could however divorce *them*), although in practice, in some states, women could get legal separations from bed and board from husbands who abused or abandoned them. It should always be remembered that the American Revolution was a war for political independence, not a war to change social arrangements or family relationships. The Founders retained the English practice of coverture, as they retained all other aspects of the English legal system, and that retention had far-reaching consequences for American women.

Women's legal status had other aspects, too. Because England (and therefore English colonies) were patrilineal, women were identified as the daughters of their fathers and carried their names. This differed from contemporaneous practice in Spain, France, and Russia, where women carried the names of their mothers as well. The patrilineal component reinforced coverture. Moreover, the Anglo-Saxon component in English society meant that it was patriarchal. Men ruled their families. As a result, most women spent their lifetimes in the custody of men: first their fathers', then—if they married—their husbands', and later their sons'. There was no such thing as personal independence for women in England or English colonies, or in the new nation that inherited English legal traditions.

Although in theory the legal strictures did not apply to single women or to widows, in practice all women were outside the formal and informal power structures and were, by definition, powerless. A few women succeeded in transcending societal norms and expectations by strength of will or by circumstances. To some degree, poor women had a better chance of doing that, because their tavern- or shop-keeping relieved their communities from the obligation to provide for them. Women who were not poor but who challenged the culture by their learning or by other kinds of "presumptions" experienced the same negative attitudes that women in our society did only a few years ago, and still experience in some circles. Such women were considered peculiar or "mannish," were frequently ridiculed, and were seldom taken seriously by other women or by men.

Thus, concepts of equality simply did not apply to a female half of the white population. It was beyond the Framers' comprehension or experience to link together the words "equality" and "women," although often their mothers, sisters, wives, and daughters were clearly their intellectual equals and were recognized as women of accomplishment. Indeed, Madison was considered very unusual in his advocacy of educational opportunities for women. But his mentor wrote as late as 1807 that "the appointment of a woman to office is an innovation for which the public is not prepared, nor am I." [1]

The third, and perhaps most obvious group not included in most definitions of equality were slaves and free blacks. To a limited extent, the Framers' ideas were conditioned by their stances on the question of slavery. The members of the Convention were about equally divided between slaveholders and non-slaveholders, and some were as passionate about ending America's "peculiar institution" as others were about preserving it. By 1787, there was no slavery in Massachusetts; emancipation was beginning in New Hampshire, Connecticut, Rhode Island, and Pennsylvania; and vigorous anti-slavery campaigns were underway in New York and New Jersey. The circumstance that the Convention was held in Philadelphia—the stronghold of Quaker, and thus anti-slavery sentiment—may have influenced those who were neutral on the question, if anyone fell into that category.

John Adams and John Jay, two members of the Founders' generation who were vigorous opponents of slavery were not in Philadelphia, nor was Jefferson, who opposed its extension into the western territories. George Mason, who was present, refused to sign the Constitution, partly because it did not contain a Bill of Rights and partly because it did permit the slave trade for twenty years, which he considered "disgraceful to mankind." It

---

1. Thomas Jefferson to Albert Gallatin, January 13, 1807, *The Writings of Albert Gallatin*, ed. Henry Adams (1872; rpt. New York: Antiquarian Press, 1960), Vol. I, p. 328.

may be true that most of the Framers expected slavery to die out in a generation or two, or three. But Eli Whitney's invention of the cotton gin only six years after the Convention made slavery even more profitable for slave owners, and the attainment of even a minimum of legal equality for black people was postponed for generations.

In any case, opposing the institution of slavery, or the slave trade, or the extension of slavery was not the same as believing that black people were equal in any meaningful way. None of the Framers could have anticipated the findings of twentieth century anthropologists, sociologists, or psychologists who have shown that intelligence is not linked to color any more than it is linked to gender or the size or shape of human heads. However greatly many of the Framers respected individual blacks, their experience led them ineluctably to associate black people with servile status.

Madison was probably as "progressive" as any of the Framers in acknowledging the moral equality of blacks. In Federalist No. 54, he defended the three-fifths compromise in the Constitution:

> We must deny the fact that slaves are considered merely as property, and in no respect whatever as persons. The true state of the case is, that they partake of both these qualities: being considered by our laws, in some respects, as persons, and in other respects as property. In being compelled to labor, not for himself, but for a master; in being vendible by one master to another master; and in being subject at all times to be restrained in his liberty and chastised in his body, by the capricious will of another—the slave may appear to be degraded from the human rank, and classed with those irrational animals which fall under the legal denomination of property. In being protected, on the other hand, in his life and in his limbs, against the violence of all others, even the master of his labor and his liberty; and in being punishable himself for all violence committed against others,—the slave is no less evidently regarded by the law as a member of the society, not as part of the irrational creation; as a moral person, not as a mere article of property.[2]

Moral equality, however, was not the same as political or social equality. When the question of admitting Missouri to the Union in 1820 provoked the quarrel that sounded to Jefferson "like a fireball in the night," Madison acknowledged that:

> To be consistent with existing and probably unalterable prejudices in the U.S. the freed blacks ought to be permanently removed beyond the region occupied by or allotted to a White population. The objections to

---

2. Publius (James Madison), February 12, 1788, *The Papers of James Madison*, ed. Robert A. Rutland (Chicago, 1977), Vol. X, p. 500.

a thorough incorporation of the two people are, with most of the Whites insuperable; and are admitted by all of them to be very powerful. If the blacks, strongly marked as they are by Physical & lasting peculiarities, be retained amid the Whites, under the degrading privation of equal rights political or social, they must be always dissatisfied with their condition as a change only from one to another species of oppression.[3]

Like many slave owners, Madison was troubled about slavery. He wrote in 1825 that "the magnitude of this evil among us is so deeply felt, and so universally acknowledged, that no merit could be greater than that of devising a satisfactory remedy for it."[4] Even he with all the political imagination that he possessed was unable to propose that remedy.

Thus, because the Convention was not concerned with equality for native Americans, women, or black people, we are left with white males—less than 40 per cent of the population. Even among this group, Madison did not believe in a "homogeneous" kind of economic or social equality:

In all civilized societies distinctions are various and unavoidable. ....
There will be rich and poor; creditors and debtors; a landlord interest, a
monied interest, a mercantile interest, a manufacturing interest. .... In
addition to these natural distinctions, artificial ones will be founded, on
accidental differences in political, religious, or other opinions, or an
attachment to the persons of leading individuals.[5]

The most direct evidence that we have about the views of Madison and the other Framers about political equality is in Madison's notes of the Convention. On August 7 and 8, the debate concerned whether the Constitution should specify the qualifications of those who were to elect the members of the House of Representatives, and if so, what those qualifications should be. The issue was joined over whether men with no property at all (neither land, nor commercial or manufacturing assets) should be allowed to vote, or whether the suffrage should be confined to freeholders. The debate continued for two days, and in the end the question was resolved on practical grounds. Because many of the states already granted suffrage to all free men in state and local elections, it seemed inexpedient to set up different qualifications for voting for members of this particular federal body. The result was what we know as section 2 of Article I:

---

3. James Madison to Robert Evans, June 15, 1819, *Letters and Other Writings of James Madison, Fourth President of the United States* (New York: R. Worthington, 1884), Vol. III, p. 134.
4. James Madison to Frances Wright, September 1, 1825, *Letters and Other Writings*, Vol. III, p. 495.
5. Madison to Jefferson, October 24, 1787, *Papers of James Madison*, Vol. X, p. 212.

> The House of Representatives shall be composed of Members chosen every second Year by the People of the several States, and the Electors in each State shall have the Qualifications requisite for Electors of the most numerous Branch of the State Legislature.

Madison was among those who thought that the protection of property rights required that voters meet property qualifications. Most of the states had eliminated them by 1821, and Madison had seen many of the things he had feared come to pass: agrarian (stay) laws, the cancelling or evading of debts, and other violations of contracts. Nevertheless, his own position had changed:

> Under every view of the subject, it seems indispensable that the Mass of Citizens should not be without a voice, in making the laws which they are to obey, in chusing the Magistrates, who are to administer them, and if the only alternative be between an equal & universal right of suffrage for each branch of the Govt. and a continement of the *entire* right to a part of the Citizens, it is better that those having the greater interest at stake namely that of property & persons both, should be deprived of half their share in the Govt.; than, that those having the lesser interest, that of personal rights only, should be deprived of the whole.[6]

It is impossible to say how many other members of the Convention had second thoughts about property qualifications. James Wilson, who may have been the most democratic of the Founders, died in 1798; Alexander Hamilton, who was among the least, in 1804. It should be remembered that even this degree of political equality, however limited as it was in some states, applied only to elections for members of the House of Representatives. The Constitution provided that state legislatures elected Senators, thus placing an entire political body between citizens and those who represented them in the Senate. Essentially the same procedure—and barrier—existed in the election of Presidents and Vice Presidents. Citizens voted for Electors, but only the Electors voted for the chief executive and his possible successor. The judiciary—the third branch of government—was, of course, even farther removed from election by the people.

The Founders had little, if any, confidence in direct democracy or widespread political equality. The experiences that brought them to Philadelphia in 1787 did not lead them to believe that the new nation would be secure if common people had genuine political power. Although those

---

6. James Madison, "Note to Speech on the Right to Suffrage," *The Complete Madison* ed. Saul K. Padover (New York, 1953), p. 40.

who gathered to write the Constitution were children of the Enlightenment, few were optimistic about human nature or the possibility of
disinterested political behavior. As for Madison, he thought that the security of the nation lay in balancing the interests of many "factions" and
many groups.

Political equality lay in the future, and it came not by the grace or
magnanimity of the Founders, but usually upon the demand of people
whose support was needed for the well-being of the Republic. Most white
men achieved it in the first quarter of the nineteenth century. Women
achieved political (but not legal) equality a hundred years later with the
ratification of the Nineteenth Amendment. Native Americans gained the
rights of citizens in 1924 and thus a measure of potential political equality
earlier denied them. But many black Americans could not exercise their
right to vote until after passage of the Voting Rights Act of 1965, a statute
that—unlike its predecessors—the United States Supreme Court upheld
as "appropriate" legislation to implement the Fifteenth Amendment.

The one kind of equality that the Framers did believe in and that did
apply to all white males—at least in theory—was legal equality. Two
generations ago Charles Beard and others alerted us to economic factors
that influenced the Founders and those who led the American people to
declare their independence from Great Britain in 1776. Today, however,
most of us who read the letters and papers and other documents of that
era are increasingly convinced by the evidence that constitutional issues,
rather than economic ones, precipitated the War for Independence. It
was the threat of losing their legal rights as Englishmen that fueled
America's limited, political revolution. As someone once wrote, the colonists came to believe that they could better preserve their rights outside
the British Empire than they could within it.

It is worth noting that none of the state governments established after
the Declaration of Independence, nor the government provided by the
Articles of Confederation, nor the Constitution created by the Framers
repudiated English legal traditions. The sons of England were justly
proud of those traditions because they assured due process and access to a
neutral—if not independent—judiciary for everyone and provided a
body of predictable law. Most of all, the English had established as early as
1215 the principle that the law was superior to any individual, even the
monarch. No other western nation even came close to those ideals. In
Spain and the Netherlands, religion determined access. In the Ger-
manies, hundreds of different political units had dozens of different legal
systems. There was no "Italy" as such; for people who lived in the region

now called by that name, there were at least three categories of legal systems: one dependent upon the Austrian Hapsburgs, another deriving its authority from the Papacy, and a number of others that were essentially local arrangements which varied according to their historical antecedents. In France, the legal system was both nationalized and rationalized by Napoleon in 1804—but that was years after the Philadelphia convention —after much blood had been shed in the French Revolution and in the wars that the French and Napoleon engaged in after 1789. But the beginning of a legal system common to all Englishmen and available to a greater proportion of "the people" than was the case in any other nation was then six centuries old.

It is frustrating not to be able to cite a nice, pithy paragraph by Madison or another of the Founders on the subject of legal equality. It may be a dubious proposition to assert that the reason such statements cannot be provided is because legal equality was so widely presumed that it did not seem necessary for the Framers to make speeches or write letters about it. For that kind of evidence we are dependent upon the members of the first Congress. Section 8 of the Judiciary Act of 1789 requires all federal judges to take the following oath of office:

> I ... do solemnly swear or affirm, that I will *administer justice without respect to persons, and do equal right to the poor and to the rich,* [italics added] and that I will faithfully and impartially discharge and perform all the duties incumbent on me ... according to the best of my abilities and understanding, agreeably to the constitution and laws of the United States. So help me God.[7]

The only kind of equality to which the Framers were unequivocally committed was legal equality, and it applied only to white males. That seems unacceptably limited to us who live two centuries later. The Framers are our heroes, and we wish that they believed in all the things that we believe in. Probably most Americans would like to be able to quote them today as authorities on equality so that it would not be necessary for us, personally, to define and redefine that word in order to address the crises of our time. Yet the art of history lies in learning what people in another time thought and believed, and why they did as they did, not in attributing to them what we have learned from their failures and successes. The Founders' ideas about equality were far more limited than ours. It was their belief in legal equality that eventually made it possible for other people, also, to achieve political equality.

---

7. *The Public Statutes at Large of the United States of America, 1789-1873* ed. Richard Peters, (Boston: C. C. Little and J. Brown, 1850-73), Vol. I, p. 73.

In the comfort of bicentennial hindsight it is worth remembering that, in many respects, equality was an elusive concept only twenty years ago. In 1965, no native American had won a lawsuit to regain the land unconstitutionally taken from them by the states. In 1965, few blacks in the former slave states had been able to gain the access to public accommodations that had been provided by the Civil Rights Act passed the year before. In 1965, Martin Luther King and some of the bravest of his followers had to march from Selma to Montgomery to gain a meaningful implementation of the Fifteenth Amendment. It should also be remembered that despite the civil rights supporters' demonstrated commitment to non-violence, two of them were murdered for trying to change a system that had endured for a century after emancipation. In 1965, neither the United States nor any state guaranteed even legal equality to women.

When Americans think about the changes that have come about in only twenty years, it is easier to appreciate the work of the Founders. If we are realistic about attitudes that persisted into the last third of the twentieth century, it is easier to understand why men of the eighteenth century were unable to achieve the timeless ideals of the Declaration of Independence.

It should be enough for us that the Founders created a republic with democratic potential. Their Constitution made it possible, in time, to enlarge the franchise and give effective political and legal equality to more and more groups of people within the polity without revolution. Their compromises on slavery, an institution incompatible with equality, could not prevent the Civil War. Since then, it has been possible to bring about change in ways that, for the most part, have been peaceable: by amending the original document, by statute, or through the judicial system. It is worth noting that ten of the fourteen Amendments ratified since 1805 have resulted in broadening the privileges of citizenship and strengthening legal and political rights. The thrust of constitutional development has been toward realizing the aims of the Declaration: toward achieving equality.

The United States is no longer a fragile experiment in self government. Ours is the oldest of all written constitutions, and it provides the framework for the second-oldest continuous government in the world. But the permanence of the nation and the stability of our society depend now upon our creativity, our ability to respond to change. We have not yet fully and effectively secured the blessings of equality for all Americans. That is among the challenges that the Founders left to us and, should we fail, to our posterity.

Equality: Contemporary Reflections

Henry J. Abraham

I

More or less akin to my paper-giving colleagues at the University of Dallas' Bicentennial Conference's "The Blessings of Liberty: First Principles of the Constitution," I have what is in essence an impossible assignment. Mine is to discuss "today's views" on that principle of popular government, *equality*—a principle enshrined explicitly and/or implicitly in our Declaration of Independence, our Constitution, and our political philosophy. It represents a hallowed commitment from which few members of the body politic dissent in theory, but which many members of that body politic reject in its practical application. That truism is patently self-evident, for not only does the noun "equality" invoke definitional quandaries and disagreements, it all but necessarily sooner or later comes into conflict with that other great principle of popular government, *liberty*. The denial of either "without due process of law" is specifically proscribed by the Fourteenth Amendment to our Constitution, whereas the Fifth Amendment addresses such a proscription only to "liberty" (as well as "life" and "property").

The questions raised by the Conference's managers in their charge to discuss "today's views" nicely pinpoint the vexatious nature of the issue: "Is the meaning of equality to be restricted to the formal political rights to life, liberty, and property, or must the social conditions which allow people to take advantage of their rights also be equalized? Are the rights of women the same as those of men? Does the principle of equality oblige us to equalize the average social, economic, and political fortunes of majority and minority groups?" Although I suspect that there are those who have quick and categorical answers to these intriguing *quaeres*, they are essentially characterizable as of the "have you stopped beating your wife" type. Fortunately, however, we were also advised that it would be perfectly appropriate to focus on one or two positions rather than attempt a general treatment, and I have opted to do so by essentially concentrating on one agonizing contemporary egalitarian can of worms, the affirmative action/reverse discrimination syndrome. For it is peculiarly representative of the vexatious nature of the concept of equality, of the difficulties of endeavoring to live up to both constitutional/legal and socio/political norms and commands, of the patent fact of life that there are no easy answers, that "equality" quite simply means different things to different people—regardless of what the law of the Constitution may be held to require, and regardless of such easy-answer certainties as those propounded by, for example, Harvard's Laurence H. Tribe.[1]

II

Would a dictionary definition of equality be helpful? There are, of course, numerous definitions; but for the sake of order we may focus on the three leading ones provided by the *Oxford English Dictionary* (and utilized, for example in the *International Encyclopedia of the Social Sciences*): (1) "the condition of having equal dignity, rank, or privileges with others"; (2) "the condition of being equal in power, ability, achievement, or excellence"; (3) "fairness, impartiality, equity, due proportion, proportiateness."[2] *A priori* this triad breathes conviction and common sense. Yet, as one of the "equality" entry's authors in the *Encyclopedia*, Irving Kristol, is necessarily quick to manifest, even a moment's contemplation will reveal that those three definitions, while readily consistent with common usage, are neither entirely nor necessarily consistent with one another:

> If, for example, men [and women] are unequal in power, ability, achievement, or excellence, then an adherence to definition (3) will lead to a violation of definition (1), while an adherence to definition (1) will lead to a violation of definition (3). It is only if men [and women] *are* in fact equal in power, ability, and excellence that equity preserves a condition of equal rank.[3]

In fact, however, men [and women] are *not* equal in power, ability and excellence; yet no egalitarian society can maintain an easy conscience regarding the inequalities that do exist within it. And there obtains a distinct sentiment, whether it be propelled by a sense of fairness or one of guilt, or both, that all men and women are *ipso facto* equal merely because they are men and women.

Is *equality of opportunity* the decisive yardstick *cum* answer? It is tempting

---

1. See for example, his *Constitutional Choices* (Cambridge, Mass., 1985).
2. *International Encyclopedia of the Social Sciences* (New York, NY, 1968), pp. 102-111.
3. *Encyclopedia*, p. 108, col. 1.

to respond in the affirmative because of the arguably fundamental on-its-fact neutrality, even fairness, of the concept. But it also invokes a negative contention, such as that by Felix E. Oppenheim, namely, that there is an obligation to bring the underprivileged to the "general starting line," which *ipso facto* necessitates an "inegalitarian rule of allotment" in their favor.[4] Does that philosophy, on the other hand, require the attainment of *equality of condition or result?* If so, what are the limits, both in terms of measurability and time span? Whereas equality of opportunity may well comprise considerably more than *legal* and *political* opportunity, does it include *economic* equality? If so, whose task in our democratic society is it to fashion it? The judiciary's or the representative/political/elected branches of our government? To what extent, if at all, do special privilege and/or compensatory public policies for racial, ethnic, and religious minorities and for women constitute an acceptable egalitarian policy? If favored treatment for the first three is in line with the then Associate Justice Harlan Fisk Stone's famous Footnote Four in the 1938 case of *United States v. Carolene Products Company*, exhorting special and higher judicial standards of review for what he terms "discrete and insular minorities,"[5] is it also applicable to women—who are hardly an "insular minority"? The answer seems to have become "yes," but on the basis of not quite as high a standard as race. It is seminal questions such as these that inform the wrenching case study of "affirmative action/reverse discrimination" on the frontiers of the egalitarian debate.

III

So much has been said, written, and emoted concerning the subject of "affirmative action/reverse discrimination" that it represents a veritably frustrating experience to endeavor to come to grips with it in a non-redundant, non-banal, non-breast beating manner. The difficulty is compounded by the all-too-pervasive substitution of passion for reason on that wrenching issue, one that, admittedly, invites passion. Indeed, passion informed not an insignificant number of the record filings of the 120 briefs *amici curiae* in 1978 in the first central "affirmative action/reverse discrimination" case of *Regents of the University of California v. Allan Bakke*, in which oral argument had been presented to the Supreme Court

---

4. *Encyclopedia*, p. 105, col. 2.
5. 304 U.S. 144.

of the United States in mid-October 1977.[6] It took place in a sardine-like packed Court chamber, with more than 200 putative spectators waiting in line all night in the hope of perhaps hearing one three-minute segment of that potential bellweather decision toward which the Court, in an unusual action, called for the filing of supplementary briefs by all parties concerened two weeks later in order to argue specifically the *statutory* question(s) involved in the application of Title VI of the Civil Rights Act of 1964. Passion similarly governed the denouement of the second major "affirmative action/reverse discrimination" case, *United Steel Workers and Kaiser Aluminum & Chemical Corporation v. Weber*,[7] which the Court decided in 1979, almost exactly one year after the *Bakke* holdings; again one year later, in 1980, that of the third, *Fullilove v. Klutznick*;[8] and of the fourth, handed down in 1984, *Memphis Firefighters Local Union #1784 v. Stotts*.[9] The latter, depending upon one's interpretation, either did or did not draw a partial line between *bona fide* "affirmative action" and impermissible "reverse discrimination," here relevant to neutral seniority systems. And passion, however comprehensible emotionally, has clouded the arguments and contentions of even the most cerebral professional as well as lay observers of the "affirmative action/reverse discrimination" issue, the resolution of which may well constitute a watershed in this particularly crucial aspect of the race syndrome and the idea of equality, of what Gunnar Myrdal more than three decades ago so pointedly titled an "American Dilemma."[10] Indeed, a satisfactory resolution may never take place, given the Supreme Court's policy of ducking the issue by either affirming lower court rulings or refusing to grant review in potentially promising cases designed to reach it for resolution—although the Justices accepted a trio of such cases for review in the 1985-86 term of Court.[11]

---

6. 438 U.S. 265.

7. 443 U.S. 193.

8. 448 U.S. 448.

9. 104 S. Ct. 2576.

10. Gunnar Myrdal, *An American Dilemma: The Negro Problem and Modern Democracy*, rev. ed. (New York, 1962).

11. E.g., *Bushey v. New York State Civil Service Commission*, 53 LW 3477 (1985), in which the Court fell short of one vote to agree to consider a politically volatile "reverse discrimination case," which had seen the "voluntary" ignoring of examination scores in order to promote minority candidates to attain a racial quota. (Chief Justice Burger and Justices White and Rehnquist wanted to hear the case, but the fourth vote to grant *certiorari* was not forthcoming.) On the same day in January 1984 the Court, without comment, let stand a ruling that upheld Philadelphia's system of transferring teachers to achieve racial balance among city school faculties, again based on a racial quota established in 1978, the year of *Bakke*. (Kromnick v. School District of Philadelphia, 52 LW 3475.)

Henty J. Abraham

In the hope of avoiding an abject surrender to the aforementioned passion(s), I shall do my best to discuss the matter on a rational basis while pledging to strive to eschew what Headmaster Stanley Bosworth of St. Anne's Episcopal School in Brooklyn so tellingly, if perhaps a mite expansively, once identified as "the piety, puritanism, and guilt that have combined to stir the worst semantic confusion" conceivable in this emotion-charged policy spectrum. It would thus be helpful to try to identify at the outset what we are, or should be, talking about in any attempted analysis of the constellation of what I regard as the substantive dichotomy of "affirmative action" and "reverse discrimination," and what we should not be talking about. To do that it is necessary to find what the concepts mean. "I only want to know what the words mean," once commented Justice Oliver Wendell Holmes, Jr., in many ways the judicial philosopher of our age; but he freely admitted, with E. M. Forster, that there is "wine in words." A lot of wine and other rather less consumable liquids have been poured into the notion, into the alleged meaning of both "affirmative action" and "reverse discrimination."

It is vital, therefore, at the outset to consider briefly both the events and the egalitarian philosophy that underlay the bellwether case of *Regents of the University of California v. Bakke*. Actually, it would not have become the flagship case had the Court, four years earlier (1974), been willing to reach the merits in what had loomed as the first major consideration of the "affirmative action/reverse discrimination" issue in *De Funis v. Odegaard*.[12] Marco De Funis, a white applicant, had been denied admission to the University of Washington's School of Law despite qualifications objectively superior to a group of thirty-seven non-white applicants, who benefitted from the Law School's preferential racial admissions quota program. But in a 5:4 *per curiam* decision the Supreme Court ruled the case to be "moot" on the grounds that De Funis, who had been ordered admitted by Justice Douglas in his capacity as the Supreme Court Justice in charge of that judicial circuit, and was thus attending law school while the case was winding its way through the courts, was about to be graduated. While four Justices did not consider the case "moot" at all, only Justice Douglas reached the merits of the constitutional issue. Central to his dissent was his clarion call for "color blindness" as a fundamental pre-requisite of egalitarianism and his concomitant insistence that the equal protection of the laws clause of the Fourteenth Amendment mandated "the consideration of each application *in a racially neutral way.*"

12. 416 U.S. 312 (1974).

Douglas thus echoed Chief Justice Hale of the Supreme Court of Washington, speaking in dissent in his Court's consideration of the *De Funis* case at the highest state level: Hale had asked whether the Constitution may be color conscious in order to be color blind? Citing the first John Marshall Harlan's ringing dissent in *Plessy v. Ferguson* in 1896, namely, that "[o]ur Constitution is color-blind, and neither knows nor tolerates classes among citizens,"[13] he believed not.[14]

Bakke would reach the merits, the intervening four-year period featuring intensive debate in the academic community, with propounded solutions ranging over the entire spectrum.[15] To cite two polar opposites: On the one hand, John Hart Ely counseled: "When the group that controls the decision making process classifies so as to advantage a minority and disadvantage itself, the reasons for being unusually suspicious, and consequently, employing a stringent brand of [judicial] review, are lacking."[16] On the other hand, we have the earlier argument by John Kaplan that "any legal classification by race weakens the government as an educative force"; that any "[p]reference for [blacks] can [be] expected to be a major factor in preventing the education [toward color blindness] we are trying to bring about through a host of other laws."[17]

Allan Paul Bakke, a 32-year old mechanical engineer, who had decided to embark upon a medical career, applied to the new Medical School of the University of California at Davis in 1972, four years after the latter's establishment. Davis's faculty, which had never discriminated against minorities, voluntarily instituted an "affirmative action" program in 1969, the second year of its existence, under which minorities could be considered separately from other applicants, in effect, according to different, *i.e.,* lower, academic standards. The plan was crowned with immediate success, and by the time Allan Bakke applied, sixteen percent of the entering class of 100 had been set aside for minority students. Bakke, with superior qualifications and record, was rejected in 1973. Aware of the set-aside program, he made an issue of it in his re-application for the entering class

---

13. 163 U.S. 537, at 559.

14. De Funis v. Odegaard, 507 P. 2d 1169 (1973), at 1189.

15. See the representative sampling of pre-*Bakke* commentary cited by Gerald Gunther in *Individual Rights in Constitutional Law: Cases and Materials*, 3rd ed. (Mineola, N.Y., 1981), p. 423, fn. 3.

16. John Hart Ely, "The Constitutionality of Reverse Racial Discrimination," 41 *University of Chicago Law Review* 723 (1974).

17. John Kaplan, "Equal Justice in an Unequal World—The Problem of Special Treatment," 61 *Northwestern University Law Review* 363 (1966).

of 1974. Rejected again, he reluctantly went to court. Victorious at the highest level of the California state judiciary, he saw his case accepted for review on both constitutional and statutory grounds by the U.S. Supreme Court in 1977. The rest is history.

IV

The philosophical problem the faculty at Davis had faced in establishing the special "affirmative action" program is clear. Since Davis had no record whatsoever of racial discrimination—or of any other kind of discrimination—how could it justify its special admissions program which demonstrably discriminated against non-minorities? Was this "equality" in fact, or was it, in effect, patent racial discrimination? The courts would ultimately have to come to grips, more or less, with the legal and/or constitutional response to that fundamental question. But meanwhile, what of the philosophical or moral justification *cum* imperative? The University took its cue from President Lyndon B. Johnson's celebrated 1965 commencement address at Howard University, in which L.B.J. spelled out the gravamen of his affirmative action contentions in the following now frequently-quoted sentences:

> You do not take a person who, for years, has been hobbled by chains and liberate him, bring him up to the starting line of a race and then say, "you are free to compete with the others," and still justly believe that you have been completely fair.

> Thus it is not enough to open the gates of opportunity. All of our citizens must have the ability to walk through those gates.

> This is the next and more profound stage of the battle for civil rights. We seek not just freedom of opportunity—not just legal equality but human ability—not just equality as a right and a theory, *but equality as a fact and as a result.*[18]

The Davis faculty—and after *Bakke* colleges and universities throughout the land—would take their cue, in effect, from the underlined concluding sentences of the President's historic statements, thereby introducing and adopting what would quickly become the core of the argument: Equality "as a fact" was incontestable, *i.e.* complete, total equality of opportunity at

---

18. John Hope Franklin and Isadore Starr, ed., *The Negro in Twentieth Century America* (New York, 1967), p. 226, (italics added).

the starting line and, if that equality was lacking, bring those concerned up to it by virtue of affirmative governmental action. But as for "equality as a result," that was immediately regarded as loading the dice, as diminishing demonstrated competence, of substituting the guarantees of the age-old hated *numerus clausus*—that had so often been used against other minority groups, especially Jews, in the past—both here and abroad— because once equality of opportunity existed for Jews, ultimate achievement in terms of result was all but foreordained. (As I was told, for example, by a leading Ivy League University administrator in 1951: "You are clearly entitled to be promoted, but we have already promoted a Jew in the Department this year. You understand. No offense meant.")

To those who embraced the "and as a result" exhortation of L.B.J.'s historic announcement, the charge levied against them of utilizing discrimination in order to eradicate discrimination was parried as an irrelevancy. While admitting that a De Funis or a Bakke, neither of whom had discriminated against anyone, might well be hurt in the "as a fact and as a result" conjoinage, the response was essentially the two-fold one presented by Justices Brennan and Blackmun in the *Bakke* case: (1) that all society was at fault and all must pay for the injustices of the past—even if that meant children and grandchildren had to pay for the sins of their parents and grandparents; (or, as Professor Tribe put it, "individuals who are innocent of wrongdoing must be denied opportunities because of their race, in order that individuals equally innocent be given opportunities from which their race would otherwise have effectively excluded them"); and (2) that the policy would be "temporary"—although to this day no satisfactory explanation or yardstick has been agreed-upon as to the precise or predictable nature of the adjective.

Bakke and his supporters readily conceded the need and obligation of and for "affirmative action." Their basic disagreement was, and is, the resort to what soon came to be regarded as "reverse discrimination." Thus, to permit all non-whites to compete in the candidacies for the 100 open admission slots was, of course, "equality as a fact," just as it would have been for whites. If, in order to compete for the 100 it was necessary for any members of the applicant pool to have obtained special preparatory training, even if subsidized by government funds, fine, as long as that opportunity was open and free to all on the basis of need—a theme sounded so nobly, and then amazingly successfully, in L.B.J.'s dynamic push through a reluctant Congress of his Federal Aid to Elementary and Secondary School Act of 1965, where the sole criterion of aid-entitlement was demonstrable need. What Bakke objected to was, however, that whites could participate on an "equality as fact" basis as applicants for *only 84* of the 100 slots, sixteen being reserved for non-whites, thereby guaranteeing a block of admission to non-whites under the "and as a result" equality equation, an equation that, true to Johnson's exhortation, provided *both* a handicap for a racially identifiable segment of a universe *and* a guaranteed result.

Allan Bakke's sense of injustice and his formal legal contentions in that seminal case—seminal in both constitutional and philosophical terms—was not merely a personal crusade or a selfish lawsuit. As he put the matter in a letter to the San Francisco Office of the Equal Employment Opportunities Commission, "[r]everse discrimination is as wrong as the primary variety of [discrimination] it seeks to correct."[19] And because he was convinced that it was fundamentally wrong, it was *ipso facto* wrong for anyone potentially affected by it. Bakke did not argue a *right*, be it constitutional, legal, or moral, to be admitted to medical school—or, for that matter, to any other non-government-mandated educational institution—nor did he argue that aptitude tests or grade-point-averages, should constitute the sole criterion for admission. He did argue, however, that his *claim* to admission—he stipulated that he did not have a *right* to be admitted but that he surely had a right to apply for admission—should be evaluated on the basis of everyone else's; that race should be regarded, in Justice Douglas' terms, as "neutral" and/or, in Justice Hale's words, "color blindly"; that achievements must be measured under our system by *individual* standards, not by group standards; that "racial proportionality" is at war with our principles of government, in general, and "equal protection of the laws," in particular; that there must be no guarantee that *any* individual or *any* group be numerically represented in any given school or any given profession. Quite apart from his moral posture on that aspect of the issue of equality, his position seemed to be indubitably supported, in the specific language as well as in the history of the floor debate, by the federal cornerstone legislation on behalf of civil rights, the Civil Rights Act of June 1964. It had cleared the House of Representatives with relative ease, 290:133; but its success in the Senate, by a bi-partisan vote of 73:27, was delayed until the surmounting of a 75-day Southern filibuster, with the application of the Senate's debate-limiting cloture rule on the 83rd day of the debate, by a vote of 71:29. It was the first time cloture had been

---

19. *Record*, filed with the U.S. Supreme Court, in *Bakke*, p. 281. (The Record contains the opinions, findings of fact, and conclusions of law and judgment of the State trial court in California.)

achieved on a civil rights filibuster since the adoption of the cloture rule itself in 1917.[20] One of the concessions that facilitated the Act's passage was the assurance by the bill's managers, a guarantee enshrined in the record, that there would be no requirements "on the basis of percentage or quota related to color."[21]

V

There is simply no doubt that the cardinal assumption that underlay the enactment of the Civil Rights Act of 1964, the noble joint-product society, was that, once accorded basic equality of opportunity, "equality as a fact," individuals would advance socially, culturally, economically, and politically by virtue of their own talents and abilities. It was recognized that "affirmative" action was needed to render that equality more than a hypothesis, especially in such obvious realms as recruiting, training, teaching, and so forth, even if that meant massive appropriations. However, in the words of two close observers of the issue, "[c]learly, there is no mention of this fledgling concept of 'affirmative action' of any equality that could be turned into numbers."[22] But when the post-Civil Rights Act 1960s days did not witness the achievements of blacks and some other minorities as fully or as quickly as a good many observers and well-wishers had predicted or hoped, sundry agencies of the federal government, prodded by President Johnson—assuredly the best friend in the White House contemporary blacks have had—began to move rapidly toward the philosophy of "equality as a result." Thus, the Civil Rights Act of 1964-created Equal Employment Opportunities Commission (EEOC) commenced to develop the concepts of "under-representation" and "under-utilization" in employment, based on the presence of minorities and women in the work force of a particular geographic entity. Inexorably, this led to a numbers game, based on statistical results: Equality of results promptly became the adopted yardstick, with nouns such as "quotas" (at least until *Bakke*), "goals," and "guidelines" developing into governmental tools and

20. On the bill's final roll call—on which all 100 Senators were present and voting—46 Democrats and 27 Republicans voted "aye", 21 Democrats and 6 Republicans "nay." Voting to invoke cloture were 44 Democrats and 27 Republicans; opposed were 23 Democrats and 6 Republicans.
21. E.g., Hubert H. Humphrey (D.-Minn.), 110 Cong. Rec. 7420.
22. Terry Eastland and William J. Bennett, *Counting by Race: Equality from the Founding Fathers to Bakke and Weber* (New York, 1979), p. 11.

household words. To measure numerically became *de rigeur* as the test of the now broadly governmentally-embraced and sanctioned standard of equality. Institutions of higher learning were soon in the forefront of the numbers game in terms of admissions and, not so long thereafter, in that of faculty profiles. Title VI of the Civil Rights Act of 1964, as amended in 1972 and 1978, which proscribes any federal financial assistance for institutions that discriminated on the basis of race, color, national origin, sex, or age, became a key lever in the governmental bureaucracy's development of the aforedescribed numerical tests. Yet most colleges and universities needed little prodding to adopt the equality of result notion: indeed, their voluntary efforts, including those of the professional schools, were not only as widespread as they were generous, they were patently based upon the concept of compensation for past injustices, thereby creating an additional rationale for embracing both the "result" and the "group" commitments of the equality issue. Since these now cascading practices were necessarily based on numerical standards, it was but a question of time before Congress and/or the Court would be called upon *either* to justify these preferential interpretations and approaches to the "affirmative action" syndrome *or* to proscribe them, either by legislative action or by virtue of passing the proverbial buck to the judicial branch for statutory construction and/or constitutional interpretation.

Hardly astonishingly, Congress would not or could not move decisively. While attacks on, and some defenses of, racial quotas and such desegregation tools as racial busing, were all but daily occurrences, and cluttered up the expensive pages of the *Congressional Record*, no proscriptive or repeal legislation passed both houses, and several efforts to resort to constitutional amendments failed as well. It would be up to Mr. Hamilton's "least dangerous branch of the government." As noted earlier in these pages, that branch, too, had done its best to avoid the problem—*e.g., De Funis*— but *Bakke* or, more accurately, the two *Bakkes* (*Bakke I* and *Bakke II*) did bite the bullet in the late Spring of 1978, albeit decisionally only by the narrowest of possible margins, 5:4 and 4:5.[23]

VI

In the remainder of this essay I shall endeavor to analyze the significant developments following the *Bakke* decisions and to argue, in part upon

---

23. Regents of the University of California v. Allan Bakke, 438 U.S. 265.

what I have tried to say in my aforegone presentation, and in part of what I have written elsewhere,[24] that (a) it *is* possible to distinguish between "affirmative action" and "reverse discrimination"; and (b) that *when confined to its appropriate sphere*, the former is both legal and constitutional, whereas the latter is neither.

Acknowledging the audience of these ruminations to be educated, intelligent human beings, who read, see, hear, and appraise the news that informs our *vie quotidienne*, I am comfortable in assuming a basic familiarity with the issues involved. I am also aware that and—I daresay, without exception—any listener or reader will have strong feelings on the matter. So do I. We would not be human if we did not; while they operate on a host of levels and are triggered at vastly diverse moments, we all have consciences. Stipulating these facets, I should first endeavor to make evident what permissible "affirmative action" *is* (or what "reverse discrimination" is not): (1) It *is* action, be it in the governmental or private sector, designed to remedy the absence of proper and needed educational preparation or training by special, even if costly, primary and/or secondary school level preparatory programs or occupational skill development, such as "Head Start," "Upward Bound," etc., always provided that access to these programs is not bottomed on race but on educational and/or economic need, be it cerebral or manual. (2) It *is* the utilization of special classes or supplemental tutoring or training, regardless of the costs involved (assuming, of course, that these have been properly authorized and appropriated) on any level of the educational or training process, from the very pre-nursery school bottom to the very top of the professional training ladder. (3) It *is*, of course, the scrupulous exhortation and enforcement of absolute standards of non-discrimination on the basis of race, sex, religion, nationality, and also now age (at least up to 70, with certain exceptions). (4) It *is* the above-the-table special recruiting and utilization efforts which, *pace* poo-pooing by leaders of some of the recipient groups involved, are not only pressed vigorously, but have been and are being pushed and pressed on a scale that would make a Bear Bryant and Knute Rockne smile a knowing well-done smile. (5) It *is* even an admission or personnel officer's judgment that, along with sundry other

---

24. See my "Some Post-*Bakke, Weber,* and *Fillilove* Reflections on 'Reverse Discrimination,' " in *Neither Conservative Nor Liberal: The Burger Court on Civil Rights and Liberties,* ed. Francis Graham Lee (Malabar, Florida, 1983) and "Some Post *Bakke*-and-*Weber* Reflections on 'Reverse Discrimination,' " *University of Richmond Law Review* (Winter, 1980), reprinted in *Taking the Constitution Seriously* ed. Gary L. McDowell (Dubuque, Iowa, 1981), pp. 434-44.

criteria, he or she may take into account an individual applicant's racial, religious, ethnic, gender, or other characteristics as a "plus"—to use Justice Powell's crucial *Bakke* term—but only if that applicant can demonstrate explicit or implicit merit in terms of ability and/or genuine promise. For I shall again and again insist that the overriding criterion, the central consideration, must in the final analysis be present or arguably potential merit. It must thus be merit and ability, not necessarily based exclusively upon past performance, but upon an honest, mature, experienced, realistic, no-nonsense judgment that merit and ability are in effect in the total picture either by their presence or by their fairly confident predictability.

This belief, of course flies squarely into the face of the contention by the influential Professor Ronald Dworkin who, in his controversial writings, such as *Taking Rights Seriously*, in effect rejects John Marshall Harlan's seminal plea that our Constitution is "colorblind, and neither knows or tolerates classes among citizens," by arguing that while our constitution *is* tolerant of classes among citizens, it is *merit-blind* and neither knows nor tolerates public policy based on concepts of human excellence.[25] These five aforementioned "yes's," which are all aspects of the concept of "affirmative action", are naturally not an exhaustive enumeration. Yet they are illustrative of common practices that, in my view, do *not* constitute "reverse discrimination"—always provided that they remain appropriately canalized within proper legal and constitutional bounds—for they give life to the basic American right of equality of *opportunity*, of *equality as a fact*. One of the major problems, alas, is that militant pro-"reverse discrimination" advocates insist on substituting a requirement of equality of *result* for the requirement of equality of *opportunity*—a requirement based on the unacceptable notion of statistical group parity, in which the focal point becomes the *group* rather than the individual.

This brings me to the necessary look at a quintet of what "reverse discrimination" *is* (or what "affirmative action" *is not*). (1) It *is*, above all what in the final analysis, the *De Funis, Bakke, Weber, Fullilove,* and *Stotts* cases fundamentally were all about, namely, the setting aside of quotas—be they rigid or quasi-rigid—i.e., the adoption of a *numerus clausus*, on behalf of the admission or recruitment or training or employment or promotion of groups identified and classified by racial, sexual, religious, age or nationality characteristics. For these are characteristics that are, or should be, proscribed on both legal *and* constitutional grounds, because they are *non-sequiturs* on the fronts of individual merit and ability and are,

25. Ronald Dworkin, *Taking Rights Seriously* (Cambridge, Mass., 1977).

or certainly should be, regarded as being an insult to the dignity and intelligence of the quota recipients. To refer again to that earlier lodestar: "Our Constitution is color-blind," thundered Justice John Marshall Harlan in lonely dissent in the famous, or infamous, case of *Plessy v. Ferguson* in 1896, "and neither knows nor tolerates classes among citizens."[26] His dissent, which became the guiding star of the Court's unanimous holding in the monumental and seminal 1954 ruling in *Brown v. Board of Education of Topeka, Kansas*,[27] now prompts us to re-ask the question whether, as the proponents of "reverse discrimination" urge, the "Constitution must be *color-conscious* in order to be color blind"? But to continue what "reverse discrimination" is, it *is* (2) the slanting of what should be neutral, pertinent, and appropriate threshold and other qualification examinations and/or requirements; double-standards in grading, rating, and promoting; double-standards in attendance and disciplinary requirements. It *is* (3) the dishonest semanticism of what are called *goals* or *guidelines*, which the contemporary bureaucracy has simply pronounced legal and/or constitutional on the alleged grounds that they differ from rigid *quotas* which, since *Bakke*, would be presumably illegal and/or unconstitutional. Supported by Justice Powell's dismissal of them in the *Bakke I* decision as a "semantic distinction" which is "beside the point," I submit that this distinction is as unworkable as it is dishonest—in the absence of, to use a favorite Department of Health and Human Services, Department of Labor, and EEOC term, "good faith" vis-a-vis the far-reaching efforts of affected educational institutions and employers to function under the concept of "goals" or "guidelines."

But while going to enormous lengths to deny any equation of "goals" or "guidelines" with "quotas," the largely messianic enforcement personnel of the three aforementioned powerful and well-funded agencies of the federal government—personnel that, certainly in the realm of the administration of higher education, often lacks the one-would-think-essential experience and background—in effect require quotas while talking "goals" or "guidelines." Indeed, within hours, if not minutes of the *Bakke* decision, for example, Eleanor Holmes Norton, then the aggressive head of the EEOC, announced that the Supreme Court holding would make no difference, whatever, the agency's established policies! Thus, there is extant an eager *presumption* of a lack of a good faith effort against the background-imposition of rigid compliance quotas, based upon fre-

---

26. 163 U.W. 537, at 562.
27. 347 U.S. 483.

quently irrelevant group statistics, statistics that are demonstrably declared *ultra vires* by Title VII, Sec. 703(j) of the Civil Rights Act of 1964. (4) Reverse Discrimination *is* such a statutory provision—one initially challenged and declared unconstitutional by U.S. District Court Judge A. Andrew Hauk,[28] and then upheld by U.S. District Court Judge Daniel J. Snyder, Jr., who was affirmed by the United States Court of Appeals for the Third Circuit—as that mandated under the Public Works Employment Act of 1977. Under that Act, Congress enacted a rigid requirement, adopted on the floor without committee hearings as a result of shrewd strategy by the Congressional Black Caucus, that ten per cent of all public works contracts designed to stimulate employment go to "minority business enterprises" regardless of the competitiveness of their bid. Known as "M.B.E.'s," they are identified statutorily as private businesses that are at least half-owned by members of a minority group or publicly held businesses in which minority group members control a majority of the stock. For purposes of the Act, "minorities" are defined as "Blacks, Orientals, Indians, Eskimos, Aleuts," and what is termed "the Spanish-speaking." At issue, in what quickly came to be known as the "1977 Ten Per Cent Set-Aside Quota Law," were thousands of construction jobs and billions of dollars worth of Government contracts. But when the U.S. Supreme Court initially had the case before it a few days after it handed down its *Bakke* decision, it ducked the problem on the ground that the award involved had already been consummated and the money expended, the issue thus being moot.[29] However, the Court did subsequently re-examine and uphold 6:3 the practice in 1980 in *Fullilove v. Klutznick* [30] as a Congressional prerogative under its legislative powers. And reverse discrimination *is* (5) the widely advanced notion, a favorite of officials at the very highest levels of numerous branches of government and in much of the private sector, that somehow, two wrongs make a right; that the children must pay for the sins of their fathers by self-destructive actions; that—in the words of Chief Justice Burger's dissenting opinion in the pro-reverse discrimination *Franks v. Boroman Transportation Co.* decision in 1976—"robbing Peter to pay Paul"[31] is just and, accordingly, a racial spoils system of "separate and proportionate" is somehow excusable as appropriately egalitarian.

---

28. 441 F. Supp. 955.
29. 438 U.S. 909.
30. 448 U.S. 448.
31. 424 U.S. 474, at 781.

VII

It is, of course, the latter issue—one I suggested as my fifth illustration of what "reverse discrimination" is—that lies at the heart of the matter. To put it simply, but not oversimplifiedly, it is the desire, the perceived duty, the moral imperative, of compensating for the grievous and shameful history of racial and collateral discrimination in America's past. That discrimination is a fact of history which no fair person can deny and the re-appearance of which no decent or fair person would sanction, let alone welcome. America's record since the end of World War II, and especially since the *Brown* decision, is a living testament to the far-reaching, indeed exhilarating, ameliorations that have taken place, and are continuing to take place, on the civil rights front. This is a fact of life amply documented and progressively demonstrated, and I need not do so here. I have tried to do it in my *Freedom and the Court* (now in its fourth edition)[32] which ironically, in view of my stance on "reverse discrimination," had encountered difficulties in certain parts of the country as recently as a decade ago because of its allegedly excessive liberality on the race issue. I presume it all depends "whose ox is being gored"—to use Al Smith's felicitous phrase—and at which moment in history. Anyone who denies the very real progress *cum* atonement that has taken place, and is continuing to take place, in both the public and the private sector, is either utterly misinformed or does so for political purposes—and the largest numbers, understandably, fall into that latter category. American society today is absolutely committed to the fullest measure of egalitarianism in fact under our Constitution, mandated in our basic document by the "due process" clause of Amendments Five and Fourteen and the latter's "equal protection of the laws" clause as well as in a plethora of both federal and state laws and ordinances. But that Constitution, in the very same Amendments, safeguards *liberty* as well as equality—a somber reminder that rights and privileges are not one-dimensional.

It is on the frontiers of that line between equality and liberty that so much of the "affirmative action/reverse discrimination" controversy, both in its public and private manifestations, has become embattled. It is here that the insistent, often strident, calls for compensatory, preferential, "reverse discrimination" action are issued—and, more often than not, they issue from a frighteningly profound guilt complex, a guilt complex that has become so pervasive as to brush aside as irrelevant on the altar of atonement even constitutional, let alone legal, barriers: witness, for exam-

---

32. Henry J. Abraham, *Freedom and the Court* (New York, N.Y., 1982).

ple, the opinions by Justices Brennan, Marshall and Blackman in both the *Bakke* and *Weber* rulings. To cite just one or two cases in point: One argument that veritably laces the pro-"reverse discrimination" arguments of the briefs in *Bakke, Weber*, and *Fullilove*, especially those by the American Civil Liberties Union, the Association of American University Professors, Harvard University, Stanford University, the University of Pennsylvania, Columbia University, and the NAACP, among others, is that the injustices of the past justify, indeed demand, a *"temporary"* use of affirmative action including class-based hiring preferences and admission goals" in favor of racial minorities. In other words, the record of the past creates the catalyst *cum* mandate for the imposition of *quotas* like the 16 places out of 100 admittedly set aside by the Medical School of the University of California at Davis for the "special" admissions of members of certain minority groups. What the school did is entirely straightforward and clear: it *did* establish a racial quota; it *did* practice racial discrimination; it *did* deny admission to a fully qualified white applicant, Allan Bakke, on racial grounds—which as Justice Stevens' stern opinion for himself and his colleagues Burger, Stewart, and Rehnquist, makes clear, is *ipso facto* forbidden by the plain language of Title VI of the Civil Rights Act of 1964. The University had justified its action on the grounds of redress for past racial discrimination (although it had *never* practiced discrimination— and had, and has, never been accused of such until it denied Allan Bakke's admission), on the need for compensatory action, and a commitment to "genuine equal opportunity." In the responsive, apposite words of a widely-distributed statement by the Committee on Academic Nondiscrimination and Integrity:

> Just as no one truly dedicated to civil liberties would contemplate a 'temporary' suspension of, say, the right to counsel or the right to a fair trial as a means of dealing with a crime wave, so no one truly dedicated to equality of opportunity should contemplate a 'temporary' suspension of equal rights of individuals in order to achieve the goal of greater representation. The temporary all too often becomes the permanent. It is not the ultimate ends we proclaim but the temporary means we use which determine the actual future.[33]

In *Weber*, the central issue was a similar type of quota arrangement, although it governed private employment rather than public education. The Steelworkers and the Kaiser Corporation, under contemporary pressure by government agencies to engage in "affirmative action," had

---

33. 45 *Measure* 1 (December, 1977).

devised a plan that "reserves for black employees 50% of the openings in an in-plant craft training program until the percentage of black craft workers in the plant is commensurate with the percentage of blacks in the local labor force." Both the U.S. District Court and the U.S. Court of Appeals had ruled that the plan clearly violated Title VII, Sec. 703, of the Civil Rights Act of 1964, which *specifically* outlaws discrimination in employment because of "race, color, religion, sex, or national origin" (42 U.S.C.A. par. 2000-2(a), (d), and (j)). But while admitting the presence of the plain statutory proscription, Justice Brennan in effect sanctioned its violation on the basis of the *spirit* of the law rather than its letter.

In *Fullilove*, the Court—albeit badly split 3:3:3—upheld over "a facial constitutional challenge, a requirement in a Congressional spending program that, absent an administrative waiver, ten percent of the federal funds granted for local public works projects must be used by the local grantee to procure services or supplies from businesses owned and controlled by members of statutorily identified minority groups." Chief Justice Burger's controlling plurality opinion, joined by Justices White and Powell, found justification in the reach of the spending power which he declared to be "at least as broad as the regulatory powers of Congress," and "properly tailored to cure the effects of prior discrimination."

A related, although somewhat different justification advanced on the altar of redressing past wrongs by temporarily (or perhaps not-so-temporarily?) winking at legal and constitutional barriers, on what some prefer to call the "I am not really pregnant, just a little bit," approach to the problem, is illustrated by Ronald Dworkin, Professor of Jurisprudence at Oxford University, in his following 1977 defense of the use of racial criteria in connection with the aforementioned 1974 Washington Law School "reverse discrimination" case of *De Funis v. Odegaard*:

> Racial criteria are not necessarily the right standards for deciding which applicants should be accepted by law schools for example. But neither are intellectual criteria, nor indeed, any other set of criteria. [*Sic!*] The fairness—and constitutionality—of any admissions program must be tested in the same way. It is justified if it serves a proper policy that respects the right of all members of the community to be treated as equals, but not otherwise. ... We must take care not to use the Equal Protection of the Laws Clause of the Fourteenth Amendment to cheat ourselves of equality.[34]

Which, of course, is exactly what he in effect counsels—in addition to the

---

34. Ronald Dworkin, *Equality and Preferential Treatment* (Princeton, N.J., 1977), p.42.

inequality of "reverse discrimination." In other words, the desired end justifies the means—no matter what the Constitution may command! We have here another patent illustration of the guilt complex syndrome which, not content with equal justice under law and equality of opportunity, insists upon, in Raoul Berger's characterization, the attainment of "justice at any cost." Yet it represents the gravamen of the concurring opinions in *Bakke* by Justices Brennan, Marshall and Blackmun, the controlling holding in the *Weber* case via the pen of Justice Brennan, and the opinion by Justice Marshall in *Fullilove*, which was joined by his colleagues Brennan and Blackmun.

VIII

There is one other matter *cum* issue that must be addressed as a complement to my exhortation of the legal process, the necessity of playing the proverbial judicio-governmental societal game according to its rules. That, naturally, is the role of the judiciary in interpreting the Constitution and the laws passed (and executive actions taken) under its constellation. The line between judicial "judging" and "lawmaking" is of course an extremely delicate and vexatious one: what represents "judicial activism" to some represents "judicial restraints" to others, and vice versa. All too often an observer's judgment corresponds to the answer to the question "whose ox is gored?" Jurists are human, yet they, unlike laymen, are presumed to be professionally qualified to render objective judgment on the meaning, range, and extent of constitutionally and statutorily sanctioned or interdicted governmental authority and exercise of power. To be sure, in Justice Cardozo's memorable phrase from his seminal *The Nature of the Judicial Process*, "it is not easy to stand aloof" when one deals with so controversial a policy matter as the resort to discrimination as a cure for discrimination, for, as that great jurist and sensitive human being put it so poignantly, "[t]he great tides and currents which engulf the rest of men, do not ... pass [even] the judges idly by."[35] And they assuredly have not done so—notwithstanding what would appear to be some crystal clear statutory, and some relatively clear constitutional, commands. *Au contraire*, these commands have served jurists as well as legislators and mere citizens as justifications and/or rationalizations along the pathways of coming to grips with the issue in settling fashion in either political, or

---

35. Benjamin N. Cardozo, *The Nature of the Judicial Process* (New Haven, Conn., 1921), p. 34.

socio-economic, or philosophical, or statutory, or, in the final analysis, judically constructed terms.

But there *are* demonstrable limits to subjectivity and result orientation, even when these are viewed against the notion of an obligation to heed, as Justice Holmes put it, "the felt necessities of the time."[36] One of these limits is the ascertainable intent of lawmakers in enacting legislation. *De minimis*, courts have an absolute basic obligation to examine *statutory* language and plain legislative intent as evidenced by the printed record—and the "affirmative action/reverse discrimination" field is no exception. Admittedly, the *constitutional* ground is considerably less clear: for the verbiage and the concept of "equal protection" (and, for that matter, "due process of law') defy finite or categorical definition—regrettably all-too-often depending upon the eye of the beholder or the subject and object of the aforementioned oxgoring. Yet even on constitutional *qua* constitutional grounds it is difficult to deny the verity of Justice Powell's point in his majority opinion in *Bakke I* when he noted that: "The guarantee of equal protection cannot mean one thing when applied to one individual and something else when applied to a person of another color. If both are not accorded the same protection, then it is not equal."[37]

Be that as it may, one who attempts to be a dispassionate commentator need not reach, as in effect the Court customarily tried very hard *not* to reach, the constitutional issue (here the Fourteenth Amendment's equal protection of the laws clause). For if words mean anything, the language of the basic statute involved, namely the 1964 Civil Rights Act's Title VII, would indeed seem to be crystal clear in *proscribing* the kind of racial quotas that the United States District Court and the United States Circuit Court found to have violated Brian Weber's rights, for example, but which, on appeal, the highest court of the land *upheld* in its 5:2 decision in 1979.[38] The controlling opinion, written by Justice Brennan, acknowledged the statutory, the linguistic command; but he and his four supporters found approbative warrant in the law's "spirit" rather than in its letter. For the law's Section 703(l) makes it unlawful for an employer to classify his employees "in any way which would deprive or tend to deprive any individual of employment opportunities or otherwise adversely affect his status as an employee, because of such individual's race, color, religion, sex, or national origin." And, perhaps even more tellingly, Section

---

36. Oliver Wendell Holmes, *The Common Law* (Boston, 1881), p. 1.
37. 438 U.S. 265, at 289-90.
38. 443 U.S. 193.

703(j) provides that the 1964 Act's language is not to be interpreted "to require any employer . . . to grant preferential treatment to any individual or to any group because of the race . . . of such individual or group" to correct a racial imbalance in the employer's work force. Further to buttress the historical and factual documentation on statutory grounds that the authors of the Civil Rights Act were demonstrably *opposed* to racial quotas, one need only take a glance at the voluminous, indeed repeated, documentation to that extent in the *Congressional Record* during the debates that led to the passage of the 1964 Civil Rights Act. Thus, the latter's successful Senate floor leader, Senator Hubert Humphrey (D.-Minn.), in responding to concerns voiced by doubting colleagues, vigorously and consistently gave assurance that no racial quotas or racial work force statistics would be employable under the law. In one exchange with his colleague Willis Robertson (D.-Va.), he made the following offer: "If the Senator can find in Title VII . . . any language which provides that an employer will have to hire on the basis of percentage or quota related to color . . . I will start eating the pages one after another, because it is not in there."[39]

It is difficult, indeed, it is in fact impossible, to argue with the facts of the statute's language, or with Congressional intent. Not once during the 83 days of Senate debate did any speaker, be he proponent or opponent, suggest that the bill would allow employers, voluntarily or otherwise, to prefer racial minorities over white persons. As the legislative history makes clear, speakers on both sides of the issue recognized that Title VII would tolerate no racial preference, voluntary or non-voluntary, whether in favor of blacks or whites. Justice Brennan's opinion attempted to vitiate those facts by (1) seizing upon the allegation that the joint Steelworkers-Kaiser Corporation agreement to hire one black for every white trainee was not required but was *voluntary*; and (2) that, in any event, the program would expire upon reaching statistical workforce-by-race availability-in-the-community parity. One need not embrace the angry and sarcastic language of Justice Rehnquist's dissenting opinion to support his accurately documented contentions that, as to (1) above, anyone with any knowledge of the course of "affirmative action" programs knows that they are patently Government-*required*—indeed, inspectors from the Office of Federal Contract Compliance Programs had specifically raised the question of Kaiser's compliance; and that, as to (2), provision (j) of Section 703—quoted above—(a) forbids such a program, and (b) the

---

39. 110 *Cong. Rec.* 7420.

notion that it would prove to be "temporary" is either naive or, as Rehn-quist put it, "Houdini"-like. Whatever one's personal views on the under-lying issue, whatever one's sympathies, the Rehnquist dissent, as Professor Philip B. Kurland of the University of Chicago School of Law commented, is simply unanswerable in terms of statutory construction and Congres-sional intent. To a very considerable degree it was not Justice Rehn-quist's dissent, but that by Chief Justice Burger, which comes to the heart of the matter if one wishes to abide by the imperatives of the government framework under which we function. For he pointed to the salient fact that:

> The Court reaches a result I would be inclined to vote for were I a Member of Congress considering a proposed amendment of Title VII. I cannot join the Court's judgment, however, because it is contrary to the explicit language of the statute and arrived at by means wholly incom-patible with long-established principles of separation of powers. Under the guise of 'statutory construction,' the Court effectively rewrites Title VII to achieve what it regards as a desirable result. It 'amends' the statute to do precisely what both its sponsors and its opponents agreed the statute was *not* intended to do.[40]

There is no valid rebuttal to the Chief Justice's admonition—for it assesses accurately the obligations occurring under our system's separa-tion of powers and the attendant roles of the three branches. In brief, and calling a spade a spade, the Court legislated—a function in this instance demonstrably reserved to Congress. The elusive line between "judging" and "legislating" is, of course, a monumentally difficult one to draw in a great many instances; it represents *the* basic issue of controversy in the exercise of judicial power. But there is *no* controversy in the present instance: Congress spoke and wrote with indeed uncharacteristic clarity! Nonetheless, a majority of five Supreme Court Justices, given the nature of the public policy issue at hand, would neither listen nor read accurately. The *Weber* decision, in the words of Barbara Lemer, distinguished student of law and psychology, "is a gross and blatant refusal by the Court to enforce the legislative will."[41] What the Court in effect did, as University of Virginia Professor Edmund W. Kitch put it succinctly, was simply to invalidate the delicate political compromise that led to the Civil Rights Act of 1964, namely, that that "law was to enact not a special program

---

40. 443 U.S. 216.
41. *The Supreme Court Review* 1979 (Chicago, 1980), p. 45.

of relief and assistance to blacks but a general principle of racial, sexual, religious, and ethnic neutrality."[42]

A concluding word on the desirability of "reverse discrimination" *per se*. I hope I have demonstrated what I regard as its tenets: what it *is*, and what it is *not*. Whether or not one agrees with that position, and regardless of how one perceives or reads the inherent statutory and constitutional issues, what about the merits of the proposition of adopting racial, or sexual, or religious, or nationality quotas, or by whatever other noun they may be perfumed? Responding to that *quaere*, I shall call as my star witness someone whose credentials on the libertarian front are indisputably impeccable: Justice William O. Douglas. In his 1974 dissenting opinion in *De Funis v. Odegaard*,[43] after finding that Marco De Funis had been rejected by the University of Washington School of Law "solely on account of his race," Douglas lectured at length on that classification, styling it at the outset as introducing "a capricious and irrelevant factor working an invidious discrimination," and insisting that the Constitution and the laws of our land demand that each application for admission must be considered in "a racially neutral way," a phrase he italicized and one, incidentally, quoted with approval by Justice Powell in *Bakke I*. "Minorities in our midst who are to serve actively in our public affairs," he went on, "should be chosen on talent and character alone, not on cultural orientation or leanings." Warmly he had cautioned that there:

> is no constitutional right for any race to be preferred. . . . A De Funis who is white is entitled to no advantage by reason of that fact nor is he subject to any disability, no matter his race or color. Whatever his race, he had a constitutional right to have his application considered on its individual merits in a racially neutral manner. . . . So far as race is concerned, any state sponsored preference of one race over another in that competition is in my view 'invidious' and violative of the Equal Protection Clause.[44]

That exhortation would be eloquently echoed after Douglas's death by Justices Stewart and Stevens's ringing dissenting opinions in *Fullilove*: The former called the ten percent set aside law "racist" and an "invidious discrimination by government"; the latter warned that "our statue books will once again have to contain laws that reflect the odious practice of delineating the qualities that make one person a Negro and make another white," and suggested sarcastically that now our government must devise

---

42. *Supreme Court Review*, p.3.
43. 416 U.S. 312.
44. 416 U.S. 312 at 334, 343-44.

its version of the Nazi Nurnberg laws that defined who was and who was not a Jew.[45]

Justice Douglas, who in his last book, wrote that "racial quotas—no matter how well-intentioned—are a wholly un-American practice, quite inconsistent with equal protection", had concluded his *De Funis* dissent on a note that, for me, hits the essence of the entire issue: "The equal Protection Clause," he insisted, "commands the elimination of racial barriers, not their creation in order to satisfy our theory as to how society ought to be organized. The purpose of the University of Washington cannot be to produce Black lawyers for Blacks, Polish lawyers for Poles, Jewish lawyers for Jews, Irish lawyers for the Irish. It should be to produce good lawyers for Americans . . . ."[46]

That, I submit in all humility, is the *sine qua non* of the matter. It is my fervent hope, though very far from a confident expectation—especially in view of the unsatisfactory, multifaceted, evasion-inviting response given by the Court in *Bakke II* and the high tribunal's patent violation of the language and intent of Title VII in *Weber*—that we will still, at this late hour, resolve to heed the late Justice's admonition and substitute for "lawyers" whatever educational, occupational, or professional noun may be appropriate in given circumstances in the justly egalitarian strivings of all Americans, regardless of race, sex, creed, nationality, age, or religion, for a dignified, happy, prosperous, and free life, blessed by a resolute commitment to and acquiescence in equal justice under law—which is as the cement of society.

---

45. 48 LW 4979 (1980), at 5002-07.
46. 416 U.S. 342.

Crisis in the Understanding of Liberty

John Alvis

The signers of the Declaration of Independence were prepared to pledge their lives, their estates, and their "sacred Honour" upon the truth of certain propositions they held in common with their countrymen. Chief among the truths they held was the proposition: "all men are created equal and are endowed by their Creator with certain inalienable rights." The question now arises whether the latter day descendants of the signers still hold those truths which the signers deemed "self-evident." Particularly we have cause to doubt whether the linchpin of Jefferson's revolutionary case, the equality proposition, still carries assent. I do not mean to say equality has been displaced in the political rhetoric you will hear practiced by most public spokesmen. Together with liberty and outranking prosperity, equality continues to be a standard, a goal, a watchword that we regularly invoke when we seek to identify the purposes America ought to pursue. Nevertheless there is reason to believe that what we invoke under the name of equality is not what Jefferson, Madison, Hamilton and Washington revered. The same word may have a meaning for this generation quite different from its meaning for the Framers. To see that this is so let us consider the meaning of the assertion "all men are created equal" as one encounters the statement in the Declaration, then reflect upon the understanding of equality that appears to underlie recent decisions of the Supreme Court.

The equality proposition of the Declaration asserts not the claim of a particular group of men for better treatment, but a conviction on the part of Americans that all human beings require a certain kind of treatment in accord with their human nature. The first clauses state the common human possession to consist in certain inalienable rights, and the latter part of the document—its bill of particulars against George III and his parliament—suggests these rights are violated by governments that rule without consent of the governed and without regard for those procedures known as due process of law. But consent of the governed and due process are necessary just because all men are created equal. In what sense are they equal? Not in their capacity to manage, to think, to make their way, certainly not in their deeply varying interests. The men of the founding generation most often defined equality in moral terms and in connection with liberty. Human beings are in essence rational agents, beings who by

109

their power of thought incur the responsibility of determining their course of action. Such beings stand above beasts, which need not give their consent to our management because their end is not in themselves. No set of men can be the natural rulers of other men as all men are natural rulers of all beasts. No man is good enough to rule another arbitrarily. Hence among eighteenth-century political thinkers human equality most typically finds expression in a definition of a natural moral right: freedom from subjection to the arbitrary will of another. In this conception equality and liberty are inseverable, the liberty being the natural consequence of the fact of equality.

It ought to be stressed that the notion of human equality I have described points to a political right, a claim in justice that any human being may justly expect other human beings to acknowledge as the basis for political justice. It is not a complaint against the cosmos for causing differences of intelligence and talent to exist among the various members of the human species. Acknowledgment of universal equality protects us from one another but gives us no handles upon the workings of nature, no security against the operation of the effects of nature's very unequal distribution of the physical means for securing survival or advantage. Hence it makes sense to speak of this view of equality as that which stipulates equal opportunity. The barriers of privilege should come down if a nation heeds the Jeffersonian idea, but these artificial or conventional inequalities are held pernicious because they stand in the way of the emergence of other, better founded, inequalities: better founded because arising from real differences of merit rather than from distinctions of birth or religious affiliation. Therefore, Jefferson remained faithful to the egalitarian tenets of the Declaration when late in his life in his well-known letter to John Adams he assured the Federalist Adams that America provided the political setting most conducive to fostering a natural aristocracy. Or as Madison would also argue, the democratic regime founded on the proposition all men are created equal seeks by its elimination of unnatural political inequalities to protect freedom, a large dimension of which is the operation of the unequal faculties of men for acquiring property. From the speeches, writings, and policies of the statesmen who devised the Constitution and were first to govern by it, one gathers a general agreement that equality prepares for liberty. Equality is the moral fact, liberty the moral purpose required by the fact of equality. Because men are at first equal in that no group bears at birth any title to rule others, men must be free to choose their rulers or free to govern themselves. Moreover, individuals possess equally rights to maintain life, to dispose of their labor, and to pursue happiness for their own sake, not as instruments to individuals deemed more fully human. Thus civil liberties, procedural rights, and substantive claims all derive from the principle of equality. Equality finds its complete fruition in political liberty. But, it is necessary to emphasize, all the rights devolving from the principle of equality are understood first, to have a moral character consequent upon respect for the nature of the rational human person and second, to pertain to human beings as individuals precisely because of this moral character. The rights are not simply new claims to advantage pressed by a new power, the hitherto "disadvantaged" majority of men. Not group rights but individual rights follow from accepting the equality proposition.

Now as everyone today says and as a few men of the time were prepared to acknowledge, the Constitution of 1787 did not secure at once the freedom which its first principles require. Under carefully confined terms it countenanced the continuation of slavery, and it made no provision for extending civil rights to women. As early as 1784 the anomalous status of women became clear with a provision of the Northwest Ordinance stipulating that women should enjoy full rights of inheritance. But over a hundred years would elapse before women had everywhere the basic civil right in a democracy of voting. The extension of political rights to black Americans was of course not to be accomplished until the Civil War had made possible the Fourteenth and Fifteenth Amendments. These constitutional additions carried through by the Reconstruction Congress were conceived as the installments of equality necessary to complete the imperfect provisions of the original Constitution, yet even so, the amendments were conceived in the spirit of the Constitution of 1787 and its progenitor, the Declaration of Independence. Equality still meant securing equality of rights for individuals who were, qua individuals, equal in their entitlement to justice. Due process and equal protection of the laws, the operative concepts of the Fourteenth Amendment, secure the extension of rule of law to those who had hitherto been denied that equal status. The intended beneficiaries of the amendment were the freed blacks and, later, women. The ultimate aim was the elimination of considerations based on class—racial, sexual, or otherwise—so that the subject of rights should be recognized, as both rule of law and constitutional government require, to be the individual person. The means to this end was a redefinition of the terms of citizenship. Whereas under the original Constitution citizenship in a state was prior and citizenship in the nation a derivative condition, as a result of the Fourteenth Amendment national citizenship takes precedence. Human beings born in the United States (or naturalized) enjoy all the rights pertaining to national citizenship, and hence the equality proposition of the Declaration receives a clear Constitutional expression. Moreover, equal protection of the laws came to be interpreted by the Court in such a way as to secure equal treatment for blacks under state law as well as under federal regulations. Once the Supreme Court had overcome certain anomalous applications of the Fourteenth Amendment evident in the Slaughter-House Cases at the close of the nineteenth-century, it moved fairly consistently towards a full implementation of the anti-racist potential of the due process and equal protection of the law clauses, reaching under the Warren Court and as a result of the 1964 Civil Rights Act a high point in the actualization of the Founders' ideal of equal political rights for all. The late 60's seemed to promise success in the long effort to overcome residual class discriminations in favor of a standard of political life based upon the determination to treat individual men and women solely in terms of what their character, capacities, and talents merited. Such an outcome would have meant the full fruition of equality as understood from the point of view of Jefferson, Madison, and Marshall.

Through another door, however, class consciousness and discrimination have re-entered our public counsels. The door is judicial activism of the 70's and 80's, and the new proponents of discrimination are friends to those who suffered, or whose ancestors once suffered, the effects of earlier discrimination. In decisions such as Bakke I and II, United Jewish Organizations, Castaneda, Weber, and Fullilove the Court has indicated its resolve to act on behalf of "discrete and insular" minorities by finding in favor of various programs of affirmative action. In the Weber case judicial activism seemed to reach its zenith when the Court ruled in favor of a racial quota as the proper instrument of affirmative action even though quotas were expressly forbidden in the provisions of the Civil Rights Act the Court was seeking to enforce. The affirmative action decisions of the Court have brought to sight a pattern of thought that warrants our speaking of a "new equality," or a new conception of equality quite different from—in some important respects antithetical to—the older notion of equality as the equal enjoyment by individuals of political rights. Three principles are evident in this new conception of equality: first, justice requires equal treatment of all except when unequal treatment is justified as a benefit to less favored groups; second, rights are vested in groups rather than in individuals, and membership in a group suffices to establish entitlement to protection against a majority; third, through the

Supreme Court minorities enjoy a virtual representation that aims at redressing oppression inflicted by a permanent, monolithic majority.

The first principle finds expression in the Court's rejection of Justice Harlan's guidance ("Our Constitution is color-blind, and neither knows nor tolerates classes among citizens") in favor of Justice Blackman's assumption that "in order to get beyond racism, we must first take account of race" and in favor of Chief Justice Burger's principle that members of the white majority should absorb the costs of benefitting members of minorities since previously the white majority benefitted from injuries borne by the non-whites. Setting aside a certain number of positions in medical schools for black students or a certain number of government building contracts for minority construction firms satisfies the Court's sense of a moral imperative requiring help for non-whites to be "brought up to the starting line." The jurists follow Lyndon Johnson, who complained of those who offered blacks merely equal opportunities. Johnson called for compensatory action which would undo some of the effects of long-standing discrimination and now reward minorities with unearned advantages as previously the white majority had prevented non-whites from earning their just measure. The spirit behind this new racially discriminatory jurisprudence may be benign, but however well-meaning, the re-introduction of racial quotas brings with it at least two harmful consequences. For one, the Court cannot give a clear account of its own doings since it's unclear how it may be determined when special preference for minorities has succeeded in bringing everyone even at the starting line so that genuinely equal protection of the law may begin again to be applied. This gives activism an unprincipled, ad hoc, and irregular character. Second, the Court clearly countenances inequity when it requires members of the white "majority" to pay penalties for wrongs those individuals did not inflict. The present practice violates a fundamental premise of law that only those guilty of a violation of law should suffer the penalities exacted by the law.

The second feature of the new equality—the notion that rights vest in groups rather than in individuals—also brings pernicious effects. It means parties claiming grievances need no longer establish that they have received direct and particular harm from the operation of some law, policy, or regulation. As Justice Marshall declared in the first Bakke decision: "It is unnecessary in 20th-century America to have individual Negroes demonstrate that they have been victims of racial discrimination." The converse of Marshall's proposition is that anyone identified with the dominant majority need not be convicted of any particular act of discrimination but is justly subject to the costs of reparation simply because he is white. Such reasoning substitutes class considerations for scrutiny of the particular circumstances of individuals, traditionally the proper subject for adjustments called for by equity. Moreover, by shifting the residence of rights from individuals to groups the Court encourages a view that human beings act always from narrow class interests. From such a view one risks losing the very notion of a right as an obligation morally binding every member of society; rights tend under this view to become indistinguishable from class interests and hence a product of will and power rather than a moral standard set above human caprice to regulate the workings of will and power.

The third tenet of the new equality—the Court's assigning itself the function of virtual representation—offers the most striking instance of the divergence of recent opinion from the views of equality that obtained with the Founders. Because it contends the legislative processes have proved inadequate—or by the very nature of politics may be always inadequate—to safeguard interests of minorities from violation by majorities, it falls to the judiciary to secure the good of "discrete and insular minorities" by providing such groups with a special representation beyond the means associated with voting, free speech, petition, and access to government offices. As the Framers thought, the great challenge of popular government lay in creating conditions that would produce responsible majorities. According to Madison, factions are the bane of free republics. A faction is a group motivated by an interest hostile to the rights of other citizens or opposed to the permanent and aggregate interests of the nation as a whole. Minority factions would be overcome, Madison concluded, by the majority, and therefore the crucial problem lay in protecting against majority factions. Madison counted upon the largeness of the sphere of society and the diversity of interests agitating over that expanse to prevent coalitions of interests on grounds other than justice. Besides these social conditions, the various modes of representation called for by the Constitution together with the separation of branches and division of authority between national and state governments would work so to moderate the majority coalition that the result would be a general will respectful of the rights of every segment of society. The solution, that is, consisted in rendering it unlikely that the majority could form on a basis other than justice. This was a solution consistent with the republican principle that the will of the majority must prevail; and Madison and the other Framers explicitly rejected another possible solution, that of reposing guardianship over individual rights in a body placed beyond the authority of the majority. The latter expedient was rejected not because it could not work but because such a solution was incompatible with the principle of self-government. Yet the Supreme Court now espouses that rejected expedient, arguing that the judiciary must moderate majoritarian legislation from a position beyond the reach of majoritarian authority.

The irony of this development may be appreciated by recalling our point of departure for these observations: the assertion of universal equality in the Declaration. That assertion found expression in the motto, "no taxation without representation," which calls for direct representation of the governed in the British legislature. This was an explicit rejection of Britain's argument that the colonists were adequately represented in Parliament although they sent no representative to Parliament. Britain granted the principle that constitutional government required deliberation in the legislature by the representatives of the governed, but maintained the colonists were accorded "virtual representation" in a Parliament composed exclusively of British members. We have thus come the full circle to the Supreme Court now occupying the position once taken by the British against the colonial revolutionaries. The equality proposition of the Declaration rejected the notion of virtual representation, arguing instead that the legitimate powers of government derive from the consent of the governed, an argument brought to completion in the majoritarian arrangements of the Constitution, including those arrangements designed to insure a majority respectful of minority rights. Today's Court not only maintains the consistency of its virtual representation with democratic principle, but holds moreover that for the sake of advancing the interests of "discrete and insular minorities" the Court's powers of virtual representation ought to take precedence over the majority acting through its representative legislature. Rejecting the Madisonian argument reposing trust in the deliberative justice of a majority carefully refined, limited, and open to scrutiny in its formation, deliberations, and in its subsequent actions, the Court now tends simply to degrade the majority by equating it with any interest group. Under this view every majority is ipso facto a majoritarian faction, that is, a body intent on pursuing its interest to the detriment of minority right. The dangers posed by such a view are obvious. It causes distrust of the very possibility of self-government by suggesting that we cannot count on human beings to arrive through deliberation at a common good but only at an accommodation of unjust interests. To the degree that the view takes hold and persuades Americans to view their country as divided between a continuous oppressive white majority and subjugated non-white minorities, to just such a degree will racist animosities become inflamed, intractable, and permanent. Not the particular activist decisions of the Warren Court but a new theory following in their wake has shored up racist distinctions just when they had seemed on the point of being pulled down once and for all.

What then is the crisis in our understanding of equality that appears when we confront the egalitarianism of the Founders with the new theory of equality advanced in recent affirmative action policy statements? To say that the choice rests between equality of opportunity (the Founders' view) and equality of result (the new purpose) is not untrue. The Framers did seek to open to a wider field opportunities which had before admitted only a privileged group, whereas some of today's egalitarians are content to buy a more equal status, social and political, for the hitherto disadvantaged at the cost of denying equal opportunity to others. The dichotomy, opportunity vs. result, although true, is insufficiently revealing of what is at stake. At bottom what is at stake is a concept of human nature and of the mode of government most consistent with that nature.

Popular government, constitutional government, or rule of law are almost synonymous as the Founders conceived these terms. All these designations of a form of civil life resting upon a basis more regular, just, and rational than someone's authoritative caprice, point toward a modest confidence in human reason. The belief that human beings possess a degree of rationality sufficient to make them the morally responsible authors of their doings underlies the proposition "all men are created equal." A rational nature affords the indispensable substratum for the equality of rights of life, liberty, and the pursuit of happiness. To be morally accountable is in the essential sense to be free; an agent cannot be accountable if he is simply the resultant of his interests, the pawn of sub-rational desires or of class conditioning which holds him to its course preventing his subordination of passion to a common good. A modest confidence in human reason also appears in the arrangements the Founders devised for the conduct of government. They trusted reason not implicitly, for they knew that left at large unchecked passions and partial interests will outrun prudence and fairmindedness. Theirs was rather a conditional respect for reason, conditional upon its being given a fair chance by laws, institutions, and social conditions that would prevent passion having a clear road to its objects. Under such purifying conditions the deliberate will of the majority will approximate reason and therefore ought to enjoy sovereignty. Hence, for the Framers, the majority acting through the representative legislature was the central and highest authority in a free regime. Finally, a moderate respect for reason decreed the end, the purpose, of government for the minds who espoused our founding articles of faith. The life they proposed to encourage by their constitutional provisions was one of rational liberty, individuals free to cultivate their natural capacities within bounds set by the obligation to respect the rights of others. Self-government enjoyed one by one, in each of us rationality governing passion, was the ultimate aim of self-government practiced all together through the national institutions. That is what it means to be conceived in and dedicated to liberty.

Or that is what it meant. For the new equality, the tenets of which I have attempted to sketch, calls into doubt all of the principles just mentioned. Its underlying premise is that human beings seek their interests because their situation within groups compels them not only to feel certain passions but to identify their passions with justice. Justice is simply the "rationalization" of interest, and what passes current for justice in a regime is simply the interest of the ruling class. Because human beings are class products rather than morally autonomous individuals, it makes no sense to speak of liberty as the end of political life nor of reasonable deliberation producing a majority as the legitimate means of forming public policy. Nor should we rest content with achieving equality of opportunity since that means nothing more than ratifying the haphazard distribution of talents dispensed by nature's lottery. Nature as a foundation and as a norm is rejected by the new equality. If this new concept of equality is true, one doubts that the interposition of the Court between the majority passion and its objects will serve to deter that majority for any length of time. If all groups are factions then the more powerful faction need observe no self-imposed moral restraint. The recent jurists and their theoretical mentors may be teaching the shortest way to remove a salutary restraint on the majority will. But then again, the new equality may be wrong in its view of human nature and the political precepts called for by that nature. If it is wrong, we pay for its ill-conceived program of an equality of result with a real loss of liberty.

Chapter Three

Majority Rule and Freedom:
The First Amendment

In creating a limited government based upon majority rule, the founders faced the problem of whether such a government was compatible with that freedom of conscience, thought, and speech which permits the highest human endeavors. In order to secure such freedom, does constitutional government require also the freedom to do what may be base or despicable?

On the Dangers of a Bill of Rights:
A Restatement of the Federalist Argument

Hadley Arkes

The philosopher Wittgenstein reminded us that certain questions may best be answered by the asking of another question. The style of argument here may be identified as talmudic, and when it is applied artfully—when the question is properly pointed—it is possible to reconstruct, quite tenably, the understanding that lay behind the question. Several years ago the current prime minister of Greece, Andreas Papandreou, was the leader of the Socialist opposition within the national assembly, and he offered up one day a long, tedious denunciation of NATO and American imperialism, which he flavored with praise of the Soviet Union. The prime minister at that time, Mr. Karamanlis, endured this tirade and finally responded with one short sentence, which brought laughter from the house. "When you left Greece," he asked, "where did you go?"[1] Under the regime of the Colonels, Mr. Papandreou had exposed himself to the ravages of capitalism by settling as a professor in Berkeley, California.

The prime minister's gentle question could have been replaced, rather plausibly, by a fuller commentary which ran along these lines: however much Mr. Papandreou esteemed socialism, he apparently attached a more decisive importance to the security that was afforded by a regime of law; or he apparently thought that a non-socialist economy had been far more successful in providing those material comforts which could soften, for him at least, the rigors of life. And if it were indeed more important to Mr. Papandreou that a country be "free" before it were "socialist"—that its government be subject to constitutional restraints and the consent of the governed—then the absence of those features had to imply an objection in principle to the Soviet Union that ran far deeper than any objection he could have to the United States.

All of this might have been offered, as I say, as an implication that arose from the prime minister's question. I mention this incident because I think that some of the most telling parts of the original argument against a Bill of Rights were locked away in this manner, in understandings that were evidently present, but which were never filled out or even adequately stated. They were implied, rather, in a number of talmudic questions that

---

1. Walter Laqueur, "Euro-Neutralism," *Commentary* (June, 1980), p. 25.

were posed by different writers or speakers in the court of the original debate about the foundations of the new government and the need for a Bill of Rights. I would suggest that these rhetorical questions, posed at strategic moments in the debate, would lead us back along the paths of reason that must have produced them, and if we trace back these threads or fragments of argument, we could reconstruct the understandings that lay behind these questions. And when we did, I think we would fill in some of the deeper arguments against a Bill of Rights that were never made explicitly as arguments.

The case against the Bill of rights was offered mainly by the men who were known as Federalists, while the arguments in favor of a Bill of Rights were pressed mainly by the men we identify as Anti-federalists. It is only in recent years that an attempt has been made to recover the Federalist argument or to remind us that there had indeed been a serious dispute.[2] And yet, a certain enigmatic quality still attaches to the argument drawn by the Federalists. My late professor, Herbert Storing, was one of the most thoughtful defenders of the men who led the movement for a stronger national government. But in his last work (published after his death) Storing reviewed what he took to be the main arguments made by the Federalists in resisting a Bill of Rights, and he found those arguments unpersuasive.[3] After all, the Founders had already incorporated in the test of the Constitution prohibitions on ex post facto laws and bills of attainder. If the framers were willing to descend to these particulars, how could there be an aversion in principle to setting forth several more restrictions on the power of the government, especially when these provisions could be reassuring to many people and perhaps even useful in defining the character of constitutional restraints? Storing was disposed to join the Anti-federalists in asking: what would be the harm? As Patrick Henry tauntingly put it: would this project have taken too much paper?

One Anti-federalist writer set forth his case in this way:

> We do not by declarations change the nature of things, or create new truths, but we give existence, or at least establish in the minds of the people truths and principles which they might never otherwise have thought of, or soon forgot. If a nation means its systems, religious or

---

2. For this recovery of historical memory we must be obliged most notably to Gordon Wood for his engaging book, *The Creation of the American Republic, 1776-1787* (Chapel Hill: University of North Carolina Press, 1969), especially pp. 536-43.

3. See Herbert J. Storing, *What the Anti-Federalists Were For*, Vol. I of *The Complete Anti-Federalist*, ed. Storing (Chicago: University of Chicago Press, 1981), pp. 64-70.

political, shall have duration, it ought to recognize the leading principles of them in the front page of every family book.[4]

Herbert Storing thought that this statement, with its sober and measured claims, conveyed the best case that the Anti-federalists could make
for their position: that a Bill of Rights could be "a prime agency of that
political and moral education of the people on which free republican
government depends."[5] I think the Federalists did understand that the
Bill of Rights would find its main effect in teaching, but they were
convinced that it would teach the wrong lessons: that it would narrow our
understanding of the rights that government was meant to protect; that it
would misinstruct the American people about the very ground of their
rights; and that it would make it even harder then to preserve republican
government.

As the Federalists understood, the very notion of a "Bill of Rights"
imparted the wrong cast to our conception of "rights" because it drew on
the wrong analogies. Hamilton remarked in the Federalist #84 that:

> bills of rights are, in their origin, stipulations between kings and their
> subjects, abridgments of prerogative in favor of privilege, reservations
> of rights not surrendered to the prince. Such was MAGNA CARTA,
> obtained by the barons, sword in hand, from King John . . . . Such was
> the *Petition of Right* assented to by Charles I . . . . Such, also, was the
> Declaration of Right presented by the Lords and Commons to the
> Prince of Orange in 1688, and afterwards thrown into the form of an act
> of parliament called the Bill of Rights.[6]

These arrangements bore the solemnity of a fundamental contract, but as
James Wilson and Oliver Ellsworth pointed out, a contract implies two
parties equally competent to contract. The metaphor of the contract
would suggest then that the government and the people stand on the
same plane, with two distinct interests of a comparable dignity. But that
notion would be wholly out of keeping with the character of a republic or
a popular government, in which authority emanated from the people, not
from the government, and in which the government stood, in relation to
the people, as an agent in relation to its sovereign.[7]

---

4. Quoted in Storing, p. 70.
5. Storing, p. 70.
6. *The Federalist* (New York: Modern library, n.d.), p. 558 (Emphasis in original).
7. Hamilton remarked on this point that Bills of Rights "have no application to constitutions, professedly founded upon the power of the people, and executed by their
immediate representatives and servants" (*The Federalist*, p. 558). As Gordon Wood has
shown, this theme was sounded by several other writers, including James Wilson. See
Wood, pp. 540-42. Apparently, for the critics of the Bill of Rights, this was not merely a
talking point, but a sign of mistakes that ran deep in the argument for a Bill of Rights.

If the Bill of Rights represented a certain reservation of natural rights to the people, the implication would quickly arise that the government may exercise all of those powers which had not been explicitly withheld. The paradoxical result, therefore, was that this reservation of rights might actually enlarge the total powers of the government, and it would remove from the government the burden of justifying its use of authority in a wide range of cases in which its measures were not explicitly forbidden. But as Herbert Storing points out, the Founders had not been loath to specify in the body of the Constitution that the writ of habeas corpus should not be suspended (except in cases of rebellion or invasion), or that no state may grant any title of nobility. Why was it necessary, he asked, to make *these* prohibitions explicit? Why should anyone have supposed that the Congress had the authority to suspend the writ of habeas corpus or that the States might grant titles of nobility? In their willingness to make these singular provisions within the text of the Constitution, the Founders had not betrayed any fear that they were conceding to the government through indirection all of those powers which they had not explicitly forbidden. Still, if they did suffer those apprehensions, why were their concerns here not dispelled finally by the passage of the Ninth Amendment? That Amendment read: "the enumeration in the Constitution of certain rights, shall not be construed to deny or disparage others retained by the people." Why did that provision not resolve the matter? Altogether then, Herbert Storing was moved to conclude that the Federalist argument on this point was rather "sophistical."[8]

And yet, as Storing must have known, the Founders had not shown a uniform enthusiasm for specifying principles or making prohibitions explicit within the body of the Constitution. On this matter they were affected by the same apprehensions they would later suffer over the wisdom of making stipulations in a Bill of Rights. It is curious in this respect that Storing chose to pass over the reservations expressed by Oliver Ellsworth and James Wilson when the proposal was brought forth at the Constitutional Convention to prohibit "ex post facto" laws. According to Madison's notes, Ellsworth remarked that "there was no lawyer, no civilian who would not say that ex post facto laws were void in themselves. It cannot be necessary to prohibit them." Wilson, too, was "against inserting anything in the Constitution as to ex post facto laws. It will bring reflections on the Constitution—and proclaim that we are ignorant of the

---

8. Storing, p. 67.

first principles of Legislation, or are constituting a Government which will be so."[9]

To pretend to the project of articulating the first principles of lawful government and to mention only bills of attainder and ex post facto laws was to run the risk of suggesting to those tutored in law that these were the only first principles that the American Founders knew. Or it would suggest at least that among the first principles of law, the items set forth in the Constitution stood on a higher plane of importance than the principles which the Founders had neglected to mention. And that sense of the matter would only confirm again the understanding that Hamilton feared was simply implicit in a Bill of Rights. With all respect for my late professor, Herbert Storing, I would suggest that the concerns expressed by Hamilton have been borne out quite tellingly in our experience. That they have been borne out even in the presence of the Ninth amendment may be a deeper confirmation of his argument: for in spite of the avowals in the Ninth Amendment, we have seen in a number of signal cases the casual denial of freedom and the cavalier destruction of certain rights precisely because these freedoms and rights were not apparently mentioned in the Bill of Rights or its sequelae. In other words, what has taken hold in practice is the state of mind—or the peculiar logic—that Hamilton thought was contained in the Bill of Rights; and that logic has not been overcome by the Ninth Amendment.

It was possible to add to the Bill of Rights many artful, pointed words to disclaim and reassure, but they could not easily dissolve the logic that was contained within the cast of this instrument: the Bill of Rights bore, ineffaceably, the character of a charter which listed the terms of an agreement or contract—in this case, the terms on which the American people agreed to be governed. The Bill of Rights would be seen as a list of reservations or stipulations about the rights that the people had not surrendered when they had tendered their obedience to the new government. The Bill of Rights drew, then, on the understandings associated with a "social contract." This metaphor lent itself to a number of variations, but it always assumed that individuals had stood at one time with certain natural rights in a state antecedent to civil society. Some writers have been pleased to refer to this condition as the "state of nature," and it has usually been conceived as a hazardous place: no one in the state of nature was restrained or protected by law, and as consequence any man

---

9. *The Records of the Federal Convention of 1787*, ed. Max Farrand, rev. ed. 1937 (New Haven: Yale University press, 1966), vol. II, p. 376 [August 22].

could be warranted in regarding every other man as a potential enemy. This was, as Hobbes described it, the "war of every man, against every man." Under these conditions anyone would be justified in carrying out preemptive attacks on his potential enemies: as Hobbes put it, "every man [would have] a right to every thing; even to one another's body."[10] These prospects were thought sufficiently frightening that people would be impelled to move from the state of nature to civil society; they would be willing to surrender the rights they possessed in the state of nature for a more limited set of "civil" rights, which would be rendered more secure, however, by the advent of a government which could make those rights enforceable at law.

Of course, not all political philosophers assumed that political life found its origin in a contract. Aristotle had argued compellingly that the notion of "contract" is radically unsuitable in accounting for the foundation of "law" and the justification of polity.[11] And yet, even among philosophers who have favored the analogy of a "contract," there has been a subtle but critical difference which has turned on the question of whether human beings possessed moral understanding *before* they entered civil society. The most notable denial on this point was offered by Hobbes. As he wrote in the *Leviathan*, "the desires, and other passions of man are in themselves no sin. No more are the actions, that proceed from those passions, till they know a law that forbids them: which till laws be made they cannot know."[12] That is, before the existence of law and civil society we cannot expect men to know the difference between right and wrong, or to treat that difference as one they can afford to respect.

But this understanding was rejected at the root by James Wilson, who stood, even among the Founders, as one of our preeminent juristic figures. And the ground on which Wilson rejected that argument made a profound difference for the understanding of the Bill of Rights and the kind of government to which a Bill of Rights would need to be attached. Wilson's rejection of the Hobbesian view was conveyed in one of those talmudic questions I alluded to earlier. The question was offered in his classic lecture on "Natural Rights" in response to an argument by Blackstone, and the query was followed by no further commentary. But it left

---

10. Thomas Hobbes, *Leviathan* (Oxford: Basil Blackwell, 1960; originally published in 1651), pp. 82, 85.

11. See Aristotle, *Politics* 1280a-1281a, and my extended discussion of this point in *First Things* (Princeton: Princeton University Press, 1986), ch. II.

12. Hobbes, p. 83.

no possibility of mistake about the understanding behind the question. Blackstone had remarked in Book I of his *Commentaries* that "the law, which restrains a man from doing mischief to his fellow citizens, though it diminishes the natural, increases the civil liberty of mankind . . . ."[13] To that observation Wilson responded with a simple question: "Is it part of natural liberty," he asked, "to do mischief to anyone?"[14]

That was all he said, and yet the question placed him a tradition of understanding that ran back to Aquinas and Aristotle, and which would later be reflected in Abraham Lincoln in his rejoinder to Stephen Douglas: "When Judge Douglas says that whoever, or whatever community, wants slaves, they have a right to have them, he is perfectly logical if there is nothing wrong in the institution; but if you admit that it is wrong, he cannot logically say that anybody has a right to do a wrong."[15] By this logic, which is nothing less than the logic of morals, we could never claim a rightful "liberty to do mischief." Apparently, for Wilson it was possible even in the state of nature to recognize the difference, say, between an assault that was provoked or unprovoked, justified or unjustified. The inflicting of a harm without justification could be judged quite clearly as a wrong, even before the existence of government. In that sense Wilson separated himself decisively from Hobbes: the advent of government did not mark the advent of morality. Even in the state of nature men did not have a natural right to assault or rape or commit injustice of any other kind. And obversely, even people in the state of nature had a right not to

---

13. William Blackstone, *Commentaries on the Laws of England* (Chicago: University of Chicago Press, 1981; originally published in 1765), Bk. I, pp. 121-22.

14. Wilson, "Of the Natural Rights of Individuals," in *The Works of James Wilson* (Cambridge: Harvard University Press, 1967), vol. II, p. 587.

15. Lincoln, debate with Douglas at Quincy, Illinois (October, 1858), *The Works of Abraham Lincoln*, ed. Roy P. Basler (New Brunswick: Rutgers University Press, 1953), vol. III, pp. 256-57.

suffer these wrongs.[16] It was not the existence of the government which created these rights; it was the existence of these rights which called forth and justified the existence of the government. Wilson was quick to note then that the purpose of government was not to create "new rights by a human establishment," but rather "to acquire a new security for the possession or the recovery of those rights" we already possess by nature.[17]

At the same time, the advent of law marked no diminution of freedom. The law which forbids a man to rape or to steal does not restrain him from doing anything he was ever rightfully free to do. And so if the question were put to Wilson: what "rights" do we give up when we leave the state of nature and enter civil society; the answer, unequivocally, was: none. Since we never had the right to do a wrong, even in the state of nature, the law which restrains us from doing wrong deprives us of none of our rights. And since no rights are surrendered in joining civil society, nothing needs

---

16. It is worth noting that not all of the responses of the Founders on this question were left to inference. Over a dozen years before the controversy over the Bill of Rights, a precocious Alexander Hamilton saw the need to address Hobbes's argument explicitly as he sought to appeal to natural rights and vindicate the rights of America in relation to Britain. The 19-year-old Hamilton wrote: "[Hobbes] held ... that [man in the state of nature] was ... perfectly free from all restraints of law and government. Moral obligation, according to him, is derived from the introduction of civil society; and there is no virtue, but what is purely artificial, the mere contrivance of politicians, for the maintenance of social intercourse. But the reason he ran into this absurd and impious doctrine, was, that he disbelieved the existence of an intelligent superintending principle, who is the governor, and will be the final judge of the universe. ... Good and wise men, in all ages, have embraced a very dissimilar theory. They have supposed, that the deity, from the relation we stand in, to himself and to each other, has constituted an eternal and immutable law, which is, indispensably, obligatory upon all mankind, *prior to any human institution whatever*." "The Farmer Refuted." (February, 1775), in *The Papers of Alexander Hamilton*, ed. Harold C. Syrett (New York: Columbia University Press, 1961), vol. I, pp. 86-87; emphasis added.

Some writers recently have sought to build an understanding of the Founders and the Constitution on the assumption that the Founders had accepted the "modern" notion of natural rights put forth by Hobbes, and that understanding encompassed the notion that rights were in fact surrendered in entering civil society. It should be clear, however, that this understanding cannot be true in relation to Hamilton and Wilson, and if it is not true in relation to them, it is hard to see how this understanding can be attributed, with any confidence, to "the Founders." If we did not grasp the point that Hamilton and Wilson had indeed rejected this implication of modern natural rights, we could not give a coherent account of the objections they framed against the Bill of Rights.

17. Wilson, p. 585.

to be reserved in a Bill of Rights.[18] But if the concern for rights is merely tacked on to the end of the Constitution, in a list of "reservations," this understanding of Wilson's would be overturned: we would indicate rather dramatically that the protection and enlargement of our rights is not in fact the central and animating purpose of the government. We would seem to suggest that the main purpose of the government must be found elsewhere: perhaps the polity would be seen largely as an alliance for the protection of property or for the cultivation of a manly, military honor. Or it might be seen far more modestly, as a government dedicated to the protection of certain minimal rights, but a polity whose range of moral concerns must be regarded as notably truncated, even in comparison with those governments which have been known as "limited," constitutional governments.[19] And yet the Founders were clear that the mission of the political order was nothing less than the protection of natural rights; and as Wilson described them, with a sober precision, they seemed to take in the full sweep of those rights. Man has, he said, "a natural right to his property, to his character, to liberty, and to safety"[20]—which is to say, he has a right to be protected, so far as practicable, from virtually all species of injustice.

That understanding of our "natural rights" extended well beyond any list that could be set down in a Bill of Rights, and one concern of the Federalists was that the understanding of rights would indeed be narrowed to the list of things that the First Congress thought to mention in the Bill of Rights. But the concern ran even more deeply, and it touched, as I have suggested, our understanding of the source and logic of these rights. When the Bill of Rights was brought forth in the First Congress, it encountered the irascible dubiety of Theodore Sedgwick of Connecticut,

---

18. Hamilton made the point explicitly: "Here, in strictness [i.e., under the new Constitution], the people surrender nothing; and as they retain every thing they have no need of particular reservations." Hamilton, *The Federalist* #84, p. 558. In the same vein, Dr. Benjamin Rush commended the framers for avoiding the incoherence of attaching a Bill of Rights to the Constitution: "As we enjoy all our natural rights from a pre-occupancy, antecedent to the social state," it would be "absurd to frame a formal declaration that our natural rights are acquired from ourselves." Quoted in Herbert J. Storing, "The Constitution and the Bill of Rights," in *How Does the Constitution Secure Rights?* ed. Robert A. Goldwin and William A. Schambra (Washington: American Enterprise Institute, 1985), p. 30.

19. This understanding of the American founding has indeed been offered in a celebrated essay by Martin Diamond, "Democracy and the Federalist: A Reconsideration of the Framers' Intent," *American Political Science Review*, vol. 53 (1959), pp. 52 ff.

20. Wilson, p. 592.

who responded to this project with another set of talmudic questions. Sedgwick first expressed his impatience by wondering just why the House was descending to such trifling details: if people have the right to speak, they must surely have the right to assemble for the purpose of speaking. But then why was it even necessary to specify that in a regime of law and constitutional liberty people had the right to speak? Sedgwick was moved to ask sardonically: why not also specify that "a man should have a right to wear his hat if he pleased; that he might get up when he pleased, and go to bed when he thought proper?"[21]

The questions were artfully placed, but in his impatience Sedgwick did not bother to fill out the understanding that lay behind the questions. Without that statement of his argument, Sedgwick's criticism was likely to be misread as a concern mainly for redundancy. And yet, once again, I think the questions implied an understanding that reached more deeply. I think Sedgwick was suggesting, first, that the people who produced this list of rights did not apparently understand the difference between a principle and the instances in which a principle may be manifested. They reveal the state of mind described by a colleague of mine when he refers to the people who would apparently believe that the series of positive integers were discovered *one at a time*. These people could go on forever listing the variety of circumstances in which our rights could be violated, but without understanding the logic that stands behind the list of rights. And so, to the current list contained in the Bill of Rights we could conceivably add the right not to be stopped and searched in our automobiles, the right not to have our briefcases and luggage examined without our consent, the right not to have blood removed from our arms in the search for legal evidence. These kinds of specifications would be no less plausible than many of the provisions already contained in the Bill of Rights, and at the same time, they would be no more illuminating.

When the Founders spoke of our "natural right" to life, liberty, and property, they never meant to suggest that the government could secure to us life everlasting, or that the government would never be warranted in restricting our freedom or taking our property (in the form of taxation). If there is a fire on a nearby street and the fire department closes off the street to pedestrians, the pedestrians are restrained in their freedom, but their natural rights have not been violated. For this restriction of freedom was made for a justified end, and as we have seen, when freedom is restricted justly people are not deprived of anything to which they have a

---

21. Sedgwick, *Annals of Congress*, 1st Cong., vol. I, p. 731 (August 15, 1787).

"right." It might be said then, more precisely, that we have a natural right to be treated justly: we have a right not to have our lives taken, our freedom restricted, our property extracted, *without justification*. The problem in all instances will pivot on the question of whether the government is restraining our freedom for reasons that are justified or unjustified; and it adds nothing to our understanding of the problem merely to elaborate in a Bill of Rights a somewhat fuller list of the kinds of cases in which we are apt to face this question.

For example, if we consider the right to "assemble" that was mentioned in the First Amendment, it should be apparent that the right is not defined as soon as we identify a group that gathers in the street and fits the description of "assembling." They could be assembling with burning crosses outside the home of a black family. They could be assembling without violence, but in the middle of the main intersection in town at the height of the rush hour. The critical question is not whether a group meets a description of "assembling," but as Congressman Page said in the First Congress, the question is whether people are assembling "on their lawful occasions" for legitimate ends.[22] The issue turns then on whether people are assembling reasonably or unreasonably, for purposes that are justified or unjustified. In the same way, the Bill of Rights does not bar *all* searches and seizures, but only those which are "unreasonable" or unjustified. The same qualification would have to attend all of the rights mentioned in the Bill of Rights, because any "right" must pivot, as I have said, on a moral judgment and not merely on a factual description of bodily movements. For that reason it would be equally useless or unilluminating to add to the list by providing, say, for our "right" not to be stopped *without justification* in the street, to have our automobiles searched *unreasonably*, to have our suitcases inspected *without cause*. We could go on endlessly listing the kinds of cases in which our freedom may be restricted wrongly, and we could do that without clarifying anything more about the matter that is truly decisive—namely, the grounds on which we are able to

---

22. Page, in *Annals of Congress*, p. 732.

distinguish between rightful and wrongful ends, between restraints on our freedom that are justified or unjustified.[23]

Theodore Sedgwick recognized the mindless quality of laying out an inventory of cases when he asked his colleagues: why not specify that "a man should have a right to wear his hat if he pleased; that he might get up when he pleased, and go to bed when he thought proper?" His colleagues felt the sting of his humor without understanding his point, and so Congressman Page remarked that Sedgwick's proposal might not be entirely inapt. He observed, rather portentously, to Sedgwick that "a man has been obliged to pull off his hat when he appeared before the face of authority."[24] Let us assume for a moment that Page managed to express here a plausible concern, that the abuse of legal authority might express itself in unjust, preemptory orders to a citizen to remove his hat in the street. There is a point to be made in considering just how a problem of this kind might have been addressed through the Bill of Rights. A passage might have been added, perhaps in the Second Amendment, stipulating that "the government may not require people unreasonably to remove their hats in public or to wear them under compulsion." Two hundred years later this scene would have been predictable: we would have found lawyers and judges straining their arts of argument over the question, is a motorcycle helmet a "hat" within the meaning of the Constitution? When a legislature requires motorcyclists to wear hats, would that provision violate the understanding expressed in the Bill of Rights?

This kind of exercise has become all too familiar, and it is worth noticing the nature of the shift that has taken place: instead of deliberating about the question of whether the regulation of headgear may be justified or unjustified—instead of focusing, in other words, on the sub-

---

23. In another essay on the Bill of Rights, Herbert Storing glimpsed—though he did not pursue—the alternative understanding I am putting forth here. "Without a bill of rights," he wrote, "our courts would probably have developed a kind of common law of individual rights to help to test and limit governmental power." As Storing recognized, those rights would be defended against the power of the government by an appeal to natural rights; and on the other side, the government would bear the burden of showing that it is restricting rights in any case for the sake of *ends* that are *legitimate*. And in that way he partially anticipated my argument: "Might the courts thus have been compelled to confront the basic questions that 'substantive due process.' 'substantive equal protection,' 'clear and present danger,' etc., have permitted them to conceal, even from themselves? Is it possible that without a bill of rights we might suffer less of that ignoble battering between absolutistic positivism and flaccid historicism that characterizes our constitutional law today?" See Storing, pp. 25-26.

24. *Annals of Congress*, p. 732.

stantive moral question—lawyers and judges often spend their time in empirical puzzles: is a motorcycle helmet a hat; are movies and peep shows "speech"? If we can subsume peep shows under "speech" we can bring the peep shows under the protection of the Constitution—but without addressing the substantive question of whether the law can reasonably ban peep shows, even if they are a form of "expression."

In the same way, the question we would not face on the matter of motorcycle helmets is whether the government would be justified in restricting personal freedom and compelling people to wear protective covering for their heads. At the time of this writing, a case is before the Supreme Court involving an orthodox Jew who insists on wearing his yarmulke in the Army. It should be evident that his "right" to choose the covering for his head will pivot on the kinds of considerations that the Army can bring forward in explaining why it is necessary to the discipline or safety of troops to wear only the headgear that is specified in the regulations on "uniforms."[25] One way or another, these are the kinds of questions the Army will have to address in showing why it is *justified* in restricting the freedom of its servicemen. But as I have tried to suggest, this is the form of the question that must be raised in relation to any effort on the part of the government to restrain personal freedom; and to that essential problem the Bill of Rights adds nothing. It furnishes no guidelines and it does not augment in any way our means of addressing these questions. Just to test this argument, we might consider two kinds of cases. In one, a man makes harassing, obscene phone calls in the middle of the night, and the question is whether the government may restrain this use of "speech." In another case the government announces that people should go to their homes and not venture out into the streets without the permission of the authorities.

The first case arises over the use—or misuse—of speech, and so it appears to many people that it involves the preeminent freedom mentioned in our First Amendment. In the second case the government would restrict a rather elementary freedom to move about in the public streets and engage in commerce outside the home. In effect, it would impose a kind of detention or house arrest, and yet it does not touch any freedom that was mentioned specifically in the Bill of Rights. The question may be put: must the government carry a heavier burden of justification in the first case than in the second; must it come forth with a far more compelling justification when it restricts a freedom that was mentioned in the Bill

---

25. See *Goldman v. Weinberger*, Doc. No. 84-1097.

of Rights? And yet it is hard to see why the government should be allowed to confine us to our homes for reasons any more casual or less compelling than the justifications it would be obliged to offer before it restrains our speech. For it would be hard to argue that our freedom to venture into public, to engage in a world—including a political world—outside the household would be any less "fundamental" than our right to speak.

But if there is no difference in the kinds of justifications we would demand in these cases, we would have to reach the sobering recognition that the Bill of Rights would make no difference in guiding our judgment: regardless of whether the freedom involved in any case was mentioned in the Bill of Rights, the questions we would have to pose, the tests we would have to apply, would be exactly the same. Those questions, or those tests, would not be furnished to us by anything written in the Bill of Rights. In both of the cases I have described here, we would ask whether people were inflicting a harm without justification, and whether the government would be justified in restraining these unwarranted acts.

In the case of the phone calls we have no problem in distinguishing between the caller who torments people for his own pleasure and the caller who phones in the middle of the night to convey news of a death in the family. In both cases speech becomes the cause of hurt, but we can distinguish between a hurt that is inflicted for the pleasure or benefit of the assailant and a hurt that is inflicted as a regrettable part of a decent and legitimate purpose. In the case of confining people to their houses it would make a difference if the government were acting for the public safety in a time of riot or insurrection, or if the government were alarmed at the prospect of the Republicans winning elections and was trying to keep people safely at home on election day.

Differences of this kind are not inscrutable. They form the ground of judgments we have to make very day, and they reflect the kinds of questions we would have to bring to these judgments in the law even if there were no First Amendment—and *even if there were no written Constitution.* These questions are simply built into the logic of legal and moral judgment, and so they were the questions that were brought to these cases before we had our current Constitution. The men who founded this republic and framed our second Constitution knew a world of law that antedated the Constitution. They had experience in reflecting on legal questions and reaching legal judgments before they would appeal to the Constitution and its Amendments. They understood then that they possessed sources of judgment outside the Constitution, which they often referred to simply as "the principles of law." And so, in one of the earliest cases before the Supreme Court, Justice Chase could point out that the wrongness of ex post facto laws had been understood long before the Constitution. That recognition was established as part of our understanding of law by the jurists and writers who had reflected most ably on "the true principles of government."[26]

In framing a Constitution, the Founders naturally drew upon these "true principles" of law and government, and some of them were taken as so evident and necessary that the seasoned jurist would almost be embarrassed to make them explicit. But when questions were raised, those principles could be explained by showing that they were indeed "necessary," that the law could not be conceived coherently without them, even if they had not been written down. As one notable example here, no maxim of the law has become more familiar than the notion that persons accused of crime must be presumed innocent until they are proven guilty. That aphorism comes readily to the lip of every schoolboy, so widely has it been absorbed in the public understanding. And yet, it is nowhere set down within the Bill of Rights or within the main text of the Constitution. What is our ground of surety then that this cardinal maxim will be preserved in our law? Could it be anything other than the conviction, rooted in the understandings of lawyers and citizens, that this maxim is bound up with the logic of constitutional government itself; that it would be incoherent for any government of law to arrange its trials on a radically different premise? To ask how confident we are that this maxim of the law will be preserved, even though it is not "guaranteed" by the Bill of Rights, is to ask how likely it is that our legislators could replace this maxim with a premise of this kind: that all people must be presumed guilty of virtually any crime until they carry the burden of establishing their innocence; that in the absence of clear proof of innocence, any person must stand in peril of legal punishment.

We know that in the judgment of the Founders the prohibition of ex post facto laws, or "retrospective" legislation, was another one of those principles which were necessary to any constitutional government. In Article I, Sections 9 and 10, the Constitution registered that understanding by barring ex post facto laws to the States as well as to the Federal government. In that respect John Marshall thought that the Constitution already "contain[ed] what may be deemed a bill of rights for the people of each state."[27] In his opinion for the Court in *Fletcher v. Peck* the Chief

---

26. Calder v. Bull, 3 U.S. 3 Dallas 386, at 391.
27. Fletcher v. Peck, 6 Cranch 87 (1810), at 138.

Justice went on to show that the protection offered in the same part of the Constitution against laws "impairing the Obligation of Contracts" flowed as a logical implication from the principle on ex post facto laws. Marshall explained that "an *ex post facto* law is one which renders an act punishable in a manner in which it was not punishable when it was committed." The punishment may be constituted by "penalties on the person" or it may inhere in "pecuniary penalties" or fines—which is to say, claims made on the property of an individual. To say that a legislature may not enact a measure of this kind is to say that a legislature is "prohibited from passing a law by which a man's estate, or any part of it, shall be seized for a crime which was not declared, by some previous law, to render him liable to that punishment." But Marshall then asked: what would be the distinction between that arrangement and one in which the legislature claims the power of "seizing, for public use, the estate of any individual in the form of a law annulling the title by which he holds that estate?" He saw, in fact, no distinction:

> This rescinding act [in Georgia, in *Fletcher v. Peck*] would have the effect of an *ex post facto* law. It forfeits the estate of [the buyer] for a crime not committed by himself, but by those from whom he purchased. This cannot be effected in the form of an *ex post facto* law, or bill of attainder; why, then, is it allowable in the form of a law annulling the original grant?[28]

I am not entirely clear that it was necessary for Marshall to flex his genius in this way in order to establish the nature of the wrong in "impairing the Obligations of Contracts." There were separate moral grounds on which he could have explained what was wrong in injuring people who had innocently staked their interests on the promise that a contract would be respected. But by casting his argument in this form Marshall was able to teach one or two uncommon lessons in the law. He managed to suggest, first, that the propositions we regard as principles of law bear logical connections to one another, that they could be extracted through deduction and the force of the syllogism. They could be extracted in that way because they found their origin in the same source: they could all be drawn ultimately from the logic of law itself or the character of a constitutional government. Judges who began with this understanding knew that they had access to standards of judgment quite apart from the provisions that were stipulated in the Constitution. Marshall then took care to note that the wrong of ex post facto laws was rooted

---

28. Fletcher v. Peck, pp. 138-39.

in "the general principles of our political institutions" as well as in "the words of the constitution."[29] The case in *Fletcher v. Peck* had arisen from the state of Georgia, and Marshall thought it important to make the point that the validity of the legislation would have been in serious doubt even if Georgia had been a "single sovereign power."[30] That is, even if Georgia had not been subject to the explicit restraints of the Constitution, the legislation would have been called into challenge by "the general principles" of a constitutional government. On this point Justice Johnson, in his concurring opinion, was even more emphatic: "I do not hesitate to declare that a state does not possess the power of revoking its own grants. But I do it on a general principle, on the reason and nature of things: a principle which will impose laws even on the Deity."[31]

When Marshall suggested that the first principles of law could be drawn deductively, he did not stamp himself as an eccentric among the jurists of his time. James Wilson had made the same point 17 years earlier, in the first substantial opinion produced by the Supreme Court.[32] In our own day, of course, this willingness to speak seriously of "first principles" and moral truths is bound to be regarded as quaint. And in a jurisprudence that has suffered the ravages of positivism and the philistinism of Critical Studies, the notion of extracting principles through the syllogism is likely to inspire a round of derisive mirth. But the curious concession that the new jurisprudence must make to the old is that it cannot reject as implausible the project of reasoning that Marshall inscribed in the law with such a large hand. The modern exponents of the Bill of Rights persistently resort to a style of argument that must move within that same cast: there is surely nothing in the First Amendment which marks off the burning of draft cards or the pitching of tents outside the White House as forms of "symbolic speech" that the Constitution was meant to protect. And yet those who would protect these acts of "expression" would have to imply that there is something contained in the character of the First Amendment which could be connected—not frivolously or arbitrarily, but plausibly and logically—to these odd instances which are nowhere specified in the First Amendment. The exercise in reasoning commanded by this enterprise could hardly be less extravagant than the project described by

---

29. Fletcher v. Peck, p. 139.
30. Fletcher v. Peck, p. 136.
31. Fletcher v. Peck, p. 143.
32. See *Chisholm v. Georgia*, 2 Dallas 419 (1793), at 453-54, 464-65. Compare, also, Hamilton in *The Federalist* #31, p. 188.

Marshall, the project that is widely regarded today as illusory by conservatives as well as liberals: that jurists may validly connect their legal judgments to the first principles of lawful government, and that they can draw those principles from postulates which are not entirely set down in the Constitution.

Men who were tutored in this discipline of jurisprudence had access to an understanding of law that was not rooted in the Constitution. For that reason even the advent of the Bill of Rights did not make a profound difference for the jurisprudence of the founding generation. The Bill of Rights did not cause John Marshall to alter his understanding of the principles of law or the ends of republican government. Instead, Marshall read the Bill of Rights in the light of his understanding of the principles of law or "the general principles of our political institutions." In that perspective he could address questions of speech, or the restriction of any other kind of freedom, with a mind that had not been distracted yet by the cliches that would grow out of the Bill of Rights. And so Marshall could proclaim, without a hint of apology, that anyone who writes or publishes a libel in this country "may be both sued and indicted"[33] —he may be subject to the judgment of the law in both civil and criminal actions. Marshall evidently understood that speech could be an instrument of wrongdoing quite as much as any other medium by which human beings were able to carry through their acts. Speech could be used to assault and terrorize—it could be used, in other words, to inflict harms without justification—and when it was, the law could judge and restrain these assaults carried out through speech, as it could judge any other species of assault.

Marshall and the jurists of his generation were quite far then from the disposition found in our own day to confuse "speech" with a "principle": they knew that speech could not be *categorically* innocent and good, and therefore, they could not regard speech as categorically more important or more deserving of protection than any other uses of personal freedom. One man could engage honestly in the legitimate trade of a tailor; another man could use his speech viciously, for illegitimate ends. For jurists such as Marshall it was hard to see why the freedom to engage in a legitimate calling did not deserve the same concern and security as the freedom to engage in acts of speech. And here, one might say, was the

---

33. Marshall, "Address on the Constitutionality of the Alien and Sedition Acts," in *The Political Thought of American Statesmen*, ed. Morton Frisch and Richard Stevens (Itasca: Peacock Publishers, 1973), p. 113.

obverse side of the skepticism borne by the Federalists toward the Bill of Rights. They did not regard speech as sacrosanct, but neither did they think there was anything trivial about other uses of our personal freedom that placed them beneath the concerns of the law. They were not persuaded that the freedoms mentioned in the Bill of Rights stood on a higher plane than others, but neither were they willing to narrow the protections of the Constitution to the freedoms that could be set down in a Bill of Rights. In his tart comments on the Bill of Rights, Theodore Sedgwick suggested that we have a claim to all aspects of our freedom— not merely to our freedom to speak and assemble—so long as our freedom is not being used to inflict harms without justification. As a literature would come to accumulate over the First Amendment, it would become common for scholars to insist that the Amendment meant to protect mainly *political* speech and discussion, not tawdry displays in the street, and not merely the crass speech by which vendors seek to hawk their wares in public. It was not until the 1970's that the Supreme Court came to the recognition that a public interest could be served by certain kinds of commercial advertising on the part of pharmacists and lawyers. With that step the judges came to the threshold of recognizing that if people are engaged in a legitimate calling they should have a presumptive right to use any decent speech which becomes necessary or useful to their practice of a lawful business. And yet why should that have come as such a momentous surprise? That understanding was contained in Theodore Sedgwick's rejoinder to his colleagues on the Bill of Rights: why should there be any ground for doubting that, in a constitutional order, in a regime of liberty, we have a right to speak, just as we have a right to any other form of our personal freedom, so long as that freedom is not used for a wrongful end? And if the speech used to promote a legitimate business is not used maliciously to injure without warrant, this speech should be no more open to restriction than any other innocent act.

To pick out certain uses of freedom, such as speech and assembly, for a special mention in the Constitution runs the risk then of disparaging by implication the freedoms that have not been mentioned. That was the warning posted by the Federalists, and we would be obliged to consider seriously whether their fears have not in fact been borne out: has there not been cultivated within us a sense that the rights mentioned in the Bill of Rights are more fundamental than others? Are we not more inclined to notice the violation of those "rights," and at the same time, have we not blocked from our view whole classes of rights—and whole classes of victims—which have not been mentioned in the Bill of Rights, but which may be quite as deserving of our concern? The Bill of Rights says nothing, for example, of the right to practice a legitimate calling. In many states people who have been trained as physicians, lawyers, or optometrists, and whose competence can be certified, are nevertheless barred from their professions by barriers of "licensing." The aim of these procedures is to restrict the number of professionals for the sake merely of propping up the income of the people who are already in the field. There is in nature no "principle" that establishes the correct price for a pair of pants; nor is there a principle that can establish the right or "just" income for lawyers and optometrists. No guesses, then, about the level of incomes for lawyers and optometrists could possibly establish a justification for barring people from the practice of a legitimate profession in which they have been properly trained. To an earlier generation of jurists, these arrangements in licensing would have been recognized as a patently arbitrary use of the law in restricting personal freedom.[34]

The right to practice a legitimate business cannot be reckoned as any less fundamental than the right to speak, and yet it is not a right which seems to excite the concern of our jurists or civil libertarians (unless the business in question happens to be an abortion clinic). When John Marshall stated the logic of an ex post facto law, that logic was not confined to laws which carried a *criminal* penalty. His understanding could encompass laws which acted retrospectively in imposing penalties on people in the form of heavy fines or ruinous confiscations of their property. In this respect Marshall's understanding was shared by Madison, Oliver Ellsworth, Roger Sherman, and others among the Founders, who thought that the logic of ex post facto laws extended to the field of commercial relations.[35] From this perspective, the concern for ex post facto laws could very plausibly embrace the kinds of penalties and confiscations that come along with wage and price controls. But the civil libertarians of our own day have not been much excited by the serious restrictions of freedom—even the effective denial of the right to earn a living—which may be imposed through controls on wages and prices. The civil libertarians will quickly concede that they are less interested in these "regulations of the economy" than in the protection of what they call "fundamental free-

---

34. There could be no clearer statement on this point than Justice Field's dissenting opinion in the Slaughter-House cases, 16 Wall. 36 (1873), 83-111. See also Bernard Siegan, *Economic Liberties and the Constitution* (Chicago: University of Chicago Press, 1980), ch. 5.

35. See, on this point, Siegan, p. 76 and *passim*.

doms." But in that admission they confirm one of the main points in the argument of the Federalists: the celebrants of the Bill of Rights would actually protect a range of rights far narrower than the rights that the Founders thought they were protecting under the Constitution.

What I am suggesting is that this floundering, this difficulty in identifying the rights engaged here, is not an accident. We encounter this problem because there has been a masking of the jural landscape: certain kinds of rights have been made indistinct to us or placed outside our vision, and this masking effect has something to do with the way in which our jural vision has been formed by the Bill of Rights. In spite of the Ninth Amendment, the rights mentioned in the Bill of Rights have in fact made a stronger impression on our legal sensibilities, and they have commanded a larger measure of our concern, than the rights that were not named in the first eight Amendments.

If this argument may still seem a bit speculative, we need only consider whether we do not have, every day, fresh evidence of the casualties produced by the legal perspective I have described here. If anyone would ask just where this understanding has made a practical difference in our law and in the lives of our people, we could hardly offer an example more dramatic than the judicial reasoning of Mr. Justice Blackmun in *Roe v. Wade*.[36] As Blackmun understood the problem of that case, the question was not: on what grounds would we be justified in regarding the human fetus as less than a human being; and on what grounds would we be justified in removing the protections of law from children before they were born? The problem was not set forth in this way, in a manner that would focus on the substantive moral justification for the taking of fetal life. Mr. Justice Blackmun argued, rather, in this way: that the Constitution protects the lives of "persons," but it is nowhere specified in the Constitution that the term "persons" refers to people before they were born.[37]

Blackmun noticed that whenever the Constitution referred to "persons" it was to persons who were engaged in activities such as voting or migrating or escaping or being extradited—activities that were possible only for people outside the womb. From those clues he concluded that "persons" did not refer to people before they were born and mobile. By the same reasoning, of course, "persons" would probably not refer to people who were crippled or retarded, confined to their beds or wheelchairs. And indeed it turns out that these inferences are not being made

---

36. 410 U.S. 113 (1973).
37. See Blackmun in 410 U.S. 113 (1973), p. 157.

about people who are retarded. These handicapped people are now being drawn into that class of beings who are thought to lack what Mr. Justice Blackmun refers to as "meaningful life." Their diminished intellect is taken as a justification for abortion in unborn children and for the withdrawal of feeding and medical care from children who are newly born. Before the passage in 1984 of the legislation on Baby Doe, the burden in the courts was placed on those who would treat retarded infants as "persons" within the protection of the law. And even now, after the passage of legislation, the courts may still resist these efforts to invade the "privacy" of parents for the sake of protecting infants who are retarded. For these children, inside or outside the womb, the Constitution has not been the source of a legal discipline which requires lawyers and parents to justify the destruction of their lives. Instead, the Constitution has been the container of a formula which allows these people to be removed from the protections of the law if they are not explicitly listed among the "persons" that the Constitution would seek to protect.

It is arguable then that the warnings raised by the Federalists were not rendered "academic" by the passage of the Ninth Amendment. But rather, that Amendment was overborne by the logic which was embedded in the Bill of Rights. Our absorption of that logic may be seen today in the language that now reflects the staples of our thought on these matters. Is it not common to hear people speak of that "freedom of speech we possess *through* the First Amendment"? And do we not hear even lawyers speak of our "First Amendment rights"? The sense in both cases is that these rights flow to us distinctly through the First Amendment: the necessary implication is that in the absence of the First Amendment we should not have these rights. There is in this outlook both a libel on the Founders and the most curious understanding of the Constitution they produced. If the Constitution was not made, as James Wilson said, for the purpose of securing and enlarging our natural rights—*all* of our natural rights—for what purpose was it made? Is it really conceivable that the Constitution framed so carefully by the Founders did not encompass the recognition that citizens had the right to speak and assemble and to be free from unreasonable searches? Were these rights never imagined until they were tacked on, as an afterthought, in Amendments to the Constitution?[38]

These kinds of assumptions must be regarded as part of the deep misunderstanding fostered by the Bill of Rights, and the fruits of this miseducation may be visible to us today, even in domains that seem to be removed from constitutional law. Several years ago there was a public "Appeal to the Government of Vietnam," signed by Staughton Lynd, Joan Baez, Aryeh Neier, and many others who had been active in the antiwar movement. These people were repelled by the evidence of "systematic violations of human rights" in Vietnam—most notably, the holding of prisoners without charges or trials because of their political or religious convictions. The signers of the Appeal were apparently surprised to discover that the Communist regime in Vietnam had no commitment to the notion of habeas corpus, or to any of the other more refined conventions that arise for defendants and prisoners in a regime of law. What was strange about the "Appeal" was that the signers seemed to expect the refinements that emerged from a constitutional government, but without the underlying structures from which those refinements emanate. There were in Vietnam no free elections and no independent courts of law in which the government could lose cases. In short, there was in Vietnam no government restrained by law. Why then, should the signers of the Appeal ever have supposed that a Communist regime would respect these rights which grew distinctly out of a government of laws?

The answer, apparently, is that they had been given assurances on these

---

38. In fairness, Herbert Storing reminded us that the decision to attach the Bill of Rights as an appendage to the Constitution was made at the behest of Roger Sherman, who bore no enthusiasm for making these additions in the first place. The partisans of a Bill of Rights preferred to have the rights declared, as principles, in the preamble of the Constitution. There these maxims could take the position of founding principles, from which the character and powers of the government could be drawn. But Federalists such as George Clymer preferred to keep the amendments distinct from the body of the Constitution so that "the world would discover the perfection of the original and the superfluity of the amendments." Storing apparently thought that this change was more compatible with the ends of the Antifederalists than their own design would have been: the Bill of Rights was converted from a grand statement of natural rights into the operative principles of a constituted government. As I have suggested, we may properly doubt that this distinction made any substantive difference for the judging of rights in the law. But Storing would help make the accounts clearer: to the extent that the confusions of the Bill of Rights have emanated from this decision, to place the protection of natural rights as an appendix to the Constitution, the responsibility for this miseducation must lie with some of the Federalists themselves. See Storing, pp. 31-34.

points by Communist leaders during the war. That they were gullible is quite clear, but their gullibility cannot be attributed merely to personal sources. It is worth considering, after all, just why these children of America thought it was possible to speak of human rights in the abstract, detached from the legal institutions which reflect the moral premises behind those rights, and which furnish in turn the most favorable structure in which those rights can be secured. Is it not at least politically interesting that the signers of the Appeal did not understand "human rights" in the way those rights were understood by the men who drafted and signed the Declaration of Independence: they did not understand that, as soon as we begin speaking of rights natural to human beings, the most fundamental of those rights were the rights of human beings to be ruled only by their consent, in a government of free elections, a government restrained by law. But to point these things out is virtually to restate Hamilton's argument about the understandings that had to be passed by in the "injudicious zeal for bills of rights." Staughton Lynd and his friends failed to understand that the most fundamental human rights were already reflected in the very structure of a constitutional government—that "the Constitution," as Hamilton said, "is itself, in every rational sense, and to every useful purpose, A BILL OF RIGHTS."[39]

Anyone who contemplates the mind and sensibility reflected in the opinion of the Supreme Court in *Roe v. Wade*, anyone who measures the understanding contained in the "Appeal to the Government of Vietnam," may grasp the dangers that the Federalists saw in a Bill of Rights. It might be said that the concerns of the Federalists at their deepest level were with the lessons that would be taught, with the kind of legal sensibility that would be cultivated, by the Bill of Rights. The teaching of the Bill of Rights threatened to affect the citizens of this republic with a brittle, almost childish literalism; it would misinstruct them about the grounds of their rights and the breadth of those freedoms which were protected under the Constitution. It would produce in later generations lawyers, judges, and statesmen who no longer knew how to deliberate about questions of justice. These men and women of the law would lose the aptitude for deliberation because they would have forgotten the main questions of jurisprudence, and they would no longer know the difference between a principle and the circumstances in which a principle may be manifested. And so, two hundred years later we find judges confronting a private college that rejects, in its code, dating and marriage across racial lines.

---

39. *The Federalist* #84, pp. 560-61.

The judges deny a tax exemption to this school; but they still cannot come to a judgment on whether racial discrimination is *wrong in itself*—wrong in principle, regardless of whether it takes place in the choice of housing or sexual partners—and whether this discrimination in the domain of sex is quite as wrong when proclaimed by the Bob Jones University or by the "personal ads" in the *New York Review of Books*—whether the wrong of this discrimination is to be found only in some material harm that is inflicted on black people *in schools*. Judges who suffer these confusions will of course find it hard to establish the principled ground for their judgments, since they are not entirely sure that they can recognize a principle when they see it. The life of the law for them will be found in the memorizing of slogans and formulas, and since they know no ground of judgment outside these formulas, they can only convert the task of judging into a game of making ingenious connections between new cases and old descriptions. (Are movies "speech"? Are infants in the womb "persons"?)

Whatever can be said about lawyers of this type, it must be said that they will have become notably different in the cast of their minds from the men who created this political order. Ironically, we know it was the aspiration of the Founders to make themselves as a class dispensable. They sought to fashion a government that would not depend on having at its head at all times statesmen who were philosophers, or men like themselves who could reason about first principles. They hoped to create a system of institutions which could survive even bad times and venal men. But through the agony of our Civil War—and through the example of Lincoln —we came to learn a different lesson: that the polity may be corrupted to the point of dissolution if statesmen and their constituents are not schooled to understand the principles on which their constitutional freedom is ultimately founded. When Stephen Douglas said that he did not "care" whether slavery was voted up or down, when Senator Pettit of Indiana declared that the proposition "all men are created equal" was not a self-evident truth, but a "self-evident lie," it was clear that a large portion of the political class no longer understood the premises on which their own free government was founded. Those men could not be relied on to preserve republican government for the next generation.

What Lincoln represented was the reappearance of a man of the same stature as the Founders, a man who was able to preserve this political order because he could do—and do even better—what the Founders sought to do, and that was to trace his judgments back to the first principles of lawful government. Sober men may have to acknowledge that the legal culture fostered by the Bill of Rights is more likely to produce a Mr.

Justice Blackmun, or the typical lawyers of the American Civil Liberties Union, and that it is less likely to produce lawyers like Abraham Lincoln and John Marshall. Of course, no man of prudence would urge us to repeal the Bill of Rights, but we might seek to free ourselves from the constricted vision of the Bill of Rights by restoring to our jurisprudence the understanding of our first generation of jurists. And yet it must be admitted that this task of restoration has been made far more difficult with a legal profession that has been shaped, in its sensibilities, by the formulas of the Bill of Rights. The most damning thing that might be said then, finally, about the Bill of Rights is that it has been part of a curriculum of civic education in this country which has made it far less likely that we will bring to positions of authority people with the same furnishings of mind—with the same capacity to trace their judgments back to first principles—as the men who founded this republic.

Misapprehensions and the First Amendment

George Anastaplo

During the contest of opinion through which we have passed, the animation of discussions and of exertions has sometimes worn an aspect which might impose on strangers unused to think freely and to speak and to write what they think. But this being now decided by the voice of the nation, announced according to the rules of the Constitution, all will of course arrange themselves under the will of the law and unite in common efforts for the common good. All, too, will bear in mind *this sacred principle that, through the will of the majority is in all cases to prevail, that will, to be rightful, must be reasonable:* that the minority possess their equal rights, which equal law must protect and to violate which would be oppression. Let us then, fellow citizens, unite with one heart and one mind. Let us restore to social intercourse that harmony and affection without which liberty and even life itself are but dreary things. And let us reflect that, having banished from our land that religious intolerance under which mankind so long bled and suffered, we have yet gained little if we countenance a political intolerance as despotic, as wicked, and capable of as bitter and bloody persecution . . . .

> —Thomas Jefferson, First
> Inaugural Address (1801)
> (emphasis added)

I

The First Amendment labors these days under various misapprehensions, and this contributes to problems for those who would regard and use it properly. Some of these misapprehensions contradict others, depending on whether the critic of the First Amendment is "conservative" or "liberal" in his orientation.

There is probably some basis for each of the misapprehensions relevant here: they are not simply irrational. This can be reassuring in that it points to why freedom of speech is good for us. I will be using "freedom of speech" to refer to what the First Amendment calls "freedom of speech, or of the press." I will do little more than touch upon the Religion Clauses of the First Amendment on this occasion, although they too are illuminated by some of my analysis.[1]

The question posed for this chapter indicates various more or less conservative reservations about the First Amendment today. Before considering these reservations in some detail, we should also notice the liberal reservations about the First Amendment today. I trust that it becomes evident from my discussion here that some of these complaints, whether labelled "liberal" or "conservative," may not really be against the First Amendment but rather against certain interpretations of it.

We begin then with a catalogue of the misapprehensions about the First Amendment, or about the nature of community and of moral training, upon which the complaints of liberals depend:

1. It is assumed by some liberals that wealth is needed in order to get oneself heard, that only the monied interests are able to take advantage of the First Amendment. (This assumption is reflected in the problem of "access," including debates as to whether government should subsidize dissent. It is reflected as well in legislation controlling campaign contributions and expenditures.)

2. It is assumed that there is considerable censorship, or repression, all around us, much of it informal but nevertheless effective. This repression is seen both as direct (as manifested in concerns about public school textbooks) and as indirect (as manifested in concerns about resources needed for effective communication).

3. It is assumed that "freedom of expression" is necessary for the full flowering of the "individual." (This assumption is intimately related, as may be others, to one of the conservative complaints about how freedom of speech impedes the efforts of a community to provide a proper moral training for citizens.)

4. Indeed, it is assumed that the community has no right to pass judgment upon a people's morals or state of character, but only upon

---

1. It suffices to say here that the Religion Clauses pronouncements by the courts have been unpersuasive. That is, they are very much in need of serious discussion. See George Anastaplo, "The Religion Clauses of the First Amendment," 11 *Memphis State University Law Review* 151 (1981).

See, generally, on the Speech and Press Clause of the First Amendment, my article on Censorship in the *Encyclopaedia Britannica* and my book, *The Constitutionalist: Notes on the First Amendment* (Dallas: Southern Methodist University Press, 1971). See, also, Anastaplo, "William H. Renquist and the First Amendment," *Intercollegiate Review*, Spring 1987, p. 31 (based on a Bicentennial Program talk given at the University of Dallas, Nov. 23, 1986).

actions that clearly (that is, physically?) hurt others. This position is taken partly because moral judgments are considered to be subjective and relative. And so, it is insisted, we should not be "judgmental."

5. It is assumed that such forms of expression as pornography and obscenity cannot hurt people, or at least that they cannot be *shown* to hurt people. It may even be good for us to remove crippling inhibitions, thereby permitting the full human flowering which is yearned for. In fact, it is believed to be difficult to show that anything *said* can hurt, or that it is any government's business to be concerned about such things.

6. It is assumed, furthermore, that the less government there is, the better, at least with respect to matters having to do with morality. (Conservatives tend to call for more government here.) And so limited government is called for, whatever may be said about the need for government intervention with respect to welfare and with respect to racial discrimination. (Conservatives tend to call for quite limited government *here*.)

7. It is assumed by some liberals that there is a natural goodness to mankind independent of anything government or society need do—and that men ought to be allowed to choose what they wish.[2]

I will return, if only briefly, to these liberal concerns.[3] But, first, we must deal with the concerns of conservatives.

II

As I have indicated, the question posed for this chapter reflects characteristically conservative concerns. It begins with the observation that "republican government poses the problem of how to reconcile majority rule with minority rights," and then describes the topic for our discussion in these terms:

In creating a limited government based upon majority rule, the

---

2. There is something Rousseauistic about this assumption, and perhaps about one or more of the other liberal assumptions as well.

3. I have dealt with these liberal concerns at considerable length in several publications: See, for example, "Psychiatry and the Law: An Old-Fashioned Approach," in Lawrence Z. Freedman, *By Reason of Insanity: Essays on Psychiatry and the Law* (Wilmington, Delaware: Scholarly Resources, Inc., 1983); a review of Franklyn S. Haiman's *Speech and Law in a Free Society*, in *The Windsor Yearbook of Access to Justice*, vol. 3 (1983); "Pornography and the Scope of the First Amendment," *Women's Law Reporter*, Summer 1985 (Loyola University School of Law); "Obscenity and Common Sense," in Anastaplo, *Human Being and Citizen: Essays on Virtue, Freedom and the Common Good* (Chicago: Swallow Press, 1975).

founders faced the problem of whether such a government was compatible with that freedom of conscience, thought, and speech which permits the highest human endeavors. In order to secure such freedom, does constitutional government require also the freedom to do what may be base or despicable?

Various misapprehensions of the constitutional situation are evident here, misapprehensions (or partial truths) which are generally held among conservatives and of which this provides but a specimen. These misapprehensions can be conveniently catalogued in this fashion (recognizing as we do so that, just as in the case of the liberal misappprehensions, there is here, too, considerable overlapping):

1. It is assumed by some conservatives that a limited government was established by the Constitution. (Although conservatives do not consider this altogether bad, they do tend to regard it as dubious, at least with respect to several critical functions of government.)

2. It is assumed that if the majority is not kept from having its way, there will be effective government (or at least as effective a government as its limited powers permit).

3. It is assumed that freedom of speech is designed for, or at least has the effect of, crippling government.

4. Therefore, it is assumed that government, to be effective, must restrict discussion of public policies. That is, it is because of the unrestricted talk protected by the First Amendment that government is kept from being effective.

5. It is assumed that the First Amendment licenses one to *do* various base things.

6. It is assumed that the First Amendment also licenses one to *say* virtually all that one is moved to say, including the most base things. (Included among the improper things which are licensed by the First Amendment may be radically irresponsible talk, if not even treason.)

7. It is assumed by some conservatives that the rights guaranteed by the First Amendment are "minority rights," the exercise of which has to be reconciled with "majority rule." The most conspicuous, and questionable, minority is made up of those who want to say base things and to do (or permit the doing of) terrible things.

III

In some ways the difficulty here is that conservatives have all too often accepted some of the liberals' errors and have reacted against them as authoritative accounts of what the First Amendment is and does.

The first three of these conservative assumptions are the easiest to deal with. I touch upon each in turn here:

The government of the United States has great powers, virtually unlimited (although not exclusive) powers with respect to the matters assigned it—which include the vital matters of the commerce (that is, the economy) of the country, the defense of the country, and the relations of this country with other countries.

The exercise of these powers will not lead to effective government by their mere uninhibited exercise. If they are not exercised sensibly, they are likely to be anything but effective. I trust this is obvious enough—when one stops to think about it.

Does, then, freedom of speech cripple government? Or does it rather empower it? That is, does it not represent and reinforce the considerable power of the government of the United States, especially if that government is not considered a thing apart from the community at large?

IV

We will return to these considerations, but first we should touch upon the final three items in our catalogue of conservative misapprehensions related to the First Amendment.

These three assumptions are the hardest to deal with—hardest to deal with because of some silly things which have been said over the years by courts (and by others). Each of these assumptions, too, I touch upon in turn here:

Contrary to what some have said, the First Amendment does not license anyone to "do" anything but speak. No other kind of doing is provided for, no actions or conduct, not even what is often called "symbolic speech." No doubt, one may very much want to "say" things by *doing* certain things, but that does not warrant First Amendment protection, however justifiable if not even laudatory it may be on other grounds. Certainly, one cannot *do* with immunity various of the things one may be able to talk about with immunity.

Nor does the First Amendment license anyone to say anything, or virtually anything, he pleases, including the most base things. In fact, strictly speaking, it does not apply to art, obscenity, advertising, or commercial speech generally. Rather, the First Amendment is primarily for the protection of full public discussion of political issues—of the matters the community must discuss if it is to be able to govern itself. (Thus, the First Amendment is not concerned with "freedom of expression," as many seem to think. The looseness with which the First Amendment can be spoken of may even be seen in the reference in the topic of this chapter to "freedom of conscience, thought, and speech.") All this is to suggest that the primary purpose of the freedom of speech provision in the First Amendment has been lost sight of, leading to tensions within the constitutional system. [4]

When the primary political-discussion purpose of the First Amendment is recognized, it becomes evident why it is not sound to assume that the rights guaranteed by the First Amendment are "minority rights," the exercise of which has to be reconciled with "majority rule." These are not rights of the minority primarily, nor for that matter of the majority—but rather they are the rights (that is, the power) of the community as a whole, as it tries to assess what the community needs and what the government is doing.

Sometimes one person invokes that right, sometimes a minority, and sometimes (most of the time) everyone. Indeed, freedom of speech may be one of the few privileges in the Bill of Rights which is exercised "all the time" by the community. Relatively few of us ever have to draw upon most of the other privileges enumerated in the Bill of Rights, such as those privileges related to "cruel and unusual punishments," to "excessive bail," to "trial by jury," to a "speedy and public trial," and to the quartering of soldiers.

V

An appreciation of the proper purpose of the First Amendment helps us deal sensibly with the central item in our catalogue of conservative misapprehensions about the First Amendment, the assumption that the government, if it is to be effective, must occasionally restrain the discussion of public policies.

---

4. See Appendix II, "On What the First Amendment Does and Does Not Do." See, also, Anastaplo, "Notes toward an 'Apologia pro vita sua,'" *Interpretation*, vol 10, p. 319 (1982), at pp. 344-345; Anastaplo, "How to Read the Constitution of the United States," 17 *Loyola University of Chicago Law Journal* 1, 37-49 (1985).

It should be evident to the reader that "speaking" includes "printing" (or the press) in this paper.

This usually comes down to the majority curbing the speech of some minority. (In a few cases it can require the curbing of all public speech. We are not concerned, however, with the rare emergency, for which there are adequate constitutionally-provided responses.)

No doubt, it is tempting to shut off complaints and disagreements. But dare we risk as a routine response anything which keeps us from a full public consideration of the issues we consider relevant in our capacity as a sovereign people?

Full discussion of public issues is no panacea: it can still lead to mistaken judgments and harmful decisions. But how can it be safer to rely upon opinions that have not been exposed to thorough public discussion and to all arguments—that is, to a scope of examination and discussion *not* determined by officials who prefer to see their positions maintained? Is not that even more dangerous than occasional irresponsible criticism? To permit interested parties (in government or out) to curb public discussion is to make ourselves even more subject to chance than a democratic (or any but the very best?) regime may naturally be?

Certainly, people can more easily be led to see why they should run risks in permitting uninhibited political discussion than they can be led to see why they should permit public indulgence in base things.

The majority (or, rather, the community) itself cannot exist—cannot be a self-conscious public body—without genuine freedom of speech. Without full discussion, and an uninhibited consideration of all possibilities, the community cannot know its mind, cannot know what it truly wants or what it should do. That is, the majority does not know what it wants or needs or *is* until there has been enough freedom of speech to clarify the issues and to illuminate the alternatives that bear upon the common good. Thus, rather than crippling majority action and effective government, freedom of speech permits them to be truly what they should be.

Some may say, however, that the community can sufficiently *be* and *act* through its government. But who should make up that government and with what mandate? Eventually, governmental power and legitimacy, at least among us, must be rooted in a people who know what they are doing. Otherwise, that which is done in selecting and maintaining a government tends to be a matter of chance. Thus, the First Amendment is not primarily to protect personal desire but to permit the community to function as a community under a republican form of government. Even so, there is no question but that the majority can have its way in regulating men's conduct. The First Amendment does not stop that, however much it may permit inquiries into and questions about what has been done and by whom. Consider, for example, how vigorously and for how many years, conservatives were able to denounce as disastrous the deficit financing permitted by liberal administrations in Washington. It would have been unthinkable, of course, to try to curb officially such denunciations by that temporary "minority," and to do so in the name of what some temporary "majority" considered to be effective government programs dedicated to the general welfare and to the common defense.

If, then, the people *is* to be sovereign, how can it know what is and should be done, and what is right or wrong about what has already been done, but through virtually unlimited (that is, "absolute") freedom of speech with respect to the matters that it, as a people, must deal with? And how can the people be properly confident that it is still on the right course if it does not know that those who believe themselves to know better are still free to come forward to challenge what has been said, believed, or done by the majority of the day? Thus, only with a generally recognized freedom of speech can the people reasonably believe that it has done all *it* can do in order to be informed; only thus can it come as close as a people may come to knowing that it does know.

It should be emphasized that actions are not prevented by such freedom of speech, however much they are subject to examination. Pornography, for example, can be suppressed, but not the right to discuss whether it should be (or whether it should continue to be) suppressed. We do not want ourselves to be "locked into" error, whether in the form of a foolish war or of a foolish economic program or of foolish prohibitions of one kind or another.

I have long been struck by how things sort themselves out when people can keep talking. I am again and again reminded, as I watch Americans deliberate, how many resources there are available in any group, how many diverse and useful things they somehow share which can be put to good use. And this may be so even though there may be no one in the group who is truly thoughtful.[5] I suspect that things tend to sort themselves out even with respect to such "technical" matters as bear upon the proper selection and use of military equipment. The people, if properly

---

5. Thus, William T. Braithwaite (a colleague at the Loyola University of Chicago School of Law) reports that it is said by experienced trial lawyers that one can expect everything testified to by the various witnesses in the course of a trial to be remembered by someone on the jury. That is, some will remember this, others will remember that, and still others will remember something else—all of which can be drawn upon in the course of jury deliberations. (I suspect, however, that some things may be "remembered" as well which were not testified to.)

counselled, can make as responsible a judgment as "the government" is likely to make in determining which of the proffered expert opinions makes most sense in the circumstances. [6]

All this may be still another way of saying that the Legislative Branch (for which freedom of speech is vital) is, and should be, superior to the Executive Branch (for which resolute action may be critical).

VI

Freedom of speech is particularly important in modern nation-states: the larger they are, the more apt they are to be moved by *forces* rather than by arguments (or reason).

A recognition of this is reflected in comments made by Winston Churchill, at the end of the First World War, to a group of visiting American journalists. He began by noticing the exaggerated sense of self-importance that journalists often have: "The Press has played an extraordinary part in the war, at the outset rigorously excluded from even a public show of the military operations, but afterwards taking charge of the whole front."[7] But he at once added these observations:

> It is not possible to fight a great war like this except with a highly-intelligent democracy, and it is not possible to act upon the consciousness of a highly-intelligent democracy, except through the agency of a gigantic and innumerable Press. We have owed to the Press of this country a good many harsh criticisms and a good many rough turns, but in the main it has been the great vehicle which has expressed the national will. [8]

Thus, this great "conservative" recognized that it was only through the workings of a free press that "the national will" could be properly developed and made known.

We all have enough examples of inadequate discussion, and with it an inadequately formed national will, which affected the proper conduct of a

---

6. After all, goverment personnel can be much more hampered than the people at large are apt to be by self-interest, if only the self-interest of having one's career or reputation "invested" in a particular weapons system.

7. H. M. Swetland, *American Journalists in Europe* (New York: United Publishers Corporation, 1949), p. 23. See, also, Anastaplo, "Legal Realism, the New Journalism, and *The Brethren*," 1983 *Duke Law Journal* 1045 (1983). See, on Winston Churchill and freedom of speech, Anastaplo, "Freedom of Speech and the Silence of the Law," 64 *Texas Law Review* 443 (1985).

8. Swetland, *American Journalists in Europe*, p. 23.

major national effort both at home and abroad. That deeply-flawed undertaking known as the First World War led, in reaction, to a thought-less pacificism and thus to an inability to arm properly thereafter. (In the First World War, massive sacrifices had continued to be called for long after the ultimate purpose of the war had been lost sight of.) Similar assessments can be made of our Indochinese efforts in recent decades, efforts which our government concealed from full view (that is, did not discuss properly) until things got so bad that the eventual national discussion led to disengagement. This has given freedom of speech a bad name among those who yearned for a decisive military victory, even though their recriminations should perhaps be directed at those who tried to secure such victory without properly informing the American people of what was intended and what it would require.

Thus, the more dreadful consequences are likely to follow, among us, from too little (or too late) discussion rather than from too much discussion.[9]

All this bears on the problems of the Soviet Union today. Without effective public discussion, the Soviet government and the Russian people cannot learn and cannot reliably know how things truly are. (It is this kind of inability which seems to have contributed to the crisis the past decade in Poland.)

Related to this is the recent complaint by our President that he has not been able to get "equal time" in the Soviet Union's mass media. One must wonder who is most deprived here? Is it not the Soviet government as well as the Russian people? On the other hand, is it not good for us to hear what the Russians have to say and to subject their leaders, as much as we can, to questions from our press, and this without regard to whether there

---

9. See Appendix I, "On the Need for a Public Records Access Act in Illinois." This is a statement prepared by me for use before the House Judiciary Committee, House of Representatives, General Assembly, State of Illinois, Springfield, Illinois, April 30, 1975. (The Committee chairman was Harold Washington, then a Representative from Chicago.) I had helped draft a proposed "Public Records Access Act" as Research Director and Advisor to the Governor's Commission on Individual Liberty and Personal Privacy, State of Illinois (1974-1976). The House Judiciary Committee voted for this bill, but not the House of Representatives. Later, however, our bill was used by the Washington administration in Chicago in preparing an executive order with respect to public access to city records.

See Anastaplo, "The Occasions of Freedom of Speech," *Political Science Reviewer*, vol. 5, p. 383 (1975), esp. 398-401. See, as well, Anastaplo, "Preliminary Reflections on the Pentagon Papers," *University of Chicago Magazine*, January-February, March-April 1972 (reprinted in the July 24, 1972, issue of *The Congressional Record*, vol. 118, p. 24990).

is reciprocity in the Soviet press? Compounding the difficulty for the Soviet Union is the crippled state there of Due Process, which makes it difficult for the Russians to be able to rely upon one another and the system, something which is essential if there is to be an efficient use of economic resources in the modern world. All this tends to make the Soviet Union weaker, over the long run, than conservatives are inclined to believe. On the other hand, Russian reform with respect to these matters would generally make them seem less threatening as adversaries.

In any event, our relaxed confidence in *our* institutions does help, including confidence as to what the First Amendment is for and what it does and does not do. Such confidence is no doubt generated and sustained by our considerable success in governing ourselves for some two centuries now. Since we know what we can do, we need not become desperate.

VII

No doubt, there are abuses of the First Amendment, abuses both by the people exploiting freedom of speech and by the government regulating it. Perhaps the most effective protection against such abuses is the informed criticisms of citizens, citizens who are protected in "blowing the whistle."

Besides, it should be recognized that no matter what system is established or what arrangement is made respecting freedom of speech, there will be abuses, or at least prospects of abuses. Is not that of the very nature of political things? Certainly, there can be no guarantee against mistakes either in using or in suppressing freedom of speech.

Thus, it is difficult to know what to do about the inevitable abuses of that discussion of public affairs which is at the heart of the First Amendment. What else can we do (except in the most extreme emergency, when various constitutional processes have to be temporarily suspended)— what can we do but point out and try to deal politically with those who abuse their (and our) privileges? Thus, we depend here upon the good sense, as well as upon the fairness (and the sense of enlightened self-interest), of the American people.

Still, it should be noticed that the worst abuses of freedom of speech among us in the Twentieth Century have not been by people who have been indicted from time to time but rather have been by those who are, for practical purposes, immune from chastisement (at least until the next election).

156

George Anastaplo

VIII

Something more should be said about the widespread assumption that the Constitution provides for "limited government." The basis that this assumption does have may be found in the significant place left in our constitutional system for the States. But the General Government under the Constitution of 1787 was delegated virtually unlimited powers with respect to several matters, with its extensive Commerce Power providing a broad foundation for its domestic authority.[10]

Also assumed from the beginning was a nationwide freedom of speech: it is evident in the Constitution of 1787—and this the First Amendment may have done little more than confirm—it is evident from the outset that the people have an inalienable right to assess public policies, choose and dismiss officers of government, and even pass upon the Constitution itself. The Declaration of Independence makes this clear enough.

Americans to this day sense that political discussion unhampered by government sanctions is necessary for "the system" to work. This is reflected in how the depredations of Senator Joseph McCarthy are routinely regarded these days even by conservatives.[11] But even such a Senator and his contemporary imitators do have to be put up with, so long as their overbearing efforts take the form only of speech, speech which others in the community can oppose (in attempting to inform the majority) without running the risk of suffering retribution at the hands of government.

The question remains, of course, as to why we do depend upon majority rule. Perhaps, since such rule does require freedom of speech, it may be more apt in our circumstances to lead to actions that are generally examined and hence are more likely to be rational. It also makes it more likely that the programs decided upon are supported by sufficient public

---

10. The extent of the Commerce Power was long lost from view, in part because of desperate efforts by pro-slavery elements to play down the domestic authority of the General Government. See Anastaplo, "Mr Crosskey, the American Constitution, and the Nature of Things," 15 *Loyola University of Chicago Law Journal* 181 (1984). See, also, Anastaplo, "Political Philosophy of the Constitution," in Leonard W. Levy, Kenneth L. Karst, and Dennis Mahoney, eds., *Encyclopedia of the American Constitution* (New York: Macmillan Co., 1986). See, as well, Anastaplo, "The United States Constitution of 1787: A Commentary," 18 *Loyola University of Chicago Law Journal* 15 (1986). This Commentary, which includes a bibliography of various of my things bearing on constitutional matters, is scheduled to be published in book form by the Johns Hopkins University Press in 1988.

11. See, for example, the lead editorial in the *Wall Street Journal* of February 4, 1985.

approval to be able to withstand the shocks and sacrifices which follow upon their implementaion.

IX

We can now return, if only briefly, to the liberal misapprehensions about the First Amendment.

It may well be that the liberal misapprehensions here are more serious than those of conservatives. Various of the conservative misapprehensions tend to be self-correcting: a sound people can generally be led to see that repression tends to be self-defeating.

Liberal misapprehensions, on the other hand, tend to go much deeper. They are *not* limited to misapprehensions about the constitutional system and how it works (which may be seen as well in conservative circles). Rather, they are misapprehensions also about the objectivity of the things called "values," about the ability and right of government to make moral judgments, and even about the legitimacy of the community itself. Questions are in effect raised about the nature and conditions of civilization.

It should at once be added, however, that one major reason liberals go wrong (in wanting to cripple government, for example) is because of the experience they have had, or believe they have had, at the hands of conservatives. Still, it is sometimes necessary to remind liberals that the First Amendment upon which they rely does presuppose government: it is not designed merely for personal satisfaction and for personal experiments in "going it alone." Rather, as I have again and again argued, it permits the community to inform and to organize itself properly.

Our troubles have come, in part, because well-intentioned people have been careless in accepting fashionable doctrines about the First Amendment. Liberals have misled conservatives by making as much as they do of "freedom of expression" and of self-realization. Conservatives, on the other hand, have been imprudent in permitting suppression of genuine political discourse—and this has helped lead to an insistence by liberals upon a much broader protection than is needed (or, at least, than is constitutionally required) for all forms of speech. Indeed, it can be said, those who suppressed American Communists in the 1940s and 1950s probably contributed to the unhealthy liberation of American pornographers in the 1960s and 1970s.

If the First Amendment is seen primarily as licensing self-expression, then it does make it less likely that there will be a properly prepared community—and hence a majority that can act responsibly: for individuality will have been promoted at the expense of citizenship.[12] But citizenship is also subverted by the insistence that it is dangerous to hear out, again and again, the arguments (including the disloyal arguments) that may be relevant to the decisions made by the community.

The subversion of citizenship opens the way to tyranny. Whether it is tyranny of "the right" or tyranny of "the left" may depend upon chance. But in neither case would most American liberals or most American conservatives be happy.[13]

Appendix I

On the Need for a Public Records Access Act in Illinois*

George Anastaplo

It seems to me fitting and proper that this legislative committee, on the day of the final collapse of American policy in Indochina, should be considering a Public Records Access Act for the State of Illinois. Can we not learn and thus take heart from this unprecedented national debacle? Permit me to make the following suggestions:

Perhaps the most decisive criticism one can make of American policy in Vietnam is that it was never really an *American* policy. That is to say, it was never a policy faced up to and deliberately endorsed by the American people. Thus, only last week, the Chicago *Tribune* observed (in its lead editorial of April 22): "For more than a decade, our policy in Indochina has been conceived thru rose-colored glasses and marked by deceptive statements which led to secrecy which in turn led to worse lies."

Is it not likely that if Presidential policy in Indochina had been properly discussed in public, the American people either would have refused to go along with that policy or would have prosecuted the war in a radically different manner? And would not either result have been much better

---

12. This is related to my proposal that broadcast television be abolished in the United States. See "Self-Government and the Mass Media: A Practical Man's Guide," in Harry M. Clor, ed., *The Mass Media and Modern Democracy* (Chicago: Rand McNally, 1974).

13. See Anastaplo, *The Artist as Thinker: From Shakespeare to Joyce* (Athens, Ohio: Swallow Press/Ohio University Press, 1983), pp. 254, 474-475. See, also, *ibid.*, p. 322f, 331f. See, as well Anastaplo, *Human Being and Citizen*, pp. 226-227.

* A statement prepared for use before the House Judiciary Committee, House of Representatives, General Assembly, State of Illinois, Springfield, Illinois, April 30, 1975. See note 9, above.

than what did happen? What *can* be said for opening up to public view the workings of government? A self-govening people needs to know, and to believe itself to know, what its governments are doing. This requires that there routinely be made available to people the information generally available to its public servants.

Both so-called hawks and so-called doves, it seems to me, should be able to agree that inadequate public discussion and a persistent lack of candor on the part of "the White House" led in the case of Indochina to disastrous policies. Inadequate public discussion also meant that an effort could be made to fight that war without paying for it—and for this shortsighted economic calculation we have paid with a demoralizing inflation and with chronic unemployment.

You will have noticed, I trust, that I have put the emphasis in what I have said thus far upon the failures of the Executive Branch of government in Washington, rather than upon the shortcomings of a passive Congress. In these matters, it is important to take due account of the critical differences between, and the distinctive failings of, legislatures and executive officers. The doings of legislatures have always been intrinsically more public than those of governors, presidents and other administrators. There are a number of reasons for this difference—not all to the credit of legislators, of course.

A recognition of this natural difference may be seen in the bill before you. It explicitly provides at the outset that the public bodies regulated therein do not include the judicial or legislative branches of government. Indeed, one could say that the purpose of this act is to permit the people of this State to learn as much about what administrators are doing as it already knows about the doings of legislators. All this is provided for in such a manner as not to impede unnecessarily the ability of administrators to act with vigor, with dispatch, and (where essential) with secrecy.

The doings of the legislature which I have observed down here thus far this week have been far more sensible than I had been led from reports over the years to expect. That is to say, I have found remarkable the ability of legislative committees to make quick, often not unreasonable, judgments on the multitude of bills before them. You realize even better than I do, of course, that those judgments are not invariably correct—and that the motives of legislators are not always irreproachable. I am sure you also realize that the calendar to which you subject yourselves may not always be a sensible one.

But be that as it may, legislatures do depend, by and large, upon arguments which are more or less public—and a monument to that fact is the two-foot-high pile of bills one can see upon each legislator's desk, a pile surrounded by stacks of memoranda, newspapers and amendments. To the extent that there have been shortcomings here in Springfield this week, they have been by and large because of your failure to get to one another the information and documents needed for sensible considera-tion of the issues you deal with. The complaint which you yourselves voice again and again—that you do not know what is going on—is precisely the complaint which citizens all too often make in trying to pass judgment upon the workings of their governments.

I have suggested that you, as legislators, know what discussion is like and how critical it is if you are truly to act in the public interest. You also know, I suggest, how critical informed discussion is if the people of this State are to be able to make responsible judgments about the laws you enact and about the public servants who administer those laws.

The bill now before your committee attempts to help citizens learn what they are entitled to know about the workings of their government. In preparing this bill, the Privacy Commission and its staff had the benefit of considerable discussion of this subject by other legislatures as well as the benefit of numerous articles in the press, both scholarly and popular.

The version of the bill before you is different in several decisive respects from comparable legislation elsewhere. There is in this bill careful provi-sion for the personal privacy of citizens; the provision governs except where there is "a compelling, demonstrable and overriding public interest in disclosure." Further respect for privacy may be seen in the protection of personal working papers provided to public servants, papers which are developed solely for their own use. Thus, there is respected the integrity of the research stage and deliberative process in the day-to-day working of government. What is important is that there be made clear to the public what *has* been decided and done, rather than all the speculations and deliberations which may have led up to the final decision, except to the extent that such preliminary work is evident in, or is used to justify, the final product.

In addition, this bill is simpler and clearer than what is available elsewhere with respect to the procedures to be followed by agencies in dealing with requests for information. An effort has been made to help everyone involved to learn where they stand: the agency is both allowed to avoid unreasonable burdens and required to explain why it does not supply what is requested. All in all, it is a moderate bill you are consider-ing: it recognizes that openness is necessary for informed deliberation and responsible decision, an openness which is guided by practical rules and which is aware of obvious risks. This kind of realistic openness can contribute to a useful faith in one another—and head off, it should be noted in passing, other legislation which is not apt to be as carefully drawn or as mild-mannered as is this bill.

Permit me to observe, as I prepare to close this personal statement, that this bill provides what Illinois citizens have, for a long time now, understood to be available from their governments. Indeed, for many public bodies in this State, this bill may do no more than ratify what is already everyday practice. But everyday practice all too often does give citizens the impression that what they get from administrators they get as a privilege, not as a matter of a right which public servants have a duty to respect.

Thoughtful public servants should welcome legislation which confirms their proper relation to the citizens they serve. After all, public servants, in exercising the powers and in performing the duties entrusted to them, do depend upon the confidence of the community. They cannot be sure of such confidence if the people at large remain uninformed, or believe themselves to be uninformed, about what is being done in government and why. The known availability for public inspection of most public records can help remove many causes of suspicion and cynicism in a community, allowing public servants to perform their duties as well as—it is only prudent to assume—they really want to do.

Appendix II

On What the First Amendment Does and Does Not Do*

George Anastaplo

We begin with what we can all agree upon: Americans, as a self-governing people, are entitled and obliged to discuss fully all issues of public interest. They need to do so if they are to be able to act sensibly as citizens, both one by one and altogether.

The primary purpose of the First Amendment, then, is to protect and encourage citizens in their discussions of the issues of the day. The Framers of the First Amendment were primarily concerned to keep government from interferring with the inquiries into public matters and with the criticisms of public servants that citizens make. The evidence in support of this as the primary concern of those who demanded and

---

* An article distributed on August 30, 1985 by Public Research, Syndicated, Claremont, California, as part of its *New Federalist Papers* series.

ratified the speech and press guarantees of the First Amendment is so massive that it is hard to imagine any informed student of the Constitutional Period denying it.

In fact, it is most unhistorical to assume otherwise—that is, to regard the First Amendment as protecting various other kinds of talking and writing in addition to the unfettered discussion of public matters. Some say, however, that the First Amendment covers advertising and other commercial speech, pornography and obscenity, and even many "expressive" acts and displays. But this is not only unhistorical, it is also unpolitical, because this approach to the First Amendment can make it virtually impossible for the community to minister to moral character, to serious education, or to the arts.

Misreading the First Amendment in this fashion may mean that those measures cannot be taken that make it possible to produce and to perpetuate a people equipped to use properly the considerable freedom that Americans do have as a people. And this can mean, in turn, that as freedom is misused by a people not properly prepared to use it, freedom itself will come to be regarded by many as immoral, antisocial, and even dangerous. Thus, in the name of an unthinking liberty, freedom itself can come to be repudiated and subverted.

Of course, there are no simple or unchanging answers to questions about what should be done from time to time about advertising or art or entertainment or any other such thing. A sensible community weighs the consequences both of doing nothing and of doing the wrong things in response to whatever is to be seen and heard all around. Our traditional freedom of speech permits a community to be as sensible as it possibly can be, as it hears all relevant discussion about what would be done, as well as about what has already been done. It is primarily such discussion which the First Amoendment is intended to encourage and to protect.

Americans must be vigilant, then, lest the right and duty of free and full discussion be undermined either by the fearful or by the reckless—that is, either by those who are willing to run no risks or by those who are willing to run all risks. The fearful, in their willingness to suppress threatening political discourse, lend support to the reckless—that is, to those who argue that the safest way to proceed is to strip government of all power over anything anyone might say on any subject. Thus, the reckless, too, are fearful, in that they dare not trust the community to use its powers responsibly. Nor do they trust their own ability to counsel the community in how its powers are to be used. And yet, the prudent use of powers does depend upon our ability publicly to inform and to counsel each other as to what should or should not be done.

We conclude, therefore, as we began, with what we can all agree upon: Americans, as a self-governing people, are entitled and obliged to discuss fully all issues of public interest.

Concluding Essay

Sarah Baumgartner Thurow

Both Hadley Arkes and George Anastaplo were asked to address the topic of "Majority Rule and Freedom: The First Amendment." Their at first glance quite different ways of doing this bring out the complexity of the issue. We are all aware that the American political system rests upon the twin principles of liberty and equality, and that it is a system of majority rule with minority rights. We are also accustomed to considering the original Constitution as the document which established the institutions of majority rule, and the Bill of Rights as the appendix necessary to secure minority rights. What is less often noticed or discussed are the links between equality and majority rule and between liberty and minority rights, and the inherent conflict between these two sets of principles. It is often said that conflict was built into the American system, but that observation seldom looks beyond the institutional organizational principle of separation of powers and checks and balances. In fact, the deeper and more serious—because unavoidable—source of conflict in the American system is imbeded in our founding principles themselves.

Majority rule rests upon the premise that all men are created equal—at least insofar as political right is concerned. If all are politically equal then the will of the community can only be determined by finding the will of the majority. As Hobbes put it, it is a tug of war in which the side with the greater number will determine which way all are to go. But liberty—whether understood as the absolute freedom of a Hobbesian state of nature or the more limited Lockean right to determine one's own conduct in accordance with natural law—requires a curb on majority rule. Hobbes' solution was, on the one hand, to remove from the citizens all but the most private exercise of freedom and, on the other hand, to require the majority to constitute a truly rational sovereign, that is, a monarch. Only then would all be equally free. Locke, however, sought to devise a government in which all would be equally free by being equally obliged to obey laws made by a body of representatives in which the majority would rule. In Hobbes' system, as in contemporary Marxism, freedom is sacrificed for the sake of equality: the government's rule is absolute even over religious practice, but all the subjects are absolutely equal in their subjection. In Locke's system some measure of equality is sacrificed in entrusting the making of law to a minority of the citizens, but a greater measure

165

of liberty is retained by restricting the scope of the law and by allowing more than one to participate in legislation.

Our Constitution has been said to be based upon Locke's principles with perhaps a greater degree of democratic equality in the extent of the suffrage. Our founders chose to attempt to preserve both liberty and equality. Therefore, many of our disputes over the meaning and intention of the Constitution can in fact be seen to be arguments over whether a given clause is meant to promote liberty or equality to a greater degree.

The First Amendment may serve as a good example. In prohibiting Congress from interfering with freedom of speech, the First Amendment clearly promotes both liberty and equality. That is, all citizens are to be equal in their right to speak freely. But the issues which arise in the practical application of this right point up how complex it is. For instance, does the First Amendment require that all kinds of utterances be equally unrestricted by law or rather, as Anastaplo argues, that all citizens be equally and absolutely unrestricted in speaking about political matters only? The first argument is based on an essentially Hobbesian conception of freedom as being unhindered in doing whatever one wishes, while the second argument rests upon a conception of liberty as participation in self-government, a conception developed more fully in Arkes' essay.

Secondly, does the First Amendment require the government in the person of the court to see to it that the minority voice is not silenced by an overwhelming majority? This question leads us to the rest of the Bill of Rights and how it is as a whole meant to protect the minority of citizens from the majority and the people as individuals from the collective person that is the government. Both Arkes and Anastaplo question this understanding of the purpose of the Bill of Rights, and Arkes makes this a central concern of his essay.

There is a tendency today to associate minority rights not with liberty but with equality. Today "minority" is often taken to mean the weaker, but not necessarily numerically smaller, group (e.g. women are a "minority" and white males are a "majority"). "Rights" are understood as entitlements or claims, things which must be given, rather than as liberties, things which must not be taken away. Hence "minority rights" has come to refer to those things which the stronger are obliged to give to the weaker in order to achieve equality (usually understood as equality of conditions). But formerly "minority rights" referred to the injunction to the legislative majority not to tyrannize over those who have been outvoted. That is, although the majority had the right to make and enforce laws governing the conduct of all, there were limits to what those laws could forbid or compel. As Anastaplo shows, the most fundamental "right" was the liberty to hold and express political opinions and thereby participate in self-government whether or not one was on the winning side in any given vote.

Arkes' thesis in his essay is that the Federalists were right to oppose the Bill of Rights, that it was unnecessary and has in fact miseducated the American people. This miseducation has taken the form of what I will call two inversions of political principle. First, the principle of popular sovereignty according to which the government is derived from and empowered by the people is inverted by the implicit logic of a bill of rights as a contract stipulating the conditions under which subjects agree to obey a monarch. This logic leads to the idea that the only rights the people have are those spelled out in the Bill of Rights, and that this is the only limit to the power of the government. To Arkes' examples of the prevalence of this logic in contemporary judicial reasoning, I would add the invention of a right to privacy. Finding that the Bill of Rights says very little about the rights and liberties of normal daily life (as Anastaplo observes), and convinced that the Constitution is the only legitimate source of right, the Court found it necessary to invent a new right and argue that it was implicit in the Bill of Rights, or ought to have been. Thus the document intended to limit government power has in fact provided the occasion for the usurpation by the Court of the very constitution-making power which is at the heart of popular sovereignty.

Arkes seems to conclude from this that we should scrap the contract theory of government altogether. In making this argument, however, Arkes does not consider the variety of kinds of contract. The understanding of the Bill of Rights to which Arkes objects is that it is a contract in which a stronger party agrees to refrain from using its power against a weaker party in certain matters. But the Constitution as a whole need not be understood in these terms, nor is this the only way to understand the Bill of Rights, nor has either document always been understood this way in the past. There is another kind of contract in which a person delegates power to a representative to act in his stead. Such power must be understood as derivative: it is limited and may be revoked or modified by the will of the grantor. Arkes is strangely silent about the difference between Hobbes' and Locke's conceptions of the social contract implicit in Locke's right to revolution. Whether or not the American founders were consciously Lockean, this view of the Constitution as a delegation of limited power is certainly preferable to the Hobbesian sovereighty claimed by the contemporary Court. Indeed, even the staunch Federalist, Justice Joseph

Story, while he denied that a constitution is a contract, argued for an understanding of the Constitution in terms almost identical to Locke's two contracts. Furthermore, there is a kind of contract called a partnership in which a number of equally powerful and equally competent persons agree to do something in common and to abide by a common set of rules. This is the character of Locke's first social contract, the one which remains even in the event of revolution. This also might be the character of the Bill of Rights, as I take Anastaplo to be arguing. Thus we do not necessarily have to abandon the traditional understanding of the Constitution as a contract in order to correct the inversion of popular sovereignty.

The second political principle which has been inverted by the miseducation produced by the Bill of Rights has to do with the purpose of government. Arkes argues that the existence of a bill of rights suggests that the rights of the people are derived from their government, that without government these rights would not exist. He points out that even among social contract theorists some have argued that human beings possessed moral understanding before they entered into society, that there is a natural law which determines right and wrong even apart from government and positive law. He also points to the Aristotelian understanding of man as political by nature by virtue of his capacity for speech. If our rights are derived from our government—that is, if our government exists for the purpose of creating rights for us—then we can have only those rights which can be found in our basic law, and in order to obtain a new right we must change the law. This reasoning leads those who are dissatisfied with the extent of our civil rights either to reject the Constitution altogether or to read into it those rights which they wish us to have without feeling the need to justify them by reference to some external standard. This reasoning also leads others to the naive assumption that all that is required to enforce human rights in other nations is the establishment of governmental institutions resembling ours.

Susan Leeson raised the crucial question in her comment on Arkes' paper at the conference when she asked who Arkes would have determine the first principles, the rights which do not depend upon the existence of government. If one does not believe in natural law and in a natural reason capable of apprehending it, then the only alternative to government-created rights is a Hobbesian free-for-all in which individual or group might —including the power of expertise—makes right. On the other hand, Anastaplo's faith in the ability of ordinary citizens to make reasonable choices if they just discuss things long enough reflects a confidence not only that natural law exists, but that the reasoning power of the common man is sufficient to apprehend enough of it for most purposes. For one who denies natural law, some bill of rights is essential in order to protect the weak from the strong. For one such as Anastaplo, a bill of rights is not essential, but is useful as a guide for public discussion. Ironically, Anastaplo's understanding of the First Amendment exemplifies that correct understanding of the purpose of government to which Arkes opposes the miseducation of the Bill of Rights. But if one has neither the conviction that the natural law does not exist nor the confidence that the people can be counted on to know it, some sort of contract seems preferable to leaving the judgment of right up to "a small coterie of professionals." This, I take it, is Leeson's position.

The Hobbesian solution was devised to deal with the impossibility of establishing without doubt the content of the natural moral law. Because men could not be expected to agree upon the truth, truth had to be abandoned in favor of authority as the basis for right. With truth went nature, for as Hobbes put it, the only thing all men share by nature is the fear of violent death and the capacity to kill one another. Aristotle, in contrast, argued that all communities are based upon moral agreement because the one thing all men share by nature is the capacity to make moral distinctions and the desire for the good. It is communal consensus about what is good and what is evil which articulates those first principles to which Arkes would have us refer. And it is partnership in attempting to secure that which has been agreed to be good which produces the constitution of the community.

In Aristotelian terms what Hobbes did was to found a community upon the lowest form of moral agreement, agreement that violent death is bad, and to derive from that agreement a partnership aimed only at preventing violent death. Thus, there is no reason why we cannot attempt to understand our community in Aristotelian terms, whether or not the founders were Hobbesian and whether or not the Constitution and Bill of Rights are contracts. To revert to first principles, as Arkes advocates, means to ask ourselves what exactly we as a community believe is good and what bad. This does not require a degree of philosophy beyond the ability of the common man, for what is required is not to find out the best first principles, but only those which are ours. As William Murchison argued in his comment at the conference, the real power is not in the written documents of a community nor in its wisest members, but in the continued practice of the community, including the interpretation of its documents by its elected officials.

To revert to first principles when those principles have been obscured by even one generation of neglect is like taking up a musical instrument one has not played for years. Practice is necessary before one can play it well again. To base our judicial decisions upon first principles without first becoming adept again as a community at reasoning from first principles would indeed mean either allowing the ill-founded opinion of the majority to rule over the minority, however wise, or subjecting ourselves to the equally ill-founded opinion of any minority capable of claiming a Hobbesian authority. If we could revive a civic education along more classical lines we might be able to correct the flaws of the Bill of Rights without losing its salutary effects. If we were to adhere to Anastaplo's understanding of the First Amendment, we could arrive at a communal consensus in which the minority alternative was preserved. And if we were to direct our public discourse, as well as our public education, toward discussion of the first principles of our Constitution, we could move away from the Bill of Rights as the only basis for judgment of right without thereby subjecting ourselves to the subjective opinions of a professional elite.

Chapter Four

Citizenship and Human Rights

Do non-citizens have civil rights? The Declaration of Independence states that the purpose of government is to secure men's unalienable rights. But these natural rights are transformed by the Constitution into civil rights—the rights of citizens. How is citizenship to be understood? What does our citizenship require of us that is not required of human beings generally? Do we have rights as citizens that we are not entitled to as human beings?

The Constitution and Civil Rights in the Founding

Ellis Sandoz

John Dickinson, writing as Fabius during the ratification debate, explained that "liberty is the sun of society. Rights are the beams."[1] With the Constitution and Bill of Rights as the focus of discussion, I shall follow the clue provided by Dickinson to consider the liberty embraced by Americans of the founding generation, the ways in which it is embodied in the Constitution, and close with some attention to the ratification controversy that ends in adoption of the formal Bill of Rights in 1791 as the articulation of liberty into civil rights.

I

It is customary to stress the essential continuity of American liberty, among much else, with English liberty. There is general validity in this custom. But there are complications, as we shall see. Edmund Burke's famous and still stirring words undoubtedly go to the heart of the matter before us. The Americans, he said to the House of Commons in March 1775,

> are descendants of Englishmen. England, Sir, is a nation which still, I hope, respects, and formerly adored, her freedom. The colonists emigrated from you when this part of your character was predominant; and they took this bias and direction the moment they parted from your hands. They are therefore not only devoted to liberty, but to liberty according to English ideas and on English principles. Abstract liberty, like other mere abstractions, is not to be found. Liberty inheres in some sensible object; and every nation has formed itself some favorite point, which by way of eminence becomes the criterion of their happiness. It happened ... that the great contests for freedom in this country were from the earliest times chiefly upon the question of taxing.[2]

---

1. John Dickinson, *Letters of Fabius*, 1788: Letter IV in *The Bill of Rights: A Documentary History*, ed. Bernard Schwartz (New York: Chelsea House, etc., 1971), vol. I, p. 549.
2. *Edmund Burke: Selected Writings and Speeches*, ed. Peter J. Stanlis (Chicago: Gateway Edition, Henry Regnery, 1963), p. 158.

II

The sun of liberty shooting its beams of rights through the pages of Sir William Blackstone's *Commentaries on the Laws of England* (1765-1769) is clouded over with the pale cast of corruption, in American eyes. His doctrine is better than the ministry's performance; and even the doctrine itself (when read with the words of the Declaratory Act drumming in American ears, asserting "the power to bind in all cases whatsoever") becomes subversive of true English liberty and the Ancient Constitution upon examination. Law as simply the *command* of the sovereign, whether proceeding on the basis of Stuart divine right claims or parliamentary sovereignty, especially absent representation of the affected community, stinks of tyranny. The divorce of human law from natural and divine law that later comes to be called Positivism and is essentially the *will* of the sovereign, reduces politics to power and strips away the moral and onto-logical moorings of governance that Blackstone himself implicitly depre-cated and explicitly sweeps aside as "airy metaphysical notions ... started by fanciful writers."[3] Legal philosophy is on the road to John Austin's utility deity, and the view that "to say that human laws which conflict with the Divine law are not binding, that is to say, are not laws, is to talk stark nonsense. The most pernicious laws, and therefore those which are most opposed to the will of God, have been and are continually enforced as laws by judicial tribunals. . . . The existence of law is one thing; its merit or demerit another."[4]

Perhaps this is the simple truth of the matter. But it is unacceptable truth to Americans of the founding generation. Rejection arises from multiple sources, not all of them consistent with one another, but all fervent and determined not to embrace the hateful principles of passive obedience and arbitrary government. In the Revolution, from the first thunderbolt of James Otis's mighty speech against the writs of assistance in the early 1760s down to the bitter quarrel over ratification of the Constitution and its merits, the Americans are clear that it is a *rule of law* and not of men they want, one wherein liberty is served and justice of the highest order institutionalized as the *real* criterion of positive law. The civil and religious leadership of the country set themselves against a declension of Truth in the world, whether civil or religious. In the rather amazing process, they manage to decry tyranny in a three-penny tax on

---

3. Blackstone, *Commentaries on the Laws of England*, vol. 2, p. 3.

4. Austin, *Lectures on Jurisprudence*, 5th ed., ed. R. Campbell (London: John Murray, 1885), vol. 1, pp. 214-15n.

tea, as Madison remarked in his old age. They trace its origins as policy not merely to the ministry and King George III, but to the Stuarts of the previous century, back through distant centuries to the Normans of 1066 who subverted the Ancient Constitution first woven by the mythical descendants of Brutus of Troy (as Sir Edward Coke thought) and the ancient Saxons (as Otis and Jefferson, not to mention Montesquieu, believed). Thus not only do Otis and those after him in the period quote Scripture and the classics but also the historiogenetic argument:

> The law of nature was not of man's making, nor is it in his power to mend it or alter its course. He can only perform and keep or disobey and break it. The last is never done with impunity, even in this life, if it is any punishment for a man to feel himself depraved, to find himself degraded by his own folly and wickedness from the rank of a virtuous and good *man* to that of a brute, or to be transformed from the friend, perhaps father, of his country to a devouring lion or tiger.

Otis then continues as follows:

> Few people have extended their inquiries after the foundation of any of their rights beyond a charter from the crown. There are others who think when they have got back to *Magna Carta* (A.D. 1215) that they are at the beginning of all things. They imagine themselves on the borders of chaos . . . and see creation rising out of the unformed mass or from nothing. Hence, say they, spring all the rights of men and of citizens. But liberty was better understood and more fully enjoyed by our ancestors before the coming in of the first Norman tyrants than ever after, till it was found necessary for the salvation of the kingdom to combat the arbitrary and wicked proceedings of the Stuarts.[5]

The commonplace of the British constitution that "in an Act of Parliament every Man's consent is included"[6] holds no validity in American eyes

---

5. Otis, *The Rights of British Colonies Asserted and Proved* (Boston, 1764), 31; in *Pamphlets of the American Revolution 1750-1776*, ed. Bernard Bailyn (Cambridge: Harvard University Press, 1965) vol. I, p. 441. For the Old Saxon constitution see pp. 52-54 and the literature cited therein. Also, Demophilus (George Bryan?), "The Genuine Principles of the Ancient Saxon, or English Constitution" (Philadelphia, 1776) in *American Political Writing During the Founding Era, 1760-1805*, ed. Charles S. Hyneman and Donald S. Lutz (Indianapolis: Liberty Press, 1983), vol. I, pp. 340-67: "That beautiful system, formed (as Montesquieu says,) in the German woods, was introduced into England about the year four hundred and fifty" (p. 341). See J. G. A. Pocock, *The Ancient Constitution and the Feudal Law: A Study of English Historical Thought in the Seventeenth Century* (1957; rpt. New York: W. W. Norton, 1967); for Coke's Brutus of Troy and the origins of Parliament in King Arthur's Knights of the Round table see pp. 40-42.

6. Bacon, *New Abridgement of the Law*, I:79; quoted in James H. Kettner, *The Development of American Citizenship, 1608-1870* (Chapel Hill, N.C.: University of North Carolina Press, 1978), p. 32n.

Ellis Sandoz

on the principle of virtual representation rooted in the electoral corruption derided by Old Whig writers as Robinarchy and subsequently
offered to the colonials.[7] Consent has to be real and effective in linking the
few with the many in all matters of policy, but most especially in matters of
taxation, if sacred liberty is to be preserved. The matters of taxing and
property are not only the issues of the Revolution, but the point of honor
and test of constitutional right reason and true law in the British tradition, as Burke remarked.[8] While the Constitution of 1787 attends, as *The
Federalist* argues, to all the salient issues demanded in the name of liberty
against England, the provision for direct taxation and the scheme of
representation both are heated subjects of debate in the ratification
controversy, as jeopardizing the people's rights. It is not solely over the
absence of a Bill of Rights that ratification is strongly contested. In fact,
defusing the clamor of the Anti-federalists by conceding a Bill of Rights is
something of a sop and harmless concession to blunt an attack that
threatens the entire scheme of effective national government. Everybody
favors liberty and essential political rights, but not everyone favors a
powerful national government at the expense of the States' autonomy.[9]

III

To notice the pragmatic spirit of the Federalist decision to support a
Bill of Rights in the First Congress is to be reminded that politics is a
human affair and the art of the possible. It is not to denigrate motives,
least of all those of James Madison. He led the drive for constitutional
amendments in the new government by introducing the subject into
Washington's first *Inaugural Address* as a legislative matter of vital importance to the country, and by forcing the issue in a House of Representatives preoccupied with the urgent problems of inventing institutions and

7. Bernard Bailyn, *The Ideological Origins of the American Revolution* (Cambridge: Harvard
University Press, 1967), pp. 44-54 and *passim*. This book is a revision of the "General
Introduction" to Bailyn, ed., *Pamphlets of the American Revolution*, vol. 1. See Nathan O.
Hatch, *The Sacred Cause of Liberty* (New Haven: Yale University Press, 1977), Chap. 2,
"Robinocracy and the Great Whore of Babylon...."
8. Stanlis, ed., *Edmund Burke*, pp. 158-59, 170-75.
9. See Storing, "The Constitution and the Bill of Rights," in *How Does the Constitution Secure
Rights?* ed. Robert A. Goldwin and W.A. Schambra (Washington and London: American
Enterprise Institute, 1985), p. 19; also Herbert J. Storing with Murray Dry, *What the
Anti-Federalists Were For* (Chicago: University of Chicago Press, 1981).

procedures to start the country operating under the Constitution. It is sometimes hard to remember that grandiose Founding Fathers such as Madison, Jefferson, and Washington are consummate politicians, too. To Madison's initial litany of objections to amending the Constitution and doubt that any such "parchment barriers" to abuse of liberty will do significant good, for example, Jefferson crisply responds point by point in advocating such amendments: "Half a loaf is better than no bread. If we cannot secure all our rights, let us secure what we can. . . . A brace the more will often keep up the building which would have fallen with that brace the less."[10] Madison later on, in the course of debate on the floor of the House, subtly reminds his colleagues what all know and he and his Baptist supporters at home clearly appreciate: "amending the Constitution" in the several ways pending before them is *required by our constituents*." He continues:

> Have not the people been told that the rights of conscience, the freedom of speech, the liberty of the press, and trial by jury, were in jeopardy; that they ought not to adopt the constitution until those important rights were secured to them. . . . [A]s *a friend to what is attainable*, I would limit [our proposals] to the plain, simple, and important security that has been required.[11]

Shortly afterward he explains to a correspondent that "If amendts. had not been proposed from the federal side of the House, the proposition would have come within three days, from the adverse side. It is certainly best that they should appear to be the free gift of the friends of the Constitution rather than extorted by the address & weight of its enemies." By so proceeding, the Bill of Rights being thus offered "will kill the opposition every where . . . putting an end to the disaffection to the Govt."[12]

While eleven states have by this time (the summer of 1789) ratified the Constitution, a number did so only because of a tacit understanding that suitable amendments would be forthcoming from the First Congress. Massachusetts ratified by a vote of 187-168 after the Federalists agreed to a proposal for a bill of rights; Maryland ratified in April of 1789 after proposing a bill of rights. South Carolina ratified and attached a list of proposed amendments to the Constitution. Virginia was among the last

---

10. Jefferson to Madison, Mar. 15, 1789, *Papers of James Madison*, ed. W.T. Hutchinson et al. (Chicago: University of Chicago Press, 1962).

11. From the *Congressional Register* for Aug. 15, 1789, 2:215-16, in *Papers of James Madison*, p. 342.

12. Madison to Richard Peters, Aug. 19, 1789, *Papers of James Madison*, p. 347.

four states to ratify, and Patrick Henry led the opposition. Madison served in the ratification convention and was certain that Virginia only finally ratified because of the Federalists' promise to seek amendments securing rights; even so the vote was 89 for to 79 against, so that a switch of six votes would have blocked ratification. New York finally ratified by a mere three vote margin, despite the mighty efforts of Publius. North Carolina and Rhode Island remained out of the Union, the former refusing to act until a Bill of Rights was proposed by Congress: the state convention adjourned until November when it reconvened and ratified. Rhode Island finally called its convention and ratified in 1790.[13] In sum, eight states offered over 200 amendments during ratification deliberations, including nearly one hundred different substantive provisions. Madison managed to incorporate into his initial proposal to the House of Representatives fourteen out of twenty-two amendments proposed by four or more states. But he was more than a mere draftsman and played a highly creative role in combining and refining concepts and language so that the Federal Bill of Rights would be "both an eloquent inventory of basic rights and a legally enforceable safeguard of those rights."[14]

The task of establishing liberty as law, in James Madison's eyes, is substantially achieved by the provisions of the Constitution as woven together with an institutional design that serves to ally human nature and the cause of good government. The theory of scientific government there in place, along with the necessary qualities in the country and the people, augur well for justice and liberty, not least of all because the Constitution and laws made pursuant to it are the supreme law of the land. Madison's distrust of the states as repositories of sound government leaves him unsure, however, that liberty and justice in government can be maintained without additional power in the national government, especially since the veto of state legislation had been rejected by the Federal Convention. Faced with the *political* necessity of a Federal Bill of Rights, he accepts from Jefferson ideas that promise to make such a set of additions to the Constitution substantively desirable after all. The general reliance on "jealousy" and adversarial checking and balancing, Jefferson thinks, will be enhanced by a Bill of Rights, especially when viewed in light of the

13. See A.E. Dick Howard, *The Road From Runneymead: Magna Carta and Constitutionalism in America* (Charlottesville: University of Virginia Press, 1968), pp. 224-31. For Madison and his Baptist supporters, see Madison to George Eve, Jan. 2, 1789, *Papers of James Madison*, vol. 11, pp. 404-406; Madison to George Washington, Nov. 20, 1789, vol. 12, pp. 451-54.
14. Bernard Schwartz, *The Great Rights of Mankind: A History of the American Bill of Rights* (New York: Oxford University Press, 1977), pp. 156-59.

division of powers between the state governments and the national government. It is true, Jefferson agrees with Madison, that the "limited" powers of the federal government and jealousy of the subordinate governments afford a security which exists in no other instance. The jealousy of the subordinate governments is a precious reliance. But observe that those governments are only agents. They must have principles furnished them whereon to found their opposition. *The declaration of rights will be the text whereby they will try all the acts of the federal government.* In this view it is necessary to the federal government also: as *by the same text they may try the opposition of the subordinate governments.* And Madison has overlooked a cardinal point:

> In the arguments in favor of a declaration of rights, you omit one which has great weight with me, the legal check which it puts into the hands of the judiciary. This is a body, which if rendered independent, & kept strictly to their own department merits great confidence for their learning & integrity. In fact what degree of confidence would be too much for a body composed of such men as Wythe, Blair & Pendleton? On such characters like these the "divium ardor prava jubentium" would make no impression. [Horace: "The man tenacious of his purpose in a righteous cause is not shaken from his firm resolve by the frenzy of his fellow-citizens bidding what is wrong."]][15]

These arguments are not forgotten in Madison's speech of June 8, 1789, in the House of Representatives, but structure his presentation. What is important is to notice Madison's logic. The people expect the Congress so to amend the Constitution as to "expressly declare the great rights of mankind secured under this constitution." This is not unreasonable to do since "all power is subject to abuse," and it is proper "to satisfy the public mind that their liberties will be perpetual, and this without endangering any part of the constitution, which is considered as essential to the existence of the government by those who promoted its adoption." After listing proposed amendments, Madison points to the misconceptions about protections of liberty under the British constitution. The principal defect is that only the executive is restrained and the legislature remains omnipotent.

> Altho' I know whenever the great rights, the trial by jury, freedom of the press, or liberty of conscience, came in question in [Parliament], the invasion of them is resisted by able advocates, yet their Magna Charta does not contain any one provision for the security of those rights,

---

15. Jefferson to Madison, Mar. 15, 1789, *Papers of James Madison*, vol. 12, pp. 13-17; the translation in brackets is given on p. 17n. Italics added.

respecting which, the people of America are most alarmed. The freedom of the press and the rights of conscience, those choicest privileges of the people, are unguarded in the British constitution. . . . [I]t may not be thought necessary to provide limits for the legislative power in that country, yet a different opinion prevails in the United States.

Some of the key liberties are natural rights, others political rights. Madison continues: "Trial by jury cannot be considered as a natural right, but a right resulting from the social compact which regulates the action of the community, but is as essential to secure the liberty of the people as any one of the pre-existent rights of nature." Whether embraced in statements of rights or protected by checks and balances of the constitutions in the several states, the universal purpose of the concern for liberty is to restrain government:

the great object in view is to limit and qualify the powers of government, by excepting out of the grant of power those cases in which the government ought not to act, or to act only in a particular mode. They point these exceptions sometimes against the abuse of executive power, sometimes against the legislative, and, in some cases, against the community itself; or, in other words, against the majority in favor of the minority.

Even considering it is valid to say the Constitution is one of the enumerated powers and the "great residuum" of rights and powers not surrendered remains with the people, Madison continues, there is the "necessary and proper" clause that introduces discretion in the exercise of enumerated powers. This can lead to abuses of powers at the expense of liberty. On the other hand, the enumeration of some rights and silence about others can tend to disparage those rights retained but unmentioned, but a specific provision to guard against that ought to be included (Ninth Amendment). It is also to be hoped that rights incorporated into the Constitution will be objects of special attention from "independent tribunals of justice" that:

will consider themselves in a peculiar manner the guardians of those rights; they will be an impenetrable bulwark against every assumption of power in the legislative or executive; they will be naturally led to resist every encroachment upon rights expressly stipulated for in the constitution by the declaration of rights.

Beside this security, there is a great probability that such a declaration in the federal system would be enforced; because the state legislatures will jealously and closely watch the operations of this government . . . the greatest opponents to a federal government admit the state legislatures to be sure guardians of the people's liberty.

While there is some irony in Madison's last statement, we have noticed that he is a politician as well as a statesman. There is no doubting his intention to create legally enforceable rights, however. It is his intention that all governments face the prospect of a "general principle that laws are unconstitutional which infringe the rights of the community." In a further echo of Jefferson's persuasive counsel sent from Paris, Madison holds out the hope that the "paper barrier" being proposed to secure rights will "have a tendency to impress some degree of respect for them, to establish the public opinion in their favor, and rouse the attention of the whole community, it may be one mean to controul the majority from those acts to which they might be otherwise inclined."[16]

IV

Gordon S. Wood speaks for a significant consensus among scholars in stating that "republicanism as the Americans expressed it in 1776 possessed a decidedly reactionary tone. It embodied the ideal of the good society as it had been set forth from antiquity through the eighteenth century."[17] Apart from the ideological swipe that *reactionary* makes at our subject, the liberty and rights to which the Founders are devoted plainly bear out Wood's generalization. The movement from colonies in a limited monarchy, through a brief small republic phase during the Revolutionary War and Confederation, into the extended compound mixed republic of the Constitution did little if anything to affect the fundamental convictions of Americans about liberty and rights. The self-evident truths of the Declaration are the common sense of the subject in 1787 as well as in 1776. The conviction of human equality before God and the law persists; the self-evident truth that human beings who are created equal are endowed by their Creator with unalienable rights to life, liberty, and the pursuit of happiness persists; and so also does the notion that governments exist primarily to secure these rights, rest upon the consent of the governed from whom all their powers arise, and can be altered or abolished if faith is not kept with the people.

The near horizon of liberty is articulated into the array of rights

---

16. Speech of Madison in House of Representatives, June 8, 1789, in *Papers of James Madison*, vol. 12, pp. 197-210.
17. Gordon S. Wood, *The Creation of the American Republic, 1776-1787* (1969; rpr. New York: W. W. Norton & Co., 1972), p. 59.

secured by laws in various jurisdictions, especially in the common law received by the states as the formal basis of their jurisprudence, more grandly in constitutions and bills of rights, culminating in the Federal Bill of Rights and Constitution as the supreme law of the land. That the vast array of rights secured by law compose the texture of free government and emanate from the personalities of the individuals who collectively compose the *People* is a fundamental conviction in America. Civil rights may arise directly from natural rights *or* indirectly from them through the medium of a social and political order contrived out of the *consent* of the people given in constitutions and statutes. Immemorial usage and natural liberties are not readily discriminated since both emanate from human nature's reason as created and ordered by God. The achievement of James Madison and his colleagues is to devise a resourceful and substantially self-equilibrating set of processes and structures to legally enforce rights and supply standards of judgment for their realization in America. What these processes and structures consist of in detail is, in large part, the subject matter of the constitutional theory of the country. The founders institutionalize rights in such a way as to make the Constitution as amended *itself* a legally enforceable higher law, now brought down out of the clouds and firmly planted on the earth. We have seen that Madison and others viewed these developments as critical improvements over the British constitutional arrangements and anticipated the role of the judiciary through judicial review and guardianship of the fabric of fundamental rights that eventuated.[18] Liberties thereby become the birthright of all Americans with citizenship dated from adoption of the Declaration of Independence.[19] Whether comprising freedom *to* or freedom *from*, the thrust of rights is to protect the individual and limit intrusion into private life especially (but not exclusively) by government.

"Sacred liberty," as the founding generation called its heritage, encompasses constitutionally protected rights but as natural law and natural rights cannot be enforced per se in the country's courts. The emphatic legalizing of rights witnessed in the Founding served both to give them practical effectiveness (more formally after the process of absorption or

---

18. Some attention is paid the role of higher law in American jurisprudence in Ellis Sandoz, *Conceived in Liberty: American Individual Rights Today* (North Scituate, Mass.: Duxbury Press, 1978), esp. Chaps. 1, 2, 5.

19. See Madison memorandum entitled *Citizenship*, May 22, 1789, in *Papers of James Madison*, vol. 12, pp. 178-82.

incorporation began in 1925 in *Gitlow v. New York*),[20] *and* to reinforce the tendency, remarked in Blackstone and matured in Austin, of divorcing law from philosophical and ethical theories to make it an autonomous body of doctrine and knowledge. Because of the strength of the higher law tradition in American civilization, however, and the integral experience of reality that shapes the Founding and subsequent history, this tendency to a pure theory of law (or legal positivism with a vengeance) has not so far won a monopoly of American legal theory. But these are matters beside the point of the present discussion.[21]

The point to be stressed is that sacred liberty as it emerges with such force in the formative period is a philosophical and religious symbolism evoking the hierarchy of being and its order. It is not merely political. It spills over the boundaries of the legal and constitutional categories as a controlling mode of Truth. Sacred liberty is the freedom experienced by persons living in accordance with highest truth of the reality in which they participate. It is the pattern announced by Jesus: "you shall know the truth and the truth shall make you free." This is the saintly life lived in process of redemption. Its analogue is the Philosopher's contemplative life of Plato and Aristotle as the best life for man *qua* man that results from the conversion of the soul toward highest Good, such as is marked by the *periagoge* in the Parable of the Cave.[22]

Whenever experiences of this class are tied into large scale social movements, then one *possibility* is the kind of apocalyptical millenarianism and chiliasm that characterize the Civil War period in Seventeenth Century England and carry over into America to become a social force in the American Revolution. This happens when a significant number of people endow the tribulations of the time with eschatological meaning: the translation of time into eternity, the Second Coming of Christ in power and glory is at hand! As Pocock has largely shown, this is a prominent ingredient of republicanism in its modern career from the time of Machiavelli

---

20. 268 U.S. 652. See Sandoz, *Conceived In Liberty*, pp. 43-81; Berns, "The Constitution and the Bill of Rights," in *How Does the Constitution Secure Rights?*, p. 52.

21. For contrasting discussions, see H. L. A. Hart, *The Concept of Law* (New York and London: Oxford University Press, 1961); and Harold J. Berman, *Law and Revolution: The Formation of the Western Legal Tradition* (Cambridge: Harvard University Press, 1983); also, Ellis Sandoz, "H. Berman, *Law and Revolution*: A Review," *Louisiana Law Review* 45 (1985), pp. 1111-1131.

22. John 8:39. Plato, *Republic* VII.1 (515C).

and Savonarola in Florence.[23] The "revolution of the saints" is the mark of Cromwell's enterprise and of the English Commonwealth, the dawn of Anglo-American republicanism. Thus, a former governor of Massachusetts, Sir Henry Vane, writes in *A Healing Question* (1656), one of the classics of civil and religious liberty, that Godly union must be perfected "by a spirit of meekness and fear of the Lord ... to uphold and carry on this blessed cause ... that is already come thus far onward in its progress to its desired and expected end of bringing in Christ, the desire of all nations, as the chief Ruler among us." The expectation is "the setting up of the Lord himself as chief judge and lawgiver among us."[24] In the wake of the American Revolution, similar expectations rise and fall; the war ends and not the Lord but post-war depression and normalcy appear, thus dashing apocalyptic hopes. One writer has delineated the meaning of liberty for such Americans in these words:

> For evangelicals, liberty meant the total denial of the self and the obliteration of self-interest by the creation of a pure and perfectly united political community. Liberty thus was not thought of in terms of individuals but of the public collectively. For evangelical republicans, political liberty became synonymous with piety and true virtue, for only the moral reformation of the entire people would make possible the regeneration of the political world as well. Liberty thus became the freedom to be pure and virtuous, free from corruption and from sin.... Republicanism in 1776 involved nothing less than the attempt by many Americans to bring about the regeneration of American society and politics. ... The Revolution of the American saints failed. By 1780, Samuel Adams, the arch-revolutionary of the country, had begun to despair even of Boston, since all the vices and sins of pre-revolutionary years had reappeared.[25]

The pathos is captured in Sam Adams's question to Richard Henry Lee in 1785: "Will the Lion ever associate with the Lamb or the Leopard with the

23. J. G. A. Pocock, *The Machiavellian Movement: Florentine Political Thought and the Atlantic Republican Tradition* (Princeton: Princeton University Press, 1975), pp. 104-116, 294-95, 317-18.

24. Vane, *A Healing Question* in *American Historical Documents*, Harvard Classics vol. 43 (New York: Collier & Son, 1910), pp. 126-46 at pp. 141-43.

25. Philip Greven, *The Protestant Temperament: Patterns of Child-rearing, Religious Experience, and the Self in Early America* (New York: New American Library, 1977), pp. 346-47, 354, 358. Basic to Greven is Alan Heimert, *Religion and the American Mind from the Great Awakening to the Revolution* (Cambridge: Harvard University Press, 1966.) See Edmund S. Morgan's scathing review of Heimert's book in *William and Mary Quarterly* 24 3rd Series (1967), pp. 454-59.

Kid," asked the great republican Christian, "till our favorite principles shall be universally established?"[26] Such millennialist utopianism fades, and its epitaph as a dominant political movement is written in the Constitution, perhaps, whose political theory is not altogether removed from a modern skeptic's reaction to lions lying down with lambs: "That's O.K., son, so long as you add fresh lambs now and again."[27]

The word for the feverish zealotry that contributes so much to the country's unity in the Revolutionary War and then, paradoxically, becomes an obstacle to effective government on a continental scale is *enthusiasm*. The trouble with it, as Publius says, is that "the noble enthusiasm of liberty is too apt to be infected with a spirit of narrow and illiberal distrust."[28] This impedes rational deliberation, for "men ... blinded by enthusiasm" cannot take account of matters that are being analyzed from a pragmatic perspective.[29] The consequence is that sacred liberty must be preserved against both vulgar liberty (the clamor of the base passions that urge you to do whatever you will), on one side, and from world-annihilating millennialism and related fanaticisms, on the other side. Apocalypticism is a *possibility* in revelatory experience requiring rational balancing, as in Augustine. Millennial hope, an essential feature of biblical faith and of the Christian vision more specifically, points toward the fulfillment of time in eternity. But it is not a program to be carried into effect on a knowable timetable. Madison and his fellows are *not* choosing between empire and virtue, for virtue remains *essential* to happiness and to the operation of the social and political order ordained by the Constitution. But the framers are rejecting the "temptation of God" (in John Witherspoon's phrase)[30] by either doing nothing and counting on divine deliverance or by building a Tower of Babel out of purely worldly means.

---

26. Quoted from Hatch, *Sacred Cause of Liberty*, p. 182.
27. Jack Crabb in Thomas Berger, *Little Big Man* (New York, 1964); see James West Davidson, *The Logic of Millennial Thought: Eighteenth-Century New England* (New Haven: Yale University Press, 1977), p. 232.
28. Alexander Hamilton in *The Federalist*, ed. Jacob E. Cooke (Middletown, Ct.: Wesleyan University Press, 1961), p. 5 (No.1).
29. *Federalist*, p. 565 (No. 83). The standard study is Ronald A. Knox, *Enthusiasm: A Chapter in the History of Religion, with Special Reference to the XVII and XVIII Centuries* (New York: Oxford University Press, 1961). Also Norman Cohn, *The Pursuit of the Millennium: Revolutionary Millenarians and Mystical Anarchists of the Middle Ages*, rev. ed. (New York: Oxford University Press, 1970); Eric Voegelin, *The New Science of Politics: An Introduction* (Chicago: University of Chicago Press, 1952).
30. Witherspoon, *Works of the Rev. John Witherspoon*, 4 vols., 2nd Ed. (Philadelphia: William W. Woodward, 1802), vol. 3, p. 41.

One effect of their work is to purge apocalyptical excesses from faith through reason. The creation is intended to be lived in, and man's dominion over it is an augury of progress and the development of civilization, even of empire. The protection of property (*dominium*) is fundamental to a reality in which mind and spirit are founded in physical bodies of persons and are not imperceptible shades flitting about in ethereal existence. Life is given by God and meant to be lived, fostered, and enjoyed. In a sense, then, matter is spirit-bearing and property no mere impediment to man's existence in truth but its necessary condition. Witherspoon's analysis is to the point. It provides an eclectic synthesis commanding wide assent and reflecting a balanced vision of faith and reason:

> If we take tradition or Revelation for our guide, the matter is plain, that God made man lord of the works of his hands, puts under him all the other creatures. . . . Private property is every particular person's having a confessed and exclusive right to a certain portion of the goods which serve for the support and conveniency of life. . . . [I]n civil society full formed, especially if the state is at all extensive or intended to be so, private property is essentially necessary, and founded upon the reason of things and public utility. The reasons are (1) without private property no laws would be sufficient to compel universal industry. There never was such a purity of manners and zeal for the public in the individuals of a great body, but that many would be idle and slothful and maintain themselves upon the labor of others. (2) There is no reason to expect in the present state of human nature, that there would be a just and equal distribution to every one according to his necessity, nor any room for distinction according to merit. (3) There would be no place for the exercise of some of the noblest affections of the human mind, as charity, compassion, beneficence, &c. (4) Little or no incitement to the active virtues, labor, ingenuity, bravery, patience, &c.[31]

The liberty of person and property are so intimately connected as to be inseparable, by this view: "There is not a single instance in history in which civil liberty was lost, and religious liberty preserved entire. If therefore we yield up our temporal property, we at the same time deliver the conscience into bondage."[32] Consonant with this view is that the *citizen*

---

31. Witherspoon, *Lectures on Moral Philosophy: An Annotated Edition* ed. Jack Scott (Newark, N.J.: University of Delaware Press, 1982), pp. 126-27 (Lec. X.) For the problem in Augustine see Voegelin, *New Science of Politics*, p. 109, with reference to *City of God* XX.7, 8, 9. For discussion of apocalypse, transfiguration, and the problem of balance see Ellis Sandoz, *The Voegelinian Revolution: A Biographical Introduction* (Baton Rouge: Louisiana State University Press, 1981), pp. 233-43 and citations therein.

32. Witherspoon, *Works*, vol. 3, p. 37.

qualified to participate in politics as voter or official must possess an "independent will," a quality long measured in some kind of property qualification. This mark especially is valued in those who serve in offices of trust, where the more propertied classes are generally prevalent in American assemblies, for the obvious reasons that such people have more leisure time to devote to public affairs, understand the complexities of business and government better, have a demonstrable stake in society, and evince "superior virtue by being able to amass and retain a certain amount of property. This presumably took discipline, sobriety, hard work, and a certain amount of intelligence—all of which are essential civic virtues."[33] The national regulation of commerce, assuring the validity of contracts, maintaining uniform monetary and taxing policies as facets of the economic powers of the central government under the new Constitution all served to foster material well-being and prosperity as essential means to the expansion of national power and prestige no less than to the happiness of the people.

V

The universal purpose of bills of rights is to place certain liberties beyond the reach of majorities on the premise that deprivation of these rights diminishes the civil standing or very humanity of persons so affected. American government is conceived as a habitation fit for free men. The pursuit of happiness of the Declaration is a goal fostered under the Constitution by maximizing security and protecting liberty so that individuals and groups can seek their satisfactions with minimal interference from public entities. Whether *the* end of politics is happiness or justice is a puzzle as old as Aristotle, and that puzzle remains with the American founders. The end of government is justice and the end of life is happiness, under our constitutional theory. Both entail the process of *education* whereby civic, moral, intellectual, and existential virtues form character, mind, and spirit so as to perfect the properly human in each person. It is evident that laws founded on justice can conduce to these ends. It is also evident that the achieving of sacred liberty in individuals and the community involves living in accordance with truth and goodness as far as that is possible of human beings, and that means, as a

---

33. Donald S. Lutz, *Popular Consent and Popular Control: Whig Political Theory in Early State Constitutions* (Baton Rouge: Louisiana State University Press, 1980), pp. 101-104, 205.

starting point, liberation from base passion (unlike Aristotle's slave by nature, for instance) and *desiring the truly good* so as to be a friend to oneself. A reason for the marriage of millenarianism and republicanism is the recognition that the rule of the many normally will be the rule of the largest part of the soul, which is the passions. Unless these are perfected through discipline and grace, the free rule of men by consent will necessarily degenerate into the disorder that beckons the demagogue and elevates the tyrant, as Plato long ago argued. The rule of the people will reflect the order and disorders of their lives. Hence, cultivation of moral goodness and intellectual excellence is essential to the well-ordered society, especially where consent of the people is so thoroughly *the* fundamental of social and political operations as in a republic whose premise is majority rule.

Great ingenuity and concern are lavished by the Founders on the solution of this set of problems. In the Bill of Rights, protection of what Madison calls the sacred rights of conscience occurs in the First Amendment and might from the first have been secured in a comparable amendment proposed for the states had the Senate not declined it. Madison's entry into politics when twenty-five years old began with a key revision of the liberty of conscience clause of the Virginia Declaration of Rights in 1776, made while he was serving as the Orange County delegate to the Virginia Convention and General Assembly. From that beginning through his career, he and Jefferson led the nation in advocating intellectual and religious liberty, including the provisions of the First Amendment. It becomes an American principle through this effort and as a general rule, that the pursuit of happiness and highest liberty as the end of the intellectual and spiritual dimensions of human existence (i.e., those aspects distinctive of humanity itself) will be primarily conducted *privately* under the protection of the Constitution.

While that solution to the vexed problems of religion and politics is ambiguous and paradoxical in a society formed by Christian civilization, it is theoretically acute and pragmatically sound. It reflects the general characteristic of the human condition that, neither beast nor divine, men live in the ambiguities of the In-Between reality and partake of all levels of being. A politics that is purely secular perverts existence for such beings, no less than one which attempts to leap out of the human condition and proclaim the superman on a theistic *or* atheistic premise. To acknowledge the supremacy of the life of the mind and spirit, and make it available to every person and community only on condition of preserving peace and not infringing others' rights, is the Founders' *institutional* solution of the vexed problem of the place of highest things in the American order. This is without doubt a great solution under the conditions of the time, one of the greatest achievements of the entire founding. *But* it is a solution of men of faith, not of radical secularists.

The sacred cause of liberty thereby finds a resting point in the new constitutional order where liberty is law. To borrow from Burke, "This kind of liberty is, indeed but another name for justice, ascertained by wise laws and secured by well-constructed institutions."[34] For Americans, whose rearticulation of Western civilization in the founding reasserted the classic and Christian experiences—symbols of transcendent reality— in a way that runs directly counter to radical modernity and provides a noble alternative to it, the commonsense wisdom of Poor Richard is the philosopher's stone: "*Work as if you were to live a hundred years, Pray as if you were to die Tomorrow.*"

---

34. Burke, *Letter to Charles-Jean Francois Dupont*, Nov. 1789, in Robert B. Dishman, *Burke and Paine: On Revolution and the Rights of Man* (New York: Charles Scribner's Sons, 1971), p. 74n.

The Rights of We the People Are All the Rights There Are

Benjamin R. Barber

There can be no right without a consciousness of common interest on the part of members of society.

—Thomas Hill Green

Liberty may be endangered by the abuses of liberty as well as by the abuse of power.

—James Madison

Preface

The essays in this collection are nominally divided into the views of the Founders and today's views. For my purposes here, this is a distinction without a difference. For although current controversies suggest that the intentions and texts and principles of the Founders can be easily identified and distinguished from our own interpretations of them, it is my view that interpretation must always infect, nourish, condition, and redefine what are taken to be the Founders' views. Their views are irrevocably lost to us as pristine authoritative sources of immutable principle. And insofar as we can divine them, their intentions are as varied and antagonistic as those of their modern interpreters. To the degree that the Founders had intentions, these were to draft a constitution sufficiently flexible and ambiguous to allow for ongoing reinterpretation and adaptation. The Constitution itself was widely understood to be an experiment which, in John Marshall's words, was "intended to endure for ages to come and to be adapted to the crises of human affairs."

Whether we are Supreme Court Justices, scholars, or even the Attorney General of the United States, we must finally rely on interpretation: our own views as buttressed and justified by competing interpretations of the words, intentions, and principles of the Founders. In fact, the Founders rather resemble the great political theorists, and their legislative products resemble the great books, in that they are rich, dialogical, ambiguous, and paradox-strewn political icons subject to diverse and contested subsequent understanding.

This is by no means to say that interpretation is purely subjective or arbitrary, any more than political and philosophical discourse are subjective or arbitrary. But it is to say that political discourse is not scientific discourse. Rights are not like triangles or the Second Law of Thermodynamics: the issue is not truth and error but at best right opinion, intersubjective agreement, and common ground. This is the framework for all discussions of the Founding, and is the setting for my remarks on rights and citizenship here. These remarks aim only at discourse—at political persuasion. They presume however that discourse is a more reliable guide to politics than Truth, and that political theory as a quest for Truth issues more often in dogmatism than in understanding.

We The People

The People of the United States ordained and established their Constitution to form a more perfect union, to establish justice, to insure domestic tranquility, to provide for the common defense, and to promote the general welfare. However, the Preamble to the Constitution concludes, they also established a government in order to "secure the blessings of liberty."

This final phrase echoes the Declaration of Independence and anticipates the Bill of Rights, recalling to the young nation the contractarian origins of America in a philosophy of natural rights. And although the Federal Constitution employs the word right only once (in I.8.8), numerous state constitutions and the Declaration itself avow that it is solely to secure their unalienable rights that men institute governments, which must thus derive their just powers from the consent of the governed. Federalists and Anti-federalists alike agreed that government is preceded by and founded upon right, which becomes its central rationalizing principle and the measure by which all of its institutions, acts, and laws are legitimated.

The rights upon which the American Constitution was founded were natural inasmuch as, like all rights, they were "deduced from the nature (i.e., the needs and the capacities) of men as such, whether of men as they

190

now are or men as they are thought capable of becoming."[1] Yet if rights were thought to attach to men as such, they could be exercised only by citizens: by men living together in a polity capable of enforcing the mutual recognition of those rights. If government was founded to secure the rights of natural men and the blessings of natural liberty, it was only insofar as natural men became citizens that these precious rights and liberties (the right *to* liberty) could be actualized. Men may "have" rights in some abstract generic sense as a consequence of what they are theorized to be in isolation and solitude, but their rights acquire political significance and recognizable power only in the context of social relations. Rights may, as Ronald Dworkin says, trump other claims, but only in the poker game called politics, and only insofar as the rules of the game recognize their priority. In other words, it is only as a citizenry that "We the People"—by "securing" the right to liberty—give it meaning.[2]

Yet where the Declaration and the Preamble to the Constitution, and later, the Bill of Rights, are explicit about the rights to liberty on which all government rests, they remain remarkably silent about citizenship and the character of the citizenry upon whom rights depend. Who exactly "We the People" are is one of the unspoken puzzles of the Founding, the solution for which occupied Congress and Court for the subsequent century and a half. The entire social contract tradition is marked by universalistic rhetoric ("*all* men are born free and equal," government depends upon the consent of *The* Governed) that fails to specify concretely the actual qualifications for citizenship. Locke's general language is universal, but we are left to suspect that citizenship may be reserved to, if not the propertied, the rational and industrious, who are neither "contentious" nor "quarrelsome."[3]

In the American tradition, the rhetoric is also formal and universalistic: "all men are created equal," reads the Declaration; "We the People"

---

1. C.B. MacPherson, "Natural Rights in Hobbes and Locke," in *Political Theory and the Rights of Man*, ed. D. D. Raphael (Bloomfield: Indiana University Press, 1967), p. 14.
2. Walter Berns writes: "Commanding nothing, for these are not laws in the sense of commands that must be obeyed, the laws of nature (for Hobbes, for Locke, and for the Americans of 1776) point to government as the way to secure natural rights, government that derives its 'just powers from the consent of the governed.' " "The Constitution as a Bill of Rights," in *How Does the Constitution Secure Rights*, ed. Robert A. Goldwin and William A. Schambra (Washington, D. C.: American Enterprise Institute, 1985), p. 57.
3. Locke distinguishes the "industrious and the rational" to whom God gives the world and the "quarrelsome and contentious" who, it would seem, are entitled neither to property nor to citizenship. John Locke, *Second Treatise of Civil Government*, chapter 5 (On Property).

begins the Constitutional Preamble. Yet the category seems to be empty: its contents are passed over in silence. The Articles of Confederation (Article 4) at least specify that "the free inhabitants of each of these States, paupers, vagabonds, and fugitives from justice excepted, shall be entitled to the privileges and immunities of free citizens in the several states," thereby expressly excluding slaves as well as a certain economic underclass from citizenship. Neither Negroes nor women are mentioned however, and since there were free blacks in several states, they would seem to have qualified for citizenship under the Articles. Women, though not eligible to vote, presumably also enjoyed such partial rights as the individual states afforded them.

The Constitution, on the other hand, offers no explicit account of citizenship at all. In Article I, section 8 it includes among the powers delegated to Congress the right to "establish a uniform law of naturalization," and in Article II, section I it delimits the requirements for eligibility to run for the Presidency in language distinguishing natural-born and naturalized citizens. Slavery is treated with a discretion that leaves it unmentioned by name, though alluded to in a number of places—not least in the unsatisfactory three fifths compromise that made representation in the House and direct taxation apportionable by adding to (in each state) "the whole number of free persons, including those bound to service for a term of years, and excluding Indians not taxed, three fifths of all other persons" (Article I, section 2).[4]

By treating slaves as an embarrassing residual category, the Founders expressed their own ambivalence about slavery and their reluctance to strong-arm the South, leaving it to their successors to interpret their intentions. In the Dred Scott decision in 1857, Justice Taney took it upon himself to do just that: "Negroes," he wrote, "were not intended to be included under the word 'citizen' in the Constitution, and can therefore claim none of the rights and privileges which that instrument provides for and secures to citizens of the United States." This applies to all Negroes, whether "emancipated or not." Herbert Storing and others have been at pains to demonstrate that Taney's decision was a "gross calumny on the

---

4. Article I, section 9 of the Constitution bars the Federal Government from prohibiting the importation of slaves for at least 20 years; Article IV, section 2 upholds the right of property in slaves, and compels return of fugitive slaves to their home states. Other than these two articles, only the three-fifths compromise (Article I, section 2) counting slaves as three-fifths of a person for purposes of representation and taxation directly address slavery in the Constitution.

Founders."[5] Yet in their intentional vagueness and misdirection, the Founders invited such calumnies, which were surely apposite to at least some of them.

Indeed, it required the Fourteenth and Fifteenth Amendments (and the Civil War that produced them) to clarify the Constitution in a fashion that included Negroes as full citizens. Women had to wait another fifty years for a similar clarification, at least with respect to their voting rights. The Fifteenth Amendment was drafted in particularistic language meant to address the Negro question directly: "the rights of citizens of the United States to vote shall not be denied or abridged by the United States or any State on account of race, color, or previous condition of servitude." It was intended to protect the right to vote of those already counted as citizens under the Fourteenth Amendment. But the Fourteenth itself resorts again to the universalistic language of the Declaration, assuming this time—at least with respect to males—the literal meaning of the words: "All persons born or naturalized in the United States and subject to the jurisdiction thereof are citizens of the United States and of the States wherein they reside." Surprisingly, this is the first explicit conferral of citizenship. By encompassing all persons (even in the Constitution, Negroes were persons, that is to say, "other persons"), it offers a general description of citizenship. Only a half century later is the "all" extended to include women fully (in particularistic language that mimics the Fifteenth rather than the Fourteenth Amendment).[6] In both the Fifteenth and the Nineteenth Amendments, the particularistic prohibition against "denying" the vote on the basis of race or gender has the flavor of a "clarification." Oh yes, the Amendments seem to read, the framers really meant "all persons" when they wrote the Declaration, and there is no reason to think that men of color or women of every color are other than persons for all relevant purposes of citizenship.

The fundamental question about the relationship of rights and citizen-

---

5. Arguing that slavery is extrinsic to the Constitution, Storing writes: "Slavery is the creature, Southern as well as Northern judges said again and again, of positive law only; it has no support in natural law or in transcendent principles of justice." "Slavery and the Moral Foundation of the Republic," in *The Moral Foundation of the American Republic*, ed. Robert H. Horwitz (Charlottesville, Virginia: University of Virginia Press, 1977), p. 218. My argument follows Storing to a point, but draws very different conclusions.

6. The Nineteenth Amendment, ratified in January, 1919, reads "The rights of citizens of the United States to vote, shall not be denied or abridged by the United States or by any state on account of sex." The provision does not assert that *all* humans can vote, or that *all* humans are citizens, only that women who are citizens cannot be barred from voting.

ship raised by the American tradition and the theory of natural rights on which it is founded is then this: are we to believe that our forebears regarded Indians, women, and Negroes, to varying degrees, as noncitizens because they were not fully persons and thus incapable of having rights attached to them as persons? That (as the language of the Constitution might suggest) "other persons" actually signified "other *than* persons"? And that what was required was not the conferral of citizenship on Negro persons (as the Fifteenth Amendment suggests) but the conferral of personhood on Negroes (as the Fourteenth Amendment suggests)? Or are we to concur with such admirers of the Founders' handiwork as Herbert Storing, and allow that the personhood of Negroes and women was never in doubt, and that only the conferral of full political citizenship (as per the Fifteenth and Nineteenth Amendments) was wanting? More generally, what is the relationship between natural rights and citizenship? How are we to specify the character and conditions of citizenship in regimes founded on naturalistic metaphors and a conception of natural man that purports to be universalistic? Does the right to liberty mean the right *of* the free; or does it mean the right of all men to *be* free? Does the right to property mean the right *of* the propertied, or the right of all to acquire and hold property? Do rights confer citizenship, as the theory would seem to insist? Or does citizenship confer rights, as the historical practice seems to demonstrate?

It is the aim of this essay to explore these connections. As will be apparent, it is my view that social contract theory and its attendant notion of natural rights are essentially metaphoric in character: a powerful rhetorical and polemical device—a new abstract language for advancing concrete political claims—that once helped to emancipate England from the tyranny both of its kings and of religious persecution, and America from the tyranny of England, but a device which simultaneously conceded the real dependency of rights on citizenship—a lesson learned the hard way by Negroes, women and others who, persons or not, enjoyed only degrees of political servitude until they acquired full citizenship. Women may have been somewhat better off than Negroes initially in that their status at law under state statutes gave them at least some of the attributes of citizens. But history after the Civil War suggests women became—at least in formal legal terms—even worse off than Negroes, since the judiciary argued repeatedly after that time that the Fourteenth Amendment could not be construed to overrule state statutes barring women from the polls and from political office. In short, the deference to state statutes

Benjamin R. Barber

which prior to the Civil War slightly advantaged women, after the War
seriously disadvantaged them.

History and theory alike seem to show then that the road from rights
leads to citizenship, and the road from citizenship back to rights. In what
follows, I hope to traverse this road in both directions.

From Rights to Citizenship

Immigrants to the New Eden may have been escaping religious and
political persecution in the old world, but they brought with them the
Enlightenment political philosophy of natural rights that was its finest
product. When, in the Declaration of Independence, Jefferson posited as
self-evident truths "that all men are created equal, that they are endowed
by their Creator with certain unalienable rights"—which included life,
liberty, and happiness—he assumed familiarity with and acceptance of
English and French natural rights thinking. Indeed, such thinking had
already infused state constitutions and such documents as the Virginia
Declaration of Rights. Thus, standard texts like that of Corwin and Peltason repeat that "the bill of rights did not *confer* rights but merely *protected*
those already granted by the natural law."[7]

Some Anti-Federalists regarded natural rights as so powerful that even
in the absence of a Bill of Rights individuals might be able to "take
advantage of a natural right founded on reason" and "plead it and
produce Locke, Sydney, or Montesquieu as authority."[8] Herbert Storing
speculates that without a Bill, the courts still would have developed a
"common law of individual rights" that served the same purpose.[9] Among
Federalists, much the same logic prevailed, though in the name of a
different strategy. They justified their opposition to a Bill of Rights not by
belittling rights, but by belittling the need to incorporate rights explicitly
into what was already an explicitly rights-based Constitution.

"Why," queries Hamilton in *Federalist* #84, "declare that things shall not
be done which there is no power to do?" Since, he reasons, the very

---

7. Edward S. Corwin and Jack W. Peltason, *Understanding the Constitution*, (New York: Holt,
   Rinehart and Winston, Inc., 1976), p. 176, emphasis in original. For a useful discussion
   of the evolution of rights language in Revolutionary America, see Daniel T. Rodgers,
   Contested Truths, (New York: Basic Books. 1987).
8. Herbert J. Storing, "The Constitution and the Bill of Rights," in *How Does the Constitution
   Secure Rights*, p. 26.
9. Essay by "A Farmer," *Maryland Gazette*, February 15, 1788.

Preamble to the Constitution makes it clear that the People ordain and establish their Constitution to secure the blessings of liberty, surely the People already possess "a better recognition of popular rights, than volumes of those aphorisms which make the principal figure in several of our State Bills of Rights, and which would sound much better in a treatise of ethics than in a constitution of rights."[10]

Federalists and Anti-Federalists were united in their distrust of government and their belief that rights represented the ultimate safeguard against tyranny. For the Federalists, tyranny lay in untutored public opinion and in rampant majorities, which could be best counterbalanced by constitutional mechanisms such as the separation of powers and the device of representation. To them, the Constitution itself was a bill of rights that needed no appended declarations to exhibit its devotion to the rights of men. Indeed, such appendages might weaken the commitment to rights by leading the skeptical to believe that only those rights that were explicitly enumerated were actually protected. To the Anti-Federalists, centralized government was the adversary, to be hemmed in by constraints and restrictions that were necessarily extrinsic to the Constitution. Thus, while Madison—once he converted to the cause of a Bill of Rights—fought in the first Congress to integrate its provisions into the Constitution itself, the Anti-Federalists argued for its inclusion in the style of a number of state constitutions, as a principled Preamble that would both set and limit the terms of the following document. Neither side prevailed, and the compromise placing the Bill outside of but after the main body of the Constitution suited no one very well. But the Bill of Rights did explicitly subordinate government to liberty, making it not merely liberty's servant, but its offspring.

American practice seemed in a certain sense to confirm natural rights theory. Rights grounded in something other than mere law or command were required in order to give them a moral force that secures them from the abuse of centralized governments and tyrannical majorities. Free and equal by nature, men possess in the abstract, rights to those attributes which constitute their humanity. As a contrivance of human volition to secure that humanity, government is always instrumental with respect to rights, which are the source of all political legitimacy.

This understanding of Rights was of course hardly engendered *in vacuuo*. It was critical to the ideology of resistance that developed in the Sixteenth and Seventeenth Centuries as a response to ecclesiastical and

---

10. *The Federalist Papers*, Number 84 (Alexander Hamilton).

secular absolutism. Human volition was too weak and temporal a force to challenge, let alone trump, the mandate of kings and bishops. Rights deemed to be "discovered" in "nature" acquired the power of the new physical laws of nature, and gave mere men an ally in their struggle for emancipation. God might be the author of governments but not because he mandates the rule of kings, but rather because he endows men with rights by nature and then gives them the reason to contract with one another to secure those rights. Natural rights theory in effect steals God away from the cause of the divine right of kings and, by casting Him as the Creator of nature and the rights nature confers on men, makes Him the ally of popular government.

The doctrine of natural rights served then as the first philosophical foundation for a politics of emancipation from arbitrary government and resistance to illegitimate rule. Legitimacy found a standard in nature accessible to human reason, and government became a contrivance of reason, accessible to human will. In the new formula, however, there was an inadvertent coupling of power with tyranny and liberty with anarchy that affected the practice of rights in subsequent generations—not least of all, in the New World. The rights upon which government was made to depend appeared not only as prior to government but as inimical to it. The new natural standard of legitimacy was so pure that it tended to cast as illegitimate not just arbitrary government but *all* government. These incipient anarchist tendencies of liberal rights theory infected much of what passed as liberal practice in the following centuries.[11] What served the politics of emancipation and resistance well did not necessarily serve the politics of constructing a commonwealth at all. When facing tyranny, the motto "the government which governs least governs best" may make sense, but when facing the tasks of constitution-making it can—as the Federalists learned—be an obstacle to prudent government. What served the resistance to capricious English rule in 1776 did not serve the creation of self-government in 1789. Historians have often commented on the turning away of America from revolutionary rhetoric between 1776 and

---

11. The more extreme Anti-Federalists possessed an almost anarchist fear of governmental authority; thus, in 1788, Samuel Chase wrote to John Lamb: "A delegation of rights alone will be of no essential service. Some of the powers must be abridged, or public liberty will be endangered and, in time, destroyed." Issac Leake, *Memoir of the Life and Times of General John Lamb*, (Albany: J. Munsell, 1850), p. 310. I have explored the anarchist tendencies of liberalism at some length in Part I of my *Strong Democracy: Participatory Politics for a New Age*, (Berkeley: University of California Press, 1984).

1789 as if nothing other than reaction were involved.[12] But while buildings can be razed they cannot be raised with bulldozers, and 1789 was less a Thermidor than the victory of political architecture over political anarchy —of political liberty over political liberation.

In fact, the evolution of American political thinking from 1776 to 1789 responds to a profound dilemma—a singular inadequacy—of rights theory. For those rights that resistance ideology insisted had to be adversary to government were shown by political realism also to be the products of government. To be emancipatory rights had to be grounded in nature, but to be of political significance they had to be grounded in social relations. Where liberation theory cast rights as the parent of government, realism cast them as its offspring.

Jeremy Bentham offered the political realist critique of natural rights theory in characteristically extravagant language: "Rights," he inveighed, "is the child of law: from real laws come real rights, but from imaginary laws, from 'laws of nature,' come imaginary rights ... natural rights is simple nonsense, natural and imprescriptible rights rhetorical nonsense, nonsense on stilts."[13] The Federalists used rights rhetoric, but their concern was with effective government, which, they appeared to believe, secured rights by facilitating the rule of law. They accepted Hobbes' dictum that the greatest liberty was to be found where the laws were silent, and did not need the Tenth Amendment to persuade them that the government established by their Constitution had only those powers explicitly delegated to it. Nonetheless, when a Federalist like Hamilton tells the people of New York (in *Federalist* #84) that "the constitution is itself in every rational sense, and to every useful purpose, a Bill of Rights," he means not simply that it confers only delegated powers on the government, but that it secures rights by writing them into the very structures of popular sovereignty. Is it not plain, he asks, that what advocates of a Bill of Rights demand is already "done in the most ample and precise manner in the [Constitution's] plan of the convention"? And if it is "another object of a bill of rights to define certain immunities and modes of proceedings, which are relative to personal and private concerns," this too is "attended to in a variety of cases in the same plan."

---

12. Crane Brinton comes closest to identifying the constitutional era as a Thermidor in relation to the preceding revolutionary era (in his *The Anatomy of Revolution*), but historians generally have divided the two eras and labeled them radical and nation-building (or conservative or reconstitutive).

13. Jeremy Bentham, *Anarchical Fallacies*.

The Anti-Federalists worried that too much government would submerge the liberties in whose name government was constituted. But the Federalists worried in turn that too much liberty, too great a focus on radical rights, would submerge the government on which liberty ultimately depended for its security. "Liberty may be endangered by the abuses of liberty as well as by the abuses of power," wrote Madison in *Federalist* #63.[14] Edmund Pendleton was more explicit still: "There is no quarrel between government and liberty," he writes. "The war is between government and licentiousness, faction, turbulence, and other violations of the rules of society, to preserve liberty."[15] The Rights tradition, evolving as a response to absolutism, had come to identify government with the suppression of liberty. But the Federalists suspected that anomie was a still greater enemy of freedom and that isonomy and the rule of law, in overcoming anomie, would nourish freedom.

Even such modern critics of positivism as Ronald Dworkin—who allows that "it makes sense to say that a man has a fundamental right against the government, in the strong sense, like free speech, if that right is necessary to protect his dignity"—nevertheless acknowledge that rights are not "a gift of God, or an ancient ritual, or a noble sport," but rather "a complex and troublesome practice that makes government's job of securing the general benefit more expensive."[16] Since securing the general benefit enhances the security of freedom, the Federalists may be excused for wondering whether an overly zealous concern for rights might not ultimately undermine liberty.

Bentham exposes only a mild deficiency of natural rights theory when he portrays its fictitious derivation from a non-empirical version of nature. More fundamentally, rights are compromised in the very characteristic that purportedly makes them significant: their supposed immunity to relativism. For if rights are attached to a certain conception of human nature and thus human need, what counts as a right becomes all too easily as variable as human nature and human need. Almost all of the very considerable modern controversy that surrounds the issue of human rights derives from debate and disagreement over what is to count as essentially human and what is to count as a genuine human need: wants?

---

14. Madison was discussing the six year term for the Senate here and, once again, arguing against those turbulent and contentious factions that are the bane of *Federalist* #10.

15. *Debates in the Several State Conventions on the Adoption of the Federal Constitution*, ed. Jonathan Elliot, vol. 3, p. 37.

16. Ronald Dworkin, *Taking Rights Seriously* (Cambridge: Harvard University Press, 1977), pp. 198-199.

desires? the requisites of survival? of growth? of flourishing? As Rousseau saw long ago and D. D. Raphael has noticed recently, "in general, material and moral progress produces a continuous expansion of needs ... [and] what is thought to be a luxury today may be regarded as a necessity tomorrow."[17] Most modern social progressives, arguing that "people now are vulnerable to kinds of threats and need forms of protection that were inconceivable in the eighteenth century," include subsistence rights, rights to employment and education, and even the right to a paid vacation in their international human rights agendas.[18]

These claims are worthy of notice here because in recalling the contestable character of needs and wants, they exhibit the intrinsic contestability of all rights claims deriving from a conception of human nature and human need. It is the putative universality of rights that gives them their potency in challenging governments; yet in practice, their universality yields to the particularism of specific conceptions of need that change over time. In rooting themselves in concrete human nature, they lose the abstract universality that is their claim to attention.

There is a further dilemma, even more troubling than the one precipitated by the relativism of needs. In order to ground right in a moral and metaphysical imperative beyond the pale of those positive laws for which right is to be the legitimating measure, the naturalistic tradition had to push it beyond the pale of human will and thus, in political terms, of popular sovereignty. Although originally rights were a legitimate device of popular government against absolutism, volition organized communally as popular government in time became the danger to which rights became the response, so that to secure rights became for advocates of natural rights theory to bridle the very autonomy (in its mutualist manifestations) that rights had once helped to establish. Rights had, ironically, to be defended against political autonomy—the will to self-determination of a united people—that many regarded as their finest expression. Liberty exercised becomes the enemy of liberty—or so it would seem.

On the other hand, positivists went too far in the other direction. Applying Hobbes with one-eyed diligence, they subsumed rights entirely

---

17. D. D. Raphael, "Human Rights, Old and New," in *Political Theory and the Rights of Man*, p. 65.

18. Henry Shue, "Subsistence Rights," in *How Does the Constitution Secure Rights*, pp. 74-75. Those who have argued for the expansion of rights to encompass economic needs like subsistence and employment include C. B. MacPherson, D. D. Raphael, and Christian Bay. Most modern rights documents include economic as well as civic rights, although it is not clear that such rights are anywhere adjudicated or enforced.

to human will, to the laws yielded by sovereign command, and thereby appeared to rob rights of all of their radical or subversive force. If rights are merely random claims recognized by the sovereign, then they have no status as legitimators of sovereign will. Only a standard prior to sovereignty can be utilized to measure sovereignty. Rights issuing out of human volition are too weakly engendered to bring tyrants to heel or keep an impulsive people from running amok.

There then is the most poignant dilemma of rights: rooted in nature and the nature of man, they are secured from tyrannical public opinion, from sovereign miscreants, and from the willfulness of those who pretend to be their authors; yet rooted in nature they reinforce the fiction that we do not or should not govern ourselves in common, and they nourish the illusion that we can preserve our liberties only by refraining from exercising our liberty. Too malleable and evanescent as poor creatures of the law, rights are too deterministic and rigid as reflections of universal nature. Thus it was that the Federalists, though in their rhetoric they acknowledged the priority of rights to law, in their practice did all they could to subsume rights to their Constitution by incorporating them into its structural provisions. Thus it was that the Anti-Federalists aspired not merely to attach a Bill of Rights to the Constitution as a caveat and a constraint on the powers of the sovereign people, but to "abridge" where they could such powers as were delegated to the people's government.[19]

The political tangle into which the quarrel between naturalists and positivists—as well as between Anti-Federalists and Federalists—propels us can be mediated by consulting the language of rights usage. Even the most zealous naturalists acknowledge that rights need to be secured or recognized or enforced in order to acquire operational force in the real world. As John Dunn has observed, Americans "possessed their rights by historical and political inheritance as a product of—at a minimum—almost two hundred years of constitutional history. And that history offers no license for viewing their possession of these rights as in any sense prior to the claims of political authority."[20] If rights exist by nature, it is only *in potentia*. As claims, which is what they are as long as they are merely asserted in nature by individual persons, they do not yet possess

19. See note 11 above.
20. John Dunn, *Political Theory*, (Cambridge: Cambridge University Press, 1984), p. 11. It may be useful to recall here that Rousseau, that consummate rights theorist, understood rightful authority as *conventional* rather than natural (cf. *The Social Contract*, Bk. I, Ch. 4).

the normative character that gives them the status of legitimizers.[21] They acquire legitimacy only when they are recognized.

T. H. Green addresses the implications of what it means to recognize rights in a fashion that lays bare their essentially social character: "There can be no right without a consciousness of common interest on the part of members of a society. Without this there might be certain powers on the part of individuals, but no recognition of these powers . . . and without this recognition or claim to recognition there can be no right."[22] In still more elemental terms, one can say that recognition entails the mutuality of a common language, common conventions, and common consciousness—minimally, what is understood as sociability or civility—perhaps even political relations defined by law. Against others, solitary persons can advance only claims. Citizens alone possess rights which, in Green's words "attach to the individual . . . only as a member of a society of free agents."[23] When Green argues that "a right held against society, in distinction to a right to be treated as a member of society, is a contradiction in terms," he may be saying in philosophical terms very much the same thing as Edmund Pendleton is saying in political terms when he says "there is no quarrel between government and liberty."[24]

Rights attach and pertain to citizens rather than abstract persons, whose evolving natures and needs generate evolving *claims* that become rights only inasmuch as they succeed in eliciting the mutual recognition of citizens bound together by common interests, and thus a common political community. To recognize a right is to confer it. The ordaining of government transforms claims into rights. To become a citizen is to engage in acts of common consciousness that entail the mutual acknowledgement of individuality and personhood that we call rights. The Constitution could be considered to be in and of itself a Bill of Rights because in breathing air into the American polity it gave life to rights. The "we" of "We the People" entailed a prior mutuality and common understanding that issued in those rights upon which, in turn, the legitimacy of the

---

21. "A right is a claim," writes Bernard Mayo; and although it is a "justifiable" claim, its justifiability derives from mutual undertakings that are part of a social context. Mayo, "What are Human Rights," in *Political Theory and the Rights of Man*, p. 75.

22. Thomas Hill Green, *Lectures on the Principles of Political Obligation*, (London: Longmans, 1941), paragraph 31, p. 48.

23. Green, paragraph 138, p. 143. Green is not arguing that the state creates rights, but he is suggesting that it "gives fuller reality to rights already existing," and that these exist by virtue of prior social relations (paragraph 133, p. 138).

24. Green, paragraph 99, pp. 109-110.

People's well-ordained government was thought to depend. If rights were prior to government, mutuality was prior to rights.

Thus, for example, it can be argued that the resistance ideology of Seventeenth Century commonwealthmen was the invention not of solitary individuals asserting natural rights, but of partisans already bound together by doctrine, convention and common cause—by ties with a history dating back to Magna Carta and beyond. The rights in the name of which they rebelled were the byproduct rather than the premise of their civil association.

The source of legitimacy that endows claims with the status of rights would seem then to be civility rather than solitude, human convention rather than nature, artifice rather than God-given human character. Right precedes the formal structures of the Constitution and may there-fore be thought to constrain and condition those structures, but they are in turn preceded by the informal structures of the social polity, which ultimately may be thought to constrain and condition right. We contrive through common consciousness the "natural" rights with which we affect to constrain the political artifacts of common consciousness. There is no harm in this magnificent illusion as long as the pretense of the lexical priority of rights is not permitted to manacle the political arms of the people whose sleight of hand accomplished the trick in the first place.

If the tyranny of unchecked majorities constitutes one of the gravest of those "abuses of power" against which Madison warned in *Federalist #63*, rights absolutism rooted in metaphysical naturalism constitutes the grav-est of those other equally malignant "abuses of liberty" about which he worries in the same place. Rights not only lead to citizenship, which is the condition of their recognition and which thus not only secures but entails them; they also attach exclusively to citizens, who enjoy them as a result of their civic membership in a polity constituted by common consciousness and common recognition.

The current controversies in which members of the Reagan Adminis-tration such as Attorney-General Meese and members of the Supreme Court have become embroiled revolve precisely around this issue. Meese argues for a kind of textual absolutism that construes the Constitution, as mediated by the intentions of its Framers (whatever those are), as immuta-ble dicta that at one and the same time are unambiguous in their com-mands and prohibitions *and* beyond the interpretive powers of the Court or the people. Justice Brennan and others deny that such self-evident dicta are to be found in what is in any case an antiquarian tradition that *must* be interpreted if it is to be made pertinent to the changed circumstances of our own radically altered world.[25] (One might argue that if this is the case, it is the legislative and not the judicial branch that ought to adapt the old, intentionally flexible, constitutional tradition to the new circumstances; but that is another matter.)

The analysis thus far suggests a resolution to the Constitution's ambiguity about the place of certain outsiders (Negroes, Indians, women) in its scheme of rights. It makes little difference whether such individuals were regarded as human beings or persons. As long as they did not count as citizens they were without significant rights. For whatever the metaphysical origins of rights, it was understood well enough in practice that they attached to and could only be enjoyed by full citizens. All men might be born free and equal, and all women too for that matter, but such universalistic rhetoric was empty and could not change the simple political reality that until all men, black, white and red alike, and until all women too, acquired citizenship, their personhood or membership in the human race even if granted was a meaningless abstraction. Membership in the human race did not confer citizenship, but citizenship did confer human rights. Better to be a naturalized cat or dog than a Negro or a female born free and equal but without the full prerogatives of citizenship. It took the particularistic language of the Fifteenth and the Nineteenth Amendments to concretize the rights of citizenship conferred in the Fourteenth Amendment. It was not by being admitted into the human race but into full political citizenship and its prerogatives that the two outcast classes acquired rights.

By the same token, the futility of much of what passes today as human rights talk and international rights talk is due less to tyranny and injustice than to the absence of a common international citizenship, a common international polity, or a common international framework of recognition. There can be no human rights until what we call humanity ceases to be a philosophical abstraction or the holographic projection of a Kantian imagination, and becomes a genuine, identifiable People—a "We" woven together by invisible threads of common understanding, shared convention, acknowledged commonality, and mutual recognition. We would like world government to arise naturally out of the logic of human rights; but in reality the logic of human rights will fall into place only when world government has found a practice.

Rights lead then to citizenship; they are entailed by citizenship, they are

---

25. Edwin Meese et al., *The Great Debate: Interpreting Our Constitution*, (Washington, D. C.: The Federalist Society, 1986).

the essence of citizenship—its finest product. Does the road from citizenship to rights traverse the same territory? That question requires that we examine citizenship itself, initially without regard to the problem of rights.

The Road From Citizenship to Rights

We have become accustomed to thinking of politics as a spectator sport and of citizenship as a passive, watchdog function that is exercised only episodically in the election of those who actually govern in the name of "We the People." Obviously, if citizenship entails only the periodic accountability of voting, it will be a weak source of legitimacy and thus a questionable foundation for rights.

By focusing on the network of mutual consciousness and mutual interests that constitutes the real meaning of civility, T. H. Green's analysis suggests a richer and more subtle account of citizenship. In his analysis, it comprises attitudes as well as actions, and it exhibits itself in a capacity for public thinking and public judgment that is wholly at odds with the capacities of individuals or private persons to act on their own behalf. Citizenship in this sense is defined by what may be called "we" modes of looking at the world that have much in common with what Rousseau understood as the General Will. Citizens are individuals who have reconceived their identities in a public language; private persons who have reconceptualized their interests in a rhetoric of public goods; strangers who have come to recognize in others facsimiles of themselves as a result of common belonging to common communities.

As isolated individuals, as manifestations of gender, as religious sectarians, as creatures of intelligence, as physical beings, we are anything but equal. I am bigger, she is brighter, he is more devout, we are quicker, they have more staying power. It is only as citizens that we acquire equality. Jefferson's 'all men are born equal' expresses an aspiration—a longed-for norm. In truth, all men are *born* unequal, but are given the opportunity of equality through membership in a democratic polity. By nature, some are weak, some strong, some black, some white, some male, some female, some stupid, some clever, some industrious, some lazy, some accommodating, some contentious. All are free by nature but only insofar as their natural power allows. None have rights—not because, as Hobbes had it, right is a pure creation of positive law—but because right depends on a system of mutual recognition that the abstract solitariness of man's natural condition precludes. Liberties become rights when individuals become citizens. Citizenship is the device by which natural inequalities and God-given differences are overstepped and artificial categories of likeness are invented to promote a fragile but essential equality. It is the We-ness of community that confers and extends the notion of right intuited by nature but given life only by arduous artifice.

Here the linkage between rights and legitimacy alluded to above is fully visible. What legitimates the actions of a citizenry deliberating in common—the so-called General Will—is that will's generality, its inclusiveness, and its encompassing of separate wills in a single, unified will. This will identifies those who participate in it as occupying common ground— as equals at least with respect to their shared interest. It is then this we-ness, this commonality of a will, that legitimates it.

The arguments of the social contract tradition, anxious to ground right in nature and legitimacy, in something beyond positive law, construe men as rights-bearing by nature. But as we have seen, while there may be natural liberty and natural power, there cannot be natural right in the same sense. For right is a product of power legitimized, and legitimacy is conferred by mutual consent—that is to say, citizenship. There is something suspiciously oxymoronic about the phrase individual rights, for to posit a right is to imagine a world of artificial kith and kin who recognize themselves as alike in their claim to liberty (if nothing else). As a *me*, I can make claims; but only as part of a *we* can I possess and acknowledge rights. Citizenship is, among other things, a kind of self-redefinition in which, with respect to the polity, we rethink who we are and what is good for us. Empathy and imagination are the psychological faculties necessary for identification with the Other, and it is these same faculties that underlie the acknowledgement of rights.

Now if citizenship is understood in the wan terms favored by some advocates of liberal representative democracy; empathy, imagination, the confluence of intèrests, and the pursuit of a common good can play only the slightest of roles. Elsewhere, I have developed an extended argument in favor of "strong democracy" as the only viable form of democratic government: not government by all the people all of the time over all public matters, but government by all of the people some of the time over some public matters.[26] Critics of this and other versions of participatory

---

26. In *Strong Democracy*, I have distinguished strong democracy both from representative democracy, and a virulent parody of direct democracy that I have called unitary democracy.

government have often cited the antipathy of direct democracy to rights as one of its chief defects. But the argument here suggests rather the opposite: that a form of strong democracy focusing on mutualism, active pursuit of common goods, and creative common action—because it nourishes empathy and imagination—is more likely to be hospitable to rights than a form of thin democracy that waters down citizenship and encourages passive accountability, mutual suspicion and adverserial bargaining. The linkage between the preservation of rights and democracy is suggested in Madison's initial conviction that self-government is the only true guarantor of individual liberty. As Storing sums it up: "The basic justification for the absence of a bill of rights was that the main business of a free people is to establish and conduct good government; that is where the security of freedom must be sought. ... [T]he rhetoric of bills of rights might serve as a delusive substitute for the hard tasks of self-government.[27]

The quarrel I have with Madison and such current critics of rights as Walter Berns and Herbert Storing, is that the kind of self-government that accommodates and succors rights requires a great deal more democracy than they are willing to contemplate. Self-government means on-going civic participation by a citizenry enfranchised in more than name and engaged in more than voting. Madison correctly envisions the dependency of rights on the devices of the Constitution, yet devotes most of his energy to transforming those devices into checks on popular government. Walter Berns argues that virtue serves liberty better than abstract rights can serve it, but then becomes queasy at the thought of conferring on a citizenry an exercise of power sufficient to cultivate its civic virtue.[28] Herbert Storing and Nathan Tarcov wisely demonstrate that the Constitution omits the conferring of rights on Negroes and women but does not commit the sin of reading them out of the human race by nature; yet they do not notice that Negroes and women are thereby deprived of rights as

---

27. H. J. Storing, in *How Does the Constitution Secure Rights*, p. 34.
28. See Walter Berns, *Freedom, Virtue, and the First Amendment* (New York: Henry Regnery, 1965).

effectively as if they had been declared non-persons and read out of the race.[29]

There is a good deal of interesting historical evidence in favor of the claim that where notions of citizenship have been most firmly entrenched, the need to devise extrinsic guarantees of rights have been least often felt. Neither the Green republics nor participatory democracies like the Swiss Confederation or the Raetian Republic had significant records of rights abuse in spite of the absence of declarations of rights. The United States, on the other hand, experienced an unsettling number of rights abuses from the Alien and Sedition Acts of the late Eighteenth Century to Lincoln's suspension of habeas corpus during the Civil War—and this in spite of an explicit Bill of Rights. Indeed, although intended to protect States and individuals from the abuses of a centralized Federal Government, the Bill of Rights in fact was never used for this purpose in the Nineteenth Century (the first case was *Gitlow vs. New York* in 1925). Nor would any such use have been conceivable in the absence of the broad language (equal protection and due process) of the Fourteenth Amendment—in other words, until after the Civil War. As Tocqueville had observed, the real spirit of liberty had to be regarded as local, depending upon an engaged citizenry rather than an abstract declaration.[30]

Intolerance, manipulated opinion, factionalism, privatism, and the abuse of liberty we call licentiousness are the real enemies of right.

---

29. Tarcov argues "the political arrangements of the constitution excluded enslaved Blacks and autonomous Indians [he does not mention women], rather than Blacks or Indians as such." "American Constitutionalism and Individual Rights," in *How Does the Constitution Secure Rights*, p. 113.

   Herbert Storing cites Frederick Douglass to similar effect: "I hold that the Federal Government was never, in its essence, anything but an anti-slavery government. Abolish slavery tomorrow, and not a sentence or syllable of the Constitution need be altered . . . If in its origin slavery had any relation to the government, it was only as the scaffolding to the magnificent structure, to be removed as soon as the building was completed." Douglass, cited by H. J. Storing in "Slavery and the Moral Foundations," p. 221.

   There are two problems with this approach as a resolution to the question of rights: first, it is belied by history; it took 75 years and a civil war to make the Constitution do for Negroes (and 150 years for women) what Douglass and Storing want to argue it meant, "in essence," to do in the first place. Second, the Constitution *is* a scaffold and not an essence. It contains a practice, but its provisions are all so much scaffolding. What the scaffolding omits to do, is not done. If rights depend on the conferring of citizenship, then the Fifteenth and Nineteenth Amendments are no mere rectifications of oversight, but fundamental alterations in the character of American citizenship.

30. See Alexis de Tocqueville, *Democracy in America*, and J. J. Rousseau, *The Social Contract*, Books 3 and 4.

Participatory self-government—active citizenship nourished by civic virtue—is calculated to diminish the force of such enemies, and is thus a friend to rights. In eras of intolerance and the abuse of liberty, it is not to our rights but to our democracy that we need to look. When, as seems to be happening in this era of prosperity and privatism, we cease to respect each other as citizens, when the differences spawned by our private identities overwhelm the equality engendered by our civic identities, when civic virtue is displaced by wholly private interests, it is then that our rights become most precarious. These rights belong not to individuals but to citizens: To "We the People." This is why it can be argued, as I have done here, that the rights of "We the People" are all the rights there are.

Concluding Essay

Rogers M. Smith

In many respects the essays on citizenship and human rights of Ellis Sandoz and Benjamin Barber are not in sharp conflict. Professor Sandoz stresses that the framers believed natural rights were derived from divinely-authorized higher law, and he sees the civil rights they established as practical devices to further the ends of that law. Professor Barber agrees that the founders subscribed to higher law, but he contends that *only* their political actions gave those beliefs concrete significance. And he notes that their actions left many apparent injustices standing, which he counts as evidence that a more participatory democracy might do a better job of actualizing human rights in practice.

Barber's political prescription reflects in part a serious philosophic disagreement in the papers that was brought out well by the commentators and the general discussion at this panel, as it was throughout the conference. Conceding that the framers founded their rights of citizenship on ideals of natural rights, can we and should we today strive to sustain their higher law perspectives? Professor Sandoz did not address this question, although clearly he finds the founders' views attractive. Professor Barber argued that we cannot and should not maintain their beliefs in natural rights. He describes those beliefs as myths, metaphors, at best as a way of expressing what are really only shared social values. The central thrust of the critical commentary his paper received was to argue that this view makes human rights matters of preference and political influence, even social whim. Many maintained that we need to accept the existence of transcendental moral standards in nature if we are to be able to evaluate and oppose unjust social beliefs.

This issue is clearly a profound one. It must be conceded, I think, that the existence of a need for transcendental standards does not provide us with a reliable way of discerning them. Indeed, honest doubts about whether such principles can be ascertained have become pervasive in our intellectual culture since the founders' time. Very little of the discussion at the conference addressed those doubts. Instead, it was simply noted repeatedly that the founders did not share them. Even so, if we have become less than sanguine about the capacity of practicing politicians to grasp immutable philosophic truth, it seems prudent to assume initially that all posited legal rights express influential political judgments more than transcendental insights, as Professor Barber contends.

210

Those of his mind can also argue that the absence of clearly discernable, immutable natural standards does not leave us without moral standards at all. We can still argue among ourselves about what values we find attractive or compelling, identifying our reasons. If we reach agreement, that consensus can serve as the foundation for our moral principles, including our beliefs in human rights.

Such a view has a healthy realism about it, but it cannot entirely dispel fears that turning our attention away from possible higher sources of morality may doom us to miss what is truly meaningful in life. Furthermore, if we truly believe that the outcomes of our discussions are our proper political guides, we may tend to succumb too quickly to results that in fact have been determined by force, error, or mystification. Thus, while at present Barber's more pragmatic position seems able to muster more intellectual ammunition than can the seekers of higher law, the arguments each view presents against the other possess genuine force. So perhaps it is best that this debate continue in the earnest and lively fashion with which it was conducted at the conference.

But there are other descriptive and normative issues concerning citizenship and human rights, in the founders' world and our own, that were not so well ventilated in this session. Here and at other panels it was noted that Americans long denied full citizenship to blacks, women, and Native Americans; and all discussants appeared to accept that these practices represented, at best, a failure to fulfill the ideals of the Declaration of Independence completely and immediately. Several speakers stressed that most of the founders regarded all these members of the population as human beings fully possessed of natural rights, even if the framers thought it inappropriate to bestow full civil rights on them at that time. But why was it inappropriate? How did Americans justify these exclusions to themselves?

The leading implicit answer at the conference seemed to be that the sincerely liberal and/or Christian framers felt compelled to bow to the popular prejudices and economic necessities of their day, while striving to set the nation on the course to full civic equality eventually. I am aware that this was Lincoln's view of the framers' attitude toward slavery, and I have no doubt that several of the leading founders possessed such sentiments to a significant degree. But recent research suggests that the universalistic, Lockean, liberal conception of political membership that the conference's discussions focused on was by no means the only notion of citizenship influential in the founders' thought. Exploration of the other discernable conceptions sheds further light on the arguments about the proper form of citizenship that the papers at this panel considered.

Conceptions of American citizenship inevitably express a sense of civic identity, of what is involved in being an American. At the commencement of the debates with England that led up to the revolution, most colonial leaders saw themselves as loyal British subjects, concerned to preserve their constitutional rights as Englishmen. Only in the course of that debate did they come increasingly to describe themselves as Americans, as republicans, and as possessors of human rights. Those three descriptions, moreover, expressed senses of American civic identity that were united in their support for the revolutionary cause, but distinguishable in their implications for the forms of citizenship the revolutionaries would establish.

Perhaps because it was somewhat less prominent in the founders' rhetoric, perhaps because we are uncomfortable with it, modern scholars tend to give the least attention to the conception of their common identity that may have been most potent for many revolutionaries: their sense of themselves as bearers of a special ethnocultural heritage. As Bernard Bailyn and others have noted, the colonists believed that "they, as Britishers, shared in a unique inheritance of liberty." Like all Englishmen, they were proud descendants of Anglo-Saxon peoples who had historic traditions of political, personal, and intellectual freedom that were culturally, if not biologically, central to their race. Anglo-Saxons, they believed, had a unique responsibility and capacity to sustain political liberty in the world. This view of their special Anglo-Saxon ethnocultural identity was undoubtedly heightened in America by the presence amidst the colonists of Afro-Americans and Native Americans, whom British Americans generally took to be unfit for civil liberty, at least without considerable tutelage.[1]

And as they saw the British parliament and king violating what they took to be their traditional English liberties, American leaders increasingly gave this conception of their ethnocultural identity a more nationalistic content. England, it seemed, had become corrupt. Therefore Americans were left alone as the last pure repositories of Anglo-Saxon freedom,

---

1. H. Kohn, *American Nationalism* (New York: Macmillan and Co., 1957), pp. 13,21,28; J. Higham, *Strangers in the Land* (New York: Atheneum Press, 1966), pp. 9-11, 133-134; B. Bailyn, *The Ideological Origins of the American Revolution* (Cambridge: Belknap Press, 1967), p. 66; P. Gleason, "American Identity and Americanization" in *Concepts of Ethnicity*, ed. William Petersen, Michael Novak, and Philip Gleason (Cambridge: Belknap Press, 1980), pp. 59-60.

giving them a mission to keep that legacy alive for the future. America's special material, historical, and social circumstances, shaped by the hand of providence, were also credited with maintaining and enhancing their natural aptitude for freedom.[2]

From this ethnocentric view of themselves as uniquely blessed "modified Englishmen," it was easy to arrive at laws of citizenship of the sort the founders created in the 1780s and 1790s—laws which tolerated slavery, granted free Afro- and Native-Americans second class citizenship at best, expressly limited naturalization to whites, and consigned women to the traditional, politically subordinate "domestic sphere." The fact that the more liberal-minded of the framers were troubled by some of these restrictions should not obscure the truth that for many others, these relative statuses reflected a natural order of things that expressed itself in distinctive ethnocultural identities and roles. After all, similar views can claim broader, more longstanding, more enduring acceptance in human thought than can any rigorous liberal egalitarianism. Hence when we consider the founding generation's understanding of nature and political identity, the prominence of this Anglo-Saxon ethnocentrism should not be dismissed or ignored.

But as many have discussed, the revolutionaries had trouble sustaining their case against Britain simply through reliance on their hereditary status and rights as Englishmen.[3] Constitutional developments in England after 1688 and the various precedents of parliamentary legislation for the colonies all gave the British claim of parliamentary sovereignty significant support. So Americans increasingly appealed instead to both Enlightenment and Christian ideals of universal human rights, as Professors Sandoz and Barber each noted. There are certainly important tensions between Enlightenment rationalism and even a Protestant Christian faith, tensions evident in, for example, the unsteady compromises of Jeffersonian deism. But I am inclined to agree with the general theme of the papers and the discussion—that most leading framers were confident of the existence of a higher law that could be alternatively discerned in Locke or in the New Testament, and that the Declaration of Independence was a concise summary of these higher law views. I agree, too, that the Declaration's procla-

---

2. M. Gordon, *Assimilation in American Life* (New York: Oxford University Press, 1964), pp. 72-73, 89; W.D. Jordan, *White Over Black* (Chapel Hill: University of North Carolina Press, 1968), pp. 336-339; J. Higham, *Strangers in the Land* (New York: Atheneum Press, 1975). p. 20.

3. Bailyn, pp. 185-188; J. Kettner, *The Development of American Citizenship* (Chapel Hill: University of North Carolina Press, 1978), pp. 132-133, 165-172.

mation of human equality in terms of basic immutable rights was and is a powerful weapon with which to challenge many conventional inequalities, as well as a stirring statement of admirable political ideals. Yet here, too, we must not be oblivious to the support these liberal views could provide for social conditions that seem, at least in principle, inconsistent with the Declaration's goals.

To be sure, the Lockean Enlightenment heritage rejected all claims that one's political identity, as an Englishman, American, or anything else, was in any sense "natural." On Locke's view, a human being is born "a Subject of no Country and Government," and so must become a citizen by tacit or express consent at the age of majority—a view more anti-naturalistic than American law has ever explicitly embraced.[4] But at the same time, such liberalism does strive, as Professor Sandoz observed, to remove a range of economic, intellectual, and spiritual activities from public life. And in so doing, it can allow for the perpetuation and increase of "private" economic and social inequalities that render persons' formal equality in terms of legal and political rights hollow. While the solution to this familiar difficulty is not readily visible, it should not therefore be forgotten. Furthermore, the Enlightenment's fascination with cultural and anthropological differences has sometimes proven usable for "scientific" theories of racial and gender inequality of the sort that tempted Jefferson.[5] Locke's contention that rational labor was needed to create property rights also was often cited to deny the land claims of the allegedly "nomadic" Native Americans.[6] A full treatment of the liberal conceptions refracted in the Declaration, then, has to acknowledge the sanctions they provided for unequal civic statuses, as well as the challenges to such inequalities that are, one hopes, their dominant legacy.

Like the Declaration itself, Locke's liberalism said little about the appropriate form of government, other than insisting that legitimate governments should comply with the principles of social contract theory. On such issues the founders looked instead to the tradition of republican thought, which Professors Carey McWilliams, Lance Banning, and Drew McCoy, among others, examined at the conference as they have in their

---

4. J. Locke, *Two Treatises of Government*, Book II, ed. Peter Laslett (New York: New American Library, 1965), pp. 391-392.
5. T. Jefferson, *The Portable Thomas Jefferson*, ed. Merrill Petersen (New York: Viking Press, 1975), pp. 186-193; M. Gruber, *Women in American Politics* (Oshkosh: Academic Press, 1968), p. 4.
6. W.E. Washburn, *Red Man's Land/White Man's Law* (New York: Charles Scribner's Sons, 1971), pp. 38-41.

writings. The discussions on citizenship, however, did not explore in detail the view of many contemporary scholars that republicanism offered a notion of civic membership very different from the privatistic, property-oriented Lockean liberal conception. As Gordon Wood, J. G. A. Pocock, and others have stressed, a republican citizen should display his civic virtue, his dedication to the common good, through active participation in public life.[7] That republican legacy was reflected in the clear recognition of the founders that all their new governments, including the federal Constitution, must be ultimately popular, however indirectly the people might participate, and must also be free of any titles of nobility or other forms of hereditary aristocracy. However limited its achievements, republicanism could and did serve as an impetus and instrument for successive democratizing movements in American life, a feature that Benjamin Barber wishes to build upon in his evocation of older republics as partial models for American participatory democracy.

But the Greek republics held slaves and restricted aliens, while the Swiss ones have been marked by sharp ethnic divisions often manifested in law. Those facts should not be surprising, for the republican tradition contained at least two basic tenets that have long served to support inequalities in civic statuses in theory and in America's political practices. First, republican thought always insisted that to sustain the social solidarity that promotes public-spiritedness, republics must possess considerable social homogeneity.[8] Hence a republic's governors can properly insist on considerable conformity in political ideology, education, religion, and national origins. In American history, derivative arguments that various groups were too culturally and politically dissimilar to participate effectively in America's republican institutions have repeatedly been used to urge limits on access to citizenship for Catholics, blacks, Native Americans, Asians, southern Europeans, and Hispanics.[9]

The need for a homogeneous citizenry was also used in republican thought to argue that republics must remain small, connected to other regimes, if at all, through a loose defensive and commercial confederation

---

7. G. Wood, *The Creation of the American Republic* (Chapel Hill: University of North Carolina Press, 1969), pp. 28-42, 69; J.G.A. Pocock, *The Machiavellian Moment* (Princeton: Princeton University Press, 1975), pp. 4, 75; L. Banning, *The Jeffersonian Persuasion* (Ithaca: Cornell University Press, 1978), pp. 30-31.

8. H. Storing, *What the Anti-Federalists Were For* (Chicago: University of Chicago Press, 1981), pp. 19-23.

9. Higham, *Strangers*, pp. 6, 40-41, 109, 132-133, 165-186.

or imperial domination.[10] The argument on behalf of small republics was a chief tenet of the anti-Federalists, and it has since been a staple of state's rights interpretations of the Constitution.[11] The insistence that the states must retain extensive powers of self-governance and self-definition has in turn been used to challenge national interference with discriminatory state institutions such as those denying the franchise to blacks and women and limiting the economic opportunities of aliens. Furthermore, Americans have at times proved willing to extend a republican "empire of liberty" over those—first Native Americans, then Filipinos and Puerto Ricans—who were labelled incapable of self-governance, at least for a seemingly interminable "present."[12]

My point, again, is not to deny the moral or political value of the liberal egalitarian ideals of the Declaration of Independence, or of republican calls for popular self-governance. It is to note that liberal and democratic sentiments formed only part of the observable strains in the thought of the founders concerning citizenship, and that these different strains on balance make inequalities in civic statuses that seem unacceptable today appear quite natural in the late 18th century and long after. If we are to explore the founder's thought on citizenship fully, then, the intellectual and political force of all these disparate traditions must be examined. As we undertake such studies, we may become more cautious about contending that either the "natural law" or the "participatory republican" elements in earlier American thought can be relied upon unproblematically today.

Finally, I would note that while Barber may be correct to argue that we have no certain access to the framers' views, only to our own interpretations of those views, that point requires us to pay more attention to the notions of citizenship that have become prominent in American thought —our thought—since the founders' times. As Milton Gordon, John Higham, Philip Gleason, and other scholars have documented, a new understanding of American civic identity came to the fore in American public life during the 1950s and especially the Great Society of the 1960s. That position, which may be termed "democratic cultural pluralism,"

---

10. Pocock, pp. 491-492, 509-511.
11. Wood, pp. 97-107, 120-122; T. Bender, *Community and Social Change in America* (New Brunswick: Rutgers University Press, 1978), pp. 82-85.
12. Pocock, pp. 510-511; F. Jennings, "The Indians' Revolution" in *The American Revolution*, ed. Alfred F. Young (Dekalb: Northern Illinois University Press, 1976), pp. 322-324; J. Cabranes, *Citizenship and the American Empire* (New Haven: Yale University Press, 1979), pp. 29, 41.

builds on the democratic pragmatism of the Progressive era's left-liberal intellectuals, especially John Dewey—as does Barber's own perspective.

Such pragmatism rejects the higher law elements of American liberal thought as lacking intellectual credibility, but it thereby only accentuates the longstanding liberal emphasis on tolerance and freedom for diverse ways of life. It also accepts arguments that inherited ethnocultural identities are often tremendously important to persons, and that democratic participation is normally integral to personal and political liberty. But it insists on permitting persons to seek fulfillment through whatever ethnocultural group memberships they find sustaining, while attempting to make it possible for members of all ethnic and economic groups to participate in a democratic public life on an equal basis. Great Society programs such as the 1964 Civil Rights Act, the liberalizing 1965 Immigration and Naturalization Act, the 1965 Voting Rights Act, the 1968 Bilingual Education and Indian Civil Rights Acts, among others, are often cited as examples of the influence of this egalitarian yet pluralistic conception of American civic identity.[13]

But attractive as this ideal initially seemed in theory, it has proven difficult to realize in practice. Unable to shirk the economic and technological imperatives that have driven us to ever-larger units of social and political organization, American democratic pragmatism has arguably been more successful in supporting the instrumental rationality of the modern bureaucratic state than in promoting any vividly participatory civic institutions. Barber's own work on "strong democracy" suggests that creating means of effective public deliberation in modern life that approach the democratic participation of the Athenian assembly is as difficult a task as discerning transcendental verities.[14] And in practice, modern policies promoting democratic pluralism are often criticized for encouraging loyalty to ethnic, religious, economic and other subgroup identities over commitments to a national political community—thereby fostering a divisive politics of interest-group conflict instead of truly common endeavors, egalitarian diversity, or a genuine concern for individual rights. Ironically, democratic pluralism—which portrays the nation-state as essentially a common arbiter that insists on equal concern and respect for all groups—is held to support equalizing governmental interventions that heighten group tensions, such as busing and affirmative action, while it also erodes any sense that democratic participation may

---

13. Gordon, pp. 16, 85-86, 132-159; Higham, *Send*, pp. 59-60, 220; Gleason, pp. 119-121, 142.

14. B.R. Barber, *Strong Democracy* (Berkeley: University of California Press, 1984).

require not just self-expression but also the sacrifice of certain subgroup interests for the national good.[15]

I cannot examine here how far these charges may or may not be sustainable, but they are clearly important for any analysis of contemporary American citizenship, particularly ones that attempt to advance Deweyite participatory democratic ideals. The conference's focus on the content and authority of the founders' views appeared to limit somewhat the extent to which these pressing modern issues were developed and debated. In sum, the papers and discussion usefully explored several essential questions concerning citizenship and human rights in America's past and present. But inevitably, perhaps, those topics are far more complex and troubling than either those relatively brief essays, or this even briefer one, have indicated.

---

15. Higham, *Send*, pp. 230, 246; S.H. Beer, "In Search of a New Public Philosophy" in *The New American Political System*, ed. Anthony King (Washington, D.C.: American Enterprise Institute, 1978), p. 44; C. B. Keely, "Immigration and the American Future" in *Ethnic Relations in America*, ed. Lance Liebman (Englewood Cliffs: Prentice-Hall Inc., 1982), pp. 28-65.

Chapter Five

Economics and the Constitution

Does the form of government established by the Constitution rest upon particular economic requirements or a particular economic system? Was the Constitution intended to give political sanction to an existing economic order? As Federalist #10 *makes clear, the framers thought that the character of economic life was important to the success of constitutional government; but as the quarrel between the Republicans and the Federalists makes clear, what that character should be was a matter of dispute. Can today's economic disputes be understood in terms of the debate over the larger principles of constitutional government?*

"Economic Liberties" and the Foundations of American Constitutionalism: The Federalist Perspective

Jennifer Nedelsky

> The most rapid Advances in the State of Society, are produced by Commerce. Commerce once begun is from its own nature progressive. . . . It requires not only the perfect security of property but perfect good Faith. Hence its effects are to increase civil and diminish political liberty.
>
> Governeur Morris

The question of whether the American Constitution requires a particular economic system or a particular conception of economic liberties has been continuously and often fiercely debated since at least the 1880s. At one level the issue might seem settled. In 1937 the Supreme Court decided that the Constitution did not require the particular conception of economic liberties associated with the laissez faire ideology of the turn of the century.[1] Since that time the power of the government to regulate the economy has been used increasingly and has been widely accepted as legitimate. Yet the debate continues over the extent to which private rights of property and contract set limits to the legitimate scope of governmental action.

The conservative right argues that we have abandoned the economic underpinnings of the Constitution and thus threatened the very foundation of our constitutional system. They urgently advocate a recognition of private property and unfettered "private"[2] economic decisions as essential components of our constitutional liberties, indeed prerequisites for them. Egalitarian liberals, on the contrary, argue that the state has not gone far enough in reforming the unequal distribution of wealth and power our system has wrought. The Constitution certainly permits, and according to some even requires, not only regulation, but redistribution. The radical left may agree with the right that "free enterprise" (and its

---

1. West Coast Hotel v. Parrish (300 U.S. 379) is the conventionally recognized turning point.
2. Throughout this essay I will use quotation marks to denote a common usage whose implications I do not accept.

iniquities) are integral to the American political system, but concludes that the constitutional structure is therefore irredeemable.

Each argument makes claims about the relation between our constitutional form of government and a particular economic system. Many of these arguments make at least implicit recourse to "the tradition" of American constitutional government. The right explicitly claims to be urging a return to the true intent of the Framers. While the problems of determining the "intent" of the Framers are probably insurmountable (and the jurisprudential significance at least debatable), an examination of the origins of the Constitution can help us to understand the ways in which conceptions of the economic order of the new republic helped shape the constitutional structure.

At the core of the debate over economic liberties and the Constitution is the question of the constitutional status of the rights of property and the related rights of contract. In looking at the debates over the Constitution in 1787 it is obvious that the protection of property was a central concern. That fact alone, however, cannot answer the question of property's constitutional status. We need to know more about the nature of that concern: why the focus on protecting property, what did they mean by property, how did they propose to protect it? James Madison and Gouverneur Morris, two of the most important Framers at the 1787 convention, can help us understand the Federalist answers to those questions. Madison is the most thoughtful of the Framers on these questions, and he is also the most characteristic of the dominant mode of thought at the convention (in part because he was so influential). The Constitution that emerged from that convention is in important ways a Madisonian document. Morris is less characteristic than Madison, but he is the most directly interested in the relation between economic and political institutions. His views are sometimes starker than those of his fellow Federalists, but his candid arguments reveal widely shared assumptions in Federalist thought and choices implicit in the constitutional structure.

In the first two parts of this essay, I will use the thought of Madison and Morris to shed light on the role played by the Federalist conception of property in the formation of the Constitution. In the final part, I will explore the significance of these origins for current debates about economic liberties and the Constitution.

I

James Madison revealed the importance he accorded to property in the preamble he wanted to affix to the Constitution. He would have returned property to the trilogy of rights Jefferson had amended in the Declaration of Independence; life, liberty and the pursuit of happiness were incomplete without property:

> government is instituted and ought to be exercised for the benefit of the people; which consists in the enjoyment of life and liberty, with the right of acquiring and using property and generally pursuing and obtaining happiness and safety.[3]

And, of course, Madison's famous *The Federalist*, No. 10 proclaimed the "protection of the different and unequal faculties of acquiring property" as the "first object of the government."[4] These general claims about the purpose of government correspond to Madison's actions in the 1787 convention—a consistent focus on the capacity of the new republic to protect property.

The importance of property in Madison's perception of the problems of republican government is revealed most clearly in his famous discussions of faction in *The Federalist*, No. 10. He argued there that all minorities are vulnerable in a republic and that majority factions may form around a great variety of issues and differences. But "the most common and durable source of factions has been the various and unequal distribution of property." And this inevitable conflict would also form the chief task of government: "The regulation of these various and interfering interests forms the principal task of modern legislation." Both Madison's analysis of the problem and the solution he held out addressed the general problem of the vulnerability of all individual rights. But property was the central instance of the problem, the example that Madison considered most serious and that would be the central issue for governments. If the

---

3. Speech in the House of Representatives, June 8, 1789, in *The Mind of the Founder: Sources of the Political Thought of James Madison*, ed. Marvin Meyers, The American Heritage Series (Indianapolis, 1973), p. 215 (hereinafter cited as Meyers).

4. Madison also said that there were not one, but two "cardinal objects of government: the rights of persons and the rights of property." (Remarks on Mr. Jefferson's Draught of a Constitution," October, 1788, Meyers, p.58.) Understanding the priority Madison accorded to property in the context of this dual concern is a particularly fruitful way of understanding his political thought and his plans for the Constitution. It is, however, beyond the scope of this essay. Here I will be focusing on the nature of Madison's concern with property, leaving out some of the problems that focus posed for him. For a fuller consideration, see my chapter on Madison in Jennifer Nedelsky, *Private Property and the Formation of the United States Constitution* (Chicago: University of Chicago Press, forthcoming).

new Constitution could not solve the problems posed by the vulnerability of property, it could not provide a successful foundation for the republic. A failure to protect property would be a failure to meet both the immediate challenge and the most basic objectives of republican government.

Property was a compelling symbol of the problems of republican government, and focal point for their solutions, in part because it was not merely symbolic. Madison thought the security of private property was itself extremely important. Most of his arguments about the importance of the problem were aimed at instructing his audience about the dire consequences of a failure to provide adequate security. He did not spend time explaining why property was a fundamental right. He assumed that that basic belief was shared. What people failed to understand was what constituted a violation of property rights, and the threat such violations posed to the republic itself.

The lesson Madison most often tried to teach was the relation between property and stability. The security of property was essential to economic and political stability, and stability was essential for the survival of the republican government:

> The instability, injustice and confusion introduced into the public councils have, in truth, been the mortal diseases under which popular governments have everywhere perished.[5]

Paper money and debtor relief laws were the most common form of instability, injustice, and confusion in the public councils of America. Madison repeatedly urged the need to control such "internal vicissitudes of State policy, and the aggression of interested majorities on the rights of minorities and of individuals."[6]

Legislation that threatened the security of property had an inevitably destabilizing effect: "One legislative interference is but the first link of a long chain of repetitions, every subsequent interference being naturally produced by the effects of the preceding."[7] Such constant shifts in laws governing entitlements and transactions would have a devastating effect on the economic order. They would make returns on investment uncer-

---

5. *The Federalist*, ed. Jacob E. Cooke (Middleton, Connecticut, 1977), (No. 10), p. 56-57.

6. To Washington, April 16, 1787, in *The Writings of James Madison*, in 9 vols., ed. Gaillard Hunt (New York, 1900-1910) vol. 2, p. 346 (hereafter cited as *Writings*. See also letters to Jefferson and Randolph advocating the need for a federal veto on state legislation. Together they make clear that he had paper money and debtor relief in mind when he made his frequent references to the "vicissitudes of state policy." Ibid, p. 326 and 339.

7. *The Federalist*, No. 44, p. 301.

tain and undermine confidence in both public and private contracts—all prerequisites for long term enterprise.

Madison was in essence arguing that the republic required a certain kind of economic order, one in which his conceptions of property entitle-ments and the obligations of contract were consistently embodied in the laws. The economic order that Madison saw as essential for both justice and stability required the proper legal framework. The fluctuations and injustice that had characterized state legislation under the Articles of Confederation would ultimately destroy the republic. In the long run, such legislation would undermine the "national character," that is, the character necessary for an effective market economy: a character that respected the obligations of contract and the rights of property.[8] Even in the short run people might not tolerate the insecurity and instability of the vicissitudes of state policy: "was it to be supposed that republican liberty could long exist under the abuses of it practiced in some of the States?"[9] If a republican solution could not be found, people would turn to other forms of government that could guarantee security and a sound economy.

The arguments I have discussed so far have focused on the conse-quences of threats to property rights. Contemporary advocates of "eco-nomic liberties" also make that sort of consequential or instrumental argument. Their major emphasis, however, is on the relation of economic liberties to individual freedom. Although, Madison offered little by way of direct articulation of such claims, it is possible to reconstruct his concep-tion of property rights and their basic value.

Once again, *The Federalist*, No. 10 is particularly revealing. Madison's claim for the priority of property is a very particular and unusual one: the first object of government is the protection of "the faculties of men from which the rights of property originate," namely, "the different and unequal faculties of acquiring property." The argument from which this claim emerges makes clear that the exercise of these faculties is a basic part of man's liberties.

He had argued that there were two ways to remove the cause of faction. One was to destroy liberty. The second was to ensure that every citizen had the same opinions, the same passions, and the same interests. If liberty were not destroyed, there were two aspects of liberty itself that

---

8. See *The Federalist*, Nos. 37 and 26.
9. *The Records of the Federal Convention of 1787*, ed. Max Farrand, rev. ed. in 4 vols. (New Haven, 1966) vol. 1, p. 134.

would make the second alternative impossible: the free exercise of man's reason and the free exercise of his faculties for acquiring property. To limit either dimension of freedom would be to return to the first alternative, "a remedy worse than the disease." Despite the fact that "the most common and durable source of factions has been the various and unequal distribution of property," Madison did not seriously consider the possibility of limiting the exercise of the faculties that led to this unequal distribution.

This now opens a question central to our modern debates over economic liberties: what did it mean to protect the different and unequal faculties of acquiring property? Madison was never explicit, but he gave some indication in his 1792 article on property: "That is not a just government, nor is property secure under it, where arbitrary restrictions, exemptions, and monopolies deny to part of its citizens that free use of their faculties and free choice of occupations which . . . are the means of acquiring property . . . ."[10] Government should, apparently, ensure the free exercise of the faculties of acquisition by preventing unwarranted restrictions on this freedom. No citizen should be denied the opportunity to exercise his faculties.

It was thus opportunity and, implicitly, equal opportunity that the phrase "faculties for acquiring property" suggested. But it was explicitly opportunity for *unequal* faculties. Madison even suggested that the rights of property had their origin in the natural inequality among men: it was the different and unequal faculties from which the rights of property originate. Madison's conception of property thus appears rooted in inequality. He was in any case explicit that, "from the protection of different and unequal faculties of acquiring property, the possession of different degrees and kinds of property immediately results."[11]

Madison made it equally clear that the resulting unequal possessions were entitled to protection: "the personal right to acquire property, which is a natural right, gives to property, when acquired, a right to protection, as a social right."[12] It is interesting, and important for the current debate, that Madison noted this distinction between the natural right to acquisition and the social right to possession. The whole thrust of Madison's arguments, however, was to invest that social right with the sanctity of the natural right from which it derived. As *The Federalist*, No. 10 made clear,

10. "Property," *National Gazette*, March 29, 1792, Meyers, p. 245.
11. *The Federalist*, No. 10, p. 58.
12. Speech in the Virginia Constitutional Convention, December 2, 1829, Meyers, p. 512.

unequal possessions were the natural result of liberty; the protection of liberty implied the protection of possessions.

Madison's fear and condemnation of redistributive schemes such as paper money and debtor relief are now clearer still. Such policies not only had terrible consequences, they were fundamental violations of both justice and liberty and thus intrinsically evil. *The Federalist*, No. 10, for example, referred to "a rage for paper money, for an abolition of debts, for an equal distribution of property, or any other improper or wicked project."

We can now also see something more about Madison's basic conception of property. It was clearly not simply land or even material goods. His choice of the phrase "the faculties for acquiring property" emphasized a non-material dimension of property. Similarly, the sort of attacks on property that he repeatedly warned against were not straightforward confiscations, but the more indirect infringements inherent in paper money and debtor relief. Those interferences with the security of expectation and transaction were the dangers the republic had already experienced and would be likely to be plagued with if adequate precautions were not taken. They were both more likely and more invidious than direct confiscations because the violations of property rights were less overt. One of Madison's chief concerns was to make it clear that such indirect attacks were nevertheless violations of basic rights, and that it was therefore crucial that the new Constitution prevent them. Madison's understanding of property thus went far beyond the focus on land that we associate with the traditional image of the yeoman farmer. It had a modern, sophisticated quality, whose echoes we can recognize in the opinions of the *Lochner* era.

Madison did not, however, envision a government that simply took a "hands off" attitude toward property. On the contrary, as everyone familiar with *The Federalist*, No. 10 knows, "the regulation of those various and interfering [property] interests forms the principal task of modern legislation." Mediating competing economic interests for the public good and providing the legal framework necessary for a prosperous market economy were a large part of what government was for. The obvious question, and the one around which debate has swirled for the past hundred years, is on what basis one distinguishes between appropriate regulation that is the proper task of government on the one hand, and choices among competing interests (e.g., debtors and creditors) that amount to violations of property rights, on the other.[13] Madison clearly thought he knew the difference. He did not, however, try to offer a systematic explanation of that difference. He did try to make clear that the redistributive consequences of paper money and debtor relief laws of the 1780s placed them in the unacceptable category. And he had some hopes that the contracts clause in Article 1 would prevent such abuses. But his real hope lay not in defining categories for constitutional prohibition, but in ensuring that the sort of men who would know the difference would end up in the new offices of the federal government—and giving the federal government a veto over state legislation.

Whatever the ambiguity about the precise dimensions of Madison's conception of property rights, it is quite clear that he wanted the new government to treat that conception as sacred and inviolable. It is important for our understanding of the constitutional status of property to recognize the implications of that objective: Madison wanted a structure of institutions that could effectively thwart the wishes of the majority. The desire of the majority for a greater share of property was not merely a passing whim (although the demands for particular forms of debtor relief might be temporary excesses). The propertyless would ultimately be a majority who would "secretly sigh for a more equal share of life's blessings."[14] Madison wanted to prevent the implementation of an essentially permanent desire of the majority for redistribution in their favor.

Madison did recognize majority rule as a basic principle, but one in tension with other values:

> True it is that no other rule exists, by which any question which may divide a society, can be ultimately determined, but the will of the majority; but it is also true that the majority may trespass on the rights of the minority.[15]

Majority rule would inevitably conflict with the basic value of justice. And the injustice of the majority had no higher moral status than the more obvious evils of a tyrannical minority. In short the will of the majority was not itself a standard of legitimacy for governmental action. To take the "interest of the majority [as] the political standard of right and

---

13. The discerning reader may have noted a similar ambiguity in my earlier statement that Madison thought that government should prevent *unwarranted* restrictions on the exercise of faculties for acquiring property. The real question is, of course, which restrictions are unwarranted. Madison provides even less of an answer to that question.

14. Farrand, vol. 2, p. 422.

15. *Memorial and Remonstrance Against Religious Assessments*, 1785, Meyers, pp. 9-10. See also *The Federalist*, No. 43.

wrong" would be to re-establish "under another name and a more specious form, force as the measure of right."[16] The proper standard was provided by "the rules of justice,"[17] which stood above the will of the majority.

The conflict between the sanctity of property rights and majority rule was thus resolved at the level of principle (leaving open how it was to be institutionalized). Madison clearly thought that the rules of justice required the protection of property. The rights of property were based on natural rights. Majority rule on the other hand, "does not result . . . from a law of nature, but from compact founded on utility."[18] Republican principles must always be understood in the context of the highest object of government: "Justice is the end of government. It is the end of civil society. It ever has been and ever will be pursued until it be attained, or until liberty be lost in the pursuit."[19]

This clear ordering of priorities is crucial in understanding the role property played in Madison's conception of republican government. It does not, however, take us very far in resolving any specific dispute over exactly what limits the rules of justice set. Madison never offered a definition of justice. As with "property," he seemed to consider the meaning of these central concepts unproblematic. Indeed, it seems to be Madison's uninquiring certainty about property and, more broadly, justice that allowed him to treat them as setting bounds to the legitimate choices of the majority. Had he seen these concepts as fundamentally contested—rather than merely misunderstood or neglected—the problems of treating them as standards against which to measure the will of the majority would have been far more obvious and troubling.

The priority Madison accorded to property over majority rule was no doubt eased by his confidence that his understanding of justice and the rights of property would work to the benefit of all. He clearly believed that in placing property above majority rule, he was not placing the interests of the few above those of the many. Part of his confidence was based on the belief that the existence of poverty did not suggest any injustice in the system. Poverty was inevitable in any country fully peopled. Madison was acutely aware that for society as a whole to benefit from an economic system based on private property, most would end up without property

---

16. To James Monroe, October 5, 1786, *Writings*, vol. 2, p. 272.
17. The phrase is from *The Federalist*, No. 10, p. 57.
18. To Jefferson, February 4, 1790, *Writings*, vol. 5, p. 440.
19. *The Federalist*, No. 51, p. 352.

and some without even employment.[20] But the inevitable presence of that "unfavored class of the community" did not mean that the government had failed in its obligations. Redistribution could not overcome the problem of poverty. On the contrary, the redistributive schemes the majority were likely to clamor for would only make matters worse.

A proper legal framework, providing just and stable laws of property and contract would ultimately be to the benefit of all. Indeed, only such a framework could serve the long run interests of the poor. The responsibility of the statesman was, therefore, to resist the unjust and destructive demands of the poor for encroachments on the rights of property. That was the challenge that the inevitability of poverty posed to the new republic.

We can now see the basic dimensions of the role property played in Madison's constitutional thinking. The free exercise of the faculties to acquire property was an essential element of liberty; the protection of the unequal possessions resulting from such free exercise was required both by the fundamental rules of justice and the prudential requirements of economic and political stability. Threats to property were certain to arise in a republic, and such threats were intrinsically evil, dangerous, and indicative of the most fundamental problem of republican government. The ability to contain those threats and the broader problem of majority oppression was a top priority for the new Constitution. The implications of that priority are clearer still in the political thought of Gouverneur Morris.

II

Morris' primary interest in designing a new constitution was to ensure that it provided the framework for mutually sustaining economic and political institutions. He was certain that the republic could not endure if it undermined its economy, and he had a clear sense that the kind of economic order he envisioned required certain political institutions. Indeed, it seems that Morris' primary commitment was to his vision of a

---

20. "Let the lands be shared among [the people] ever so wisely, and let them be supplied with labourers ever so plentifully; as there must be a great surplus of subsistence, there will remain a great surplus of inhabitants, a greater by far than will be employed. . . . What is to be done with this surplus?" To Jefferson, June 19, 1786, in the *Papers of James Madison*, ed. William T. Hutchison and William M.E. Rachal, in 10 vols. (Chicago, 1962-77), vol. 9, p. 767 (hereafter cited as *Papers*).

free market economy; republican institutions were desirable because, if properly controlled, they could best foster that economic order. As a result, Morris paid more attention to the interaction between the economic and political realm than did many of his fellow Federalists, who shared his general vision, if not the starkness of his priorities. He also addressed the questions of economic policy very directly, so that we can get a clearer sense of his vision of the economic order.

The foundation of the political and economic order was private property. It was property, not life or liberty, for which men joined together in government.[21] Indeed property was the basis for all progress, all advantages of civilized life:

> property in Goods is the first Step in Progression from a State of Nature to that of Society. Till property in Lands be admitted Society continues rude and barbarous. ... Progress will be accelerated in Proportion as the Administration of Justice is more or less exact. ... [T]he state of society is perfected in the Proportion as the Rights of property are secured.[22]

The unequivocal priority Morris accorded to property was not characteristic of the Federalists, but the rest of the picture sketched in the quote above is. The security of property was linked not only to all the benefits of society, but to the basic principles of justice and morality. These principles were embedded in his political-economy.

Commercial society, in Morris' view, could only thrive if justice were ensured. Commerce thus fostered as well as demanded the basic virtues of justice and morality. But these virtues were not compatible with unrestrained political liberty:

> The most rapid Advances in the State of Society, are produced by Commerce. Commerce once begun is from its own Nature progressive. ... It requires not only the perfect Security of property but perfect good Faith. Hence its effects are to increase civil and diminish political liberty.[23]

Morris had a strikingly modern notion of property rights, one that emphasized free use, rather than possession:

> The spirit of Commerce requires that property be sacred. ... It requires that every Citizen have the Right freely to use his property.[24]

---

21. Farrand, vol. 1, p. 533.
22. "Political Inquiries," undated manuscript, probably after 1800, in the Gouverneur Morris Collection, Columbia University Libraries Special Collections, New York (hereafter cited as GMC).
23. Ibid.
24. Ibid.

Morris wanted this conception of property rights to replace wrongheaded notions of economics and of publicly enforceable morality. Thus he defended money lenders against the charge that they were an unsavory lot making profit in unseemly ways. He criticized sumptuary laws and price regulations.[25] Like many of his counterparts today, Morris' arguments alternated between appealing to the basic rights of property and to more pragmatic arguments that interferences with free use would have undesirable consequences. Freedom of use and productivity went together and were the foundation of a free and open society in which opportunity would abound.

Like Madison, Morris wanted the institutions outlined in the new Constitution to be able to control and contain the popular pressures for redistribution. They shared the belief that the redistributive measures the people were likely to demand would violate rights, undermine the economy, and ultimately threaten the republic. However, Morris differed from Madison in ways that reveal the implications of the importance the Federalists attached to the protection of property.

First, Morris was considerably more straightforward about the consequences for the poor of the system of government he advocated. He did believe, as Madison did, that his vision of the market republic would provide more for the poor than any other system. An economy based on the secure protection of the rights of property, in particular the free use of property, offered both the greatest prosperity and the greatest opportunity. If the economy was in good shape, the least well off would benefit; if it were harmed by pernicious redistributive policies, the poor would suffer. Morris' belief in this form of "trickle down" theory, did not, however, prevent him from clearly seeing that his system was designed to keep the majority from getting what they wanted: more of the necessities and some of the comforts of life. The poor were misguided in their judgments about the policies that could better their lot, but they were not fundamentally mistaken in seeing their interests in permanent and hostile conflict with those of the propertied. The propertyless wanted to get a greater share of the resources the propertied had acquired; the propertied wanted to prevent them from doing so. For Morris class conflict was not a misperception, but the basic reality of political life.

He was also very clear that while the people would have a greater share of political power in his market republic than in any other form of government, their political liberty had to be restricted. A complex com-

---

25. Farrand, vol. 2, p. 344.

mercial society was simply incompatible with democracy. The people were not capable of governing a modern market economy. They could not be relied upon to understand its requirements:

> Arts produce a Change as essential as Population. In order that Government decide properly it must understand the subject. The Objects of Legislation are in a rude Society simple in a more advanced State complex. Of two things therefore one. Either Society must stop in its Progress for the Purpose of preserving political liberty or the latter must be checked that the former may proceed.[26]

Morris also explicitly recognized, as few of his fellow Framers did, the consequences of economic inequality: the poor would not really enjoy an equality of rights. He saw the tension between the republican rhetoric of equality and the inevitable reality of economic inequality:

> Man is a creature of sense, and governed invariably by his feelings. Now you can easily make him feel, that in point of rights he is equal to every other man. Vanity may even whisper to him that he is so in point of talent, and if vanity were remiss, the prompter flattery is at hand. But the more he feels his equality of rights and talents, the more must he feel his inequality in point of possessions. Where these are wanting, he has rights which he cannot exercise, talents which he cannot employ, desires which he cannot gratify, and in consequence resentments he cannot allay.[27]

Morris was, of course, unshaken in his conviction that economic inequality was necessary for the advantages of civilized society; he concluded that the rhetoric of equality was dangerous.

Finally, Morris differed from his fellow Federalists in one somewhat surprising way. While sharing their concerns about the threats the people posed to property (and more broadly to the secure foundations of a market economy), he did not see that threat as the greatest danger. Rather the greatest danger came from the rich. In a commercial republic, the rich would have advantages that outweighed the numerical power of the poor. Economic power would inevitably be translated into political power and could undermine the republic. The new Constitution should be able to counter the threats from the rich as well as the poor. Morris was never able to persuade his fellows at the convention to share this point of view. His

---

26. "Equality; comments on the rights of man," a reply to the declaration of rights of man by the London Corresponding Society, ca 1796, GMC.
27. To William Carmichael, November 5, 1792, in *The Life and Correspondence of Gouverneur Morris*, ed. Jared Sparks, 3 vols. (Boston, 1831), vol. 2, p. 246-47 (hereafter cited as Sparks).

arguments that failed at the convention reveal to us some of the consequences of the property-centered Federalist perspective and stand as an important critique of the ability of the American political system to deal with the relation between economic and political power. If one could have asked Morris the twentieth century question of whether a "free market economy" was the necessary foundation of American constitutionalism, he would clearly have answered in the affirmative. But the question would not really have been well-tailored to his views. A market economy was an intrinsic part of the regime he hoped to institute in America. His vision of the republic was that of a *market* republic. The question would have sounded odd because achieving the freedom, openness, fluidity, prosperity, and strength of a market economy was not a prerequisite for the republic, but its objective. He had considerable ambivalence about democracy, but believed that a republic was the form of government best suited to the economic order he sought. In particular he seemed to think that an aristocracy (which he was in some ways temperamentally drawn to) would not foster the openness necessary for all the advantages of a market economy. An entrenched elite would only want to consolidate its power and privilege.[28] Morris would sooner have said that a republic was necessary for the market than the other way around. But he did, of course, also believe, as all his fellow Federalists did, that if the republic failed to provide the necessary foundations for a market economy, the republic itself could not long survive.

The sharp priority Morris gave to the economy was not characteristic of the thought that shaped our Constitution. What was characteristic, was the hierarchy of civil and political liberties that Morris articulated so clearly. Civil rights, particularly the rights of property and contract upon which the market economy rested, were the true ends of government.[29] Political rights were merely the means of achieving those ends. In any conflict, the ends should, of course, take priority over the means. From this perspective we get a different slant on the question of whether economic rights are part of the foundation of the Constitution: those rights were a major part of what the Constitution was designed to protect. It wasn't exactly that the Constitution required them, but that they were part

---

28. One can see these views in his discussions of the need to avoid policies that would foster a landed nobility and in his hostility to slavery as an aristocratic institution. See, for example, Farrand, vol. 2, p. 222.

29. But not, of course, exclusively those rights. The Federalists also wanted the new republic to protect the full range of rights later outlined in the Bill of Rights.

of the purpose of the Constitution. And the success of the Constitution did require the security of those rights, because the insecurity and instability that would result from systematic invasions of those rights would prove intolerable. Violations of the rights of property—including free use and respect for the obligations of contract—would be intolerable in part because of the economic consequences, in part because of the sense of insecurity such violations would create, in part because sustained official injustice was itself intolerable.

When we move to this more general sense of the consequences of failures to protect "economic liberties" (as they are called today), we leave behind any of the idiosyncracies of Morris' thought and are squarely within the Madisonian mainstream of Federalist thought. One of the important differences between Madison and Morris was that Madison never had quite such a clarity or confidence about his priorities. Like Morris, he thought that the protection of the rights of persons and property were the proper ends of government and the mechanics of republican representation merely the means. But he remained far more uneasy than Morris about the limitations on political liberty this hierarchy implied. He also never ascribed to property a priority *in principle* over the rights of persons, although the institutions he advocated would surely have given greater protection and representation to property than to persons.[30] He found the task of balancing the rights of persons, the rights of property, and the requirements of republican principles to be the most difficult task of politics. And he never found a wholly satisfactory solution to this problem. The solution he proposed in 1787 would have given significant priority to property in practice, and considerable priority of civil over political rights in principle as well as in practice. It would also have left a certain vagueness about all the priorities.

The Constitution adopted by the 1787 convention left the question of priorities vaguer still. It did prohibit state governments from issuing paper money or impairing the obligation of contracts. These had been the chief sources of the violations of rights the Federalists were so concerned about. The safety of these rights at the hands of the federal government, however, was not secured by efforts to place them beyond the reach of the legislature through prohibitions. Rather the security of the federal government lay in its structure.

The institutions were designed to maximize the likelihood that the right sort of men would be elected to office. (Both the Federalists and the

---

30. This argument is spelled out at length in Nedelsky, *Private Property*.

Anti-Federalists agreed that the size of the election districts meant that even the House of Representatives was likely to be composed of the elite. To the Anti-Federalists this was a betrayal of republican principles; to the Federalists it was the sensible way to design a government.)[31] And the increasingly mediated structure of institutions would put a whole series of checks between the desires of the people and their implementation. But it was not until the establishment of judicial review that the hierarchy of civil over political rights was directly institutionalized in the form of rights as enforceable boundaries to the legitimate power of the government.

This is not the place to discuss fully the rise of judicial review. It *is* important for our purposes here that the protection of property, especially through the contract clause, was central to the establishment of judicial review. Judicial review became firmly established during a time of intense partisan conflict between the Jeffersonians (the heirs of the Anti-Federalists) and the Federalists (the heirs of their 1787 namesake). When the Jeffersonians won the elections of 1800, it seemed to the Federalists that the carefully crafted structure of the Constitution was not enough to assure the protection of basic rights and the foundation of the economic order. Despite the Federalist victory in 1787, the structure of the economy and the meaning of the rights underpinning that structure, proved to be fiercely contested. And the wrong side seemed to have just won overwhelmingly. The foundations of the political-economic system needed to be insulated from the conflicts of politics, and the Federalist-controlled courts offered the means of doing so.

Under John Marshall's leadership, the Supreme Court claimed to be authorized to define constitutional rights and to enforce them as limits on the legislatures. This claim was particularly effective with respect to property rights. Who better to know what property rights consisted in and when they were violated than the courts, the age old interpreters of the common law of property? If the meaning of property was disputed, if the polity was divided on whether a particular law constituted a violation of property rights, the judiciary could convincingly claim to be particularly well suited to resolve the dispute. In the first decades of the nineteenth century, the Court successfully established the authority to draw the line between the realm of politics, in which shifting, conflicting views of policy were to be hammered out, and the realm of law, in which constitutionally

---

31. See Jennifer Nedelsky, "Confining Democratic Politics: Federalists, Anti-Federalists and the Constitution," *Harvard Law Review*, 96 (1982), pp. 340-360.

protected (and judicially defined) rights were to be insulated from the vagaries of political conflict.

This transformation of hierarchies of principle into institutionally enforceable boundaries is among the most important legacies of the importance of property at the founding. In America, the idea that rights can and should form limits to what government can legitimately do was given a powerful institutional manifestation in judicial review. Just as Madison's struggle to find solutions to the conflicting principles of republicanism—personal rights, property rights, and political rights—was shaped by his focus on protecting property, the establishment of judicial review took place to a great extent around the protection of property and, more broadly, of the foundations of the economic order. Both the idea and the institutionalization of rights as limits have thus grown up around property as the central instance and symbol of rights which can legitimately limit the will of the majority. "Economic liberties" did serve as a foundation of American constitutionalism in the sense of this pivotal link between property and limited government.[32]

III

We can now turn to what all this tells us about the ongoing debate over the status of economic liberties in the Constitution. There is no question that the Federalists thought that property was a basic right and that the rights of property and contract were linked to other liberties. Their concern with protecting property did not, however, lead them to build into the Constitution a set of specific prohibitions or commands. The Constitution does not explicitly spell out the economic foundations the Federalists considered so essential. It does not try to define the rights of property. The contracts clause was an important prohibition, but there was no attempt to define, and thus fix, what constituted an impairment. The Constitution relies instead on the very structure of its institutions. The result is both that it is hard to point to the document to show that it

---

32. There is one important difference between what is usually meant by "economic liberties" today and the kinds of rights the Federalists were concerned with. The Federalists gave little attention to freedom of contract in the sense of an absence of regulation of the terms under which one sells one's labor. They were concerned about the free use of property, and about upholding obligations entered into contractually. Neither of these concerns centered on labor power. However, the free use of one's labor power fits easily within Madison's concern for protecting the faculties of acquiring property.

requires a certain interpretation of economic rights, and that the implications of the Framers' original preoccupation with protecting property go
very deep. The whole structure is designed to achieve that protection. It
may thus be that while the left and the right agree that our constitutional
system was founded on a particular economic system, the left may be
correct about the ways that foundation has tinged the whole system, while
the right is wrong in its claims that particular economic rights can be
shown to be built into the Constitution.

There have been two important consequences of this original importance of property that I will only note here without trying to present the
arguments. The first is implicit in Gouverneur Morris' thought. In their
preoccupation with protecting property from the poor, the Federalists
neglected the problem of protecting the poor from the propertied. More
generally, they gave little attention to the ways in which economic power
can be wielded in the political sphere. They were simply not persuaded by
Morris' arguments that in a *commercial* republic the advantages of the rich
would make them, not the poor, the major threat to the republic and to
the rights of its citizens. Neither our institutions nor the dominant traditions of our political thought has been well suited to deal with that
problem. The second consequence is that the same preoccupation produced a neglect of the problem of participation. With the focus on
containing the threat the people had posed to property, it is not surprising that there was little attention paid to fostering their participation in
politics. The objective was to contain, not enhance popular power.

The third consequence of the original importance of property is one I
have already discussed briefly: in America, the concept of limited government developed around property as the central instance of a right that
stood beyond the legitimate reach of the majority. It is this consequence
that has the greatest implications for the challenge our regulatory-welfare
state poses to the status of property and the idea of boundaries. I shall
return to this issue as I address the question of what our Constitution, or
perhaps better, our form of constitutionalism, requires.

Does the Constitution *require* a particular conception of economic liberty or a particular economic system? I think, as indicated above, that it
would be very difficult to claim that the document itself explicitly man-

dated either.[33] Our constitutional system might nevertheless require a particular economic system in order to function or to give effect to its basic values. In this sense the Federalists clearly thought that the republic whose institutional framework they were creating required "economic liberties." They believed that a failure to protect the basic rights of property and the obligations of contract would result in economic and political chaos, would create a cycle of instability and a widespread sense of insecurity in the population. All of these beliefs are, however, not claims about principle, but about political reality. If they are wrong, they lose their force. One might argue that the kinds of incursions on the traditional rights of property and contract that have come to characterize our administrative state have not in fact had these effects (although some would surely argue that they have). If the dire consequences anticipated did not come to pass, then we could dispense with the many Federalist arguments that were essentially consequentialist in nature.

Of course, the Federalists also believed that there was a more fundamental connection between property and liberty. The use and acquisition of property were basic elements of liberty. Again, there are various arguments one can make about why we should be unpersuaded by particular beliefs of the Federalists about the requirements for our constitutional system. One might say that the nature of the relation between property and liberty has changed in the era of modern corporate capitalism, or that we have now seen the relationship more clearly. In some ways, the Supreme Court's shift in 1937 amounted to an acceptance of the argument that to protect liberty effectively for all, the traditional meaning of property and contract had to be reconceived.[34] But despite the significance of the change in the scale of economic power at the turn of the nineteenth century, I am not persuaded that it raised issues fundamentally different from those the Federalists were concerned with. The voices of the *Lochner* era and of modern day Friedmanite conservatives are, in important ways, faithful echoes of the Federalist conception of rights. I think the "changed circumstances" argument cannot carry one very far in

---

33. The issues discussed here raise questions about the proper theory of constitutional interpretation, but I shall not try to delve directly into the complicated issues of what beyond the document might constitute "the Constitution" or what the authoritative sources for its interpretation are.

34. One could make this argument despite the fact that the history of property law in the nineteenth century hardly looks the way the laissez faire ideologues would have had us believe.

the move to reject the Federalists' judgment about the nature of the threats of egalitarian demands.[35]

One can also argue that property was always only a means to higher ends. The argument starts from the claim that the Constitution really protects liberty and perhaps some other core values such as autonomy or privacy. Property, the argument goes, held the position it did in the Federalists' views because they saw property as essential to give effect to those values. If we find that these core values are best protected by means other than private property, the Constitution should be interpreted in light of that perception. Property would then lose its privileged status because it does not serve the function or have the qualities that were the basis for that status.

Another argument for transforming the role of property and "economic liberties" in the Constitution is that we should simply reinterpret property to mean whatever we think should count as entitlements. The Framers had ideas about entitlements which no longer comport with our best moral theory. We can comfortably disregard these ideas both because we should follow our best moral theory and because the Constitution requires us only to respect property and contract, not any particular definition of those terms.

All these arguments make me uneasy. One need not subscribe to any simplistic notion of the clear, determinate meaning of the Constitution, much less of the ascertainable and binding "intent of the Framers," in order to be uneasy about claims that the Constitution means whatever it would be best for it to mean. I think that the chief contribution of an understanding of the origins of the Constitution is that it gives us warnings about the implications of radical departures from the tradition. The response I offer to the debate over "economic liberties" or the economic foundation of the Constitution is the sense of the warnings that emerge from my picture of Federalist thought.

Of course, there has not just been one tradition of American constitutional thought. The Anti-Federalists lost in 1787, but their concerns were submerged, not obliterated. They have remained an undercurrent in American political thought. But the Federalists did win in 1787 and again with the establishment of judicial review, and their perspective has largely

---

35. However, it is possible that the failure of the polity to manage the problem of the political power that economic power brings would have made Madison sympathetic to the need to mitigate the disproportion in the power of labor and capital. He was after all a Federalist in 1787, but a Jeffersonian later.

dominated American political and legal thought. Most importantly, their clear hierarchy of civil over political rights provided the principled underpinning for the institutionalization of rights as limits in judicial review. Property was the central symbol and instance of those limits. As such, it provided a focal point for thinking about the central question of the legitimate scope of the state. For about 150 years Americans approached the question of what the state could and could not do with property as a clear example of a protected right: the government cannot take what's mine; a man's home is his castle; if it's mine, I can do what I want with it. It does not matter that none of these sentiments accorded precisely with the legal reality of eminent domain, reasonable search and seizure, or even nuisance law. Property both defined and symbolized a protected sphere into which the government could not enter. The welfare-regulatory state now threatens to destroy the boundary that defined that sphere. Egalitarian claims directly challenge the idea that property rights should in some basic way be off-limits. In the modern state, property is increasingly the subject of governmental action, rather than the limit to it. The judiciary expresses this shift in the reversal of the presumption of constitutionality: governmental "interferences" in the economy are no longer treated as probable violations of rights, but as valid unless completely "irrational."

These challenges to the traditional status of property are important despite the fact that they have done relatively little to change the distribution of wealth and the fact that the American political economy is clearly still based on private property. They are important because they ask us to rethink the most basic question of the proper nature and purpose of the state. They ask us to assign priorities to rights and to justify rights as limits to majority rule in the absence of a faith in natural law or even a common good. That is an enormous task.

The task is one I think should be undertaken, and arguably has been in process since 1937. Many people point to the famous footnote in *Carolene Products* as the articulation of the jurisprudence that has replaced the property centered tradition.[36] While judging economic regulation with the minimal standard of "rationality," Stone suggested that stricter scrutiny would be appropriate where (1)a statute touched upon a specific prohibition in the Constitution, or (2)where the political processes were interfered with or restricted, or (3)where statutes were directed at particular minorities or the prejudice against discrete and insular minorities

---

36. Footnote 4 by Justice Stone, United States v. Carolene Products Co., 304 U.S. 144 (1938).

might interfere with their effective use of the political processes. *Carolene Products* does indeed provide an outline for an alternative jurisprudence, but, again we should not underestimate the magnitude of the transformation being called for.

First, the case implicitly calls for an ordering of priorities among constitutional prohibitions (those involving economic rights have comparatively low priority), without articulating the grounds for such a priority. Not only would it turn the status of property on its head, but, on some interpretations, would invert the hierarchy of civil over political rights. What the Constitution really protects, we are told, is not substantive rights, but the political process.[37] This might be a good political theory, but it is not the one the Constitution grew out of. If we are to abandon the status property held for 150 years and replace it with new protected rights, or if we are to replace the very idea of substantive rights as limits on the outcomes of democratic processes with guarantees for those processes, then we will need a new political theory. If we are to retain substantive rights as limits, we will need a new way of justifying those limits against the powerful claims of democracy and new grounds for ordering priorities among competing rights. If we are to transform our constitutional system into one that protects the political process only, we will undertake a fundamental transformation of our system of constitutionalism. The very meaning of the state, of individual rights, of collective power and obligation will have to be reexamined. And the new theory will have to be integrated with our existing institutions, or the institutions themselves will also have to be revamped. Such a basic rethinking may be good and necessary, but it is, I repeat, an enormous task. When conservatives talk about the post-1937 jurisprudence as shaking the foundations of our political system, I think they are basically right. In my view, they have history, if not justice, on their side.

One of the most effective challenges to the argument I have outlined is the following: "Isn't the Supreme Court doing just fine despite the abandonment of traditional property rights? Or, isn't *Carolene Products* providing a perfectly workable framework for their decisions? In short, there doesn't seem to be any crisis on the horizon. If the transformation is profound, isn't it proceeding along quite smoothly?"[38] In a way, of course,

---

37. The best known exponent of this view is John Hart Ely, *Democracy and Distrust*, (Cambridge, Mass., 1980).

38. I am here leaving aside the question of whether the Court under Burger and Rhenquist is in the process of reversing the fifty year trend I have been discussing, and the possibility of a major reverse if the composition of the Court were to change further with the Reagan appointees.

the answer is yes. Our constitutional system has sustained a profound transformation. The judges are not paralyzed in the absence of a full blown political theory to justify their actions. Civil rights other than economic rights are being protected. Judges have turned greater attention to protecting the political process (without, however, showing any signs of accepting that as their sole task). Nevertheless, I think the strain is showing.

Judicial review is premised on the belief that there are boundaries to the legitimate scope of the government and that the judiciary is capable of discerning those boundaries in some legitimate, articulable way. I think there is an increasing sense of uncertainty about whether there are any clear boundaries, or whether there is only a process of "balancing" which it is increasingly difficult to distinguish from the proper task of legislation. The dilemmas of the modern state and of the Court's own acceptance of egalitarian claims has repeatedly pushed it to the edge of acknowledging affirmative obligations of the state to make possible the exercise of equal rights (or the equal exercise of rights).[39] The courts are stumbling along making decisions, sometimes along discernable paths of principle. But the welfare state increasingly presents them with the question of how they are to draw the lines between legitimate and illegitimate governmental action when they cannot follow the tradition of the Framers. One sees an increasing number of legal scholars finding that the logic of their analysis pushes them toward the awesome task of creating, or at least articulating, a foundational philosophy. The appeal of the conservatives becomes clear: if we want our judges to draw lines, let them do so in accordance with a long established tradition.[40] The country as a whole is, in important ways, operating outside that tradition and to the extent that it is, it does so without clear purpose or limits.

The lesson that the Federalists have to teach us is not, in my view, that we should stick with their vision of the republic, intertwined as it was with a particular conception of the economic order and the priority it accorded to property and "economic liberties." The lesson is that their vision *was* so intertwined, and unraveling the threads is no simple task. The fabric of

---

39. The clearest example is *Harris v. McRae*, 448 U.S. 297 (1980). *San Antonio Inc. School Dist. v. Rodriguez*, 411 U.S. 1 (1973), raises similar issues. The claims made in these cases are just the sort of consequences Morris might have predicted from increasing talk of "equal rights."

40. Again it does not matter that property never actually defined clear boundaries. It served as an effective focal point for the task. It was part of a well articulated, if not fully coherent, tradition that defined the purposes of the state and its corresponding limits.

our constitutional system is in some ways a whole, and expecting to keep the parts we like, such as the very idea of rights as limits to government, while discarding the values that once formed the core of that conception is likely to prove difficult—both conceptually and in practice.

One increasingly hears calls for a resurrection of our tradition of civic republicanism. This dimension of American republicanism is a part of the tradition that I referred to earlier as submerged. It seems useful to me to turn to it for insight and inspiration, and to try to foster its resurgence. I feel suspicious of such calls, however, when the message is that this is our "true" tradition. That claim seems dangerous to me because it threatens to underestimate the kind of change in our political system and habits of political thought that it implies. It always seems important to me to recognize the magnitude of the change being proposed. Otherwise we are far less likely to be able to anticipate the consequences and costs of those changes, or to understand what will be necessary to bring them about.

The Framers envisioned a society characterized by an inequality many of us today find unacceptable. If we are to overcome the economic and political inequality that the Federalists' market-republic has spawned, we will have to fundamentally rethink the meaning and status of property and the relation between "economic liberties" and freedom. But in doing so we will *not* be making minor alterations in the deepest structures of the American constitutional system. We will be rethinking the nature of the state, the meaning of public and private, and the kinds of separation that are possible between individual rights and collective power. Perhaps we will be giving better effect to the highest values the Constitution has within it (including the concern with equality added in the 14th amendment), but we will be doing so in a way in which we will have only partial guidance from the dominant tradition of political and legal thought, and with little help from the institutions shaped by that tradition.

Capitalism, Socialism, and Constitutionalism

John Adams Wettergreen

The Framers of the Constitution were not capitalists. They were not socialists. The two great political alternatives of our time, commonly called "communism" and "capitalism," or "socialism" and "free enterprise," were unknown to them.

They were unknown, not just because these terms originated in the middle of nineteenth-century, but also because the problems of political economy to which these terms refer were not of central importance to the Framers. That is, they did not suppose, as today's capitalists and communists do, that economics is politically fundamental. Nevertheless, the fact that the Framers were not—and could not be—aware of what we regard as fundamental does not make them any less interesting to us. On the contrary, as I shall now argue, because the Framers were not caught up in the prejudices of capitalism and communism, they are better aids for understanding today's problems of political economy than today's capitalists, socialists, free enterprisers, and communists.

Communism and Capitalism

Etymologically, socialism and communism are actually older than capitalism. They are terms which emerged in the 1830s and 1840s in France, England, and the United States to express dissatisfactions with modern free societies, and above all with the highly commercialized or industrialized economy of these societies. As their very name indicates, the first socialists were defenders of "society," which they understood to be threatened by "individualism." The American Transcendentalist, Catholic, and socialist, Orestes Brownson, expressed this dissatisfaction nicely: "Society without individuality is tyranny. Individuality without society is individualism."[1] So the first socialists were not theoretic materialists; that is, they did not, like Marx, suppose that the whole of human life was determined by the means of production. In fact, they were appalled by the material-

---

1. Orestes A. Brownson, *Works* (New York: AMS Press, 1966), vol. XIII, p. 13. Cf. Robert Bellah et al., *Habits of the Heart: Individualism and Commitment in American Life* (Berkeley: University of California Press, 1985), pp. 244, 303, 334.

ism—the devotion to wealth-getting and to the enjoyment of physical gratifications—which individualism seemed to inspire.

The first socialists were especially distressed by the transformation of social life brought on by industrialization. In one sense, industrialization is the greatest success of modern civilization: it resulted in the vast increase of human wealth or power which the sixteenth and seventeenth century apostles of modern technology had promised.[2] However, in another sense, industrialization was a disappointment, because the new wealth brought with it, not only solutions to some of the problems of pre-modern societies, but also new problems. The political inequality between nobility and commoners was replaced by a new inequality, apparently an economic one, between employer and employee. At the same time, families became less important as centers of production, being replaced by factories, and more important as private centers of rest and moral education, replacing such social institutions as saloons, schools, theaters, and in part, churches.[3] Moreover, modern society's highly commercialized way of life looked vulgar to the early socialists. In general, the first socialists did not long for a return to the social solidarity of feudal society, but they did hope to restore that solidarity on a modern foundation.

The development of modern free societies distressed the first socialists as much as it did the European Right. Typically, socialists (including Marxists) and rightists both advanced the claim of social order against the claims of individual freedom.[4] Individual economic freedom, both said in the nineteenth-century as they do today, incites society's members to sacrifice every other human good to the production and enjoyment of wealth. In the event, they claimed then as now, communities, families, and even Nature itself are uprooted and destroyed, manual laborers are exploited, human health and sanity are degraded, and so on—all for the

---

2. See Francis Bacon, *The New Organon*, ed. Anderson (Indianapolis: Bobbs-Merrill Co., 1960), pp. 80 (Bk. I, aph. #84), 90 (I, 92), 93 (I, 95, 96), 94 (I, 98), 97 (I, 103), 98 (I, 105); and Rene Descartes, *The Philosophic Works...*, trans. Haldane and Ross (Cambridge: Cambridge University Press, 1911), I, 61 (in "Rules for the Direction of the Mind") and II, 253 (in "Principles of Philosophy").

3. Alexis de Tocqueville, *Democracy in America*, trans. George Lawrence, ed. J.P. Meyer (Garden City, N.Y.: Doubleday & Company, 1969), pp. 572-600. Cf. Christopher Lasch, *Haven in a Heartless World: The Family Besieged* (New York: Basic Books, 1977), pp.3-12.

4. In America, the leading rightist critics of capitalism are Irving Kristol, *Two Cheers for Capitalism* (New York: Basic Books, 1978) and George Will, *Statecraft as Soulcraft* (New York: Simon and Schuster, 1983).

sake of that increase of wealth called profit. Indeed, the socialistic Left and the Right have been distressed by the same thing: final authority over all modern social relations seems to be vested in the individual member, as distinguished from and even as opposed to society and its government, and that member's exercise of his individual authority does not always seem to be enlightened. The European Right was and is appalled by the individual citizen's ignorance of "tradition," *i.e.*, of whatever fragments of the feudal regime remained in the nineteenth-century. The socialists were and are appalled by the individual citizen's vulgarity or provincialism, by his preference for the amelioration of his material life, or at the utmost, of the life of his country over the universal goals of humanity. So the social-ists, just as much as their opponents on the Right, have denied the capacity of the individual human being to rule itself.[5] Both deny, that is, the core of truth that is to be found in individualism, the core whose most beautiful expression is to be found in the Declaration of Independence: "All men are created equal." The socialists have differed from the Right only by virtue of their promise that a socialistic society, once established, would produce humans capable of self-government; no such transformation of human nature has been promised by the Right.

Unlike socialism, capitalism did not begin as a comprehensive critique of modern society. The term was coined in the later half of the nineteenth century to describe the political program preferred by capitalists. At that time, a capitalist was not someone who professed capitalism. In those days before the establishment of highly centralized and highly regulated national banking systems, the capitalist enjoyed a social status somewhere between loan-shark and corporate financier, which derived from his eco-nomic function: the capitalist was an individual citizen who had capital to loan for interest, especially to those commercial enterprises which could not get credit anywhere else because of their newness. Although the great, private, commercial banking houses of Morgan and of Kuhn, Loeb were founded by capitalists, probably the best known American capitalist in this strict, original sense of the word is the gunfighter, Wyatt Earp, who had his profession listed as "Capitalist" in the San Francisco telephone directory. Such citizens still exist, of course, but are called "venture capi-talists" in order that they not be confused with the ideologues. Not until

---

5. The European Right in America, i.e., the defenders of slavery, understood quite well their common cause with the socialists. See George Fitzhugh, *Sociology for the South* (Richmond: A. Morris, 1854), p.147: "The Southern farm is my beau ideal of communism."

Marx were the rather practical preferences of these fellows (for the continued existence of at least some financial markets free from official supervision) elevated to the status of *Weltanschauung*.

Marx was certainly correct in this limited respect: the existence of capitalists is the economic symptom of a modern free society. Individual economic freedom—capitalism in a strictly economic sense—exists wherever legal title to any external good can be acquired on the open market, that is, by the free consent of an individual buyer and an individual seller. So it is fundamental to such an economy that the material means to acquire or produce external goods—capital—be available on the open market or commercially. In contradistinction, the feudalistic societies preferred by the European Right and the socialistic societies preferred by the Left restrict possession of external goods for the sake of the established social order. Accordingly, both kinds of societies rely upon wage and price controls; in feudal societies they are administered in the name of "the just price" and in socialistic societies in the name of "central economic planning." Neither kind of society tolerates the existence of capitalists: feudal societies forbid usury and socialistic societies flatly prohibit all possession of private capital. Thus, the existence of capitalists really is distinctive, and even definitive economically, of modern, free societies. Indeed, even in the freest, most highly commercialized cities of antiquity, private capitalists were almost unknown. Before the modern era, the sole source of capital was almost always the government (in the case of republics) or the royal family (in the case of monarchies).[6]

To repeat, Marxism elevated the relatively narrow economic interests of the capitalists to the status of a political principle. That is, when radicalized, the economic interest of capitalists is, just as Marx argues, *laissez faire* capitalism: the belief in the strict non-regulation by government of all commercial decisions and activities, if not of all matters of individual interest. In the same way, Marx saw that, as a matter of political principle, socialists ought to favor communism: the abolition of all the institutions supportive of the existence of the autonomous individual—especially private property, the family, religion, and the state—for the sake of social

---

6. "The Failure of Capitalism in the Ancient World," in *Max Weber on Capitalism, Bureaucracy, and Religion*, trans. Andreski (London: George Allen & Unwin, 1983), p.55.

solidarity.[7] Of course, for most capitalists and most socialists and indeed for most American citizens, such matters of political principle never arise in practice. That is, in the practice of American politics, one seldom, if ever, observes even the advocacy of *laissez faire* capitalism or of communism. Indeed, "socialism" and, albeit to a lesser degree, "capitalism" are not quite terms of polite political discourse in the United States today. Yet, strangely, the failure of the Marxian dichotomy—*laissez faire* capitalism vs. communism—to explain American reality has not yet led to its rejection. On the contrary, the Marxian dichotomy informs most of the journalistic and academic discussions of economic issues today, as shall now be indicated by a brief discussion of the outstanding political economists of our time, John Kenneth Galbraith and Milton Friedman.

Galbraith and Friedman

For a generation, John Kenneth Galbraith has preferred to identify himself as a liberal, not a socialist, but he has built his career as an economist on arguments for increasing the size of the public sector, both absolutely and relative the private sector. More than any other intellectual, he has provided the public justification for the vast expansion of spending and programs of the central government which began in the 1960s and has continued ever since. That justification is twofold. First, according to Galbraith's claims, Americans should use their great wealth to purchase public goods as well as private ones. So, in his writings of the 1950s, Galbraith pointed to potholes in roads and the shortage of schoolrooms as symptoms of what he called "public poverty" in the midst of private affluence. In today's tracts, he argues for ever increasing federal expenditures for "the poor." Secondly, Galbraithian economics uses some of the arguments of John Maynard Keynes to encourage American politicians to believe that private prosperity is caused by government spending,

---

7. Marx differed from the first socialists (Mayhew, Godwin, Reybaud, Owen, Sainte-Simon, etc.) or what he called the "utopian socialists," above all by his unrelieved hostility to religion. See "Socialism: Utopian and Scientific," in Marx and Engels, *Basic Writings on Politics and Philosophy*, ed. Feuer (Garden City: Doubleday, 1959), pp.75, 85, 91 and Gertrude Himmelfarb, *The Idea of Poverty* (New York: Knopf, 1984), pp. 171, 312-70, 355, 229-30, 237-8, 411.

especially by deficit spending.[8] For example, in 1964 Lyndon Johnson and Hubert Humphrey followed Galbraith by claiming that by "fine tuning the economy" with federal spending, full employment and rapid economic growth would continue indefinitely; the only problem would be getting rid of ever increasing federal revenues.[9] Such arguments are not overtly socialistic, but, since Galbraith and his followers have never favored reliance upon the private sector for any purpose, all with eyes to see have understood that they are socialists. In fact, by 1973, Galbraith not only advocated socialism openly, but even claimed that it was inevitable.[10] Nevertheless, in the popular press of the day, Galbraith continues to be regarded as a "liberal" who advocates "Keynesian economics."

Although Milton Friedman was a well known academic economist in the 1950s, it was the manifest failure of "Keynesian economics" after 1974 that made him a celebrity and Galbraith's capitalistic counterpart. According to the opinions elaborated by Galbraith in the 1950s and 1960s, advanced industrial economies could be threatened by inflation or they could be threatened by unemployment, but they could not be threatened by both together. American liberals thought the two conditions to be mutually exclusive: the steps to cure unemployment—more government spending—might cause inflation, and the steps to cure inflation—less spending—might cause unemployment, but nothing could cause both together. From this point of view, growing unemployment, low or negative economic growth, and high inflation ("stagflation") should not have happened—certainly not together with the ever-increasing federal expenditures of the 1970s. Of course, those of Galbraith's persuasion claimed that governmental spending and the public sector had not grown fast enough in the late 1960s and early 1970s, but they would have said that even if there had not been stagflation. Friedman offered another explanation. He claimed that the supply (and price) of money had been poorly administered by the Federal Reserve Board: too much money (at too low a price) encouraged inflation, but did not encourage productive employment of labor and capital, because in inflationary circumstances income could be

---

8. For both points, see, above all, John Kenneth Galbraith, "The Dependency Effect and the Social Balance," *Private Wants and Public Needs*, ed. Phelps (New York, 1962), pp. 13-36. Cf. *The Affluent Society* (New York: New American Library, 1958), pp. 149, 196. Roads and schools were traditionally local concerns in America. So Galbraith's program was as much an attack on decentralization as on "public poverty."

9. See *New York Times*, Sept. 9, 1964, 1:2; Sept. 25, 1964, 28:5; Sept. 27, 1964, 65:4.

10. See *Economics and the Public Purpose* (Boston: Houghton Mifflin Company, 1973), pp. 274-285.

more easily had by borrowing than by working. Friedman's monetarism seemed to offer a means to salvage the welfare state: the economy could be fine tuned by the Federal Reserve Board's careful, scientific regulation of the supply (and the price) of money.

Although his economic policies became popular as a means to rescue the American welfare state, Friedman himself is a *laissez faire* capitalist. Accordingly, Friedman's journalistic writings are filled with examples of the failure of federal regulations and programs to supply the desires of individuals as well as individuals themselves can.[11] However, his most brilliant and extended treatment of such examples is *A Monetary History of the United States, 1867-1960*.[12] There he demonstrates that, in the period in question, private bankers were better able to regulate the supply (and price) of money than was the Federal Reserve Board, and that the mistakes of the Federal Reserve Board turned a contraction of the economy into the Great Depression. And yet, of all governmental regulations of the economy, Friedman finds those of the Federal Reserve Board to be most acceptable! Just as Galbraith attempted to adapt radical anti-individualism to the American system by proposing those incremental increases in the power and authority of the central government which are most likely to be acceptable at any given time, so has Friedman attempted to sustain radical individualism in the face of the proto-socialistic state created in the 1960s and 1970s.

Nowhere does the difference between the two economists' views appear to be more stark than in their evaluations of individual choice. Galbraith never conceals his contempt for the ordinary individual's capacity for freedom, even in the simplest matters. "The economy," he asserts, "for its success requires organized public bamboozlement."[13] That is, he supposes that only deceptive advertisements can explain the consumption not only of cigarettes and power ashtrays but also of color televisions, private automobiles, and the whole array of "consumer goods" which is the mainstay of the American economy. Of course, if the individual consumer is incapable of economic sovereignty, how much less is the individual citizen capable of political rule! It is no wonder that Galbraith seems to

---

11. Milton Friedman, *There Is No Such Thing As A Free Lunch: Essays on Public Policy* (Lasalle, Ill.: Open Court, 1975), pp. 120-142, 208-232.
12. Milton Friedman with Anna Jacobson Schwartz (Princeton, N.J.: Princeton University Press, 1963).
13. *The New Industrial State* (New York: New American Library, 1967), p. 286. See also pp. xviii, 203-11, 266-7; *Economics and the Public Purpose*, pp. 97-98, 134-38, 137-40; *The Affluent Society*, pp. 124-6, 144, 189-90.

prefer bureaucracy, that is, the fully centralized administration of society, or socialism, to free government.[14] He seems ignorant of the fact that the worst tyrannies of this century have been, and have claimed to be, socialistic. Certainly he does not see that socialism's tyranny is an economic necessity: socialist societies are not just stagnant ("no-growth") economies of the kind produced by Galbraithian economic policies in the 1970's; even when fully developed, they are incapable of producing the wealth necessary for their own self-sufficiency without resorting to forced labor on a massive scale.

Milton Friedman, on the other hand, is a libertarian. For him, the sovereignty of the individual is absolute; any individual choice is a sound choice *because* it is an individual choice. Yet, strange though it might seem to some, such radical individualism is no more the principle of free government than Galbraith's socialism. Friedman holds that individual "freedom includes ... freedom to promote communism," even though "communism would destroy all our freedom."[15] Friedman is as blind to the morality of individual freedom as Galbraith, but Friedman's blindness consists in the inanity that slavery can be freely chosen. Thus, the leading capitalist and the leading socialist of our time are incapable of an adequate defense of human freedom, including economic freedom. For this reason, the Framers' understanding of political economy is particularly relevant today.

Beyond Socialism and Individualism

Perhaps it is more obvious that the principles of American Constitutionalism are opposed to *laissez faire* capitalism than that they are opposed to socialism. For the Constitution itself says, without equivocation, that the central government shall exercise the power "To regulate Commerce with foreign Nations, and among the several States, and with the Indian Tribes" and the power to "regulate the Value" of money (Article I, Section 8). Nor did the Framers suppose that constitutional government's influence upon commerce would be minimal. In *Federalist* 10, for example, Madison declares, "The regulation of ... various and interfering [economic] interests forms the principle task of modern Legislation."[16]

---

14. See, e.g., *Economics and the Public Purpose*, pp. 283-5, 142-4.

15. *Capitalism and Freedom* (Chicago: University of Chicago Press, 1962), p. 20.

16. Hamilton, Madison, and Jay, *The Federalist*, ed. Cooke (Middletown: Wesleyan University Press, 1961), p. 59.

Indeed, the chief business of the new government, after the passage of the Bill of Rights and the Judiciary Act of 1789, was Alexander Hamilton's economic program. Hamiltonian regulation of commerce advanced "his commitment to private enterprise and to a market economy":

> he sought to transform the American people into free, opulent, and law-abiding citizens, through the instrumentality of a limited republican government, on the basis of consent, and in the face of powerful vested interests in the status quo . . . . He set out to effect what amounted to a social revolution.[17]

In short, the primary exercise of government's power of commercial regulation established in the United States what has come to be called capitalism. Could not the same power be used today to establish socialism? Is the Constitution economically neutral?

Today, the constitutional power of the government to regulate commerce is commonly understood as a typically American compromise of capitalism by socialism, or of socialism by capitalism. Accordingly, the kind of economy resulting from regulation is said to be "mixed." It is not socialistic, because the means of production remain privately owned, but it is not capitalistic either, because the means of production are publicly controlled in decisive respects. Because regulation is understood in this ideologized manner, both the American right and left are bound to be more or less dissatisfied with any regulatory policy. Libertarians, like Friedman or Murray Rothbard,[18] opine that regulation compromises the natural right to private property; to them, the economic inefficiencies of federal regulation are a proof of its immorality. Socialists, like Galbraith or Michael Walzer, urge that regulation can never achieve the public good, because those who own the means of production must, in the final analysis, benefit from their ownership at the expense of the non-owners.[19] The contemporary center defines itself in relation to these ideologized extremes. It objects to capitalism and socialism, not on principle, but practically, as though both capitalism's freedom and socialism's equality were desirable but incompatible. However, the Framers evidently favored both equality and liberty, and provided constitutional government for the sake of both together. Therefore, it is useful to investigate just what they thought a regulated economy is. In so doing, it should become clear that a

---

17. Forrest MacDonald, *Alexander Hamilton* (New York: W. W. Norton, 1979), pp. 235, 3.

18. Murray N. Rothbard, *For A New Liberty* (New York: Macmillan, 1973), pp. 327, vi.

19. Michael Walzer, *Spheres of Justice: A Defense of Pluralism and Equality* (New York: Basic Books, 1983).

regulated economy is neither capitalistic, nor socialistic, nor mixed. A regulated economy is a truly free economy, which must be distinguished from both a capitalistic and a socialistic economy (and so from any mixture of capitalism and socialism).

At the Federal Convention of 1787, few provisions of the Constitution were less controversial than the power of the central government to regulate foreign commerce and commerce "among the several states." One may say, without exaggeration, that the need for governmental regulation of commerce was the efficient cause, first of the Annapolis convention, and then of the Federal Convention of 1787. All the delegates supposed that the commercial regulatory power proceeded from the principles of the free society for whose government they were providing. That is, the Founders did not suppose, as *laissez faire* capitalists do, that regulation of commerce could be inconsistent with free commercial enterprise. Nor did they suppose, as socialists do, that free commercial enterprise could be inconsistent with a free society. Therefore, if the Framers were correct, the power to regulate commerce is opposed in principle to both capitalism and socialism.

What does the Constitution mean by "regulation"? When the Framers wrote that Congress possessed the power "to regulate," to what kind of activity precisely did they refer? Two hundred years of constitutional litigation has not answered this question adequately, because most of the legal contention has been over whether a particular activity is "commerce" or not in the meaning of the commerce clause, and over whether or not an activity, if it is commerce, is "interstate." Because the nature of the regulatory power has never been the direct object of litigation (or of Congressional deliberation for that matter), the apparently common-sensical definition of *Gibbons v. Ogden* has had little trouble gaining general acceptance: "the power to regulate [is the power] to prescribe the rule by which commerce is to be governed."[20] Indeed, the only serious scholarly attempt to define constitutional regulation, William Winslow Crosskey's *Politics and the Constitution in the History of the United States*,[21] shows only that the Framers intended federal regulation to be "complete," both in the sense that it could touch upon all branches of domestic and foreign commerce, including manufacturing and agriculture, and in the sense that it would be a genuinely national power, not one limited to commer-

---

20. Wheaton 1, 209; see *Corpus juris secundum*, ed. Ludes and Gilbert (Brooklyn: American Law Book Co., 1952), vol. VXXVI, p. 965ff.
21. (University of Chicago Press: Chicago, 1953) 2 Vols., pp. 1410, xi.

cial transactions which happened to cross state boundaries.[22] It does not define regulation itself much more clearly than *Gibbons v. Ogden.*

Prior to about 1975, that definition was adequate for all practical purposes. However, during the past decade the bulk of the activities of the central government, whether respecting commerce or not, have come to be called regulation. "Regulation" is used to refer to the whole process of central administration which is the chief business of American government today. Therefore, a more refined or theoretical understanding might be useful as well as enlightening.

The definition of *Gibbons v. Ogden,* although more or less useful when regulation itself is not the subject of litigation, does not fit the plain language of the Constitution.[23] For, in the first place, the Constitution's language distinguishes the government's power to "regulate" from its power to "govern." Furthermore, the Constitution distinguishes "rules" from "regulations." With regard to the first distinction, the Constitution grants Congress the power to *regulate* domestic and foreign commerce and to *regulate* the value of money in itself and in relation to the money of other countries, but it grants the power to *govern* the armed services, including that part of a state's militia that is in the service of the United States, and to provide for the *government* of Washington, D.C. The second distinction, that of rules from regulations, is drawn implicitly or explicitly throughout the Constitution, but nowhere more clearly than this: "The Congress shall have Power to . . . make all needful Rules and Regulations respecting the Territory and Property belonging to the United States" (IV,3,2). To complicate the question a little further, these two distinctions are compounded in the Constitution by its grant of the the power "To make Rules," both for the "Government" and for the "Regulation" of the nation's armed services. *Gibbons'* definition confounds these constitutional distinctions, because it claims that the power to regulate is a power of governance and that a regulation is a rule. Leaving aside legal precedent then, let us consider the basis of these distinctions in the constitutional order.

Rules differ from regulations as general principles do from their application to particular cases. For example, a rule might be, "Stay healthy by eating a balanced diet," and a regulation of that rule might be, "Eat an

---

22. This limitation of Crosskey's work is especially obvious on vol. I, p. 186.
23. Crosskey deliberately refuses to analyze the plain language of the Constitution, claiming that in that way he can keep his interpretation from being biased in favor of the Framers (*Politics and the Constitution,* vol. I, p. 4).

apple every day." According to the *Oxford English Dictionary*, etymologically, both words are derived from the same Latin verb (*regulare* = to rule), and, historically, both have precise meanings originating in ecclesiastical government or, to be precise, in the self-government of monastic orders. A "rule" is a general principle for the governance of a monastic order as a whole, which might well be an article of the order's charter from the Church as drawn by the saint who founded the order. A "regulation" is the application of the rule for the circumstances of a particular monastery. There might be very wide differences, even contradictions, between regulations, but all would be made pursuant to the rules. For example, for the sake of a simple, and healthful diet, one abbot might permit and another forbid wine at meals. The rules themselves were the conditions of self-governance for the order. As happens often in the sixteenth and seventeenth centuries, there was a secularization of these terms of ecclesiastical government.

In observation of this difference between rules and regulations, the Constitution calls the States' laws setting the "Time, Place, and Manner" of elections "Regulations." In this case, the rule—"Hold regular, free elections"—is supplied by the Constitution, and the regulations—"Elections shall be at this time, in these places, by a ballot of this form"—by the States' laws. These laws, in turn, are subject to Congressional review and amendment "by Law." Nevertheless, rules and regulations are not necessarily kinds of laws. Both can and do exist independent of law, although both can, of course, be legislated. Thus, for example, the Constitution itself states "the Rules" by which bills become laws (I,7,3).

The Framers supposed that some subjects of legislation were fit only for regulations, not rules, and that others might be fit both for rules and regulations: "[Congress shall have Power] to establish a uniform Rule of Naturalization, and uniform Laws on the subject of Bankruptcies throughout the United States" (I,8). Both subjects, naturalization and bankruptcy, require nationally uniform legislation. However, naturalization bears upon the politically all-important (and ticklish) matter of citizenship, the definition of which the original Constitution left to the States. Therefore, only a *rule* of naturalization, that is, a statement of such general conditions for citizenship as would be applicable anywhere in the nation, could be constitutionally enacted into law; if Congress could make *regulations* for naturalization, then it could define who in particular could be a citizen of each state, and that would have undermined the political autonomy of the states in an important respect.

With regard to the subject of bankruptcies, as distinguished from the subject of naturalization, the distinction of rules from regulations is politically and constitutionally indifferent. That is, national uniformity—both in general and in detail—is everything in the matter of bankruptcies, because heterogeneous laws would allow bankrupts to evade their responsibilities by moving from state to state. Accordingly, by implication the Constitution leaves Congress free to legislate both the rules and the regulations in bankruptcies.

Not all regulations, and so not all rules, are properly parts of the Constitution or the laws. In the first place, the Constitution recognizes the existence of what may be called moral-political rules and regulations. For example, the infamous fugitive slave clause (IV, 2, 3) of the Constitution refers to the police "regulations," as distinguished from the laws, of the free states. Often these regulations were executed in ways which tended to preserve the liberty of run-away slaves—much to the chagrin of their legal owners, who were trying to gain their recovery with the help of the free state's police. Now these regulations were not made pursuant to any particular state's laws, but to a general rule or standard maxim of a modern free society: "No human is rightly deprived of liberty."

Second, but more important for our purposes today, are the rules and regulations by which familial, civic, religious, and commercial associations govern themselves, with or without the authority of the law. The Constitution, by granting only regulatory power over commerce, implies that the *rules* of commerce exist beyond the legislative power of the central government. The rules of commerce are like the rules of the value of money, for example, "Gresham's law." Congress might wish sometimes to legislate the monetary rules, but no law will convince citizens that worthless paper is a valuable medium of exchange. Similarly, if Congress legislated that a loss is a profit, it would be acting contrary to the rules of commerce.

The Constitution's distinction of the power to govern from the power to regulate is analogous to its distinction of rules from regulations. Governance is a comprehensive power of the government, the distinctive power of the political sovereign. That over which there exists authority to govern has no right of self-governance against the government. Speaking strictly according to the Constitution's language, the central government has the power of governance only over the District of Columbia, itself, and the armed services; this apparent paradox is explained below. Regulation, in contradistinction from governance, is a limited power of the government. Those over whom there exists only the regulatory power are and ought to be, to some extent or with respect to the purpose they serve, self-governed

John Adams Wettergreen

entities; they have or make their own rules. By granting the power to regulate commerce, the Constitution implies that government is limited from the governance of commerce.

Nowhere is this constitutional distinction of governance from regulation clearer than in the case of the nation's armed services. Since they are to serve only the purposes of the central government, and never any purposes of their own, the Constitution asserts the government's authority over them unqualifiedly: Congress has the power to make laws to govern them, as well as the power to make laws to regulate and to make rules for them. The armed services are to be self-governing in no respect whatsoever. With the same intent, the Constitution establishes the central government's authority to govern the States' militia. However, because the States are to some extent autonomous, central governance of their militias had to be somewhat qualified. The crucial qualification is the reserving to the States of "the Appointment of the Officers, and the Authority of training the Militia according to the discipline prescribed by Congress." Thus, the power to govern includes the power to legislate rules, and to organize, supply, and administer various activities. However, above all, governance is the authority to determine who in particular governs an activity from day to day, who is the administering officer. Only if Congress could name the militias' officers, especially those responsible for the daily discipline of the soldiers, only then could the central government fully govern the militia (and the states). Similarly, if the Constitution had established the power to govern commerce, and not just to regulate it, then that would have meant that the central government could charter all business enterprises and specify their purposes. However, even more importantly, that would have meant that the national government could appoint and dismiss all employees of all commercial enterprises by ordinary political means. In short, whether or not it included governmental ownership of the means of production, governance of commerce would amount to what is today called socialism.

Whatever its virtues, Crosskey's *Politics and the Constitution* simply ignores this politically crucial distinction of governance from regulation. In principle, Crosskey understands the power of regulation of commerce to be unlimited; certainly it would permit a centrally administered national economy. Furthermore, Crosskey's basic understanding of "regulation of commerce" is based entirely on British and pro-British sources. According to Crosskey, "The various statements by John Dickinson, in 1774, and by Alexander Hamilton and John Adams, in 1775," as well as statements by Madison and Jefferson, "which tend, when read uncritically to indicate that the Americans of that time had some peculiar, narrow understanding of 'commercial regulation,' " were in fact "sophistical," "falsifying," "bluffing," and contradictory.[24] However, the "true meaning of regulation of commerce" which Crosskey has in mind is that of a monarchical, not that of a republican constitution.[25] No doubt, elements of the monarchical understanding of commercial regulation continued in the popular mind for some time after Independence, just as Crosskey claims. Indeed, they continued for some time after the ratification of the Constitution, for it was precisely those elements of monarchic regulation and the monarchic economy—like entail, primogeniture, and *ex post facto* laws—which Hamilton fought to eliminate by his regulations of commerce.[26] Incidentally, in this respect, Jefferson and his followers did not disagree with the economic program of Hamilton. To repeat: the problem of political economy for some time after the Revolution was to make commerce self-governing, to eliminate the vicious circles of commercial dependency upon government which had been built up during the colonial period. Strictly speaking, American commerce did not become fully capable of self-government at least until after the Civil War; there is nothing more contrary to the rules of commerce than slave-commerce.[27]

The Constitution's distinction of regulation from governance implies that self-governing entities exist prior to or independent of government. Or, in other words, it implies that not all authority is governmental, and that some authority is personal, social, subpolitical, or transpolitical. In the case of commerce, the Constitution's recognition of the distinction of governance from regulation is, of course, a recognition of historical fact; commerce did exist prior to the government established under the Constitution. However, the constitutional priority of commerce is not only historical, but also natural. This basis for the regulatory power in the natural priority of commerce to politics is presented most clearly in the second of John Locke's *Two Treatises of Government*, a work well known to the Framers.

In Chapter IX, "Of the Ends of Political Society and Government,"

---

24. *Politics and the Constitution*, vol. I, p. 186.
25. *Politics and the Constitution*, vol. I, pp. 121-3, 125, 131-3, 147ff, 175, 178, 183-6.
26. Crosskey does not object to *ex post facto* laws for the regulation of commerce; see vol. I, p. 324ff.
27. See *Max Weber on Capitalism, Bureaucracy, and Religion*, pp. 34-6, 40, 43-51 for a good account of the economic insanity of slavery. Commerce in or with slaves simply cannot be regulated—it must be governed—because slavery itself is a violation of the rules of commerce.

government's power to regulate is identified with the "the Legislative or Supreme Power" of government. By nature, Locke argues, every human possesses the right "to do whatsoever he thinks fit for the preservation of himself and others within the permission of the Law of Nature," but the existence of government presupposes that humans have surrendered this natural power in order "to be *regulated* by [positive] Laws." Still, humans do not and cannot surrender their natural legislative power "wholly." Contrary to what John Kenneth Galbraith claims, humans always possess some residual capacity to judge whether political society does in fact preserve their lives, liberty, and property. This residue is the basis of the right of revolution, and so of the advisability of regular elections. Thus the legislative power of a free government, although supreme, cannot be absolute. In this way, the natural rights of individual humans to life, liberty, and property, which are the foundations of every subpolitical association, are also the basis of the government's regulatory power.[28]

In a special sense, government's power to govern, as distinguished from its power to regulate, is total or unlimited, because, according to the second *Treatise*, government originates by our total surrender to government of our natural power of punishing wrong-doers. However, in the Lockean or liberal view, the power of governance is instrumental to the regulatory power; it is "executive." Accordingly, in the Constitution, government's power of governance is granted only over those entities—the armed services, the District of Columbia—whose existence or purpose is wholly the creature of the government. For example, it would have been folly for the Framers to grant to Congress the power to govern the value of money; money is, of course, coined by government, but it quickly and necessarily comes to have purposes of its own, which no government can command. Similarly, government's power to make rules, as distinguished from regulations, is declared by the Constitution only over governmentally (or constitutionally) created entities. For example, Congress is declared to have the power to make "the Rules of its Proceedings." In the case of another constitutionally created entity, Congress is declared to have the power only to make "Regulations" of the Courts' appellant jurisdiction; the Courts (and the Constitution itself, of course) make their own *rules* of jurisdiction. In sum, although it might sound strange, the Constitution only grants government the power of governance over itself. That is, in the strict meaning of the Constitution's language, government

---

28. *Two Treatises of Government*, ed. Laslett (Cambridge: Cambridge University Press, 1963), pp. 397-9 (secs.129-131); emphasis supplied.

is only granted the power of governance, as distinguished from the power of regulation, over governmental entities; admittedly, government's power with respect to itself is total. With respect to everything external to the government, the Constitution grants only regulatory power.

It is important to understand why the constitutional power to regulate commerce necessarily implies a limitation from the power to govern commerce. Simply stated, the reason is that the independent existence of commercial activity, such that commerce does in fact make its own rules, is secured by government's regulation of commerce. James Madison, before all others, demonstrated this.

According to *Federalist* #10, "The protection of [the diverse, natural] faculties [of humans] is the first object of government." Because "the rights of property originate" from these natural faculties, or because wealth-getting is the most common purpose for which most citizens exercise their faculties most the time, a modern government, one representative of a majority of its citizens, must concern itself with commercial issues. To deny government the power even to regulate commerce, as *laissez faire* capitalists propose, a constitution would have to forbid the citizens from freely organizing to advance their interests, for example, by electing those who were favorably disposed toward their interests. Thus, the tyrannical practices of socialism would be necessary to establish and maintain *laissez faire* capitalism.

To repeat: Madison expected that the "principal task" of free government would be "the regulation" of the various, interfering commercial interests which naturally arise when government fosters the diverse faculties of its citizens.[29] Thus, a flourishing, diverse economy would be an important measure of the excellence of modern government, of the extent to which government in fact protected the diverse faculties. However, by Madisonian standards, material prosperity could not be the principal measure of good government, precisely because the first object of government is the fostering of natural human diversity. For example, government could not rightfully forbid citizens from exercising their faculties for other than commercial purposes—for worship, study, or contemplation—merely because by doing so more wealth and more kinds of wealth would result. Thus the regulation of commerce is not simply the promotion of commercialism. Rather, it is the promotion of the end of

---

29. Hamilton, Madison, and Jay, *The Federalist*, ed. Cooke (Middletown: Wesleyan University Press, 1961), p. 59.

commerce (wealth) in harmony with the promotion of the other goods of human life (for example, health, victory in war, domestic tranquility).

We have seen that constitutional regulation of commerce is inconsistent, in principle, both with capitalism and with socialism. However, regulation is no mere splitting of the differences between these two, resulting in a mixture. Rather, regulation, properly understood and practiced, would result in a wholly free economy. For the principle of constitutional regulation is not the radical opposition of private goods to the public good, which is as characteristic of Friedman's capitalism as of Galbraith's socialism. On the one hand, capitalism asserts the primacy of private, or individual goods; the public good is ephiphenomenal, the abstract sum of private goods. Thus capitalists, like Milton Friedman, tend to condemn all governmental regulation for arbitrarily preferring some private interests to others, since they deny that the public interest exists as a standard of preference among private interests. Socialism, on the other hand, asserts the primacy of the social good over against capitalism's individualism; theoretically, socialism asserts that every individual good is a social product. Accordingly, socialists, like Galbraith, tend to condemn constitutional regulation on the same grounds as the capitalists, namely for arbitrarily preferring certain private interests to others. In contradistinction to socialism and capitalism, the principle of constitutional regulation is harmony of private (or parochial) interests; for commerce, the public interest—for the sake of which the regulatory power is exercised—is that harmony. Therefore, constitutional regulation stands as a mean between the vicious extremes of capitalism and socialism, that is, between the non-regulation and the governance of commerce.

The Framers were opposed both to the governance and to the non-regulation of commerce, but not for commercial reasons. For them, economic matters were secondary—subordinate to morality and politics.

Instances of Constitutional Regulation

Is this rather fine distinction of regulation from governance really practical? Since the industrialization of the United States, has it really been observed in the practice of constitutional government? It is evident that, in the late nineteenth century, this understanding of constitutional regulation informed the best minds. For example, the most distinguished legal mind of the first generation after the Civil War, Senator William Maxwell Evarts of New York understood well that, according to the Constitution, "Commerce has its own laws, its own trade, its own views of equality..." In this century, such clarity about the principles of regulation has proven difficult to discover. Nevertheless, by way of a conclusion, I shall indicate with a couple of carefully chosen examples from the history of the modern American corporation that constitutional regulation of modern industrial society is possible. The creation of the modern corporation in the years immediately following the Civil War and its preservation during the New Deal show that it is still possible to go beyond capitalism and socialism. Other examples could be elaborated, but that of the corporation is crucial because it is the central institution of contemporary American commerce.

The Civil War created the political condition for the development of genuinely national commercial transactions: the end of sectional strife over the issue of slavery. This political condition made possible the progress of mass, technologized production, transportation, and communication—steel, railroads, and telegraphics. For national economic modernization requires massive capitalization in several states or sections at once. Even compared to the remarkable rate of economic modernization before the Civil War, the development of modern industrial commerce proceeded at a stupendous pace after the War. This became possible by a remarkable regulation of commerce: the creation of the modern corporation.

Prior to the Civil War, railroads were more fully developed than corporate organization. While there were more miles of rails in the United States than any other nation, these were operated by corporations chartered by a state for that special purpose and usually for a limited duration.[30] The War fostered explosive progress in rail service, because it permitted the construction of a transcontinental line, a project which had been stalled for decades by sectional and partisan rivalries. However, the progress was not only in transcontinental service: in the twenty years prior to the War, 24,000 miles of rail were laid, a very great labor; in the twenty years after the war, 100,000 more miles were produced, giving the United States more service than in all the rest of the world. This rail service was the skeleton, as the telegraph wires beside the rails were the nervous system of a genuinely national commerce.

This progress of the rails after the Civil War would have been very difficult, if not impossible, without a parallel political development which

---

30. Forrest McDonald, *The Phaeton Ride: The Crisis of American Success* (Garden City: Doubleday & Company, 1974), pp. 12-37.

made possible modern industrial organization: laws of general incorporation. Beginning around the end of the Civil War, states began to replace "special purpose" incorporation with general incorporation.[31] The new laws of incorporation granted, in perpetuity, the privilege of limited liability for debts and torts to any firm doing business for any legal purpose, whereas the old laws usually granted this privilege for the purposes and term specified by the state legislature. So these laws made it possible for investors to define their risk very precisely while leaving their opportunities almost unlimited. Furthermore, corporations were intended to be perfectly free associations, in the sense that any law-abiding citizens could form one without the specific approval of the political authorities. One can scarcely imagine a regulation better fitted for the liberation of commercial activity, or better calculated for the rapid generation of the capital necessary for modernization.[32] Accordingly, whereas prior to the Civil War there existed several hundred profit-seeking corporations, twenty years after the War there were several hundred thousand.[33]

The "any-legal-purpose" corporations which developed after the Civil War existed *de facto*, but not *de jure*, as agents of national commerce, because they were the creatures of state, not national laws. Until 1886, these corporations could and did conduct commerce on the scale of the whole nation, of course, but their legal right to do so remained ambiguous. In that year—one year before the Interstate Commerce Commission, the first national regulatory agency, was established to authorize the railroads' national rates—the Supreme Court found that corporations were legal "persons" in the meaning of the Constitution.[34] This ruling

---

31. Nader, Green, Seligman, *Taming the Giant Corporation* (New York: W. W. Norton, 1976), pp. 15-61. Like Nader et. al., Crosskey is appalled by the lack of uniformity in corporation law—*Politics and the Constitution*, vol. I, p. 21: ". . . the whole process of commercial government in this country is slow, cumbersome, and ineffective to no small degree"—although this is clearly an important element in the development of commercial freedom.

32. Hessen, *In Defense of the Modern Corporation* (Stanford: Hoover Institution Press, 1979), pp. 77-87.

33. The outstanding economic historians of the past generation, Morison and Commager, complained of the period after 1876: "National politics became little more than a contest for power between rival parties waged on no higher plane than the struggle for traffic between rival railroads. [It was] intellectually bankrupt, . . . very dull." *The Growth of the American Republic* (New York: Oxford University Press, 1942), vol. II, p. 214. Do dull politics and excited commerce go together?

34. Santa Clara County v. Southern Pacific Railroad, 118 U.S. 394.

legitimated the states' laws of general incorporation under the Constitution. That is, in principle, it brought the essential organization of modernized commerce under national law. If railroads were the material condition of national commerce, corporations were the institutional condition. Both together were necessary for the development of the modern, industrialized economy that characterizes twentieth century American society.

Because they do not understand the import of constitutional regulation, neither capitalists nor socialists have been able to appreciate the importance of the corporation to American commerce. Socialists conclude that, because corporations are creatures of the law, they ought to be agents of the government. Ralph Nader, for example, urges that Congress appoint members of the boards of directors of all major corporations, in order that the corporations could become agencies of law enforcement for the central bureaucracy. *Laissez faire* capitalists, like Robert Hessen, have responded by arguing that, even though the modern corporation is a creature of the law, it is not morally a creature of government because it could have come into being as a result of strictly private, voluntary agreement. However, even Hessen is compelled to admit that this proposition cannot be demonstrated in full. The argument falters because it is impossible to imagine how limited liability for torts could have come into being by a voluntary agreement of private individuals; no private person, who had no interest in a corporation, would agree to grant limited liability for torts to that corporation.[35] Moreover, the agreement of all who might have a tort against that corporation, that is, of every human being living today and in the future, is necessary. That is why the modern corporation can only be established by law! (Law is a surrogate for social unanimity.) The mistake of the socialists is in supposing that the corporation must be the agent of government for every purpose, just because it was created by the government. However, the capitalist, be it noted, accepts the socialist contention that corporations would be rightfully agents of the government in every respect if they were creatures of the government, but tries to deny the fact that they are creatures.

Neither understands that corporations were created by government for the purpose of regulating commerce, and that that purpose acts as a limit upon government. The socialist proposal to use the corporations to govern commerce would be a perversion of the corporation's purpose and, accordingly, would not result in a well-regulated commerce. At its worst, in the Soviet Union, governance of commerce is not only tyranny but also

---

35. Hessen, *Defense of the Modern Corporation*, p. 19.

impoverishment. In its more humane forms, in Britain or France, its virtue seems to be its incompleteness. In any case, socialism's governance of commerce has never lived up to its claim that it could master commerce's materialism for the sake of the social good. For once government undertakes the governance of commerce, all the issues of commercial life become—willy-nilly—political issues. It should not be necessary to point out that, generally speaking, commerce suffers when merely commercial issues are decided by political rules. Still, as has been indicated, socialism's attempts to govern modern commerce have been no less horrifying than an attempt to sustain an absolutely unregulated commerce would be.

We have seen that laws of general incorporation, and their incorporation into the Constitution, were brilliant pieces of commercial regulation, because they allowed the government to encourage industrialization without impairing freedom of association. While it is difficult to fault it as a form of industrial organization, the corporation is a substantial departure from the traditional forms of ownership, and so from some of the traditional forms of moral and social responsibility. The collapse of the American economy in the late 1920s and early 1930s called into question the moral basis of the modern corporation, because the first symptom of the great economic contraction seemed to be the collapse of the stock exchanges. The regulation of corporate finance by the Securities and Exchange Commission (SEC), which was established during the New Deal, saved the corporate form, and is a fine example of constitutional regulation of commerce as distinguished from the means of capitalism and socialism.

During the 1930s and thereafter, Adolph Berle was regarded as the leading expert on the corporate form of ownership. In managing the passage of the Securities Act of 1933 through the House of Representatives, as much as in advocating the Securities Exchange Act of 1935, Sam Rayburn (Dem., Texas) was guided by this crucial passage in Berle's *Modern Corporation and Private Property*:

> The spiritual values that formerly went with ownership have been separated from it . . . . Physical property capable of being shaped by its owner could bring him direct satisfaction apart from the income it yielded [in more concrete form]. It represented an extension of his own personality. [With the corporate revolution] This quality has been lost

to the property owner [much as it has been lost to the worker through the industrial revolution].[36]

Like Berle, Rayburn could not conceal his distaste for incorporated property. Real wealth, he held, is "real estate and improvements," but stock in a corporation is "a piece of paper," "a mere symbol of ownership," whose value "is coming more and more to depend on forces beyond [the stockholder's] own reach and control."

This form of property was alien to the agrarian way of life to which Rayburn and so many of his colleagues in the House of Representatives were devoted. Incorporated property was, above all, morally suspect, because it fostered "speculation," not work, as a means to success. Such demoralization was thought to threaten democracy, because it threatened to create a dependent class. Above all, Rayburn feared that "18,000,000 passive citizens," the stockholders, would be dependent upon "a few hundred powerful managers directing and controlling the destinies of corporations."[37] Franklin Roosevelt's views were not much different. "The merchandising of securities is really traffic in the economic and social welfare of our people. Without . . . an ethical foundation," Roosevelt concluded, "economic well being can never be achieved."[38]

The attempts to regulate trade in corporate securities in the early New Deal provoked, Rayburn said, "the most powerful lobby ever organized against any bill which ever came before Congress." Public attention focused upon the issue of speculation. Most of Roosevelt's Democratic supporters wanted to outlaw all speculation, for example, to forbid all short-sales and all trading on the margin. At the extreme, they wanted an agency of the central government to franchise all corporations and certify the soundness of all corporate securities as investments. The New Deal's opponents, on the other hand, were frank speculators. "I claim," Richard Whitney, the president of the New York Stock Exchange, told the Senate Banking Committee, "that this country has been built by speculation, and that further progress must be made in that line." But the capitalistic

---

36. *Economic Regulation of Business and Industry: A Legislative History of U.S. Regulatory Agencies*, ed. Schwartz (New York: Chelsea House, 1973), vol. IV, p. 2617. Hereinafter cited as ERBI. I have reproduced in brackets Rayburn's ellipses from Berle's *Modern Corporation and Private Property* (New York: Macmillian Company, 1932), pp. 66-67.

37. *ERBI*, vol. IV, p. 2617; cf. the similar view of leading Republicans at *ERBI*, vol. IV, p. 2777.

38. *Public Papers and Addresses*, comp. Rosenman (Washington: Government Printing Office, 1938-50), vol. III (1933), p. 215 (#66). Hereinafter cited as FDR's Papers with year, page, and document number.

speculators favored socialistic measures almost as strongly as the extreme New Dealers. In particular, the capitalists thought that they ought to be able to appoint at least a substantial minority (two of five) of the commissioners who would regulate the securities exchanges.[39]

To preserve free commerce, Roosevelt had to walk a line between his socialistic friends and his capitalistic enemies. He encouraged the New Dealers with quotes from Ben Franklin: "... not gambling, but work is the way to wealth."[40] Incidentally, at the time, Franklin's view struck Wall Streeters as un-American! Yet President Roosevelt understood, in a way that Rayburn never could, the necessities of corporate finance for industrialization, and the necessity, for the survival of freedom in the West, that America be fully industrialized.[41] For this reason, he aimed to "restore some old-fashioned standards of rectitude [to] the merchandizing of securities" by the operations of the SEC, but to do so without the government itself becoming the merchandiser or the guarantor of corporate securities.[42]

In order to get the SEC established, the President was willing to accept some legal restrictions on speculation, but the main business of the SEC was the "sanctioning" of the exchange of securities. The notion of "sanction" is distinctive of the kind of commercial regulation established during the New Deal; the SEC sanctions capital and the National Labor Relations Board (NLRB) sanctions labor. Governmental sanction differs from license by the fact that it is not a testimony *for* the thing, be it a common stock or a labor union, sanctioned. The SEC was intended by Roosevelt to guarantee that capital is raised fairly, but to ignore the purposes for which capital is employed. The principle of fairness to be observed by the SEC in sanctioning securities is the freedom of choice of the citizen, in the sense that fraud ought not influence the purchase of securities. As Rooosevelt intended it, the SEC could not, in any affirmative sense, direct the choices of the citizens. Rather, it would sanction the organization of capital, that is, sanctify or "legitimate" the existence of each corporation as in the public interest, as indeed each must be if it is in fact the consequence of the genuinely free choices of its stockholders. This notion of regulation as sanctioning, as the certification of the free-

---

39. It did not even occur to them that this proposal is unconstitutional, because it violates the provisions for the appointment of officers of the United States.

40. *FDR's Papers*, 1934, pp. 91 (#22) and 415 (#163).

41. He had learned this from Theodore Roosevelt. See *FDR's Papers*, 1938, p. 41 (#5).

42. *FDR's Papers*, 1933, p. 215 (#66).

dom of crucial economic associations, was the New Deal's solution to the problem of collusion between Big Business and Big Government (which is what both socialists and capitalists sought). For both free commerce and free government require that corporations (and unions) be free associations; both business and government would be compromised by government's endorsement of a particular corporation.

Although it is often blamed as socialistic or anti-individualistic, the New Deal's regulatory policy, as illustrated by the foundation of the SEC, did not depart from the principle which is basic to constitutional regulation. In the most difficult of circumstances, circumstances bordering on industrial war, Franklin Roosevelt took scrupulous care to preserve and foster the commercial autonomy of a chief institution of the modern national economy, the corporation. That Roosevelt had to do this against the powerful opposition, on the one hand, of American capitalists and, on the other, of his own socialistic supporters, both of whom wished to have commerce and government directly involved with one another, shows how difficult it is to preserve the autonomy of commerce. Theoretically, that autonomy is the very basis of the regulatory power; today, it ought to be, as it was for Franklin Roosevelt, the goal of regulation.

Conclusion

The experience of the New Deal, no less than contemporary experience, vindicates the Framers' understanding of political economy. The practical result of capitalist and socialist ideologies would be the same, because both are totalistic: capitalism reduces all civic life to individual choices, socialism to social choices. Constitutional regulation, in contradistinction to both, presupposes the existence of heterogeneous spheres of human choice, each governed by its own rules or purposes, whose mutually supportive harmony is the purpose of government.[43] All free governments must have the power to regulate commerce, because all free societies require a regulated commerce, a commerce left free to pursue its own end—wealth—insofar as it is harmonious with other public purposes.

---

43. Two contemporary moralists have attempted to articulate the importance of autonomous associations as sources of authority independent of government: George Gilder, *Wealth and Poverty* (New York: Basic Books, 1981) does this for the family and Michael Novak, *The Spirit of Democratic Capitalism* (New York: Simon and Schuster, 1982) for the corporation. Neither sees that the understanding of the Framers is harmonious with his own.

Concluding Essay

Richard M. Ebeling

The near simultaneous publication of Adam Smith's *The Wealth of Nations* (March 1776) and the signing of the American Declaration of Independence (July 1776) has often been commented on. Both documents reflected the spirit of the age: the belief in what Adam Smith referred to as "the system of natural liberty." The challenge for many of the thinkers of the Enlightenment was to devise a set of reforms of the political and economic order that would guarantee each individual personal liberty in his private, social and economic affairs while at the same time assuring that "self interest" was guided "as by an invisible hand" to serve the common good.[1]

That the founding fathers were conscious of the economic dimension of their revolution is clear from some of the grounds upon which they justified their war for independence. The King, they state in the Declaration, had obstructed the free flow of labor through various emigration prohibitions; had set up restrictive trade barriers and regulations; had imposed an extensive and expensive bureaucracy over the civilian population; and had drained the financial and economic strength of the colonies with noxious taxes imposed without the consent of the colonial population.

Nor was this only a "practical" or common-sensical understanding of the economic dimension. Intellectuals on both sides of the Atlantic viewed themselves as "citizens of the world" (the phrase originated in the 18th century). They believed that nationalism—cultural, political and economic—was a barrier to human progress; the enlightened man realized

---

1. Attention has also often been drawn to the similarity between the system of checks and balances, and decentralization of power in a competitive economy, and the division of power and authority among the branches of government as prescribed in the Constitution. As Adam Smith defined it, a "system of natural liberty," was one in which: "Every man, as long as he does not violate the laws of justice, is left perfectly free to pursue his own interest his own way, and to bring both his industry and capital into competition with those of any other man, or order of men." Under natural liberty, the sovereign, in Smith's view, had three tasks: the defense of the country from external aggressors, the administration of justice among the citizens of the country, and the constructing and maintaining of certain public works which it might not be in the interests of private individuals to undertake. *The Wealth of Nations* (New York: The Modern Library, 1937), Bk. IV, Ch. IX, p. 651.

269

that national borders were hinderances to the free flow of goods, men, and ideas. Their ideal was a world in which the customs house—the symbol of tariffs on both goods and ideas—was, if not dismantled, at least narrowed in its scope and control.[2]

The founding fathers were well versed in the writings of both the French Physiocrates and the Scottish Philosophers; they corresponded with many of them and had personally met some during travels to Great Britain or the Continent. (Thomas Jefferson, for example, served as the supervising editor for the English translation of Destutt de Tracy's *A Treatise on Political, Economy*, a lucid defense of a *laissez-faire* social and economic order.)[3]

The economic dimension of the free society arose again during the debates surrounding the ratification of the Constitution. Under the Arti-

---

2. See, Thomas J. Schlereth, *The Cosmopolitan Ideal in Enlightenment Thought* (Notre Dame: The University of Notre Dame Press, 1927). Chapter 5 (pp. 97-125) on "An Economic and Political Theory of World Order" brings out the "internationalist" flavor of many of the Enlightenment thinkers on both sides of the Atlantic.

   In our century of total war and total states, it is easy to forget that there was a time when individuals were not viewed as the property of the State and that men's actions could be considered above and distinct from "reasons of state." See F. J. P. Veale, *Advance to Barbarism* (New York: The Devin-Adair Company, 1951), pp. 89-112 and Guglielmo Ferrero, *Peace and War* [1933] (Freeport, New York: Books for Libraries Press, 1969) pp. 1-96. A classic restatement of this "cosmopolitan" view of men and ideas in the 20th century is Julian Benda's *The Treason of the Intellectuals* [1928] (New York: W. W. Norton & Co., 1969); and on the assumptions and evolution of the "nationalist" ideal that overthrew the cosmopolitan ideal, see, Carlton J. H. Hayes, *The Historical Evolution of Modern Nationalism* (New York: MacMillan [1931] 1948), *Essays on Nationalism* (New York: The MacMillan Co., 1928), and Walter Sulzbach, *National Consciousness* (Washington, D.C.: American Council on Public Affairs, 1943).

   On the economic thinking of American colonial writers in the 18th century up to the Revolution, see, Joseph Dorfman, *The Economic Mind in American Civilization* 1606-1865, Vol. I (New York: The Viking Press, 1946) pp. 111-141; and Virgle G. Wilhite, *Founders of American Economic Thought and Policy* (New York: Bookman Associates 1958); and for analysis and review of the specific economic grievances of the American colonists leading to the Revolution, Murray N. Rothbard, *Conceived in Liberty*, Vol. 3, "Advance to Revolution, 1760-1775" (New Rochelle: Arlington House, 1976). A recent discussion of the relationship between the Constitution and economic liberty can be found in Robert A. Goldwin and William A. Schambra, editors, *How Capitalistic Is The Constitution?* (Washington: American Enterprise Institute, 1982).

3. The Count Destutt de Tracey, *A Treatise on Political Economy* [1817] (New York: Augustus M. Kelley, 1970); and in a letter on May 30, 1790, to his nephew Thomas Mann Randolph, Jefferson stated that, "In political economy I think Smith's *Wealth of Nations* the best book extant . . . ." *Basic Writings of Thomas Jefferson*, ed. Philip S. Foner (New York: Wiley Book Co., 1944) p. 594.

cles of Confederation many of the economic restrictions and abuses experienced under British rule were re-instituted at the state level. The several states imposed internal trade barriers that limited the potential economic gains from free trade and exchange within the union. State laws were established requiring the use of the state's own paper currency, or penalizing the use of the currencies or monies used in other states. These state legal tender laws were often abused by the legislatures, with resulting inflationary consequences. Nor were private property rights and contract obligations strictly protected or enforced.

Overcoming the infringements upon property rights and a dampening of the volatility of governmental policy upon social and economic interaction, James Madison argued, was an important reason for adoption of the proposed Constitution.[4]

> The sober people of America are weary of the fluctuating policy which has directed the public councils. They have seen with regret and indignation that sudden changes and legislative interferences, in cases affecting personal rights, become jobs in the hands of enterprising and influential speculators, and snares to the more industrious and less informed part of the community. They have seen, too, that one legislative interference is but the first link of a long chain of repetitions, every subsequent interference being naturally produced by the effects of the preceding. They very rightfully infer, therefore, that some thorough reform is wanting, which will banish speculations on public measures, inspire a general prudence and industry, and give a regular course to the business of society.

Attempts to rectify these shortcomings of the Articles of Confederation were addressed in the body of the Constitution. The sanctity of contract was guaranteed in Article I, Section 10, along with denying the State the right to make anything but gold or silver legal tender in payment of all debts. Article I, Section 8, minimized the power of the states in imposing import or export duties on goods crossing state lines. And the Fifth Amendment to the Constitution stated that no person could be deprived of life, liberty or property without due process of law, nor could private property be taken by the government for public purposes without just compensation.

However, while the intent of the framers of the Constitution appears clear—to protect the right of the individual to his life and property and to minimize government interference or regulation in the free commercial

---

4. *The Federalist Papers* (New York: The New American Library, 1961) Paper No. 44, pp. 282-283.

and industrial intercourse of the citizenry—as Bernard Siegan has pointed out in his study of *Economic Liberties and the Constitution*, "The Constitution's most crucial terminology is elusive and nebulous, allowing the interpreter wide discretion."

> The annotations of constitutional cases readily reveal the imprecision of such seemingly straightforward terms as *speech, press, contract, religion, property*, and *commerce*, and the indeterminate character of clauses concerned with *due process* and *equal protection*.

However, as Siegan also reminds us, imprecise language requires the interpreter to look back beyond and behind the text to discern the intent of the authors. But, alas, this also has not always assured certitude as to what the framers had in mind in terms of application or implementation.[5]

In her essay, "'Economic Liberties' and the Foundation of American Constitutionalism," Jennifer Nedelsky tries to discern what exactly were the meanings and intentions of some of the Founding Fathers. Her focus of attention, in particular, is upon James Madison and Gouverneur Morris. And her conclusion is that, as reflected in the writings of Madison and Morris, the economic and ethical premises upon which the Constitution was based are fairly clear. In straight-forward Lockeian tradition, all men had natural rights, government was instituted to guarantee justice, and justice was protection of those individual rights against the intrusive attacks of both majorities and minorities (in the form of factions).

Civil society has its birth in the emergence and sanctity of property. But ownership of property would be, and was, inevitably unequally distributed. The inequality of ownerships, however, did not necessarily have its origin in the rapaciousness of man; rather, men were unequal by birth, skill, and inclination, and hence the results of those diverse abilities and exertions would generate differing results. In more modern terms, Professor Nedelsky argues that the Constitutional Founding Fathers were interested in a political order that assured equal opportunity before the law for unequal men to achieve their respective potentials; but this also meant an inevitability of inequality of outcome.[6]

---

5. Bernard H. Siegan, *Economic Liberties and the Constitution* (Chicago: University of Chicago Press, 1980) p. 8. Cf., also, Richard A. Epstein, *Takings, Private Property and the Power of Eminent Domain* (Cambridge: Harvard University Press, 1985) pp. 19-31.

6. For recent discussions of the distinction between equality of opportunity vs. equality of outcome, see Nicholas Capoldi, *Out of Order* (Buffalo, New York: Prometheus Books, 1985), Terry Eastland and William J. Bennett, *Counting by Race* (New York: Basic Books, Inc., 1979) and Thomas Sowell, *Civil Rights: Rhetoric or Reality?* (New York: William Morrow & Co., 1984).

Unequal results did not imply injustice, however, given the natural inequality among men. Nor was it detrimental to the condition or prospects of those materially less well off. Indeed, as Professor Nedelsky clearly explains, for Madison and Morris protection of property was necessary for the institutional stability and environmental certainty that fostered frugality, industriousness, and commercial expansion—the preconditions for economic advancement for all the members of the economic community, including the poor.

The hallmarks of the economics of the Constitution, therefore, were free men, free markets, and consequently, minimal government regulation of economic affairs. But while that may have been the Founding Fathers' vision of the government's relationship to economic affairs, is it a relationship that is essential to the constitutional order? Professor Nedelsky's answer is both yes and no. The protection of individual property from encroachments by majorities has been central to our constitutional process. And to radically change the inherent primacy of property protection more than has already occurred may result in a sea-change in the very nature of our constitutional form of government. But, she says, if the values and ethical premises of our modern society have moved that far from those of the Founding Fathers, then perhaps such a transformation in the constitutional order would be in order—with all its necessary consequences.

One of those consequences that Professor Nedelsky does not sufficiently draw out is one that follows from one of her own arguments. She points out that in making the case for the sanctity of property, Morris was concerned with the unscrupulous designs not only of majorities, but of wealthy, propertied minorities as well. What the recently developed "economics of politics" literature has clearly demonstrated is the ease with which special interests can capture the political process once the political institutional order has moved away from strict limitations on the powers of government to interfere with the economic affairs of its citizens. In a setting in which the government can invade the property of some to bestow favors and privileges on others, socially perverse incentives are created that threaten the political and economic health of the society.[7] A serious question arises as to whether a free society is viable other than in a framework of strictly limited government. Indeed, it is this concern that has led a growing number of political economists to investigate the possibilities for *more and not fewer* constitutional restraints on government in the economic sphere, (e.g., constitutional amendments requiring balanced Federal budgets, limits on Federal spending and taxing as a fraction of national income, and constitutional restraints on the Federal government's ability to have discretionary influence over the monetary system).[8]

John Wettergreen, on the other hand, takes a more pragmatic perspective in his essay "Capitalism, Socialism and Constitutionalism." In fact, rather than arguing that economic regulation runs against the grain of American constitutionalism, Professor Wettergreen believes that a significant regulatory role was at the heart of how the Founding Fathers saw the economic future of the United States. He, therefore, believes that the "pro-capitalist" and "pro-socialist" views of Milton Friedman and John Kenneth Galbraith, respectively, are extremes outside of what the American constitutional order was meant to be all about.

Professor Wettergreen's view rests on a particular analysis of the meanings of certain words that are used in the Constitution and supplemented in the *Federalist Papers*. Specifically, he distinguishes between the words "rules," "regulation," and "govern." To *govern*, he explains, is to have political authority to order, direct, and assign the use of men and material for particular purposes and objects in mind. *Rules*, on the other hand, specify only particular actions or events that must occur or be brought about, but the details of which are left in the hands of those to whom the rules have been given. *Regulations*, finally, specify particular procedures that must be followed in the pursuit of various rules or goals.

Professor Wettergreen interprets the Constitution as setting down var-

---

7. Mancur Olson, *The Logic of Collective Action* (Cambridge: Harvard University Press, 1965); the *Rise and Decline of Nations* (New Haven: Yale University Press, 1982); James M. Buchanan, Robert D. Tollison and Gordon Tullock, eds., *Toward a Theory of the Rent-Seeking Society* (College Station: Texas A&M University Press, 1980); Richard B. McKenzie, ed., *Constitutional Economics* (Lexington, Mass.: Lexington Books, 1984); Geoffrey Brennan and James M. Buchanan, *The Reason of Rules: Constitutional Political Economy* (Cambridge: Cambridge University Press, 1985).

8. See, Dwight R. Lee and Richard B. McKenzie, *Regulating Government: A Preface to Constitutional Economics* (Lexington, Mass.: Lexington Books, 1987); James M. Buchanan and Richard E. Wagner, *Fiscal Responsibility in Constitutional Democracy* (Boston: Martinus Nijhoff, 1978); and James M. Buchanan, Charles K. Rowley and Richard D. Tollison, eds., *Deficits* (New York: Basil Blackwell, 1987).

ious regulatory duties for government in the economy, but that government is to neither govern nor rule over economic affairs. He sees the market or economic arena as one that—given the purposes of the market and the economic participants themselves—establishes its own rules, and within these rules is self-governing.

To assure both political and economic harmony, however, the Founding Fathers saw government intervention as desirable for the establishment of procedural regulations. These are not meant to inhibit or handicap the market, but to enhance its stability and social standing in the wider political and societal environment within which the market functions and exists.

As two examples, Professor Wettergreen raises the issues of the corporation and such regulatory agencies as the S.E.C. Limited liability, he argues, has served a valuable economic service for the pooling of risk, a service that might not have come into existence (or to the same degree) without laws of incorporation. Whether corporations would have come into existence in the form they presently take without legislative acts of incorporation, of course, can never be known. But it is certainly too hasty a judgement on Professor Wettergreen's part to assume the negative just because *he* cannot see how the corporate form would have been incorporated into tort law. Historically, "the law" has *preceded* legislation and has been the foundation for the "rules" of interpersonal relationships in society.[9] It is unlikely that if some variation of limited liability were seen as a profitable form of economic enterprise, and if it were found to be consistent with the structure of common law, it would not have been adopted. If it had been found inconsistent with the existing body of law, then its failure to emerge would not necessarily be something to bemoan. (In this context, I think that Professor Wettergreen is less than fair to the arguments *In Defense of the Corporation* developed by Robert Hessen.)[10]

Professor Wettergreen's example of the Securities and Exchange Commission is an even weaker one. The history of all organized markets is that they evolve over time procedures of self-regulation to assure order in financial dealings; and they police the behavior of their recognized participants to lower the transactions costs of individual members collecting

---

9. Bruno Leoni, *Freedom and the Law* [1961] (Los Angeles: Nash Publishing Corp., 1972); also, Carl Menger, *Problems of Economics and Sociology* [1883] (Urbana: University of Illinois Press, 1963), p. 157; F. A. Hayek, *Law, Legislation and Liberty,* Vol. I (Chicago: University of Chicago Press, 1973) pp. 72-144.

10. Robert Hessen, *In Defense of the Corporation* (Stanford: Hoover Institution Press, 1979). Cf., also, my review of Hessen's book in *Laissez-Faire Books* (Fall-Winter 1979-1980).

and processing information about the conduct and standing of potential trading partners.[11] That S.E.C. regulations, from their beginning, have *hampered* and not harmonized smooth market activity is now well established.[12] Speculative markets have always seemed an arena of subterfuge and wizardry. And as a result "speculation" has often been a target of anti-market and anti-capitalist propagandists. But false impressions should not be the basis for rationalizing the implemlentation of various and sundry regulations.

The real heart of the problem, as I see it, in Professor Wettergreen's analysis is the narrow meanings that he assigns to the words "govern," "rules," and "regulate." To begin with, "to govern," in the sense of having political authority to order, direct, and assign the use of men and material for particular purposes and objects in mind, can imply either that the political authority is itself determining the uses and purposes towards which it orders and directs men and material; or that, while having such authority, the governing body has the uses and purposes for which it uses its governing power determined for it outside itself. The latter is the circumstance under which the American government "governs" under the Constitution. For the duties and powers assigned to the Federal government under the Constitution specify the purposes for which it may legitimately apply its governing power.

Secondly, Professor Wettergreen defines "rules" as the specification of particular actions or events that are to be brought about or made to occur. Thus, his use of the word "rules" fails to distinguish two subtle but crucially different meanings that this word can take on in political, social and economic discussions: i.e., rules that are end-dependent and rules that are end-independent.[13] End-dependent rules are those that are constructed and implemented for the achievement of particular tasks and goals; they specify both the end for which they are promulgated and the

---

11. Cf. the excellent theoretical and historical analysis in Henry Crosby Emery, *Speculation on the Stock and Produce Exchanges of the United States* [1896] (New York: Greenwood Press, 1969); also, the chapter on "speculation" in Arthur T. Hadley, *Economics* (New York: G. P. Putnam's Sons, 1904) pp. 997-120; and John R. McCullough, *The Principles of Political Economy* [1864] (New York: Augustus M. Kelley, 1965) pp. 258-274.

12. George J. Benston, "Security for Investors," in *Instead of Regulation*, ed. Robert W. Poole, Jr. (Lexington, Mass.: Lexington Books, 1982) pp. 207-238; see, also, Tibor R. Machan and M. Bruce Johnson, eds., *Rights and Regulation* (San Francisco: Pacific Institute, 1983).

13. See, Geoffrey Brennen and James M. Buchanan, *The Reason of Rules*, pp. 1-18; F. A. Hayek, *Law, Legislation and Liberty*, Vol. 2, "The Mirage of Social Justice" (Chicago: University of Chicago Press, 1976) passim.

procedures by which that end is to be attained. End-independent rules are those which delineate the types of actions or modes of conduct that are either permitted or prohibited by which an individual or group may or may not attain an end, without specifying the end the individual or group is to pursue within the specified rules.

Finally, this distinction between ends-dependent and ends-independent rules enables us to think more clearly about "regulation," because regulations can also be ends-independent or ends-dependent. Thus, for example, in Article I, Section 8 of the U.S. Constitution we find the paragraph that gives Congress the power, "To regulate Commerce with foreign Nations, and among the several States, and with the Indian Tribes." How the framers of the Constitution meant the word "regulate" to be understood in this context is clarified when one turns to *The Federalist Papers*, numbers 7 and 42, written, respectively, by Alexander Hamilton and James Madison.

It is clear that the two authors wish to point out to the reader historical and hypothetical circumstances in which the States have abused, or might abuse, their powers over interstate commerce to manipulate import and export duties, as well as other forms of bounties and restrictions to benefit the interests of specific groups in their respective states at the expense of the citizens or other members of the confederacy. In other words, pricing, production, and transportation regulations are ends-dependent: they are promulgated specifically with the purpose in mind of concrete actions to enhance the relative income positions of certain individuals and groups at the expense of others. Hamilton and Madison argue for Federal regulation as a remedy, but it is also clear that their desire is to put in place ends-independent regulations: rules under which trade may be undertaken by any and all who choose to trade, regardless and independent of the motives of the individual traders or the relative income results that emerge from the exchange process. It is "regulation" as an instrument for influencing specific outcomes that is rejected by Hamilton and Madison in *The Federalist Papers*. And it is "regulation," as ends-independent rules, that they see as the role of the Federal Government in interstate commerce. Or expressed differently, Federal "regulation" is meant to assure that the United States comprise one single free trade area, as distinct from protectionist-restricting "regulation" by the several States. (The fact that in later writings Hamilton endorsed various manufacturing protections against foreign trade that he deemed as threats to America's "infant industry" is irrelevant. In *The Federalist Papers* Hamilton is writing as an anonymous spokesman in defense of the Constitution. In his later writings he is advocating specific policies as a distinct individual under the Constitution.)

If this is a legitimate interpretation of "regulation" in certain passages in the Constitution, then many, if not most, of the regulatory acts passed by Congress during the last one hundred years are unconstitutional. The Interstate Commerce Commission, the Federal Communications Commission, the Civil Aeronautics Board and many of the other regulatory agencies have all concerned themselves heavily with the *outcomes* of competition—the pricing, production, and content forms of that competition —and not just the general ends-independent rules under which the competitive process is to play itself out.

Our Constitution has been more than a set of formal procedures for undertaking legislative business, and it has had a purpose beyond the checking and balancing of the various branches of government. Its purpose has been to protect and preserve the freedoms and liberties of the future generations the Founding Fathers had in mind when they did their work in Philadelphia during the summer of 1787. Key to the preservation of those liberties was the respect for and defense of private property and free commerce, for they clearly understood that without a right to property in an institutional setting of voluntary exchange, freedom is soon destroyed and distorted in an environment of abuse, plunder and privilege.

Chapter Six

The Declaration of Independence
and the Constitution

The Declaration announced the principles justifying the American Revolution. Did these principles also provide the foundation of the American Constitution? Or did the Declaration set forth democratic principles which were abandoned by the Constitution in order to protect propertied interests? And how are we to understand the founders' treatment of slavery?

"To Secure These Rights":
Patrick Henry, James Madison, and the Revolutionary Legitimacy of the Constitution

Lance Banning

We hold these truths to be self-evident, that all men are created equal; that they are endowed by their Creator with certain unalienable rights; that among these, are life, liberty, and the pursuit of happiness. That, to secure these rights, governments are instituted among men, deriving their just powers from the consent of the governed; that, whenever any form of government becomes destructive of these ends, it is the right of the people to alter or to abolish it, and to institute a new government, laying its foundation on such principles, and organizing its powers in such form, as to them shall seem most likely to effect their safety and happiness.

—Declaration of Independence

If men were angels, no government would be necessary. If angels were to govern men, neither external nor internal controls on government would be necessary. In framing a government which is to be administered by men over men, the great difficulty lies in this: You must first enable the government to control the governed; and in the next place oblige it to control itself. . . . In the compound republic of America, the power surrendered by the people is first divided between two distinct governments, and then the portion allotted to each is subdivided among distinct and separate departments. Hence a double security arises to the rights of the people. The different governments will control each other at the same time that each will be controlled by itself. . . . In the extent and proper structure of the Union, therefore, we behold a Republican remedy for the diseases most incident to Republican Government."

James Madison, *The Federalist*

Scores of patriotic speakers have reminded us, of late, that the United States enjoys the oldest written constitution in the world. Few of them have mentioned the patriotic doubts with which this Constitution was originally received, doubts so serious and so widespread that the new plan of government was only narrowly adopted in several of the largest states. Twentieth-century audiences are preconditioned to suppose that the Constitution was the logical fulfillment of the promises embodied in the Declaration of Independence. They applaud the orator who reassures them that these two great documents, so often melded and confused, together still define our highest aspirations as a people. But Patrick Henry thought the Constitution represented a betrayal of the principles of 1776, and Henry spoke for roughly half the voters of the union's largest state, seconded by several other Revolutionary fathers of Virginia. Only as their fears were answered did the Constitution come to seem legitimate in Revolutionary minds, and there is therefore much to gain from paying some attention to the way that this was done. It could make our second bicentennial a better vehicle for national renewal than the first—not merely an excuse for sailing ships and fireworks, but also an occasion for a better public understanding of the principles with which we started.

A hundred years ago, no patriotic audience would have required an introduction to Patrick Henry. In 1765, on his twenty-ninth birthday, this celebrated country lawyer, just elected to Virginia's House of Burgesses but known throughout the colony for stirring courtroom speeches, introduced the resolutions that initiated the colonial revolt against the Stamp Act. With Thomas Jefferson and Richard Henry Lee, he spurred the Old Dominion's mounting protests through the next ten years and called the colony to arms in 1775 in words that countless schoolboys memorized for the centennial of American Independence. First governor of his new state, an office to which he was reelected four more times within the next ten years, Henry was an aging patriot by 1788, when voters chose the state convention that would ratify or disapprove the Constitution. Still he gloried in his role as Revolutionary tribune of the people. And when he rose to open the attack, referring to himself as "the servant of the people of this commonwealth, ... a sentinel over their rights, liberty, and happiness," he summoned the assistance of a reputation only Washington's surpassed.[1]

The people, Henry said, "are exceedingly uneasy and disquieted" with

---

1. Robert Douthat Meade, *Patrick Henry*, 2 vols. (Philadelphia, 1957-1969); Richard R. Beeman, *Patrick Henry: A Biography* (New York, 1974). The quotation is from Jonathan Elliot, ed., *The Debates in the Several State Conventions on the Adoption of the Federal Constitution ...*, 5 vols. (Washington, D.C., 1854), III, 21.

this "alarming" plan "to change our government." Delegated to prepare amendments to the Articles of Confederation, the members of the Philadelphia Convention had instead proposed a change "as radical as that which separated us from Great Britain," a plan of government that would transform the United States from a confederation into a national republic. "You ought to be extremely cautious," Henry warned the state convention. All "our privileges and rights are [once again] in danger." "We are running we know not whither," and "instead of securing your rights, you may lose them forever.... A wrong step ... now will plunge us into misery, and our republic will be lost."[2]

Language of this sort was not adopted solely for theatrical effect. When Henry spoke, America's republican experiment was barely twelve years old. It was by no means inconceivable that monarchy and aristocracy—or perhaps some other form of tyranny—could creep, or even rush, into the fold. The standard wisdom taught that a republic should be small enough and homogeneous enough that all its citizens would share a set of common interests and could maintain a jealous watch on the ambitions of their rulers. Now, suddenly, the Constitution offered to create a national republic larger than the largest European state. It sketched a central government whose powers would be every bit as great as Parliament had ever claimed, a government that would be organized in striking imitation of the British form, where only the lower house of legislature was immediately elected by the people. "I may be thought suspicious," Henry said, "but, sir, suspicion is a virtue [when] its object is the preservation of the public good."[3]

Having given much of his career to opposition to a distant, unresponsive central government, the aging firebrand was unmoved by Federalist insistence that rejection of the Constitution might destroy the union. He was unimpressed by Federalist descriptions of the benefits the nation could expect. We are told, a colleague put it:

> that we shall have wars and rumors of wars, that every calamity is to attend us, and that we shall be ruined and disunited forever, unless we adopt this Constitution. Pennsylvania and Maryland are to fall upon us from the north, like the Goths and Vandals of old; the Algerines ... are to fill the Chesapeake with mighty fleets, and to attack us on our front; the Indians are to invade us with numerous armies on our rear, in order

---

2. This summarizes parts of Henry's first two speeches in the convention. Elliott, III, 21-23, 44-45. Throughout the essay I have expanded abbreviations, corrected slips of pen, and slightly modernized the punctuation and capitalization wherever this appeared to make a passage easier for twentieth-century readers.

3. *Ibid.*, 45.

to convert our cleared lands into hunting grounds; and the Carolinians, from the south, (mounted on alligators, I presume,) are to come and destroy our cornfields, and eat up our little children![4]

"A bugbear," Henry scoffed. The nation was at peace, rapidly recovering from devastation and depression. He would not be terrified into an irrevocable mistake when it was in Virginia's power to insist, at least, on alterations that might make the Constitution safer for the states and people.[5] Neither was he willing to concede that so much governmental power would produce the blessings some expected. "Those nations who have gone in search of grandeur, power, and splendor, have ... been the victims of their own folly. While they acquired those visionary blessings, they lost their freedom."[6] "You are not to inquire how your trade may be increased, nor how you are to become a great and powerful people, but how your liberties can be secured; for liberty ought to be the direct end of your government."[7]

On this point the venerated Revolutionary unleashed all his prowess. "Whither is the spirit of America gone?" he asked, the spirit that had checked the "pompous armaments" of mighty Britain. "It has gone," he feared:

> in search of a splendid government—a strong, energetic government. Shall we imitate the example of those nations who have gone from a simple to a splendid government? Are those nations more worthy of our imitation? What can make an adequate satisfaction to them for the loss they have suffered in attaining such a government—for the loss of their liberty? If we admit this consolidated government, it will be because we like a great, splendid one. Some way or other we must be a great and mighty empire; we must have an army, and a navy, and a number of things. When the American spirit was in its youth, the language of America was different: liberty, sir, was then the primary object.

"Consider what you are about to do," Henry pleaded. History was full of cautionary lessons, "instances of the people losing their liberty by their own carelessness and the ambition of a few." "A powerful and mighty empire," he declaimed, "is incompatible with the genius of republicanism."[8]

4. William Grayson, *Ibid.*, 277.

5. *Ibid.*, 62-63.

6. *Ibid.*, 47.

7. *Ibid.*, 44-45.

8. *Ibid.*, 48, 53, 46, 54.

While Henry was obviously engaging in a little rhetorical terrorism of his own, we would be wrong to underestimate his intellect or to attribute his alarm to an unreasoned fear of extra-local power. As a speaker he preferred a shotgun to a rapier, demolishing his target with scattershots that intermixed the trivial with the profound. In these speeches, nevertheless, he introduced a set of substantive objections which were shared by Antifederalists throughout the country and persuaded many Revolutionaries that the Constitution was essentially at odds with the principles of 1776.[9] For the majority of people, Henry thought, national glory is a poor exchange for liberty and comfort. Whatever benefits the new regime might seem to promise, it ought to be rejected—or at least substantially amended—if it would also prove oppressive for the body of the people. There seemed abundant reason for anticipating that it would.

When Henry warned that liberty was once again at risk, he meant, most obviously, that the new Constitution incorporated no specific guarantees of freedom of religious conscience, trial by jury, freedom of the press, or other privileges protected by the several constitutions of the Revolutionary states.[10] The absence of a bill of rights was certainly the commonest and probably the most persuasive reason for opposition to the Constitution. The standard Federalist response—that it had not been necessary to deny the federal government powers it had not been granted in the first place—was entirely unconvincing. In Virginia, as in other states, the clamor for explicit guarantees was so widespread that Federalists were forced to promise that a bill of rights would be prepared by the new Congress once the Constitution was approved (which means, of course, that their descendants owe this fundamental charter of their freedoms,

---

9. Antifederalist writings have recently been collected in Herbert J. Storing, ed., *The Complete Anti-Federalist*, 7 vols. (Chicago, 1981). The most important secondary studies are the general introduction to Storing's collection, available separately as *What the Anti-Federalists Were FOR: The Political Thought of the Opponents of the Constitution* (Chicago, 1981); Jackson Turner Main, *The Antifederalists* (Indianapolis, 1966); and the introduction to Cecelia M. Kenyon, ed., *The Antifederalists* (Indianapolis, 1966). For additional recent writings see James H. Hutson, "Country, Court, and Constitution: Antifederalism and the Historians," *William and Mary Quarterly*, XXXVIII (1984), 337-368.

I do not mean to suggest that Henry had no particularistic reasons for opposing the Constitution. Concern for Virginia's special interests was certainly among the most important reasons for his stand. But these considerations lie beyond the subject of this essay, and their presence does not mean that Henry and his colleagues were less than genuine in advancing arguments that Antifederalists outside Virginia also shared.

10. Elliott, III, 44.

perhaps the plainest link between the Constitution and the Declaration, more to its opponents than its framers).

For many Antifederalists, however, the promise of a bill of rights was not enough. I should think that man "a lunatic," Henry exclaimed, "who should tell me to [adopt] a government avowedly defective, in hopes of having it amended afterwards. . . . Do you enter into a compact first, and afterwards settle the terms?"[11] Henry wanted his additional security while sovereignty still rested wholly in the people and the states, not least because addition of a bill of rights would not alleviate his deeper worries. Liberty, as every Revolutionary knew, was simply not reducible to any list of privileges on which a government would be forbidden to intrude. Liberty also meant a government directed and controlled by the body of a democratic people, which seemed, in any case, the only kind of government that would be likely to abide by written limitations on its power. This sort of liberty as well appeared to be profoundly threatened by the Constitution, which is why the fiery patriot initiated his attacks by warning that the republic might be lost. He did not believe that the new government would stay within the limits of its charter or, even if it did, that this would be sufficient to assure that it would prove responsive to the people's needs and will.

"This government is so new, it wants a name," Henry complained. "We are told that . . . it is national in this part, and federal in that part, &c. We may be amused, if we please, by a treatise of political anatomy," but for ordinary purposes of legislation the central government would act directly on the people, not the states.[12] It was to be a single, national government in this regard, and it would irresistibly become more national in time. In their attempt to balance state and federal powers, the Constitutional Convention had actually produced a famous monster: an *imperium in imperio.* "I never heard of two supreme coordinate powers in one and the same country," William Grayson said. "I cannot conceive how it can happen."[13] The state and general governments, George Mason pointed out, would both possess a power of direct taxation, and they would necessarily compete for the same sources of revenue. "These two concurrent powers cannot exist long together; the one will destroy the other; the general government being paramount to, and in every respect more powerful than the state governments, the latter must give way."[14]

11. *Ibid.,* 176, 591.
12. *Ibid.,* 160, 171.
13. *Ibid.,* 281.
14. *Ibid.,* 29-30.

Sooner or later, all power would be sucked into the mighty vortex of the general government. It would be little consolation to posterity, said Henry, to know that this consolidated system had been a mixed regime in its beginnings.[15]

Concentrated, central power would inevitably be unresponsive to the people. To many Revolutionaries this was both the lesson of America's rebellion against Great Britain and the irresistible conclusion of democratic logic. The size and character of the United States were inconsistent with the concept of a single, national republic. George Mason, the most important framer of Virginia's Revolutionary constitution, may have made the argument most economically. Can anyone suppose, he asked:

> that one national government will suit so extensive a country, embracing so many climates, and containing inhabitants so very different in manners, habits, and customs? . . . There never was a government over a very extensive country without destroying the liberties of the people; . . . popular government can only exist in small territories. Is there a single example, on the face of the earth, to support a contrary opinion?

"Sixty-five members," Mason reasoned, referring to the number who would sit in the first House of Representatives, "cannot possibly know the situation and circumstances of all the inhabitants of this immense continent." But "representatives ought to . . . mix with the people, think as they think, feel as they feel,—ought to be . . . thoroughly acquainted with their interest and condition." If this were not the case, the government would not be really representative at all.[16]

Antifederalists throughout the country stressed this theme, which was nearly as ubiquitous as the demand for a bill of rights. "A full and equal representation," one of their finest writers said:

> is that which possesses the same interests, feelings, opinions, and views the people themselves would were they all assembled. A fair representation, therefore, should be so regulated that every order of men in the community . . . can have a share of it.

But the federal House of Representatives would be so small that only men of great distinction could be chosen:

> If we make the proper distinction between the few men of wealth and abilities and consider them . . . as the natural aristocracy of the country and the great body of the people, the middle and lower classes, as the

15. *Ibid.*, 171.
16. *Ibid.*, 30, 32. For Mason see Robert A. Rutland, *George Mason: Reluctant Statesman* (Williamsburg, Va., 1961) and Hellen Hill Miller, *George Mason: Gentleman Revolutionary* (Chapel Hill, N.C., 1975).

democracy, this federal representative branch will have but very little democracy in it.

With great men in the House and even greater men in the Presidency and Senate, which would be chosen indirectly, all the important powers of the nation would be lodged in "one order of men," the many would be committed to the mercies of the few.[17]

To many Antifederalists, in short, a government was either sovereign or it was not, and genuine democracy was more than just a matter of popular elections. If the Constitution concentrated undue power in the central government (or threatened to in time), and if the powers of that government would be monopolized by "representatives" unsympathetic to the needs of ordinary people, then the Constitution was profoundly flawed in its essential spirit. Unrepublican to start with, the structure of the federal government, together with the hazy wording of its charter, would operate in practice to make it even less republican in time. First in substance, then perhaps in form as well, the system would become entirely undemocratic; the Revolution might result in nothing more than the replacement of a foreign tyranny with a domestic one. Mason had already made the point in print:

> This government will commence in a moderate aristocracy; it is at present impossible to foresee whether it will, in its operation, produce a monarchy or a corrupt, oppressive aristocracy; it will most probably vibrate some years between the two and then terminate in the one or the other.[18]

Grayson reinforced the argument in the convention:

> What, sir, is the present Constitution? A republican government founded on the principles of . . . the British monarchy. . . . A democratic branch marked with the strong features of aristocracy, and an aristocratic branch [the senate] with all the impurities and imperfections of the British House of Commons, arising from the inequality of representation and want of responsibility [to the people].[19]

These were among the features Henry had in mind when he denounced

---

17. "Letters from the Federal Farmer," in Forrest McDonald, ed., *Empire and Nation* (Englewood Cliffs, N.J., 1962), 98, 104, 114. McDonald followed the traditional attribution of these letters to Richard Henry Lee, which has since been effectively challenged in Gordon S. Wood, "The Authorship of the *Letters from the Federal Farmer*," *William and Mary Quarterly*, XXXI (1974), 299-308.
18. "Objections to the Proposed Federal Constitution," in Kenyon, *The Antifederalists*, 195.
19. Elliot, III, 280.

"that paper" as "the most fatal plan that could possibly be conceived to enslave a free people."[20]

"Plan," he said, and "plan" he meant. Through all these Antifederalist remarks there courses a profound distrust of the intentions of their foes. And, indeed, in several states the natural aristocracy was so one-sidedly in favor of the Constitution that their uniform support confirmed the popular suspicions prompted by the structure of the new regime. The Massachusetts state convention, where virtually the whole elite supported ratification, elicited a memorable expression of the underlying fear:

> These lawyers, and men of learning and moneyed men, that talk so finely, and gloss over matters so smoothly, to make us poor illiterate people swallow down the pill, expect to get into Congress themselves; they expect to be managers of this Constitution, and get all the power and all the money into their own hands, and then they will swallow all us little folks like the great *Leviathan*; yes, just as the whale swallowed up Jonah![21]

Even in Virginia, whose greatest public men were rather evenly divided by the Constitution and usually avoided charging one another with conspiratorial intentions, Antifederalists occasionally expressed distaste for some of the elitist phalanx who seemed so eager for the change. Speaking as a member of the Constitutional Convention—one of three who had refused to sign—Mason made a telling thrust:

> I have some acquaintance with a great many characters who favor this government, their connections, their conduct, their political principles. . . . There are a great many wise and good men among them. But when I look round . . . and observe who are the warmest and the most zealous friends to this new government, it makes me think of the story of the cat transformed into a fine lady; forgetting her transformation, and happening to see a rat, she could not restrain herself, but sprang upon it out of the chair.[22]

Who would fill these federal offices? What did they really want? These were the questions Henry started when he warned of the ambitions of the few, when he insisted that "a powerful and mighty empire is incompatible with the genius of republicanism." They were at the quick of his demand for the "real, actual, existing danger which should lead us to . . . so dangerous" a step.[23]

---

20. *Ibid.*, 176.
21. Amos Singletary in *Ibid.*, II, 102.
22. *Ibid.*, III, 269.
23. *Ibid.*, 23.

The challenge was in earnest, and none of these suspicions can any longer be dismissed as groundless fantasies of fearful, local politicians. Henry and his allies knew the country's situation. Most of them conceded that the powers of the central government should be enlarged. But this did not compel them to agree that circumstances were so desperate as to make the unamended Constitution the sole alternative to anarchy and economic ruin, nor were they wholly wrong about the motives of many advocates of constitutional reform. Since Charles Beard demythologized the making of the Constitution, twentieth century scholarship has overwhelmingly confirmed two leading tenets of the Antifederalist position: a dispassionate consideration of the social, cultural, and economic condition of the United States during the middle 1780s does not suggest a general crisis from which it was necessary for the country to be rescued; but even cursory examination of the movement for reform does reveal that it derived important impetus from much of the American elite's increasing disenchantment with democracy.[24] "The Constitution," in the words of the most influential modern student of its sources, "was intrinsically an aristocratic document designed to check the democratic tendencies of the period." Many Federalists supported the new plan of government for the same reasons that Antifederalists opposed it: "because its very structure and detachment from the people would work to exclude . . . those who were not rich, well born, or prominent from exercising political power."[25]

Among these Federalists, moreover, were several influential individuals and groups whose discontent with democratic politics as practiced in the Revolutionary states was accompanied by dreams of national grandeur very like the ones that Henry denounced. Particularly conspicuous among the latter were economic nationalists, who had been seeking since early in the decade to reshape the central government into an instrument of economic progress, and former army officers who associated sovereignty,

---

24. The landmark studies were Charles A. Beard, *An Economic Interpretation of the Constitution of the United States* (New York, 1913). Merrill Jensen, *The Articles of Confederation: An Interpretation of the Social-Constitutional History of the American Revolution, 1774-1781* (Madison, Wisc., 1940), and Jensen, *The New Nation: A History of the United States during the Confederation, 1781-1789* (New York, 1950).

25. Gordon S. Wood, *The Creation of the American Republic, 1776-1787* (Chapel Hill, N.C., 1969), 513-514.

stability, and national prowess with a small, professional establishment.[26] Rapidly emerging as a vigorous young spokesman for both these groups was Alexander Hamilton of New York, who had spoken at the Constitutional Convention in favor of consolidated central power and lifetime terms of office for the President and Senate, who hoped to help create a thriving, imperial republic, and who conceived that national greatness would require a close alliance between the country's men of liquid capital and national rulers capable of guiding and resisting the body of the people.[27]

Mason's cat was not a phantom. Henry's dreamers of ambitious schemes of national might and splendor were entirely real—and likely to possess important offices if the Constitution was approved. Virginia ratified the Constitution, then, in spite of rational suspicions of the antidemocratic inclinations of many of its friends and over well-considered theoretical objections to its tendencies and structure. It did so, in important part, because the state convention's most impressive spokesmen for the Constitution were Federalists of quite a different sort, men who were as conscientiously concerned with Revolutionary principles as any of their foes, who did not share the vision Henry feared, but who supported change because they thought it was the only way to safeguard and perfect the nation's Revolutionary gains. To understand the Constitution's triumph in Virginia and the nation, we need to give renewed attention to the differences among its friends. We need to recognize that some of these were fully as alert as Henry to the dangers Antifederalists condemned and not at all inclined to sacrifice democracy to private rights or national greatness.

At Richmond, Henry's principal opponents were Edmund Randolph, another of the three non-signers who were present at the close of the Philadelphia Convention, and James Madison, who was more responsible than any other individual for the distinctive shape of constitutional reform. Randolph's stand and story, mentioned later in the essay, offer

---

26. See especially E. James Ferguson, *The Power of the Purse: A History of American Public Finance, 1776-1790* (Chapel Hill, N.C., 1961), Ferguson, "The Nationalists of 1781-1783 and the Economic Interpretation of the Constitution," *Journal of American History*, LVI (1969), 241-261, and Richard H. Kohn, *Eagle and Sword: The Federalists and the Creation of the Military Establishment in America, 1783-1802* (New York, 1975).

27. Biographies include John C. Miller, *Alexander Hamilton: Portrait in Paradox* (New York, 1959), Forrest McDonald, *Alexander Hamilton: A Biography* (New York, 1979), and Jacob Ernest Cooke, *Alexander Hamilton* (New York, 1982). See also Gerald Stourzh, *Alexander Hamilton and the Idea of Republican Government* (Stanford, Cal., 1970).

unexampled insight into why the Constitution was approved despite a potent fear of counter-revolution. And it is Madison, of course, to whom Americans have always turned to understand the Constitution as a Revolutionary act: the document that sealed the promises of 1776. Indeed, the latter's role in framing the new government was hardly more important than his explanation and defense of the completed plan to his enduring reputation as the Father of the Constitution.[28]

Like Randolph, Madison responded to Henry's condemnation of the quest for grandeur by *agreeing* that "national splendor and glory are not our [proper] objects."[29] And when Mason said that certain clauses of the Constitution were intended to prepare the way for gradual subversion of the powers of the states, Madison immediately broke in, demanding "an unequivocal explanation" of an insinuation that all the signers of the Constitution preferred a consolidated national system.[30] "If the general government were wholly independent of the governments of the particular states," he had already said, "then, indeed, usurpations might be expected to the fullest extent." But the general government "derives its authority from [the state] governments and from the same sources from which their authority derives," from their sovereign peoples, who would certainly resist attempted usurpations.[31] "The sum of the powers given up by the people of Virginia is divided into two classes—one to the federal and the other to the state government. Each is subdivided into three branches."[32] In addition, Madison continued, "the powers of the federal

---

28. For biographical information see Irving Brant, *James Madison*, 6 vols. (Indianapolis, 1941-1961), Ralph Ketcham, *James Madison: A Biography* (New York, 1971), and Harold S. Schultz, *James Madison* (New York, 1970).

29. Elliot, III, 135. For Randolph see *Ibid.*, 81.

30. Mason insisted that many members of the Convention *had* desired consolidation, but that Madison had "expressed himself against it" in a private conversation and that he had never heard any Virginia delegate advocate a unitary system. Madison "declared himself satisfied," and Mason finished his speech. Elliot, III, 517-530. Hugh Blair Grigsby, whose *The History of the Virginia Federal Convention of 1788* ..., 2 vols. ("Collections of the Virginia Historical Society," new series, vols. ix-x; Richmond, 1890-1891) was based in part on oral information, was being overly dramatic when he wrote that Madison "demanded reparation in a tone that menaced an immediate call to the field" (p. 90), but there can be no doubt that the framer sharply resented the remark. Madison was universally described as a man of remarkably "sweet" manners, who never lost his temper, but he was capable of flashes of hard anger—and an uncharacteristic breach of parliamentary decorum—when he thought himself accused of consolidationism or when someone seemed to doubt his commitment to republicanism.

31. Elliot, III, 96.

32. *Ibid.*, 408-409.

government are enumerated; it can only operate in certain cases."[32] Far from threatening a gradual absorption of the proper powers of the states and people, adoption of the Constitution would "increase the security of liberty more than any government that ever was," since in America the powers ordinarily confided to a single government—and sometimes even to a single branch—would be entrusted to two sets of governments, each of which would watch the other at the same time as its several branches served as an internal check against abuse.[34]

It is impossible to place excessive emphasis on Madison's denial that the Constitution would result in a consolidated system or on his disclaimer of a wish for national splendor. To him no less than to Henry, I hope to show, liberty and comfort, not riches or the might to rival European powers, were the proper tests of national happiness. And liberty meant governments that would be genuinely responsive to the people, not merely governments that would derive from popular elections and protect the people's private rights.[35] This is why he placed such stress on the enumerated powers and complicated federal structure of the new regime. He did not deny that too much power, placed in hands too distant from the people, would imperil republican liberty. He even spoke occasionally of the "concessions" federal reform demanded from the people and the states.[36] He understood as well as any Antifederalist that national representatives would be less sympathetic to the people's local needs and better shielded from their wrath or clamors than the state assemblies. Therefore, he insisted, local interests had been left in local hands, and federal representatives would be responsible only for those great and national matters—few and carefully defined—on which they could be trusted to

---

33. *Ibid.*, 95.
34. *Ibid.*, 408-409. Madison's most elaborate explanations of the partly federal, partly national derivation and structure of the new system—and of the guarantees against a further consolidation—include his speeches of June 6 and 11, *Ibid.*, 94-97, 257-259, and especially *The Federalist*, numbers 39, 45, 46, 51, 62. Page citations in later notes are to *The Federalist*, ed. Jacob E. Cooke (Cleveland, 1961).
35. "The genius of republican liberty" demands "not only that all power should be derived from the people, but that those entrusted with it should be kept in dependence on the people." *Federalist*, no. 37, pp. 233-234.
36. To Thomas Jefferson, March 19, 1787, in Robert A. Rutland *et al*, eds., *The Papers of James Madison*, 13 vols. to date (Chicago and Charlottesville, Va., 1962—), IX, 318. See also his reference in the state convention, Elliot, III, 95, to the necessity of "submitting to the inconvenience" of greater federal power.

reflect the people's needs and will.[37] "As long as this is the case," he reasoned, "we have no danger to apprehend."[38]

"Where power can be safely lodged, if it be necessary," Madison maintained, "reason commands its cession."[39] True it was that every grant of power carried with it the potential for abuse, and it was true as well that Revolutionary principles demanded constant scrutiny of rulers. Yet it was also possible to carry an appropriate distrust of power to extremes that would deny the very feasibility of a republic:

> Gentlemen suppose that the general legislature will do everything mischievous they possibly can and that they will omit to do everything good which they are authorized to do. If this were a reasonable supposition, their objections would be good. I consider it reasonable to conclude that they will as readily do their duty as deviate from it; nor do I go on the grounds mentioned by gentlemen on the other side—that we are to place unlimited confidence in [national officials] and expect nothing but the most exalted integrity and sublime virtue. But I go on this great republican principle: that the people will have virtue and intelligence to select men of virtue and wisdom. Is there no virtue among us? If there be not, we are in a wretched situation. No theoretical checks, no form of government, can render us secure. To suppose that any form of government will secure liberty or happiness without any virtue in the people is a chimerical idea.[40]

The people's vigilance, this framer argued, is the ultimate security for any democratic state. The assumption that the people would repeatedly elect only those who would betray them was really an objection to self-government itself.[41]

Apart from Mason's charge that many signers of the Constitution wanted a consolidated government, nothing angered Madison so much as Henry's hints that only men of unsound principles or questionable ambitions could support the proposed reform. "I profess myself," he awkwardly exclaimed:

---

37. *Federalist*, no. 10, p. 63. But there are any number of indications that Madison assumed that federal representatives would reflect their constituents' will, which was a logical necessity for his argument that the large republic would defeat majority faction. Among the clearest are *Federalist*, no. 46, 318-319; no. 51, p. 353; and especially no. 57, 384-387.
38. Elliot, III, 90.
39. *Ibid.*, 394.
40. Elliot, III, 536-537.
41. *Federalist*, no. 57, pp. 384-387.

> to have had a uniform zeal for a republican government. If the honorable member, or any other person, conceives that my attachment to this system arises from a different source, he is mistaken. From the first moment that my mind was capable of contemplating political subjects, I never, till this moment, ceased wishing success to a well-regulated republican government.[42]

The outburst did him little credit. He ordinarily had little use for flaming protestations of patriotic zeal. But Madison was understandably infuriated by aspersions that suggested motives nearly opposite to those he felt. For he not only thought the Constitution perfectly consistent with republican philosophy; he questioned whether there was any other means by which the Revolution could be saved.

Henry called upon the Federalists for the "actual, existing danger" that compelled so great a change. No one, then or later, could explain it more completely than the man who was primarily responsible for the original proposals from which the Constitution had emerged. The history of the Confederation, Madison insisted, offered "repeated unequivocal proofs ... of the utter inutility and inefficacy" of a central government that depended on thirteen other governments for its revenues and for enforcement of its acts, proofs confirmed by the experiences of other historical confederacies.[43] "The Confederation is so notoriously feeble," he continued, "that foreign nations are unwilling to form any treaties with us," for these had been "violated at pleasure by the states." Congress was "obliged to borrow money even to pay the interest of our debts," although these debts had been incurred in the sacred cause of Independence.[44] It was plain when the Convention met that America could not continue to entrust its "happiness" and "safety" to "a government totally destitute of

---

42. Elliot, III, 394.

43. *Ibid.*, 128-129ff. For the experiences of other confederacies see further *The Federalist*, nos. 18-20.

44. Elliot, III, 135-136. On the debts see his eloquent "Address to the States" of April 26, 1783 in *Papers of Madison*, VI, 494: "The citizens of the U.S. are responsible for the greatest trust ever confided to a political society. If justice, good faith, honor, gratitude, and all the other qualities which ennoble the character of a nation and fulfill the ends of government be the fruits of our [republican] establishments, the cause of liberty will acquire a dignity and lustre which it has never yet enjoyed; and an example will be set which cannot but have the most favorable influence on the rights of mankind. If, on the other side, our governments should be unfortunately blotted with the reverse of these cardinal and essential virtues, the great cause which we have engaged to vindicate will be dishonored and betrayed; the last and fairest experiment in favor of the rights of human nature will be turned against them; and their patrons and friends exposed to be insulted and silenced by the votaries of tyranny and usurpation."

the means of protecting itself or its members,"[45] and Revolutionary principles themselves required that independent taxing powers and independent means of compelling obedience to federal laws (should rest directly on the people, not the states.[46]

National humiliation and dishonor, though, disgraceful though these were, were only part of the impending peril as Madison perceived it. Members of a union were entitled to expect the general government to defend their happiness and safety, which were seriously damaged by the economic dislocations caused by British restrictions on American commerce. But Congress was unable to secure a power to retaliate against the British, and states attempting independent action had been checked by the competing laws of neighbors.[47] In consequence, increasing discontent with the Confederation and rising, mutual antagonisms between the states had led to serious consideration of replacement of the general union by several smaller confederacies. Madison did not believe that the republican experiment could long outlive the union. At the Philadelphia Convention he had said:

> Let each state depend on itself for its security, and let apprehensions arise of danger from distant powers or from neighboring states, and the languishing condition of all the states, large as well as small, would soon be transformed into vigorous and high toned governments. ... The same causes which have rendered the old world the theatre of incessant wars and have banished liberty from the face of it, would soon produce the same effects here. [The smaller states would] quickly introduce some regular military force against sudden danger from their powerful neighbors. The example ... would soon become universal. [Great powers would be granted to executives.] A standing military force, with an overgrown executive, will not long be safe companions to liberty.[48]

Writing in *The Federalist*, he had again affirmed the warning. "Nothing

---

45. Elliot, III, 129.

46. Madison's earliest sketch of a reform (to Jefferson, March 19, 1787, *Papers*, IX, 318-319) suggested that an independent federal taxing power would require a reconstitution of Congress on the basis of proportional representation. Jefferson approved the power and likewise insisted that the reform must "preserve inviolate the fundamental principle that the people are not to be taxed but by representatives chosen immediately by themselves." (*Ibid.*, X, 336.)

47. This was clearly the problem that first led Madison to approve a thorough reconsideration of the structure of the confederation. For elaboration and citations see Lance Banning, "James Madison and the Nationalists, 1780-1783," *William and Mary Quarterly*, XL (1983), 252-253.

48. Speech of June 29 in Max Farrand, ed., *The Records of the Federal Convention of 1787*, rev. ed., 4 vols. (New Haven, Conn., 1966 [orign. publ. 1937]), I, 464-465.

short of a Constitution fully adequate to the national defense and the preservation of the union can save America from as many standing armies" as there are states or separate confederacies "and from such a progressive augmentation of these establishments in each as will render them...burdensome to the properties and ominous to the liberties of the people." Without the general union, liberty would everywhere be "crushed between standing armies and perpetual taxes."[49] The Revolutionary order would collapse.

Henry "tells us the affairs of our country are not alarming," Madison complained. "I wish this assertion was well founded."[50] In fact, the Constitutional Convention had assembled in the midst of an immediate crisis of American union, and the union was the necessary shield for the republican experiment that Henry wanted to preserve. Nor was even this the sum of current dangers. The Convention also faced a second crisis, which Henry failed to recognize in his repeated condemnations of "the tyranny of rulers." In republics, Madison suggested, "turbulence, violence, and abuse of power by the majority trampling on the rights of the minority... have, more frequently than any other cause, produced despotism." In the United States—and even in Virginia—it was not the acts of unresponsive rulers, but the follies and transgressions of the sympathetic representatives of state majorities that tempted growing numbers of the people to abandon their Revolutionary convictions. "The only possible remedy for those evils," he protested, the only one consistent with "preserving and protecting the principles of republicanism, will be found in that very system which is now exclaimed against as the parent of oppression."[51]

With these words the framer introduced the train of reasoning that had produced his most distinctive, crucial contribution to the Founding. In every state the popular assemblies had struggled to protect their citizens

---

49. *Federalist*, no. 41, pp. 273-274 and passim. See also Elliot, III, 382.
50. Elliot, III, 399.
51. *Ibid.*, 87-88. And see, of course, the famous, earlier elaborations of the point in *The Federalist* numbers 10 and 51, pp. 56-57, 352: "The instability, injustice, and confusion introduced into the public councils have in truth been the mortal diseases under which popular governments have everywhere perished.... Complaints are everywhere heard from our most considerate and virtuous citizens, equally the friends of public and private faith and of public and personal liberty, that our governments are too unstable, that the public good is disregarded in the conflicts of rival parties, and that measures are too often decided, not according to the rules of justice and the rights of the minor party, but by the superior force of an interested and overbearing majority....Justice is the end of government. It is the end of civil society. It ever has been and ever will be pursued until it be obtained or until liberty be lost in the pursuit."

from the economic difficulties of the middle 1780s. Many of their measures—paper money, laws suspending private suits for debt, postpone-
ments of taxation, or continued confiscations of the property of former
loyalists—interfered with private contracts, endangered people's rights to
hold their property secure, or robbed the states of the resources necessary
to fulfill their individual and federal obligations. Essentially unchecked
by other parts of government, the lower houses violated bills of rights and
sacrificed the long-term interests of the whole community to more immediate considerations, calling into question "the fundamental principle of
republican government, that the majority who rule in such governments
are the safest guardians both of public good and of private rights."[52]

Although Virginia managed to avoid the worst abuses of the middle
eighties, Madison thought continentally. As the country moved toward
constitutional reform, correspondents warned him of a growing disillusionment with popular misgovernment, particularly in New England,
where Shays's Rebellion erupted in the winter of 1786. Virginia's own
immunity from popular commotions or majority misrule appeared to
him in doubt. Personally revolted by the changeability, injustices, and lack
of foresight of even Virginia's laws, he did not abandon his republican
commitment, but he did become increasingly concerned that disenchantment with democracy, confined thus far to only a tiny (though an influential) few, could spread in time through growing numbers of the people,
who might eventually prefer despotic rule to governments unable to

---

52. "Vices of the Political System of the United States," April 1787, in *Papers of Madison*, X,
354. See also "Observations on Jefferson's Draft of a Constitution for Virginia," *Ibid.*, XI,
287-288. It should be noted, though, that Madison did not consider the "mutability" of
laws to be pernicious to minorities alone. Instability, says *Federalist*, no. 62, pp. 421-422,
gives an "unreasonable advantage ... to the sagacious, the enterprising, and the mon-
eyed few over the industrious and uninformed mass of the people. Every new regulation
concerning commerce or revenue or in any manner affecting the value of the different
species of property presents a new harvest to those who watch the change.... But the
most deplorable effect of all is that diminution of attachment and reverence which
steals into the hearts of the people towards a political system which betrays so many
marks of infirmity and disappoints so many ... hopes."

secure their happiness or even to protect their fundamental rights.[53] The crisis of confederation government, as Madison conceived it, was compounded by a crisis of republican convictions, and the interlocking dangers could be overcome only by a change that would at once "perpetuate the union and redeem the honor of the republican name."[54] He therefore went to Philadelphia to urge abandonment of the Confederation in favor of a carefully constructed great republic which would rise directly from the people, would possess effective, full, and independent powers over matters of general concern, and would incorporate so many different economic interests and religious sects that majorities would seldom form "on any other principles than those of justice and the general good."[55] Although the full Convention greatly modified his original proposals, he soon concluded that the finished Constitution was the best, and possibly the final, chance to reconcile democracy with private rights and public good. He even came to think that the complicated, federal features of the finished Constitution offered valuable securities for liberty that he had not envisioned when the great Convention met.

Madison assumed a very special place among the Founders—more special, I would argue, even than is commonly believed—because he personally bridged so much of the abyss between the Revolutionary tribunes such as Henry and the aspiring consuls such as Hamilton, with whom he formed a brief and less than wholly comfortable alliance. He fully shared with higher-flying Federalists not only the determination to invigorate the union, but also the emotional rejection of the early Revolutionary constitutions and the populistic politics that they permitted—what Elbridge Gerry called "an excess of democracy." He believed, as Hamilton believed, that Revolutionary governments were so responsive to the wishes of unhampered, temporary state majorities that they endangered the unalienable rights that independence was intended to protect.

---

53. Madison's letters to Virginia from his seat in the Confederation Congress during February and March 1787 reported widespread suspicions of a growth of pro-monarchy sentiments in New England. See, for example, to Washington, Feb. 21, in *Papers*, IX, 286. His fear of this phenomenon was very near the surface of his mind when he outlined his earliest ideas about reform in the letter to Jefferson of March 19, *Ibid.*, 318, writing that "the mortal diseases of the existing constitution ... have tainted the faith of the most orthodox republicans, and ... challenge from the votaries of liberty every concession in favor of stable government not infringing fundamental principles as the only security against an opposite extreme of our present situation."

54. To Edmund Pendleton, Feb. 24, 1787, *Ibid.*, IX, 295.

55. *Federalist* no. 51, p. 353.

He agreed with other Federalists that just, enduring governments demanded qualities not found in popular assemblies: protection for the propertied minority (and others); the wisdom to discern the long-term general good; and power to defend them both against more partial, more immediate considerations.

No more than Henry, though, did Madison approve the vision of a splendid, mighty future; and unlike many other Federalists, his fear of the majority had never tempted him to disregard the dangers posed by unresponsive rulers. Hamilton and other economic nationalists hoped to use a stronger central government to speed developments that would prepare the groundwork for successful competition with the great Atlantic empires. Madison intended to "perpetuate" the union in order to *preserve* the Revolution from the European curses of professional armed forces, persistent public debts, powerful executives, and swollen taxes, as well as to invest the general government with the ability to counteract the European trading policies that seemed to him to threaten the social foundations of American democracy.[56] Some members of the Constitutional Convention may have wanted to create a system that would place as much authority as possible in rulers only distantly dependent on the people. Madison expected to create a government that would defeat the wishes of factional majorities *without* destroying the republican "communion of interests and sympathy of sentiments" between the rulers and the ruled.[57] Although he shared the hope that large election districts would favor popular selection of representatives less likely to sacrifice the general good or private rights to the immediate demands of the majority (and planned to counterbalance the assembly with even less responsive branches), he entered the Constitutional Convention *equally* determined to control potentially ambitious rulers and assure their continuing dependence on the people.[58] In *The Federalist* and in Virginia's state convention, the Constitution he defended would "break and control the violence" of popular majorities and assure superior attention to the long-term good,[59] but it would *not* produce a government that would be unresponsive to the people's needs or will. Responsibility would be secured, as always, by popular elections and internal checks and balances. For the

---

56. On the last point see Drew R. McCoy, *The Elusive Republic: Political Economy in Jeffersonian America* (Chapel Hill: N.C., 1980).
57. *Federalist* no. 57, p. 386. This number is Madison's most complete explanation of the forces that would keep federal representatives responsive to the people.
58. *Ibid.*, no. 51, p. 349.
59. *Ibid.*, no. 10, p. 56.

first time in the history of representative democracy, it would be further guaranteed by the enumerated limits and the compound, federal features of the new regime.

Recent scholarship has not placed equal emphasis on all the vital parts of Madison's attempt to understand and justify the Constitution. It credits him, of course, with an essential part in the creation of a central government that would derive exclusively from popular elections, as well as with the most elaborate defense of its republican characteristics. It devotes elaborate attention to his argument that private rights are safer in a large than in a small republic. It leans on him, indeed—more heavily than on any other individual—for its recognition that "the Constitution presented no simple choice between accepting or rejecting the principles of 1776," since the Federalists could "intelligibly picture themselves as the true defenders of the libertarian tradition."[60] In doing so, however, it commonly identifies the man too closely with the movement, makes too much of some ideas and not enough of others, and thus obscures some differences that had important consequences in Virginia and the country as a whole.

"There is something decidedly disingenuous," writes Gordon S. Wood, "about the democratic radicalism" of Federalist defenses of the Constitution, for behind this language lay an evident desire "for a high-toned government filled with better sorts of people, . . . partisan and aristocratic purposes that belied the Federalists' democratic language."[61] On balance, Wood is right, and yet a careful effort to distinguish Madison's position from that of other key reformers—one that gives full weight to his insistence on the complicated federal structure and enumerated powers of the central government, his fear of independent rulers, and his conviction that the Constitution was a wholly democratic remedy for democratic ills—both qualifies and clarifies the generalization. The Federalists did generally believe that private rights and public happiness were threatened by the populistic politics and poorly balanced constitutions of the Revolutionary states. They looked to federal reform not only as a necessary cure for the debilities of the confederation, but also as an opportunity to remedy those other ills, and they believed a proper remedy required both limitations on state governments and the erection of a general government that would be more resistant to majority demand. Madison not only shared these wishes, he was more responsible than any

---

60. Wood, *Creation of the American Republic*, 523-524.
61. *Ibid.*, 562, 615.

other thinker for defining problems in these terms and sketching leading features of the Federalist solution. But this was only part—and not the most distinctive part—of Madison's peculiar contribution.

What distinguished Madison most clearly from all the other framers was his early, firm, and intimate association of survival of the union with continuation of a republican experiment that he still defined, in insufficiently acknowledged ways, in early Revolutionary terms. The liberty he wished to save—the point requires repeated stress—was not just liberty defined as the inherent rights of individuals, but also liberty defined as popular self-governance.[62] Convinced that neither sort of liberty could be secure without the other, valuing them both, he worked from the beginning for a change that would restrain tyrannical majorities, but he never doubted that majorities should rule—or that the people *would* control the complicated structure raised by the completed Constitution. This is why he heatedly denied that he approved of a consolidated system, placed increasing emphasis on federal dimensions of the structure, and properly insisted that he had no other object than the people's liberty and comfort. He was defending a reform that he had always understood—and was still trying to define—as an attempt to rescue *both* of the ideals enunciated in the Declaration.[63]

Several observations follow, most of them intended to suggest that Madison's determination to achieve a change that would secure both private rights *and* public liberty extended far beyond adjournment of the Constitutional Convention and that his effort to legitimize the Constitution from the vantage point of Revolutionary theory was nearly as important to its triumph as his contributions to its framing. Edmund Randolph's story illustrates these points, as does the rest of Madison's career.

A close associate of Madison since 1776 and governor of Virginia when the Constitutional Convention met, Randolph introduced the plan with

---

62. *Federalist* no. 39, 250: only a "strictly republican" form of government "would be reconcilable with the genius of the people of America, with the fundamental principles of the revolution, or with that honorable determination which animates every votary of freedom to rest all our political experiments on the capacity of mankind for self-government."

63. I have developed many of these points at greater length in "James Madison and the Nationalists," *William and Mary Quarterly*, XL (1983), 227-255; "The Hamiltonian Madison: A Reconsideration," *Virginia Magazine of History and Biography*, XCII (1984), 3-28; and "The Practicable Sphere of a Republic: James Madison, the Constitutional Convention, and the Development of Revolutionary Federalism," in *Beyond Confederation: Origins of the Constitution and American National Identity*, ed. Richard Beeman et al. (Chapel Hill, 1987), pp. 162-187.

which the Philadelphia deliberations started. Like Mason, he contributed effectively to the Convention's work, but grew increasingly alarmed as the proceedings altered Madison's original proposals. Sharing Mason's doubts about a strong, re-eligible executive, a Senate dominated by the smaller, Northern states, the hazy wording of important clauses, and the motives of some of his colleagues, he became the first of three non-signers to declare that he could not approve the finished Constitution, hoping for the meeting of a second general convention to repair the oversights and errors of the first. Nonetheless, when the Virginia state convention met, Randolph startled the assemblage by immediately announcing that despite his reservations he would unequivocally support the unamended Constitution. He spoke in fact, from the beginning, as a fervent foe of even a conditional approval of the plan.[64]

What had happened in the intervening months to change his mind? Henry pressed him with this question to the point of personal exchanges that provided the dramatic highlight of the meeting.[65] The response was fundamentally uncomplicated, but revealing. "I refused to sign," he answered, and if the circumstances were the same today, would still insist on alterations that would satisfy some serious objections. Now, however, eight of the nine states necessary to initiate the system had ratified the unamended Constitution. In these circumstances, to insist on previous amendments was impossible "without inevitable ruin to the Union, and ... I will assent to the lopping of this limb, [meaning his arm], before I assent to the dissolution of the Union."[66] The old Confederation, Randolph said, "is gone, whether this house says so or not. It is gone, sir, by its own weakness."[67] The eight approving states would not recede to gratify Virginia. "If, in this situation, we reject the Constitution, the Union will be dissolved, the dogs of war will break loose, and anarchy and discord will complete the ruin of this country."[68]

---

64. A standard modern biography is John J. Reardon, *Edmund Randolph: A Biography* (New York, 1975).
65. See especially Elliot, III, 187-189. Grigsby says, 165, that in the evening after this exchange Colonel William Cabell called on Randolph as a friend of Henry, but that the convention was relieved to learn the next morning that a reconciliation had been achieved without a recourse to the field. I doubt that there was any serious consideration of a duel, though Randolph had used language that one gentleman did not use to another.
66. Elliot, III, 24-26.
67. *Ibid.*, 84.
68. *Ibid.*, 603.

Henry feared the Revolution would be lost. "I am a child of the Revolution," Randolph replied. "I would join heart and hand in rejecting the system did I not conceive it would promote our happiness." But the Constitution offered new securities against "injustice, licentiousness, insecurity, and oppression,"[69] and Virginia could not "exist without a union with her neighbors":

> Those states ... our friends, brothers, and supporters, will, if disunited from us, be our bitterest enemies. ... The other states have upwards of 330,000 men capable of bearing arms. ... In case of an attack, what defense can we make? ... Our export trade is entirely in the hands of foreigners. We have no manufactures. ... Shall we form a partial confederacy? ... Partial confederacies will require such a degree of force and expense as will destroy every feature of republicanism. ... In union alone safety consists.[70]

Randolph still believed the Constitution was imperfect. He would gladly vote to recommend amendments, but not if these amendments were to be conditions of Virginia's ratification. The approval of eight states, he said, had reduced the issue "to the single question of Union or no Union."[71] "When I see safety on my right, and destruction on my left, ... I cannot hesitate to decide in favor of the former."[72]

How many moderates (or "trimmers" in contemporary parlance) reasoned much as Randolph did? It is impossible to know—and certainly impossible to say, as we can say with surety in Randolph's case—how many were directly influenced by James Madison. It is a fact, however, that in all the narrowly divided states, the ratification contest was decided by a handful of uncertain delegates who, at the final moment, proved unwilling to insist on prior amendments at the risk of dissolution of the union. It is not unreasonable to guess that, like the two Virginians, many of them thought that democratic liberty could only thrive within the federal hedge. Many of them may have hoped, as Madison and Randolph hoped, that private rights and public liberty would both prove more secure in an enlarged, compound republic. Madison was not, of course, the only Federalist to reason in these terms, but he was undeniably the earliest and most effective spokesman for a train of thought on which, among a Revolutionary generation, the triumph of the Constitution may have turned.

---

69. *Ibid.*, 65, 67.

70. *Ibid.*, 72-80.

71. *Ibid.*, 652.

72. *Ibid.*, 66.

The victory was narrow, to be sure, and incomplete. Many children of the Revolution entered on the federal experiment with all the reservations Randolph swallowed. A few proclaimed, as Patrick Henry did, that they would work with all their power "to retrieve the loss of liberty, and remove the defects of that system in a constitutional way."[73] Madison himself, however, was far from finished with his effort to define a Revolutionary federal union. The skeptics therefore found a potent, partial ally in the Father of the Constitution, who quickly joined with Thomas Jefferson to lead most of the former Antifederalists into a party dedicated to a strict interpretation of the federal charter and a vision of the future much at odds with Hamilton's design for national glory. That Madison would take this stand is not as paradoxical as many analysts have thought.

---

73. *Ibid.*, 652.

Equality and Constitutionalism: The Relationship of the Declaration of Independence and the Constitution as Understood Today

Glen E. Thurow

At the beginning of the United States we find not one, but two great founding documents, the Declaration of Independence and the Constitution. Each authoritatively proclaims the will of the American people. The representatives who signed the Declaration speak "in the name and by the authority of the good people of these colonies." Their success allows this same people to speak in the magisterial tones of sovereignty in the Constitution: "We, the People of the United States ... do ordain and establish ...." The first declares America's freedom and independence; the second establishes a constitutional order for a united people. The independence of the United States is defended on the grounds of certain self-evident truths applicable to all men everywhere, and the one people acknowledging and acting upon these truths is formed by the Constitution into a whole capable of achieving the defined purposes of limited government. The relationship between these two documents is the relationship between the truths of human nature which justify independence and the defined purposes and constituted ways of American republican government.

Both documents exercise an immense authority in today's politics. The authority of the Constitution within the United States is evident: most of the major domestic issues of our time have been decisively shaped by reference to the Constitution, often by an explicit Constitutional decision by the courts. But the prestige, if not the authority, of the American Constitution is also evident in many other countries—not excluding the Soviet Union—who have imitated its appearance if not always its heart. The Declaration is less often given as authority in American politics, but who can doubt that the great push for equality of all sorts in our time receives much of its moral force from the implicit awareness that we are a people dedicated to the proposition that "all men are created equal"? And who can doubt that the prestige of revolution and equality in many other countries is strengthened by the claim set forth in the Declaration and the success of the nation built upon it. It is often the habit of even anti-democratic revolutionaries to speak in the Declaration's language of

305

unalienable rights until their power is sufficiently secure that the public opinion formed by the longing for freedom no longer matters.

Yet the example of these revolutionaries reminds us that documents may be misused. The greater the authority of a document the greater the need for those who would subvert it to disguise their program in its language. And, of course, a document may be unintentionally subverted simply by being misunderstood. The possibility of misrepresentation or misunderstanding is made greater in the case of our founding documents because we have two of them and because the relationship between them can be, and is, disputed. In the prevailing views of this relationship can be found the measure of our understanding of the American political order.

It is not too much of a simplification to say that in today's politics men may be divided into two groups: one group speaks in the name of principles from the Declaration of Independence while denying that those principles receive their embodiment in the Constitution; the other reveres the authority of the Constitution while denying that it is dependent upon the truths of the Declaration. Both groups agree that the two documents are unrelated.

It might seem that this division between the Declaration and the Constitution would divide us, or democratic opinion in the world, into a party of liberalism proclaiming the principles of liberty and a party of conservatism wishing to preserve the Constitution or constitutionalism. And indeed, it does to some extent. Yet it is clear that the world cannot be divided into liberals and conservatives and neither can the American public. The vocabulary of recent American politics—new left, neo-conservative, neo-liberal, new right, McGovernism, the moral majority—indicates that the old terms of liberal and conservative do not easily capture the nature of public opinion today. Those who revere the authority of the Constitution are often by no means conservative, while those who speak of the Declaration's principles are not always liberal.

In denying any principled connection between the Declaration and the Constitution, predominant opinion in today's world means to deny either that freedom requires constitutionalism or that constitutionalism rests upon the truths of human nature as understood by the Declaration. I shall argue that in making these denials, the meaning of each document taken by itself is changed and neither freedom nor constitutionalism is understood. Liberty disappears as constitutionalism recedes from sight; common purposes dissolve as human nature is denied. And what we would conserve or what we would free becomes confused.

Glen E. Thurow

A Constitution Without Constitutionalism?

Tocqueville's observation that in the United States every major political issue sooner or later becomes a constitutional issue has never been truer than in our own day. Integration, affirmative action, apportionment, abortion, law enforcement, the relationship of men and women—there is scarcely an issue in American politics which has not been decisively affected by a constitutional decision of the courts. The courts themselves have put forward broader claims than ever before of their right to be the definitive and authoritative interpreters of the Constitution and have extended the reach of their Constitutional oversight into realms previously reserved for others.[1] Old doctrines limiting the courts—limits on standing or the refusal to rule on political questions—have disappeared or been narrowed.[2] Today more than ever before, America is guided by the authority of the Constitution as interpreted by the courts. Yet the predominant view of the judiciary, and the opinion of the legal scholars who support it, is that the Constitution cannot be understood as embodying the immutable truths of human nature as found in the Declaration.

There is on the highest levels of legal reflection in the United States today an attempt to find new grounds for the distinctive authority of American courts, the authority of judicial review. This attempt has both partisan and deeper causes. It has become clear to virtually everyone who thinks about American politics that many of the revolutionary opinions of the Supreme Court during the past thirty years cannot be justified on traditional grounds. According to the traditional justification it is the proper duty of the courts as interpreters of the law to interpret the supreme law, the Constitution, when an ordinary law seems to conflict with it. This duty arises from the particular function of the judiciary—to interpret laws—and is reconciled with democracy by the observation that the courts are upholding the people's most careful and considered will, to which they wish to bind even themselves, against its accidental or deliberate infringement by the government or their own ill-considered opinions.[3]

This traditional view places a duty upon the courts to find in the words and spirit of the Constitution the justification of their rulings. Only with

---

1. In *Cooper v. Aaron*, 385 US 1 (1958), the Supreme Court for the first time in its history declared that its opinions, and not merely the Constitution, were the "supreme law" of the land.
2. See the discussion in Gary L. McDowell, "Judicial Activism: Toward a Constitutional Solution," in *Taking the Constitution Seriously*, ed. Gary L. McDowell (Dubuque: Kendall-Hunt, 1981), pp. 139-151.
3. Marbury v. Madison, 1 Cranch 137 (1803); *Federalist* #78.

such a justification can the courts be properly judicial and properly loyal to the liberal constitutional government they are sworn to uphold. However, it is very difficult to justify some of the Supreme Court's most important contemporary decisions on these grounds. The clearest example, acknowledged by virtually everyone, is the decision establishing a constitutionally protected right of abortion. In its argument the Court itself confessed that it could not say where in the Constitution the right of privacy, upon which the decision was based, was to be found; although it was certain that it was somewhere and that it knew its specific dimensions.[4] The Court more or less explicitly said that it was not necessary for it to interpret the Constitution in order to know what the proper constitutional standard was. The perception that it is impossible to defend the Court in such cases on traditional grounds has led some to attack the Court as usurping power,[5] but this has not been the predominant response of the legal fraternity. Far more have been led to search for new justifications for what they see as just decisions by the Court.[6] Partisanship has led some to seek new underpinnings for the power of the courts.

But more underlies the search for new justifications than simple partisanship, and those who have sought new justifications have not always agreed with the decisions of the Warren and Burger Courts.[7] For underlying both the casualness with which the Court approaches the Constitution and the crisis in scholarship is the widely-shared conclusion that the traditional justification does not make sense. This justification is seen to rest on one of two premises, both considered doubtful. The first

---

4. "This right of privacy, whether it be founded in the Fourteenth Amendment's concept of personal liberty and restrictions upon state action, as we feel it is, or, as the District Court determined, in the Ninth Amendment's reservation of rights to the people, is broad enough to encompass a woman's decision whether or not to terminate her pregnancy." Roe v. Wade, 410 US 113 (1973).

5. E.g., Raoul Berger, *Government by the Judiciary: The Transformation of the Fourteenth Amendment* (Cambridge: Harvard University Press, 1977).

6. Among the most important books seeking a new understanding of judicial review are: Jesse H. Choper, *The Supreme Court and the Political Branches* (Chicago: University of Chicage Press, 1980); John Hart Ely, *Democracy and Distrust: A Theory of Judicial Review* (Cambridge: Harvard University Press, 1980); Richard Neely, *How Courts Govern America* (New Haven: Yale University Press, 1981); Michael J. Perry, *The Constitution, the Courts, and Human Rights* (New Haven: Yale University Press, 1982); Laurence H. Tribe, *Constitutional Choices* (Cambridge: Harvard University Press, 1985); Ronald Dworkin, *A Matter of Principle* (Cambridge: Harvard University Press, 1985).

7. For example, John Hart Ely does not endorse the abortion decisions of the Burger Court, although he is a partisan of the Warren Court.

premise is that we should be bound to the words and spirit of the Constitution because it embodies the will of the founders. Of course, it is easy to undermine this premise (although there might be more reasons to adhere to it than appear at first glance). As John Hart Ely spiritedly notes (or, at least, it would be spirited if the dead could defend themselves): why should we be bound to the will of people who lived 200 years ago; are we not adults ourselves?[8] Whatever merit there is in this rhetorical question only makes clear that the traditional justification really depends upon the second premise: that the will of the framers as found in the Constitution embodies the basic and eternal principles of free government. Not that the Constitution is perfect and unchangeable—indeed, provision was made for its amendment—but that its basic structure and intent does reflect these principles and hence is worthy of our loyalty. This second premise is denied by much of the current legal scholarship and judicial opinion.

Indeed, one is tempted to say that all sides in the current controversy over judicial review—at least all those rooted in the legal profession—accept the denial of this premise. In seeking to determine how one should interpret the Constitution current controversialists have split into inter-pretavists and non-interpretavists, with some sophisticates claiming to straddle the dichotomy. The interpretatvists say that courts should follow the Constitution's words or what its framers meant by the words. Attorney General Meese has been the principal public figure advancing this view in today's politics. But this position is the minority one, for most think that it does not answer the question of how to interpret those passages of the Constitution which seem to contradict other passages, which seem vague and hence are open to a variety of interpretations, or which do not seem to exist at all but should. The non-interpretavists, not finding a sufficient standard in the Constitution itself but wishing to avoid being arbitrary, seek a standard of interpretation in a variety of sources: in some contemporary or historical consensus, in a distinctly American vision, in the need to preserve and perfect the methods of representative government, or elsewhere.[9] Justice Brennan has found such a standard in the notion that the Constitution should be interpreted in the light of evolving standards of human dignity.[10]

---

8. Ely, p. 11.
9. See the books in footnote 6.
10. William J. Brennan, Jr., "The Constitution of the United States: Contemporary Ratification," speech delivered at Georgetown University, October 12, 1985.

Contrary to first appearances, the quarrel between interpretavists and non-interpretavists is not a quarrel between the traditional understanding of constitutional adjudication and some new understandings. The contemporary interpretavist looks to two sources in reading the Constitution: the words of the particular passage in question and the intention of the framers of that passage. His authorities are the text and the history of its adoption. The traditional standard of adjudication, however, looked to history only as a last resort and with considerable circumspection. Rather, when a particular passage was obscure, the object was to adopt the sense which, "without departing from the literal import of the words, best harmonize[d] with the nature and objects, the scope and design" of the Constitution as "apparent from the structure of the instrument, viewed as a whole, and also viewed in its component parts."[11] In other words the traditional understanding saw the Constitution as a coherent document embodying principles which could be discovered within the text itself. To be an interpretavist today, however, does not mean seeing doubtful words in the light of the whole document and the principles it embodies.[12] Most interpretavists, just as their opponents, think it illegitimate to try to discover the principles the Constitution embodies and to interpret particular passages in the light of these principles. The hero of the interpretavists is not John Marshall but Hugo Black.

The rejection today of the view that the Constitution reflects the fundamental principles of free government contrasts sharply with the interpretation given the Constitution by Abraham Lincoln in America's greatest constitutional crisis. At the moment when it became necessary to interpret the Constitution's ambiguous injunctions regarding the institution of slavery, Chief Justice Taney of the Supreme Court ruled that the right to hold others in slavery was distinctly and expressly affirmed by the Constitution and that no power existed in the federal government to prohibit the extension of slavery into new territories. Lincoln saw and argued that such an interpretation destroyed the very heart of the Constitution. Lincoln's response might be taken to be the greatest traditional example of going outside the text of the Constitution to interpret it. He sought to convince Americans that the Constitution should be read in the light of the Declaration of Independence. The Constitution was, as he put it, the frame of silver around the apple of gold of the Declaration, meant to

---

11. Joseph Story, *Commentaries on the Constitution of the United States*, 3 vols. (1833), vol. III, pp. 285-286.
12. Ely, pp. 12-14.

enhance and secure the apple. The proper interpretation of the Constitution could emerge only when it was seen that the American people were formed not only by the Constitution, but by the Declaration as well. The proper interpretation of the Constitution was one fully consistent with its own words but also consistent with the principles of the Declaration—that slavery was an evil tolerated, but not endorsed, by the Constitution.[13]

But Lincoln did not consider himself to be engrafting the alien principles of the Declaration onto the Constitution. He understood rather that there was something more fundamental in the Constitution than any one or more of its provisions, and that was the principles upon which the Constitution and constitutional government were formed. The principles of Jefferson, he said, were the definitions and axioms of free government. Those principles were stated most clearly in the Declaration, beginning with the proposition that all men are created equal. The very basis of men's own right to govern themselves is found in recognizing this truth and its consequences. For if men are not equal, the superior have every right to rule their inferiors. The "nature and objects" of the Constitution itself cannot be understood unless one sees the Constitution's dependence upon the principles enunciated in the Declaration. Nothing is more striking about today's legal scholarship than that no one suggests that the way in which ambiguities in the Constitution ought to be resolved is by considering the principles of the Declaration. Indeed, most of the major books in recent scholarship have not even mentioned the Declaration, although they purport to go to the fundamentals of the American political order.

The change from Lincoln to our own time owes much to progressive scholarship. The view first established in American academic and legal life by the work of the progressive historians was that the Constitution was a conservative reaction against the democratic principles of the Declaration of Independence. The immediate political aim of this contention was to undermine the authority of the Constitution and to place authority rather in the Declaration. But the longer term effect of this view has been to separate the Constitution and the Declaration, for if they represent fundamentally different views one cannot be used to understand the other.

This separation, inherent in the view of progressive scholarship, was assisted by the assumption of that scholarship that history is progressive.

---

13. This theme might be said to be the theme of Lincoln's political career and is to be found stated again and again in his published speeches.

The natural laws discovered by the American founders were not the truth once and for all, but the particular ideas of a particular generation of men that could be superceded by the outlook of a later generation. The principles of the Declaration, although more attractive to the progressives than the checks and balances of the Constitution, did not in their view have a solid and immutable foundation. When the optimism of the progressive was lost amid the experience of the twentieth century, skepticism about the nation's founding principles was not abandoned, but was merely enlarged to include the progressives as well. Both the founding principles and progressivism became mere ideologies.[14]

The end result of this view, then, would seem to be the overthrow of both the Declaration and the Constitution, but events do not always (or immediately) follow the work of scholars. The disjunction between the Declaration and the Constitution and the discrediting of the Declaration as a set of principles appropriate for us has meant that the Constitution could be freed from the conservative mold into which the progressives had cast it. If the Constitution is not rooted in the permanent principles of free government, then men are free to recast the Constitution by interpretation. The Constitution can properly be made to meet our standards of justice; we do not need to conform ourselves to its.

To separate the Constitution from the Declaration leads to a fundamentally altered view of the Constitution because the provisions of the Constitution rest upon a view of human nature. In the deepest original understandings of the Constitution, the Constitution was viewed as a solution to, or at least a mitigation of, a permanent problem of human nature in political order. It was not seen merely as a solution to a particular problem of the 1780's. This is most clearly seen in the *Federalist Papers.* In *Federalist #10* Publius explains that the only ways to destroy the causes of faction, the great bane of free government, are either to destroy liberty or to give everyone the same opinions, passions, or interests. Publius knows, as the Declaration says, that men are properly free and hence to destroy liberty is a cure worse than the disease. Because men's opinions tend to support their passions and because different interests result when men's faculties are left free, men cannot be given the same opinions, passions, or interests without an oppression Publius does not care to contemplate. Neither is there any way that the causes of faction can be

---

14. See Bernard Bailyn, *The Ideological Origins of the American Revolution* (New York: Macmillan, 1967) pp. 155-159.

isolated from political life; government is men, and political men, like other men, will have their passions and their interests.

The solution to this problem stemming from human nature and political life is one which seeks to use the less-than-noble characteristics of human beings in order to mitigate the very dangers they threaten. Ambition may be used to counter ambition through the separation of powers. The danger of a single oppressive ruling passion can be lessened by unleashing as many of the different faculties of men as possible through a large republic. By refining popular opinion through representatives the bite of particular interests may be softened. The purposes of common life, Publius teaches, can be achieved only by both liberating and constraining the effects of human nature.

The view which understands the Constitution to be independent of the Declaration because the Declaration rests upon principles of natural law now discredited thus also undermines the original notion of the Constitution as a use of human nature to remedy the difficulties presented political life by that nature. To divide the Constitution from the Declaration makes it impossible to understand it as a response not only to a particular crisis in American affairs but also to a permanent problem of human life. Instead of trying to understand and perfect the Constitution in the light of the human problem it addresses, we become free to remold it in accordance with our passions—whether noble or ignoble. It is noteworthy that no two participants in the present debate over judicial review seem to agree on the standard of interpretation which should replace the traditional one. One's opinions will reflect one's passions. One is tempted to paraphrase an offer made by Publius with regard to the work of the Constitutional Convention: let us keep the old standard of interpretation not until we find a better one, but until we find another one to which men will agree.

The political implications of the current separation of the Constitution from the Declaration and the standard of nature it suggests is illustrated by one of the entrants in the judicial review debate. Harvard Law Professor Laurence Tribe entitles his contribution *Constitutional Choices*. He wishes to emphasize by this title that we have a wide latitude to make whatever choices we think appropriate about the Constitution: there is no one set of principles or one standard of interpretation to which we may repair. We are constrained neither by the words of the Constitution nor by the nature of man. The consequence is that we can give a new meaning to equality and the equal protection of the laws. The Declaration suggests that the equal creation of men means that they all have unalienable rights.

Men are equal in their possession of rights, and the purpose of government is to secure those rights against the dangers others may present to them. To protect the equal rights of all means to protect those differences among men which reveal themselves when they are free to exercise their rights in the way they see fit.

But when the standards of our nature are rejected the meaning of equality no longer hinges on a recognition of the character of human nature and the differences which exist among men. Nature itself may be judged by another standard. When found wanting, she may be captured and changed. The true meaning of equality then becomes not the protection of the rights of all (and thus the protection of their differences), but the remolding of each in the image of others. According to Professor Tribe, the law should not take account of differences between the sexes except to ensure that these differences do not result in different ways of life. If the consequence of sexual intercourse is motherhood for women but not motherhood for men, then it is the duty of the law to ensure that that need not be the consequence. Otherwise something is required of women that is not required of men. Equality requires that women not be faced with any consequences of their actions not also faced by men.[15] That this understanding of equality is the destruction of liberty can be seen clearly if the reasoning is transferred to the realm of speech. If the consequence of speaking is ridicule for one man with a squeaky voice and glory for another with a deep one, then the law must ensure that these different consequences do not result—presumably, in this case, by forbidding the good speaker to speak. The desire to be free of the principles of the Declaration is a desire to be free of the constraints of nature. But to be free of those constraints is to undermine the very notion of a government limited to protecting our rights, for the proper limits of governmental action are to be found in our character as human beings.

Equality Without a Regime?

As we have noted, in the ordinary run of American politics the authority of the Constitution is more often invoked than is the authority of the Declaration of Independence. However, the hold of the Declaration *is* often visible in times of crisis or great political change. The last American political leader to base the heart of his rhetoric explicitly on the Declara-

---

15. Tribe, pp. 238-245.

tion was Dr. Martin Luther King, Jr. His powerful invocation of the Declaration's claim that all men are created equal demonstrated the potential authority of the Declaration in twentieth century American politics. Even when not explicitly invoked, the authority of the Declaration is sometimes visible. The drive for equality of various sorts in our time, although seldom explicitly based upon the Declaration, receives potency from its resemblance to the proposition that all men are created equal. Yet it remains true that, in contrast to the Constitution, the authority of the Declaration is more often implicit than explicit, potential than actual.

It is not surprising that the reverse is the case when we turn to the world at large. Here the universal claim of human equality and the right of revolution derived from it seem to be the chief inheritances of the American founding. Often these claims are invoked not only to justify revolution and movements toward equality, but to taunt the United States for failing to live up to its own beliefs. How could we fail to support revolutions in the third world when we ourselves have a revolutionary inheritance and proclaim a right of revolution? How could we fail to support the overthrow of dictators or other regimes which oppress the people when we ourselves speak in the name of human equality? These claims and taunts are often supported by potent segments of the American public as well, for they appeal to what is our own without appearing at all selfish.

Yet there is an obvious American objection to many of the revolutions in question—it is that there is often little likelihood that they will result in constitutional government. Of the many revolutions of the twentieth century one could count on one hand those that have resulted in republican government. If our Declaration teaches us to believe in a right of revolution, our loyalty to constitutionalism ought to make us skeptical of many exercises of that right. All too often the words of the Declaration are imitated, but the regime which follows is not constitutional government but a dictatorship, communist or otherwise. The moral force of many of the objections to American reluctance to support revolutions in general rests on the premise that the principles of the Declaration do not require a particular regime, that many different regimes are compatible with its principles, and that as long as a people chooses a government for itself it does not matter what it is. It is other people's right to have what they wish. The Declaration is not bound to the Constitution or constitutional government.

This opinion stems from the mistaken view that the Declaration is merely an abstract assertion of human equality. The Declaration does assert the abstract truth of human equality—that all men are possessed of unalienable rights—but it is less directly concerned with individual rights than it is with establishing public rights and purposes. The principle that all men are created equal is not merely a statement about the nature of one particular human being, but a statement about the relationship of one human being to another. As Jefferson put it, it means that "the mass of mankind has not been born with saddles on their backs, or a favored few booted and spurred, ready to ride them legitimately by the grace of God."[16] Yet our inability to govern ourselves effectively—our inability to secure our rights from the depredations of others—means that effective self-government requires the assistance of a common government over us all. But government means not only the fact of inequality between the governors and the governed, but the public recognition of that inequality which enables some men to be good Senators and Presidents and others bad. Our consent is required to government because we must artificially establish an inequality not definitively established by our nature.

The government necessary to secure our rights must meet several criteria. To be just it must take as its purpose the securing of men's insecure rights. The people have the right—even the duty—to overthrow a government which inadequately secures their rights. Finally, because men are equal the way in which these rights are to be secured can only properly be by the consent of the governed. Just government, then, must take as its purpose the securing of men's equal rights, must effectively secure those rights, and must have the consent of the governed. Only particular kinds of regimes fulfill these requirements. Many regimes do not take as their purpose the protecting of the rights of all; some who do, do not protect them effectively; and some who desire to secure rights and do so effectively do not act with their people's consent. The Declaration rules out a regime of *nobles oblige*, or enlightened despotism, which would rule without consent, as well as popular but oppressive regimes. In the Declaration consent, benevolence, and effectiveness are all in principle bound together and require each other. These requirements amount to a requirement for constitutional government.

It is true that the Declaration does not specify the form of government which follows from its principles. Indeed, it says that a people has the right "to institute new Government, laying its foundation on such principles, and organizing its powers in such form, as to them shall seem most likely

---

16. *The Writings of Thomas Jefferson* (Washington: Thomas Jefferson Memorial Association, 1903), ed. Andrew A. Lipscomb, vol. XVI, p. 182.

to effect their safety and happiness." But this is not to suggest that a people has a right to choose whatever form of government might enter their heads. It is simply a restatement and elaboration of the requirement of consent. Because the effectiveness of institutions may depend upon particular circumstances a choice must be made as to the appropriate institutions for a given people and circumstance. Since men are equal that choice is properly made by the people themselves. But they are not free to choose a government which will not desire to protect men's rights or will not do so effectively. To freely choose means to choose deliberately and well.

Men, after all, have a right to revolt against a government they have consented to if that government does not effectively protect their rights—if it turns out that their judgment was improper and their confidence misplaced. Such was the colonists' position *vis a vis* the British government. The Articles of Confederation, too, threatened to betray the principles of the Revolution not by its bad intentions or the lack of the people's consent, but by its ineffectiveness in achieving the proper purposes of government. A continual mischoice by the people—the Americans were mistaken twice—would destroy the right of the people to choose their government by revealing their incapacity for choosing wisely. It is for this reason that Publius, at the beginning of the *Federalist Papers*, says that the choice made about the Constitution will determine whether it is possible for a people to establish good government by reflection and choice.[17] Three tries and you're out. That men can, and do, dispute the political consequences of the Declaration's principles is almost required by the principle of consent. But it does not mean that there are not better and worse answers to the question of what political institutions best fulfill the principles of the Declaration.

Today, when the understanding of equality is divorced from the problem of political choice, when it is not understood to have definitive consequences for the form of government, we find understandings of equality which could undermine not only constitutional government but also individual rights. These understandings are found on both the right and the left of the political spectrum. Some forms of Libertarianism on the right argue that each individual is equal and free to decide on a course of life for himself without any interference from government. Yet they do not suggest that men must govern themselves in the absence of being governed. The freedom to choose, according to these Libertarians, does

---

17. *Federalist* #1.

not entail the obligation to choose wisely. They would destroy human dignity in the name of human independence. Segments of the left believe almost the same thing—that every way of life is equally good. The only difference between the right and the left is that the right says we can live these ways of life by getting rid of government while the left says that it is the duty of government to make these varied ways of life equally possible for all.[18]

The greatest debate over the principle of equality today is found in the issue of affirmative action. The term, affirmative action, is sometimes used to refer to any policy which takes steps to help those who are poor, uneducated, handicapped, etc. But the meaning of affirmative action which arouses principled debate about the meaning of equality is the contention that members of certain groups as a matter of justice are entitled to privileges under the law denied to others because of the unjust discrimination that group has suffered in the past. This notion has been defended and attacked with a variety of arguments. But what view of equality does it involve?

In one sense affirmative action is clearly a policy of inequality: some people will be given rights denied to others solely because of the group into which they were born, just as in bygone years those born into the aristocracy were given privileges in the law denied to the common people. Yet affirmative action is defended in the name of equality, not inequality. The advantages some groups will get today are justified by the disadvantages they suffered yesterday. These advantages will be at the expense of groups which have had more than their share of advantages, and thus all will be made equal. The end of the new inequality is equality so conceived.

It is sometimes said that affirmative action transforms individual rights in group rights, for the rights one has depend upon the group to which one belongs. It is true that what the government gives under affirmative action is determined by one's group, but to say that this transforms individual rights into group rights is to obscure just how radical affirmative action is in terms of the traditional American understanding of equality. For the protection of individual rights, as I have already indicated, is also the protection of our inequalities. When all have equal rights, some will exercise them effectively and well and others will not. Some will be good speakers and others not. Some will be good entrepreneurs and others not. Some will be deeply religious and others not. But to develop

---

18. See, for example, Ronald Dworkin, *A Matter of Principle* (Cambridge: Harvard University Press, 1985), pp. 205-213.

one's individuality or inequality is not what groups are to do under affirmative action. Any ability of one group to outshine another is to be prevented by insisting that all must be equally awarded according to their group's proportion of the population. In affirmative action we do not have group rights instead of individual rights; we have no rights at all. The aim is no longer as it is in the traditional notion of rights the protection of human individuality (inequality) by guaranteeing the free exercise of one's rights. It is rather the direction of the exercise of one's rights in order to assure group sameness.

The argument that a group's present benefits create equality when they compensate for past denials is an argument which undermines the notion of the common good. It is a very different kind of argument from the one which justified the privileges of the aristocracy. That argument rested upon the contention that those who contributed more to the well-being of their country ought to be given more. The argument for aristocracy, whether true or false, was an argument for the common good. The usual argument for affirmative action, in contrast, is not made in the name of the common good but in the name of group entitlement. The argument that blacks should be given privileges because they contribute more to the common good than they are being paid in return is not made, although perhaps it could be. Nor is there any suggestion that those who are to receive special privileges under the law owe more in return to their country (as aristocrats were presumed to do). The policy of affirmative action is a policy of unequal benefits, without the sense of merit or of obligation which might have rendered an aristocracy tolerable.

It is proper to understand justice in the case of individuals in terms of compensation for past wrongs. If an individual has been injured, it is just that he be compensated to the extent possible. If a black has been unjustly discriminated against by a white it is proper for the white to be made to compensate him for his injury. However, the just relationship among groups in society cannot be understood in the same way. The same principle of justice applied to groups leaves the result that some who have received no injury will receive compensation, and some who have done no injury will be made to pay. Injustice, therefore, cannot be wiped out by such a policy, but only be perpetuated in a new guise. In looking at the relationship among groups in society we must rather look to what the common good requires.

The common good under affirmative action appears only in the view that every group ought to be equal to every other. But this does not in fact establish a common good, but is instead a notion of something like sovereign statehood for individual groups. Different groups are held together not as parts of one country, but for the sake of getting what they can from other groups. To cut the pies among groups in some particular way may keep the peace, but it does not create a common good, as one can see when the pies get scarce.

The change which has occurred in our politics with the change in the understanding of equality can be seen in the difference between Martin Luther King and Jesse Jackson. Martin Luther King, Jr. spoke in the name of the Declaration's equality, calling upon all Americans to live up to their belief that everyone is entitled to equal rights. As a consequence, he could form a political movement of whites as well as blacks; and many whites, not part of the movement, could nevertheless be moved by it. Jesse Jackson, on the other hand, has sought to form a Rainbow coalition. Of course there is no white in the rainbow. Jackson, unlike King, has not called upon both whites and blacks to live up to the best that is in them. Rather, he has appealed to poor and other whites to recognize that they are in reality colored. Every group which is in some way disadvantaged is to unite together in order to demand from the rest what is rightfully theirs. Farmers, blacks, old people, the poor would all be part of one political movement not because they share a view of the common good, but because they desire more from the government and the dominant whites. Where is the common good? The Republicans made an effective charge against the Democrats in the last election that they were nothing but a collection of interests. But the view of equality inherent in affirmative action leaves no common good beyond a collection of interests.[19]

Both those who want a Constitution without constitutionalism and those who want equality without a regime share much in common. When the Constitution is separated from a concern with human nature the standards for interpreting it are open. The most common standard is that of equality—but an equality not informed by an understanding of its relationship to the common good or a constitutional regime. Those who seek the new equality can wish for the kind of constitution which can be interpreted to include the new equality. At the root of both views is a loss of the sense of a common good and of our common nature which allows us to have a common good.

---

19. Compare Martin Luther King's "I Have a Dream" speech of 1963 with the speech of Jesse Jackson at the Democratic National Convention in 1984.

The Declaration and the Constitution: Concluding Remarks

Thomas G. West

I

Lance Banning begins his essay by observing that most Americans think of the Declaration of Independence and the Constitution as our two great founding documents, equally worthy of reverence by a grateful posterity. The Declaration, in this view, states our democratic ideals and principles, and the Constitution puts them into practice. Glen Thurow's essay tries to show that this popular view is also the true view. The popular view is not well received among most academics, however. Banning, a historian, follows the majority of the historians' guild (although with some reservations) by arguing that the Constitution betrays the promise of the Declaration.

The Declaration, Banning rightly reminds us, lays down two principles of just government. First, government must be by consent of the governed: the majority must rule. Second, government is to secure the rights of individuals, including the rights to life, liberty, and property. Banning accepts the formulation of Gordon Wood, the most influential modern student of the Constitution's sources, that the Constitution "was intrinsically an aristocratic document designed to check the democratic tendencies of the period." Most of the supporters and Framers of the new Constitution, says Banning, believed that government by consent was in conflict with protection of individual rights. So they tried to create a government that would protect those rights by excluding the people from political power. They abandoned one principle of the Declaration (consent) because of their preoccupation with the other (private rights).

Further, says Banning, many supporters of the Constitution shared with Hamilton a vision of America as a great power, a nation that would make its mark in the world by fostering a thriving commerce promoting wealth at home and strength abroad. The Antifederalist opponents of the Constitution, such as Patrick Henry—"Revolutionary tribunes," Banning calls them—feared that this vision would require centralization of power in the national government, a large standing army, and the sacrifice of local self-government and simple republican habits. Banning believes that this fear was justified.

The immediate point of Banning's paper is to argue that not all supporters of the Constitution shared the view of Hamilton and other "aspiring consuls"—"bad guys," if I may call them what Banning so obviously thinks them. Madison and other "good guys" who favored the Constitution were "not at all inclined to sacrifice democracy to private rights or national greatness." Madison sought curbs on the abuses of democracy, not the rejection of democracy. Madison's break with Hamilton in the 1790s, in Banning's view, is explained by Madison's constant fidelity to majority rule, which was by then being betrayed, he thought, by Hamilton and the Federalists.

We note that Banning's defense of Madison has this drawback: in order to rescue Madison from the charge of being anti-democratic he must implicitly condemn him for stupidity. For if Banning and other recent historians are right—that the Constitution "was intrinsically an aristocratic document"—then "the father of the Constitution," as Madison is known, failed to perceive the most important fact about that document.

Banning's thesis depends on his success at driving a wedge between the democratic Madison and the aristocratic Hamilton. What are the facts that damn Hamilton and like-minded Federalists in Banning's mind? For one thing, Hamilton believed in the necessity of an energetic federal government. But Madison insists upon the same need in *Federalist* 37: the Constitution combines "the requisite stability and energy in government with the inviolable attention due to liberty and the republican form."

Hamilton is also charged with caring more for the rights of individuals than for government by the majority. But again, so does Madison: "Justice [including, of course, protection of individual rights] is the end of government. It is the end of civil society. It ever has been and ever will be pursued until it be obtained, or until liberty [i.e., self-government] be lost in the pursuit" (*Federalist* 51). Further: in the extreme case of "absolute necessity," one must recur to "the transcendent law of nature and of nature's God, which declares that the safety and happiness of society are the objects at which all political institutions aim *and to which all such institutions must be sacrificed*" (*Federalist* 43, emphasis added).

Did Hamilton propose at the Constitutional Convention a President who would hold office for life? Yes, and Madison voted for it at that same Convention (and they did so arguably for the same reason: not because they were monarchists, but as a tactical move to impress upon the delegates the need for a strong executive independent of the Congress).

It is true that Hamilton was mortified over America's weakness and dishonor among nations, but so was Madison, as he emphasizes in his praise of the Senate (*Federalist* 62 and 63). In sum, Madison's whole concern was to secure a Constitution that would "blend stability and liberty" in the proper proportion—a concern shared by Hamilton, which made possible their brilliant collaboration on *The Federalist*. The differences between the two men that emerged in the 1790s did not touch these crucial points of agreement, contrary to the party rhetoric of the period.

If there was greater agreement between Madison and Hamilton than Banning would like to admit, does that mean that Madison was an aristocrat? *Is* the Constitution an aristocratic document? If we look at the Constitution itself, what do we see? How does it differ from the existing state constitutions of the Founders' time? First, it creates longer terms of office for elected officials. Most states had one or two year terms for representatives, executives, and senators. The Constitution creates two, four, and six year terms. Does that make the Constitution undemocratic? Only if *democratic* means that the government must reflect the immediate, irrational will of the people. Longer terms meant that although the popular will would ultimately prevail, the representatives would be better able to resist the people's every momentary whim and passion so that their cool and deliberate sense would be more likely to hold sway. As Madison said, "But it is the reason, alone, of the public, that ought to control and regulate the government. The passions ought to be controlled and regulated by the government" (*Federalist* 49).

When we vote for candidates in elections we try to vote for the best man. No one seriously believes the representatives ought to be average so that they will accurately reflect the average voter. (A certain Nebraska Senator once argued that a Supreme Court nominee said to be mediocre should be confirmed by the Senate because mediocre people had too little representation in government. Laughter rightly settled that argument.) We want the hearts of our representatives to be in the right place, but we also want them to have good minds and be more knowledgeable about politics and policy than the average man on the street. Is this aristocratic? No one would say so today.

Was the indirect election of Senators and Presidents undemocratic? Not by the standards of the existing state constitutions, at least, for most of these had the legislatures electing the governors.

The real issue was *how close* to the people the government should be, not whether the government ought to be responsible to the people. Supporters and opponents of the Constitution were all democratic in this sense. By showing that dedicated revolutionaries like Madison and Randolph could support the Constitution in good conscience, Banning has helped to advance the scholarly resuscitation of the Constitution from the fatal reproach of being an undemocratic and aristocratic document. One could wish he had taken the argument farther to include more of the Constitution's Framers and supporters. Rereading the Convention debates today, one is struck by the genuine dedication to republicanism of the vast majority of the delegates, who were wrestling with a very real problem of democratic government: how to secure the popular rights to life, liberty, and the pursuit of happiness within the context of government through representatives elected directly or indirectly by the people.

One might wonder why Banning, like so many historians today, is willing to think the worst of most of the Constitution's Framers. About a hundred years ago the "Progressive" critique of the founding first became fashionable. The so-called Progressives of that day believed that the Constitution stood in the way of progress because of its checks and balances. So they devised an attack on the Constitution as oligarchic and aristocratic. The specific arguments used by the various Progressives, notably Charles Beard with his economic interpretation of the founding, have been demolished by later scholarship. But the same ideas keep returning, particularly in Gordon Wood's influential book, cited with approval by Banning.[1] Are historians, and intellectuals generally, as non-partisan as they would like us to think? The Progressives were politically liberal, and most historians today are as well. Even historians who are friendly to American constitutionalism (as is Professor Banning) find it hard to stand apart from the overwhelming tendency of the guild.

II

The intrusion of partisan ideology into scholarship is a problem that Glen Thurow's paper brings out with admirable clarity. He demonstrates that the merely academic question of the relation of the Declaration and Constitution has important consequences for the contemporary debate over the meaning of equality. In particular, if the Constitution is understood as an embodiment of the Declaration's principles, then the kinds of

---

1. Gordon Wood, *The Creation of the American Republic, 1776-1787* (New York: Norton, 1972). On p. 626 Wood acknowledges that he is following the general interpretation of the Progressive generation of historians.

rights that the Constitution protects are limited by and guided by human nature as a standard. The Declaration's ultimate appeal is to the self-evident truths of human nature, and that nature is therefore the unchanging starting point for understanding government under the Constitution.

On the other side, those scholars who see no connection between Constitution and Declaration or who do not believe in the idea of human nature presupposed by the Declaration are inclined to develop novel and radical views of the rights protected by government. One such scholar discussed by Thurow is Laurence Tribe of Harvard, who believes that the laws should not permit natural differences among human beings to result in different ways of life. Thus, since childbearing has different consequences for men and women, the law ought to allow women to have abortions. This view of human nature, Thurow observes, assumes that people are to be understood as individuals who are entirely free to set their own destiny, regardless of their particular natures. If even the natural differences between men and women with regard to childbearing are to be abolished by the law, what about differences such as the ability to speak persuasively? As Thurow suggests, Tribe's view implies that the law must prevent the good speaker with a deep voice from having any advantage over the poor speaker with a squeaky voice—presumably by forbidding the good speaker to speak.

If this view were to prevail in our politics—and it already does prevail in the nation's law schools and universities—it would destroy liberty, Thurow argues. The Supreme Court, inspired by the radical views of Tribe and others, has already gone far down this path. The Court's rulings on affirmative action already permit groups such as blacks and women— *and without any showing of actual discrimination* against individuals composing these groups—to demand and receive special privileges under the law at the expense of others who do not belong to the favored groups. As Thurow says, the assumption is that all human beings are mere individuals who can be presumed to have identical abilities and to make identical choices, regardless of the actual choices made by real men and women, real blacks and whites, real strong and weak, old and young, hard-working and lazy, easygoing and high-strung people, and so on.

The rights of man announced in the Declaration that were to be secured by the Constitution protected and fostered individual differences so that people's talents could be developed free from the age-old restraints of class privilege and ethnic bias that characterized every nation in the world at the time of the American founding—and still characterize all but a handful of nations today. Protection of individual rights meant that people would be more responsible for their lives where different choices lead to different consequences. The new view of rights, which in fact does away with rights, as Thurow says—above all the right to liberty—directs "the exercise of one's rights in order to assure group sameness."

Thurow summarizes the new view of equality by speaking of the contemporary desire for "a Constitution without constitutionalism" and "equality without a regime." "A Constitution without constitutionalism" means that many contemporary interpreters of the Constitution—lawyers and judges—no longer feel bound by the documents they expound. Their interpretation of the Constitution, liberated from its text, is also thereby liberated from majority rule; for a constitutional majority rules through laws approved by their representatives, including the basic law, the Constitution itself. When judges feel free to disregard the plain meaning of the laws, they are also disregarding the will of the people. The expression "equality without a regime" refers to the current demand for equality without considering the political context in which it is demanded. It forgets that the idea of equality in the Declaration requires "consent, benevolence, and effectiveness" in government, for equality means the equal rights of human beings which government is obliged to secure and which limit government by mandating the ongoing consent of the governed. Few political regimes are capable of achieving these criteria, and adherents of the Declaration are rightly skeptical of revolutions that promise equality without a commitment to constitutionalism.

III

The two discussants at the conference spoke from opposite ends of today's political spectrum—Ross Lence on the right, Sanford Levinson on the left—but both shared an important premise. Neither man was willing to endorse fully the principles of the Declaration of Independence. Lence argued strongly for the primacy of majority rule in reading the Declaration, for he is impressed by the extent to which America has lost its sense of community by its preoccupation with individual autonomy—individual rights understood as living however one pleases. Lence evidently hopes that a sense of common purpose might be restored by a shift of emphasis from the individual to the community.

What kind of community, however, one might ask, would emerge in an America that no longer looked to the rights of man as sacred? Benjamin

Barber's remarks earlier in the conference, which seemed to some participants to point toward a totalitarian subordination of the individual to
society, may indicate the dangers of a hasty farewell to individual liberty.
Equally ominous was Lence's mention of John C. Calhoun, the Southern
apologist for slavery before the Civil War, as an authority on the correct
understanding of republican government. For different reasons but in the
name of community, the conservative Lence and the socialist Barber want
nothing to do with any inalienable rights of man that put limits on the
legitimate activity of government. The price in both cases is despotism.

Sanford Levinson also found himself unable to embrace the eternal
truths of human nature announced in the Declaration, for as he
explained, he is a child of a skeptical age and he cannot believe that
anything is eternal. As far as he can see, God is dead. But Levinson also
maintained that it is unclear what nature is. The ancient Greeks thought
homosexuality was natural, he says, while the Jews thought it unnatural:
who is to say? (Levinson seems unaware that Greek philosophers did
condemn homosexuality as unnatural, as did all philosophers before the
Marquis de Sade. Leo Strauss once wrote to a sophisticated correspondent
who made a similar error: "Please do read Plato's *Laws* on this subject.
—Do not forget the *natural* connection between sexual organs and
generation.")[2]

Levinson also has grave doubts about our Constitution. To the extent it
has a distinct meaning it is a "Byzantine system" set up by men who feared
power. Woodrow Wilson didn't like it, Levinson pointed out, and Wilson
probably had a point. But Levinson does not content himself with an
allusion to the Progressive critique of the Constitution. Instead, he
advances the novel and much more radical position that the Constitution
may not mean anything at all! Its essence, Levinson asserted, is Article 5,
the amendment power, which opens the document up to become any
form of government that the people might wish. By allowing amendments
the Constitution shows its indifference to its own form. (The oddity of this
argument is shown by applying it to our own actions. Does it really mean
we are *indifferent* to our opinions and decisions if we hold them open to
reconsideration at some future time and refuse to be pigheaded about
them?) Finally, Levinson maintained, the example of the Founders shows
that our judges are under no obligation to interpret the plain words of the
document. For the Founders themselves ignored the plain words of the
Articles of Confederation—which required the unanimous consent of all

---

2. Letter to Karl Loewith, *Independent Journal of Philosophy* 4 (1983), p. 114.

thirteen states to amend the Articles—when they stated in Article 7 that nine states only were sufficient to ratify the Constitution.

Whatever one is to make of Levinson's somewhat contradictory arguments, one thing is clear. He is eager to justify today's judicial and academic fashion that encourages judges to "interpret" the Constitution in such a way as to bring it into line with contemporary liberal ideas. But unlike the Founders, who acknowledged with manly frankness the revolutionary implication of bypassing the Articles' thirteen-state amendment procedure, Levinson prefers the surreptitious rejection of the Constitution currently in vogue in the Federal and state judiciaries and in the law schools. (If Levinson were frank, he would admit that a license for judges to ignore the plain words of the Constitution amounts to a revolutionary seizure of power by an elite against the majority ruling through elected representatives under a Constitution approved and amended by them.) The Founders justified *their* action "by recurring to the absolute necessity of the case; to the great principle of self-preservation; to the transcendent law of nature and of nature's God, which declares that the safety and happiness of society are the objects at which all political institutions aim and to which all such institutions must be sacrificed" (*Federalist* 43). In this statement Madison was echoing the language of the Declaration of Independence. Further, the Founders insisted that any revolutionary change in the government had to be approved by the only legitimate fountain of authority, the people. But Levinson and the scholars he admires no longer appeal to the Declaration and no longer defend the rule of laws approved by the majority because they no longer believe in human nature as a standard and consequently no longer believe that government must be established and operate by the consent of the governed for the sake of securing the eternal rights of humanity. God and nature are dead; let the Supreme Court rule, guided by the writings of law school professors.

For the sake of clarity we may exaggerate the positions of the two discussants as follows: Lence would embrace the Declaration's requirement of government by consent of the governed but forget its insistence on securing the rights of life, liberty, and the pursuit of happiness; Levinson would embrace a novel conception of minority rights while abandoning government by consent of the governed. Both men, and the current conservative and liberal positions they exemplify, would do well to return to the Declaration, in which *consent* and *rights* are inseparable because both flow from our common human nature in which we are all politically equal.

About the Contributors

Henry J. Abraham is James Hart Professor of Government and Foreign Affairs at the University of Virginia. He has written extensively on the judiciary and on government institutions. His most recent book is *The Judicial Process: An Introductory Analysis of the Courts of the United States, England, and France.*

John Alvis is Associate Professor of English at the University of Dallas. Along with his many articles on Shakespeare, and his original plays and poems, he is the co-editor of *Shakespeare as Political Thinker*, and the author of *Shakespeare's Understanding of Honor.*

George Anastaplo is Professor of Law at Loyola University of Chicago, Lecturer in the Liberal Arts at the University of Chicago, Professor Emeritus of Political Science and of Philosophy at Rosary College, and teaches summer seminars at The Clearing at Ellison Bay, Wisconsin. He has an extensive bibliography of articles and among the five books he has published is *The Artist as Thinker: From Shakespeare to Joyce.* His most recent work is *The United States Constitutuion of 1787: A Commentary.*

Hadley Arkes is William Nelson Cromwell Professor of Jurisprudence at Amherst College. As well as numerous articles he is the author of *The Philosopher in the City*, and *First Things: An Inquiry into the First Principles of Morals and Justice.*

Lance Banning is Associate Professor of History at the University of Kentucky in Lexington. His current work is on James Madison and the evolution of republicanism, and he recently published *The Jeffersonian Persuasion: Evolution of a Party Ideology.*

Benjamin Barber is Professor of Political Science at Rutgers University. For ten years he was the editor of *Political Theory.* His many publications include *Strong Democracy: Participatory Politics for a New Age.*

Richard M. Ebeling is Assistant Professor of Economics at the University of Dallas. He has published articles in a variety of economic journals as well as having contributed to the recent book *Subjectivism, Intelligibility, and Economic Understanding.*

Wilson Carey McWilliams is Professor of Political Science at Rutgers University. He is the author of a textbook on American government and *The Idea of Fraternity in America*.

Jennifer Nedelsky is Associate Professor at the University of Toronto Law School, and has also been Associate Professor of Politics at Princeton University. She is the author of *Private Property and the Formation of the United States Constitution* forthcoming in 1988.

Ellis Sandoz is Professor of Political Science at Louisiana State University. As well as editing *Eric Voeglin's Thought: A Symposium*, he is the author of *Americanism: Political Theory and the American Civil Theology*.

Sanderson S. Schaub has been Research Director at the Foundation for the Private Sector. He is the author of "Carl Schmitt's Critique of Liberalism" and co-author of *Marx and the Gulag*.

Rogers M. Smith is Associate Professor of Political Science at Yale University. Along with numerous articles, he is the author of *Liberalism and American Constitutional Law*, and *Citizenship Without Consent: The Illegal Alien in the American Polity*.

Mary K. Bonsteel Tachau is Professor of History at the University of Louisville. She is the author of several historical articles and *Federal Courts in the Early Republic: Kentucky 1789-1816*.

Glen E. Thurow is Associate Professor of Politics at the University of Dallas. Along with numerous articles, he is the co-editor of *Rhetoric and American Statesmanship* and the author of *Abraham Lincoln and American Political Religion*. He is currently working on a book on judicial review.

Sarah Baumgartner Thurow is the Associate Director of the University of Dallas Bicentennial Project, "Constitutionalism in America." She writes on political philosophy, English literature, and contemporary political issues.

Jeffrey Tulis is Andrew W. Mellon Preceptor and teaches in the Department of Political Science at Princeton University. He is the co-editor of *The Presidency in the Constitutional Order* and the author of *The Rhetorical Presidency*.

Thomas G. West is Associate Professor of Politics and Director of the Bicentennial Project at the University of Dallas. He is the author of *Plato's Defense of Socrates* and contributor to *Saving the Republic: The Federalist Papers and the Founding*.

John Adams Wettergreen is Associate Professor of Political Science at San Jose State University. He is the author of articles on topics ranging from the bureaucracy to political philosophy. His most recent publication is an essay titled "Demography of 1984's National Majority," in *The 1984 Election*.